"As one committed to classical Reformed theology *and* a classical approach to apologetics, and as one who has often been told that the two are inherently antithetical, I am encouraged that the resurgence of research into early Protestant orthodoxy is leading Reformed theologians to reexamine the conventional wisdom on these issues. While remaining sympathetic to Van Til and other like-minded theologians, Fesko has raised questions that cannot be ignored. Whatever one's stance on natural revelation, natural theology, or apologetics, it is hard to believe that anyone would deny that this is an important book. It may prove to be a game changer. I hope it will prove to be a mind changer."

—**Keith A. Mathison**, Reformation Bible College

"Fesko has given us a clear, scholarly, and comprehensive analysis and critique of post-Enlightenment Reformed apologetics. His work goes a long way toward restoring classical Reformed theology and apologetics."

—**R. C. Sproul**, founder of Ligonier Ministries

T0339165

REFORMING
APOLOGETICS

REFORMING
APOLOGETICS

RETRIEVING the
CLASSIC REFORMED APPROACH
to DEFENDING the FAITH

J. V. FESKO

B
Baker Academic
a division of Baker Publishing Group
Grand Rapids, Michigan

© 2019 by J. V. Fesko

Published by Baker Academic
a division of Baker Publishing Group
PO Box 6287, Grand Rapids, MI 49516-6287
www.bakeracademic.com

Printed in the United States of America

Library of Congress Cataloging-in-Publication Data
Names: Fesko, J. V., 1970– author.
Title: Reforming apologetics : retrieving the classic reformed approach to defending the faith / J.V. Fesko.
Description: Grand Rapids : Baker Publishing Group, 2019. | Includes bibliographical references and index.
Identifiers: LCCN 2018036378 | ISBN 9780801098901 (pbk. : alk. paper)
Subjects: LCSH: Apologetics. | Reformed Church—Doctrines.
Classification: LCC BT1103 .F48 2019 | DDC 239—dc23
LC record available at https://lccn.loc.gov/2018036378

ISBN 978-1-5409-6153-2 (casebound)

For
John Valero Jr.,
Robert Riley,
and
Carmen Penelope

CONTENTS

PREFACE

The first theological book to capture my attention was Josh McDowell's two-volume work, *Evidence That Demands a Verdict*.[1] I had recently graduated from college and was doing my best to ignore God's call on my life. Ever since my teen years, I had sensed that I was supposed to pursue ordained ministry but fled like Jonah. One day in a Christian bookstore, McDowell's books caught my eye. I bought them and was enthralled. Providence used these books to convince me to stop running and go to seminary. During my time in seminary, I continued to study apologetics. I double minored in historical theology and philosophy of religion and majored in systematic theology. When I wrote my master's thesis as an apologetic defense of the doctrine of Scripture against the claims of postmodern philosophy, I integrated the disciplines of philosophy and theology. During my doctoral studies, I continually encountered books and essays that dealt with the apologetics of Reformed theology in the sixteenth and seventeenth centuries, but I began to notice that there were some significant differences between what I read in the pages of Francis Turretin's (1623–87) *Institutes of Elenctic Theology*, for example, and what I heard people saying in the church. I eventually published two essays in which I recorded some of my findings, particularly as they pertained to the contemporary reception of natural theology.[2] In the years since, I have also documented some of the reasons why contemporary Reformed theologians

1. Josh McDowell, *Evidence That Demands a Verdict*, 2 vols. (San Bernardino, CA: Here's Life, 1986).
2. J. V. Fesko, "The Days of Creation and Confession Subscription in the OPC," *Westminster Theological Journal* 63 (2001): 235–49, esp. 238–39; J. V. Fesko and Guy M. Richard, "Natural Theology and the Westminster Confession of Faith," in *The Westminster Confession into the 21st Century*, ed. J. Ligon Duncan, 3 vols. (Fearn, UK: Mentor, 2009), 3:223–66.

disagreed with Reformed Orthodox teachings on natural theology.[3] Amid this ongoing research, I had opportunities to crystallize my thought when, on two different occasions, I taught a course on theological prolegomena and basic apologetics. I wanted my students to have the best of both worlds, the best of what Reformed Orthodoxy has to say on issues related to apologetics, and the best of what contemporary Reformed theologians have claimed. This book represents the culmination of my thinking about these things on and off for the last twenty-five years. I write primarily from the vantage point of systematic and historical theology, my chief areas of training and study. I do not claim to be an expert in apologetics, as there are many gifted and well-trained apologists who address technical issues quite well. Nevertheless, I address theological and historical issues that pertain to the very foundations of the art and science of apologetics, and thus I seek to reform aspects of the church's present-day apologetic enterprise.

On the whole, this book is about retrieving the classic Reformed approach to defending the faith. Categories such as *common notions* and *the order of nature* once filled the pages of Reformed works but now seldom appear. This is due, in large part, to a shift in theological convictions among contemporary Reformed theologians. There is a general distrust of natural theology. I hope to present evidence that would make people reconsider their aversion to its use in theology and apologetics. In God's providence for his church, theologians and philosophers of the last century—such as Abraham Kuyper, Cornelius Van Til, and Herman Dooyeweerd—were not shy about recalibrating Reformed theology where they believed they detected shortcomings. Van Til, for example, forcefully critiqued Old Princeton theologians Charles Hodge and B. B. Warfield, and he registered his dissatisfaction with Kuyper and Herman Bavinck on a number of points with the goal of presenting a clearer exposition of Reformed apologetics. He criticized these theologians not out of pride but out of a desire to remain faithful to Scripture. This is the manner in which I present the material that follows, as I focus on and respectfully challenge some of Van Til's and Dooyeweerd's claims. I intend this critique in the spirit of Van Til's festschrift, *Jerusalem and Athens*, in which contributors engaged in appreciative but at times critical dialogue with him. In those places where I disagree with Van Til, were he still alive, I suspect he would openly welcome the disagreement and engage in hearty dialogue. Van Til would undoubtedly agree that no one is above critique, and Scripture must always be the supreme judge by which all things in religion are determined.

3. J. V. Fesko, *The Covenant of Redemption: Origins, Development, and Reception* (Göttingen: Vandenhoeck & Ruprecht, 2016), 187–97.

I am convinced that Christians need to present their arguments from the authority of Scripture, identify false and erroneous thought embedded in unbelief, and approach unbelievers in terms of their God-defined status as covenant breakers. We must not engage unbelievers in terms of naked reason or the so-called neutral ground of bare logic. I believe Christians must approach apologetics in terms of faith seeking understanding, always mindful of the antithesis of the gospel over and against any claims of unbelief. But at the same time, my aim is to draw the church's attention back to the book of nature, so that we can use both books—nature and Scripture—in the defense of the faith.

ACKNOWLEDGMENTS

The sixteenth-century poet and theologian John Donne (1572–1631) once wrote, "No man is an island, entire of itself; every man is a piece of the continent, a part of the main." These words echo in my mind as I think of the number of colleagues and friends who have rendered their assistance along the journey that has been the writing of this book. Thanks to my faculty colleagues, students, and former students who read earlier drafts. Thanks to James Dolezal, Paul Helm, Thomas Joseph White, Keith Matthison, R. C. Sproul, Danny Olinger, David Sytsma, Richard Barcellos, Liam Goligher, Richard Gamble, John Muether, Jay Collier, Mike Allen, Stefan Linblad, Matthew Barrett, Brian Hecker, and Jeff Waddington for their helpful comments and feedback. I am also grateful to Scott Oliphint for his candid negative critique, but I respectfully dissent. I am seeking to return us not "to the vomit of Rome" (as he put it to me) but to historic Reformed confessional theology. I am especially thankful to Richard Muller, who read through two drafts of the book, offered excellent feedback, and provided fantastic camaraderie throughout the process. I owe great thanks to David Noe, who carefully read through my manuscript and made many helpful substantive and editorial suggestions. I am also thankful to Jim Kinney, Dave Nelson, Wells Turner, and the whole team at Baker Academic for their continual support. As much as I appreciate all the assistance from the aforementioned friends and colleagues, this work contains my own views and are not those of my colleagues or my employer, Westminster Seminary California.

My family deserves significant thanks and recognition: they have been Aaron and Hur to me by holding me up in prayer during the process of seeing this book to press. Thanks to my in-laws, Bob and Linda Jones; my parents, Lee and Eren Fesko; my children, Val, Rob, and Carmen; and especially my wife,

Anneke. Dearest wife, you have been a rock to me throughout this process and have continually pointed me to Christ. Thank you for encouraging me to be a better man, husband, father, and minister of God's Word.

I wrote this book chiefly because I want my children to be fully equipped for the defense of the faith. I want you always to be ready to give a reason for the hope that is within you (1 Pet. 3:15). I want you to read both of God's books with great profit, the books of nature and Scripture. So, it is to you, John Valero Jr., Robert Riley, and Carmen Penelope, that I dedicate this book.

ABBREVIATIONS

General and Bibliographic

&c. *et cetera*

§(§) section(s)

AD *anno Domini*, in the year of our Lord

ANF *The Ante-Nicene Fathers: Translations of the Writings of the Fathers down to A.D. 325.* Edited by Alexander Roberts and James Donaldson and A. Cleveland Coxe. 10 vols. New York: Christian Literature, 1885–87. Reprint, Grand Rapids: Eerdmans, 1994.

art. article

BC before Christ

BECNT Baker Exegetical Commentary on the New Testament

bk. book

ca. circa

cf. *confer*, compare

chap(s). chapter(s)

col(s). column(s)

comm. comments on

d. died

disp. disputation

div. division

EBC Expositor's Bible Commentary

ed(s). editor(s), edited by, edition

e.g. *exempli gratia*, for example

esp. especially

ESV English Standard Version

et al. *et alii*, and others

FC Formula of Concord

ff. and following

fl. flourished

fol(s). folio(s)

HWT historic worldview theory

ICC International Critical Commentary

i.e. *id est*, that is

KJV King James Version

lect. lecture

n.d. no date

NIGTC New International Greek Testament Commentary

no(s). number(s)

NPNF[1] *A Select Library of Nicene and Post-Nicene Fathers of the Christian Church.* 1st series. Edited by Philip Schaff. 14 vols. New York: Christian Literature, 1886–89. Reprint, Grand Rapids: Eerdmans, 1994.

p(p). page(s)

PNTC Pillar New Testament Commentary

PSR principle of sufficient reason

pt. part

q(q).   question(s)
r   recto
rep. obj.   reply to the objection
repr.   reprint
rev.   revised (by)
SCG   *Summa contra Gentiles*
serm.   sermon
s.v.   *sub verbo*, under the word
TAG   transcendental arguments for
            the existence of God

TOTC   Tyndale Old Testament
            Commentaries
trans.   translator, translated by
v   verso
vol(s).   volume(s)
WBC   Word Biblical Commentary
WCF   Westminster Confession of Faith
WLC   Westminster Larger Catechism

Old Testament

Gen.   Genesis
Exod.   Exodus
Lev.   Leviticus
Num.   Numbers
Deut.   Deuteronomy
Josh.   Joshua
Judg.   Judges
Ruth   Ruth
1–2 Sam.   1–2 Samuel
1–2 Kings   1–2 Kings
1–2 Chron. 1–2 Chronicles
Ezra   Ezra
Neh.   Nehemiah
Esther   Esther
Job   Job
Ps(s).   Psalm(s)
Prov.   Proverbs
Eccles.   Ecclesiastes

Song   Song of Songs
Isa.   Isaiah
Jer.   Jeremiah
Lam.   Lamentations
Ezek.   Ezekiel
Dan.   Daniel
Hosea   Hosea
Joel   Joel
Amos   Amos
Obad.   Obadiah
Jon.   Jonah
Mic.   Micah
Nah.   Nahum
Hab.   Habakkuk
Zeph.   Zephaniah
Hag.   Haggai
Zech.   Zechariah
Mal.   Malachi

New Testament

Matt.   Matthew
Mark   Mark
Luke   Luke
John   John
Acts   Acts
Rom.   Romans
1–2 Cor.   1–2 Corinthians
Gal.   Galatians
Eph.   Ephesians
Phil.   Philippians
Col.   Colossians

1–2 Thess. 1–2 Thessalonians
1–2 Tim.   1–2 Timothy
Titus   Titus
Philem.   Philemon
Heb.   Hebrews
James   James
1–2 Pet.   1–2 Peter
1–3 John   1–3 John
Jude   Jude
Rev.   Revelation

INTRODUCTION

We know God by two means: First, by the creation, preservation, and government of the universe, since that universe is before our eyes like a beautiful book in which all creatures, great and small, are as letters to make us ponder the invisible things of God: God's eternal power and divinity.

Belgic Confession, article II

Man must be twice converted, first from the natural to the spiritual life, and then from the spiritual to the natural.

Herman Bavinck

The divine library consists of two beautiful books, the book of nature and the book of Scripture. In the wake of the Protestant Reformation, theologians promoted *sola scriptura*, that Scripture alone is the sole authority in the life and doctrine of the church. As a result of this doctrinal commitment, Reformation theologians have heavily used the book of Scripture. The book has been preserved over the years; its cover and pages show signs of regular and consistent use well into the present day. However, within the Reformed community the book of nature sits on the shelf largely unused and covered in a layer of dust. In the early modern period, most notably the sixteenth and seventeenth centuries, despite the prominent use of the book of Scripture, the book of nature was still regularly used by theologians. Evidence for the use of both books appears prominently in a number of major Reformed confessions, such as the Gallican (1559) and Belgic (1561). The Gallican states that God reveals himself "in his works, in their creation, as well as in their preservation

1

and control," and "more clearly, in his word" (II).[1] Likewise, the Belgic Confession likens the creation to "a beautiful book in which all creatures, great and small, are as letters to make us ponder the invisible things of God: his eternal power and his divinity, as the apostle Paul says in Romans 1:20" (II).

Similarly, the Westminster Confession (1647) speaks of the light of nature as that which manifests the goodness, wisdom, and power of God (1.1) and provides general principles for ordering worship (1.5); as the means by which unbelievers might morally frame their lives (10.4); as a guardian against the abuse of Christian liberty (20.4); and as the means by which all people know that God should be worshiped (21.1). Early modern Reformed theologians willingly employed the book of nature for a number of theological purposes but at the same time carefully defined its limits. The Westminster Confession, for example, opens with reference to the light of nature but immediately explains: "Yet are they not sufficient to give that knowledge of God, and of his will, which is necessary unto salvation" (1.1). Reformed theologians acknowledged the reality and utility of natural revelation, namely, the knowledge of God in creation, as well as a limited and carefully defined natural theology. That is, they acknowledged that there were certain truths available to the powers of natural reason. Just as one can exegete the book of Scripture, so too one can exegete the book of nature and make true claims about God. But the Reformed theologians were clear: this knowledge is not saving but is complementary to supernatural revelation (Scripture). The book of Scripture gives knowledge of Christ and salvation and thus takes interpretive priority in the exegesis of the book of nature.[2] Natural theology is drawn from the order of nature, and supernatural theology, which transcends human reason, is drawn from the order of grace. Both forms of knowledge are revealed and are not merely a matter of human discovery.[3] From the *principium* of Scripture, Reformed theologians employed natural theology to establish general rules of morality, restrain sin, and leave fallen humanity without an excuse for rejecting God.[4] In other words, Reformed theologians made regular use of the book of nature.

Opinions about the utility and legitimacy of this book changed in the late nineteenth and the twentieth centuries. Reformed theologians began to take a decidedly negative attitude toward any use of the book of nature.

---

1. Unless otherwise noted, all quotations and references from confessional and catechetical documents come from Jaroslav Pelikan and Valerie Hotchkiss, eds., *Creeds and Confessions of Faith in the Christian Tradition*, 3 vols. (New Haven: Yale University Press, 2003).

2. Richard A. Muller, *Post-Reformation Reformed Dogmatics*, 4 vols. (Grand Rapids: Baker Academic, 2003), 1:280.

3. Muller, *Reformed Dogmatics*, 1:283.

4. Muller, *Reformed Dogmatics*, 1:286.

Enlightenment philosophy made inroads into different corners of the Reformed world, and philosophical monism in particular was influential. Eighteenth- and nineteenth-century idealist philosophers argued that a system of thought had to be deduced from one principle. In technical terms, theologians sought to deduce their systems from one central dogma, which stood in contrast to early modern models that recognized two starting points, namely, Scripture and God.[5]

Philip Schaff (1819–93), for example, explains that a dogmatic system "ought to have a central idea which dominates the several parts and sheds light upon them." Schaff identified the centers of many different theological schools of thought but ultimately opined that Christology was the only doctrine that should have this role: "The center is not the beginning, but it throws light on the beginning and the end. Christology furnishes the key for theology and anthropology." Schaff believed "the best modern systems of evangelical theology in Europe and America are tending more and more toward the Christocentric theology."[6] Schaff was not alone but was part of a greater idealist-influenced theological movement that shifted attention away from the book of nature to the book of Scripture because Christology appears only in the latter, not in the former. This theological bud fully flowered in the twentieth-century Reformed community.

Karl Barth (1886–1968) is perhaps the best-known twentieth-century Reformed opponent of natural theology. Barth famously debated Emil Brunner (1889–1966) and metaphorically pounded his shoe on his desk in Khrushchev-like fashion when he said "Nein!" to Brunner's defense of natural theology. Barth rejected any theology that differed fundamentally from Jesus Christ and whose method differed from the exegesis of Scripture. Barth believed that the church should bypass natural theology as one would pass by an abyss lest one be plunged into its foreboding depths.[7] Barth was not alone in his assessment as a wide spectrum of Reformed theologians made similar claims. Cornelius Van Til (1895–1987) claimed, "No form of natural theology has ever spoken properly of the God who is there."[8] These Reformed theologians and philosophers criticized early modern Reformed theologians for reintroducing scholasticism to the biblically pure theology of the Reformation. Their forebearers,

5. Muller, *Reformed Dogmatics*, 1:123–48, esp. 125.
6. Philip Schaff, *Theological Propaedeutic: A General Introduction to the Study of Theology* (New York: Charles Scribner's Sons, 1893), 362–63.
7. Emil Brunner and Karl Barth, *Natural Theology: Comprising "Nature and Grace" by Professor Dr. Emil Brunner and the Reply "No!" by Dr. Karl Barth* (1946; repr., Eugene, OR: Wipf & Stock, 2002), 75.
8. Cornelius Van Til, "Letter to Francis Schaeffer," March 11, 1969, 1.

they claimed, engaged in synthesizing thought, which these critics understood as an effort to combine pagan Greek philosophy with scriptural teaching.[9]

Alvin Plantinga summarizes the overall negative assessment of natural theology, which ranges from indifference, suspicion, and hostility to accusations of blasphemy.[10] In Plantinga's examination of John Calvin's (1509–64) attitudes toward natural theology, he concludes: "The Christian doesn't need natural theology, either as the source of his confidence or to justify his belief."[11] Others have come to similar conclusions through slightly different historical and exegetical routes. First Corinthians 2:6–16 is supposedly "the death blow to all natural theology," and thus "natural theology may have a place in Roman Catholic and Arminian theologies . . . but not in a theology that would be Reformed."[12] Given the contemporary evangelical antipathy to natural theology and the efforts of some to extirpate it from Reformed theology, the book of nature has been placed back on the shelf and sits unused beneath a thick layer of dust in many parts of the Reformed world.

The goal of this essay is to retrieve the book of nature primarily for use in defending the faith, or apologetics. While theologians and historians may debate the precise nature and definition of natural theology, the Reformed confessional witness clearly attests to the veracity and utility of the book of nature, or in other terms, the *light of nature*. There are many avenues by which one might investigate the history and viability of the book of nature, but I approach it via two chief subjects: common notions and their connections to the order of nature. Put differently, this essay explores the connections between the innate and acquired knowledge of God—the knowledge that God inscribes on human hearts, which they bear by virtue of their identity as divine image-bearers, and the connections that this innate knowledge has to the broader created world. As Francis Turretin (1623–87) explains, historically the Reformed acknowledged natural and supernatural theology: "The natural, occupied with that which may be known of God (*to gnōston tou Theou*), is both innate (from the common notions implanted in each one) and acquired (which creatures gain discursively)."[13] Reformed theologians constructed their concept of *common notions* from the books of both nature

---

9. E.g., B. J. van der Walt, *Heartbeat: Taking the Pulse of Our Christian Theological and Philosophical Heritage* (Potchefstroom: Potchefstroom University, 1978), 278–98.

10. Alvin Plantinga, "The Reformed Objection to Natural Theology," in *Philosophy of Religion: Selected Readings*, ed. Michael Peterson et al. (Oxford: Oxford University Press, 2001), 329.

11. Plantinga, "Reformed Objection," 333.

12. Richard B. Gaffin Jr., "Some Epistemological Reflections on 1 Cor 2:6–16," *Westminster Theological Journal* (1995): 123–24.

13. Francis Turretin, *Institutes of Elenctic Theology*, ed. James T. Dennison Jr., trans. George Musgrave Giger, 3 vols. (Phillipsburg, NJ: P&R, 1992–97), 1.2.7.

and Scripture, from the testimony of pagan authorities as well as a number of biblical passages, most notably Romans 1:19–20 and 2:14–15.

The effort to recover the book of nature for the defense of the faith begins with a positive exposition of key concepts through a historical survey of the *light of nature* in the Westminster Confession, common notions, and Calvin's views on the book of nature. Chapter 1 therefore surveys the concept of the light of nature in the Westminster Confession. The phrase appears five times but often receives scant attention from commentators. This chapter explores the concept both through the Confession as well as the lectures of a key Westminster divine, Anthony Burgess (d. 1664). Burgess presented his lectures on the law of God at the same time as the divines were writing the Confession, and thus these lectures provide significant illumination on what the Confession means by invoking the term *light of nature*. Under this category, Burgess introduces the concept of common notions (the innate natural knowledge of God) as well as delineates how human reason functions in a postfall world. This chapter therefore explores the concept of the light of nature, enabling readers to see how classic Reformed theology stands at odds with the opinions of many contemporary Reformed theologians and philosophers.

Chapter 2 delves more deeply into the subject of common notions by first exploring Burgess's exegesis of Romans 2:14–15, the chair passage (*sedes doctrinae*) for the concept. This chapter reveals both the exegetical footing and the amicable interaction that Burgess had with numerous theological and philosophical authorities, most notably Thomas Aquinas (1225–74). The chapter therefore sets forth Burgess's concept of common notions and their connections to Aquinas and then situates his views within the larger early modern Reformed context to demonstrate that Burgess's views were unexceptional. The use of common notions was no aberration but rather the majority report. Although there were holdouts in the Reformed tradition, such as theologians Charles Hodge (1797–1878) and Herman Bavinck (1854–1921), with the dawn of the Enlightenment and march into the present, the concept of common notions was cast aside.

Chapter 3 examines the views of John Calvin on the book of nature, but more specifically common notions and their connection to the order of nature. This chapter explores Calvin's views, not because they are in any way normative for the tradition, the benchmark for subsequent "Calvinists," but rather because so many in the contemporary period appeal to him. Many historians and theologians have created a Calvin of myth and ignore the Calvin of history. That is, the Calvin of myth supposedly rejected all manifestations of natural theology, began with the self-attesting Christ of Scripture as his starting point, scuttled all forms of scholasticism and synthetic thinking, and thus rejected the traditional proofs for the existence of God. This chapter challenges the Calvin of myth and seeks to recover the Calvin of history with respect to his use of the book of nature. In line with the majority report, Calvin advocated a version of common notions, namely, the Stoic concept of *prolēpsis* or "preconception," and connected this innate knowledge of God to the broader created order. The Calvin of history employs both common notions and the scholastic method, and he presents his own versions of some of the traditional arguments for the existence of God. In short, these first three chapters establish the historical legitimacy of the use of common notions and their connections to the order of nature within historic confessional Reformed theology.

Chapter 4 turns from positive historical exposition to the first of four critical issues: Aquinas, historic worldview theory, transcendental arguments, and dualisms. Contemporary Reformed theologians have made a number of claims that present hurdles that must be overcome in order to recover the book of nature for apologetics. Therefore, chapter 4 deals with a number of contemporary claims, chiefly from Cornelius Van Til, regarding Aquinas. According to Van Til, one of the supposedly disqualifying features of common notions is that they rest upon the results of synthetic thought: Aquinas built his theological foundation on philosophy instead of Scripture. Thus Aquinas and any positive appeal to him ultimately rest upon autonomous reason rather than Scripture. If Van Til's critique of Aquinas is correct, then there are significant problems for historic Reformed theology, since it has broad agreement with Aquinas on the subject of common notions. The chapter demonstrates, however, that Van Til largely misread Aquinas due to his overreliance on secondary sources and that Van Til and Aquinas actually have more in common than Van Til realized. Both theologians start from a foundation of Scripture; Aquinas is not a rationalist. Thus the Reformed Orthodox appeal to and agreement with Aquinas on common notions is not an obstacle to their recovery and utility for apologetics.

Chapter 5 probes matters related to historic worldview theory (hereafter HWT). The rise of philosophical idealism was one of the reasons why the book of nature was largely set aside, namely the idea that one must have a comprehensive view of life and the world that has a solitary starting point unfolding into a holistic system of thought. Nineteenth-century advocates of HWT believed that there was no common doctrine of man (hence no divinely inscribed common notions); thus all worldviews were incommensurable, or mutually contradictory. Evangelical and Reformed theologians—most notably James Orr (1844–1913), Abraham Kuyper (1837–1920), and Van Til— embraced elements of HWT, which diminished the role of the book of nature in Orr's and Van Til's apologetic systems. Kuyper mitigated the effects of

HWT by advocating a robust doctrine of common grace, but Van Til mostly rejected common notions because of his commitment to the idea that world-views are incommensurable due to their supposed origins in synthesis think-ing. What Van Til rejected with one hand, however, he reintroduced with the other: Van Til rejected common notions and instead argued that Christians have to appeal to unbelievers on the basis of the innate knowledge of God, their identity as divine image-bearers, and their status as covenant breakers. Van Til needlessly distanced himself from historic Reformed theology. But for all his protestations, he nevertheless advocated the same concepts under a different name. Once again, though Van Til chided the Reformed Orthodox and others such as Herman Bavinck for their use of common notions, Van Til actually employs the same concepts.

Chapter 5 also explores the impact of HWT on contemporary Reformed theology, specifically how it has unnecessarily diminished the use of the book of nature. Through exegetical argumentation I show how Paul in Romans 2:14–15 and Acts 17 employed common notions as a part of his theology and his efforts to evangelize the lost. The implication of this exegesis is that Christians must not shy away from employing the book of nature in our theology or apologetics. Common notions are a vital part of God's natural revelation and thus fundamental to good theology. Believers and unbelievers have multiple points of contact, but among them are their shared common notions—the divinely inscribed innate natural knowledge of God. Thus be-lievers can appeal to these common notions in the defense of the faith: they can appeal to God's book of nature.

Chapter 6 explores the issue of transcendental arguments, or more specifi-cally, the transcendental argument for the existence of God (TAG). Theolo-gians devoted to Van Tillian apologetics tout the Copernican nature of his contribution through his introducing the TAG, which some claim is the most biblical form of argumentation. In the simplest terms, one argues from the impossibility of the contrary. Only presupposing the existence of the God of the Bible adequately explains all reality. But the TAG has its origins in ideal-ist philosophy and is wedded to HWT. This does not mean that the TAG is therefore automatically unbiblical or should be cast aside. Van Til promoted the use of the TAG in conjunction with the use of evidence, even the traditional proofs for the existence of God, but some Van Tillians have shied away from or even rejected the use of evidence. The degree to which apologists employ the TAG apart from appeal to the book of nature is the level to which they part ways with historic Reformed theology or reveal their ignorance of its history. The TAG can be a useful argument in the apologist's toolbox, but not at the cost of the depreciation or neglect of the book of nature. At the heart of this chapter is the importance of recognizing that some proponents of the TAG have unduly emphasized the coherence theory of truth at the expense of the correspondence theory. Truth must not only systematically cohere with reality but must also correspond to it. In other words, our claims about God and the Bible must correspond to the world around us. Or we can say that the books of Scripture and nature speak with one voice, and thus we can and must appeal to both in our efforts to defend the faith. Any argument that discourages appeal to the book of nature should be rejected.

Chapter 7 addresses one of the most common objections against historic Reformed theology, namely, the accusation of being dualistic. Efforts to *distinguish* between earthly and heavenly knowledge or to acknowledge that grace presupposes nature invite accusations that Reformed theologians adopted scholasticism and the nature-grace dualism. This chapter therefore primarily interacts with the claims of Herman Dooyeweerd (1894–1977) and demonstrates that to distinguish between nature and grace and acknowledge the natural and spiritual realms—or in this case that there are two books, nature and Scripture—does not introduce a dualism of any kind. Rather, Dooyeweerd's arguments rest on an inaccurate historical-theological foundation, a failure to recognize the difference between *separations* and *distinctions*. Appealing to natural law or common grace in the process of defending the faith does not introduce a pagan dualism but simply means the apologist reads the book of nature in conjunction with the book of Scripture.

The final chapter (8) transitions from hurdling potential objections to sketching out how one can employ the book of nature in defending the faith. This chapter is not programmatic or comprehensive but is merely an outline demonstrating how the books of nature and Scripture can work together in apologetics. I address matters of epistemology (how we know) in the prefall and postfall world within the framework of classic Reformed covenant theology and demonstrate the aims of a covenant epistemology, namely, love and eschatology. I also explore the goals of apologetics, starting points, the points of contact that exist between believers and unbelievers, and the importance of the use of evidence in the defense of Christianity. This chapter shows that, as important as the book of Scripture is, Christians should also use the book of nature. And rather than make claims about exhaustive knowledge of the world, we must always seek the wisdom of Christ and present the truth to unbelievers in humility.

Due to a number of factors, including the influence of idealism on theological methodology, comprehensive views of life and the world, and taking

Scripture as the only starting point for all knowledge, the book of nature has been displaced or even set aside in some cases. While the book of Scripture must always take priority in the Christian life and doctrine, Christians can and should appeal to God's beautiful book of nature. We can appeal to the innate (common notions) and acquired natural knowledge (the world) of God in concert with Scripture. As Herman Bavinck once noted, "Man must be twice converted, first from the natural to the spiritual life, and then from the spiritual to the natural."[14] Despite contemporary aversions to natural theology, historic Reformed theology made regular and frequent use of the book of nature, and the present volume aims to recover it for apologetics. Why should Christians tie one hand behind their backs and use only one of God's two books? The books of nature and of Scripture are not enemies, nor does the book of nature belong on the list of banned books. Rather, we should read both books—perusing their pages, noting how they speak with one voice, and recognizing that the book of nature shouts out that God exists and proclaims his power and might, that he created the world, and that he made human beings in his image and inscribed his law upon their hearts. Even though these truths do not mention the gospel and the redemption that comes only through Christ, they nevertheless testify to the points of contact with unbelievers and thus have the greatest necessity and utility in the process of defending the faith.

14. Herman Bavinck, *The Philosophy of Revelation* (repr., Grand Rapids: Baker, 1979), 242.

1

THE LIGHT OF NATURE

Lay aside Reason at first and then receive truths by Faith; and afterwards improve
them by Reason, and it will excellently help.

Anthony Burgess, Westminster Divine

The Book of Scripture without doubt hath preeminence in worth by many
degrees; but that of the creatures had the precedency, and was extant long
before the written word.

John Arrowsmith, Westminster Divine

The Westminster Confession (1647) begins with the statement "Although the
light of Nature, and the works of Creation and Providence do so farre manifest
the Goodnesse, Wisdome, and Power of God, as to leave men unexcusable yet
are they not sufficient to give that knowledge of God and of his Will, which
is necessary unto salvation" (1.1).[1] What precisely do the divines intend by
the term *light of nature*? One recent commentary on the Confession claims
that the opening statement refers to one of two categories, namely, general
and special revelation, or the books of nature and Scripture, and only briefly
touches on the issue of humanity's natural understanding of the book of
nature.[2] Two other commentaries bypass the statement altogether and deal

1. *The Humble Advice of the Assembly of Divines, Now by Authority of Parliament Sitting
at Westminster, concerning a Confession of Faith* (London: Company of Stationers, 1647).
2. John H. Gerstner, Douglas F. Kelly, and Philip B. Rollinson, *The Westminster Confession
of Faith: A Guide* (Signal Mountain, TN: Summertown Texts, 1992), 1.

entirely with Scripture as special revelation.[3] Older nineteenth-century commentaries, however, devote more attention to the issue of the light of nature
and explain it by the claim "God may be discovered by the light of nature, we
mean that the senses and the reasoning powers, which belong to the nature of
man, are able to give him so much light as to manifest that there is a God."[4]
In line with this older trend, the most recent commentary on the Confession,
written by Chad Van Dixhoorn, rightly notes that it begins with the doctrine
of Scripture, but the first sentence deals with a different subject: the light of
nature. Moreover, this commentary also explains the character of this concept:
"There is the 'light of nature,' by which is meant the divine imprint which
is left on each of us by our Maker. That is, we are made in God's image and
even though we are fallen creatures, God's image remains stamped upon us.
And there are 'the works of creation and providence.' The world that we see
and the world about which we read tell us of our Creator and Provider."[5]

But even though Van Dixhoorn's analysis is correct, he only touches on
the character of the light of nature. Namely, general revelation includes both
the knowledge connected to the divine image and the works of creation and
providence. He correctly acknowledges that the divines were following the
apostle Paul's arguments in Romans 1 and 2 and statements from the psalmist
(Ps. 19). But Van Dixhoorn then concludes, "In those chapters the apostle both
reminds us of this general revelation and tells us that it leaves every person
without an excuse before God. For this reason, both in our evangelism and in
our defence of the faith, we should always remember that Christians should
never be trying to prove the existence of God to unbelievers. We are reminding
unbelievers of what they already know."[6] Van Dixhoorn's explanation of the
Confession is generally true, but his analysis of its meaning and implication
deserves deeper and more precise investigation.

Late twentieth-century Reformed theology suffered a general antipathy to
any form of natural theology. Reformed theologians were content to acknowledge the existence of general revelation and its role in rendering humanity
guilty of failing to worship God as they ought, but they were little interested in

3. G. I. Williamson, *The Westminster Confession of Faith for Study Classes* (Philadelphia:
P&R, 1964), 3–9; Rowland S. Ward, *The Westminster Confession of Faith: A Study Guide*
(Melbourne, Australia: New Melbourne Press, 1992), 11–18.

4. Robert Shaw, *Exposition of The Westminster Confession of Faith* (1845; repr., Fearn, UK:
Christian Heritage, 1998), 36; see also A. A. Hodge, *The Confession of Faith: A Handbook
of Christian Doctrine Expounding the Westminster Standards* (repr., Edinburgh: Banner of
Truth, 1958), 26–29.

5. Chad Van Dixhoorn, *Confessing the Faith: A Reader's Guide to the Westminster Confession of Faith* (Edinburgh: Banner of Truth, 2014), 4.

6. Van Dixhoorn, *Confessing the Faith*, 4.

assigning anything more to it. Instead, as in some of the recent commentaries on the Confession, theologians sprint for the doctrine of Scripture and hardly acknowledge the light of nature. While frequency statistics do not always reveal a doctrine's importance, the term *Trinity* occurs only twice (2.1; 8.2) whereas the term *light of nature* appears five times in the Confession (1.1, 6; 10.4; 20.4; 21.1). Since the light of nature is not simply a passing idea, we should seek a thicker account of this concept.

One of the best sources for understanding the concept of the light of nature comes from one of the Westminster divines, Anthony Burgess (d. 1664). Burgess participated in the writing of the Confession and also lectured on the subject when the divines were constructing the Confession's chapter on the law. In fact, some argue that Burgess's lectures in his *Vindiciae Legis* provide a window into understanding the intricate details that undergird the Confession's summary presentation of the law.[7] This is not to say that Burgess was the chief architect or author of chapter 19 on the law.[8] Nevertheless, the structural similarities between Burgess's lectures and the final product reveal the symbiotic relationship between the two.[9] Hence, an examination of Burgess's lectures on the law provides a primary-source explanation of what the Westminster divines intend by the term *light of nature*. Through the use of Burgess's lectures, this chapter demonstrates that the light of nature denotes three things: (1) natural law, (2) human reason, and (3) God's natural revelation in creation. In short, the light of nature denotes the book or order of nature written and designed by God—an important tool in defending the Christian faith, a tool forgotten by many in contemporary Reformed theology but regularly used by early modern Reformed theologians. In contrast to some recent analyses of the first chapter of the Confession, Burgess gives a full-throated explanation and defense of the light of nature as natural law and human reason.

Natural Law

In his explanation of the law, Burgess devotes five lectures to the exegetical and theological exposition of Romans 2:14–15: "For when the Gentiles which know not the law, do the things of the law by nature, these having not the

7. Stephen J. Casselli, *Divine Rule Maintained: Anthony Burgess, Covenant Theology, and the Place of the Law in Reformed Scholasticism* (Grand Rapids: Reformation Heritage Books, 2016), 12–14.
8. Casselli, *Divine Rule Maintained*, 33.
9. Casselli, *Divine Rule Maintained*, 36.

law, are a law unto themselves: which shew the work of the law written in their hearts."[10] Early modern Reformed theologians connected the *light of nature* with the natural-law concept of *common notions*. John Downame (1571–1652), for example, writes: "But the combat of conscience doth begin oftentimes long before conversion, even as soone as we have the use of reason and understanding, receiving common notions from the light of Nature."[11] Here Downame writes of the common notions *and* the light of nature, but elsewhere he speaks of the "common notions of the light of Nature."[12] Similar terminology appears in Pierre Du Moulin (1568–1658); he connects common notions with "natural light" and a "generall knowledge of the law."[13] The Confession itself uses the term *law of nature* in parallel with a similar term *light of nature* (21.1). A clear confessional witness to the connections between the light of nature and common notions appears in the Canons of Dordt (1618–19):

> There is, to be sure, a certain light of nature remaining in man after the fall, by virtue of which he retains some notions about God, natural things, and the difference between what is moral and immoral, and demonstrates a certain eagerness for virtue and for good outward behavior. But this light of nature is far from enabling man to come to a saving knowledge of God and conversion to him—so far, in fact, that man does not use it rightly even in matters of nature and society. Instead, in various ways he completely distorts this light, whatever its precise character, and suppresses it in unrighteousness. In doing so he renders himself without excuse before God.[14]

10. Anthony Burgess, *Vindiciae Legis: A Vindication of the Morall Law and the Covenants* (London: Thomas Underhill, 1647), 57.

11. John Downame, *The Christian Warfare against the Devill, World and Flesh Wherein Is Described Their Nature, the Maner of Their Fight and Meanes to Obtaine Victorye* (London: William Stansby, 1634), 2.8.9, p. 1107.

12. Downame, *Christian Warfare*, 2.9.6, p. 1110.

13. Pierre Du Moulin, *The Anatomy of Arminianisme* (London: Nathaniel Newbery, 1620), 26.13, p. 215.

14. Canons of Dordt, III/IV art. 4. The Synod commissioned a commentary on the whole Bible: Theodore Haak, *The Dutch Annotations upon the Whole Bible* (1637; London: Henry Hills, 1657). Note *Annotations*, comm. Rom. 1:19, which states: "[Namely, as much as a man can know of God, without Gods words, by nature] . . . i.e., among their wise and learned men, who have left very many cleer and wise sentences and discourses hereof in their writings, although they themselves did contrary thereunto, . . . partly by the Law of nature in their consciences, . . . partly by beholding of Gods creatures, whereby his properties are as it were felt, Ps. 19:2 and 148:4–6; Acts 14:15 and 17:24, etc." Likewise, Haak identifies the written law with nature and the "work of the law" written on the heart as having the contents of God's law (Haak, *Annotations*, comm. Rom. 2:14–15). Three delegates to the Synod also wrote a summary work of theology, the fruit of the disputation cycles at the University of Leiden. They provide a fuller explanation of the concept of common notions: *Synopsis Purioris Theologiae / Synopsis of a*

The Canons refer to the "light of nature" and "notions about God, natural things, and the difference between what is moral and immoral," which are common notions. The Synod limits the function of common notions, which are nonsaving and subject to the noetic effects of sin. But what, exactly, are common notions?

Burgess writes: "The Law of Nature consists in those common notions which are ingrafted in all men's hearts." These include belief in the existence of God and a general knowledge of the difference between good and evil. At this point Burgess positively invokes Thomas Aquinas's (1225–74) treatment of natural law to substantiate his point: "*Aquinas saith well, that what principles of Sciences are in things of demonstration, the same are these rules of nature in practicals*: therefore we cannot give any reasons of them; but, as the Sun manifests it selfe by its owne light, so doe these."[15] In other words, common notions do not require proof because they are self-evident. Burgess further explains this point by citing Chrysostom (ca. 349–407), who argues that God forbids murder and other sins apart from a specific rationale: "Thou shalt not kill" (Exod. 20:13 KJV). By way of contrast, when he enjoins the Sabbath upon Israel, he provides a reason: "For the LORD . . . rested on the seventh day" (Exod. 20:11 KJV). The Sabbath command is moral, but it is not a naturally revealed command but a moral positive command.[16]

Burgess is well aware of the questions that would immediately follow. How do common notions function before and after the fall? Burgess acknowledges that there are certainly prefall and postfall differences in how common notions function. In the prefall context, these laws were perfectly implanted in Adam's heart, but now, in a postfall world, human beings have only residual fragments of them.[17] Yet even though Burgess uses negative language to describe the postfall state of common notions, he does not completely eradicate the idea from his postfall anthropology. There were some, such as Lutheran theologian Matthias Flacius Illyricus (1520–75), who argued that God de novo infuses common notions into human beings when he regenerates them. He

---

Purer Theology, ed. Dolf te Velde et al., trans. Riemer A. Faber, 2 vols. (Leiden: Brill, 2014), disp. 18; see also Donald Sinnema and Henk van den Belt, "The *Synopsis Purioris Theologiae* (1625) as a Disputation Cycle," *Church History and Religious Culture* 92, no. 4 (2012): 505–37.

15. Burgess, *Vindiciae Legis*, 62; cf. Thomas Aquinas, *Summa Theologica* (repr., Allen, TX: Christian Classics, 1948), Ia-IIae q. 94 art. 2. For an overview of Aquinas on natural law, see Michael Baur, "Law and Natural Law," *The Oxford Handbook of Aquinas*, ed. Brian Davies and Eleonore Stump (Oxford: Oxford University Press, 2012), 238–54; Clifford G. Kossel, "Natural Law and Human Law (Ia IIae, qq. 90–97)," in *The Ethics of Aquinas*, ed. Stephen J. Pope (Washington, DC: Georgetown University Press, 2002), 169–93.

16. Burgess, *Vindiciae Legis*, 62.

17. Burgess, *Vindiciae Legis*, 62.

held this view because he wanted to demonstrate how original sin completely eviscerated God's image in fallen human beings. In fact, Illyricus believed humans bore the image of Satan, not God, as a consequence of the fall, a position confessionally rejected by the Lutheran churches in the Formula of Concord (1577).[18] Burgess also mentions "a godly man, in his Book of *Temptations*," who holds the same view.[19] Burgess, therefore, rejected Illyricus's idea that the fall completely obliterated common notions from the human heart.

Burgess does acknowledge, however, the difficulty of determining the precise boundaries of the law of nature. There are four opinions regarding where these boundaries lie:

1. *The general principles in which man and beast agree, such as self-defense and the desire for life.* Burgess rejects this version because it excludes ethical categories such as honesty and righteousness. Beasts are incapable of sin and obligation to the law. This view was held by ancient Roman jurists.[20]

2. *The general custom of the nations, or* ius Gentium. Burgess rejects this claim because not all people agree on what, precisely, constitutes a vice or a virtue. This was the view of Isidore of Seville (ca. 560–636).[21]

3. *The reason in every person.* This too is uncertain because people disagree on many ethical questions.

4. *The will of God declared to Noah in seven precepts and later to Moses in the Decalogue.* Burgess objects because the law of nature thus extends from first principles to deduced conclusions.[22] This was the view of rabbinic scholars.[23]

Instead of these four opinions, Burgess opts for identifying the law of nature as it is revealed in the moral law delivered by Moses at Sinai. But he quickly

18. Matthias Flacius Illyricus, *De Peccati Originalis aut Veteris Adami Appellationibus et Essentia*, in *Clavis Scripturae S. seu Sermone Sacrarum Literarum* ([Basel]: Eusebius Episcopius, 1580), 370; see also Robert C. Schultz, "Original Sin: Accident or Substance—the Paradoxical Significance of FC I, 53–62 in Historical Context," in *Discord, Dialogue, and Concord: Studies in the Lutheran Reformation's Formula of Concord*, ed. Lewis W. Spitz and Wenzel Lohff (Philadelphia: Fortress, 1977), 38–57.

19. Burgess, *Vindiciae Legis*, 63.

20. Justinian, *Justinian's Institutes*, trans. Peter Birks and Grant McLeod (London: Duckworth, 1987), 1.2, pp. 38–39.

21. Isidore, *The Etymologies of Isidore of Seville*, trans. Stephen A. Barney et al. (Cambridge: Cambridge University Press, 2006), 5.4, p. 117.

22. Burgess, *Vindiciae Legis*, 62–63.

23. David Novak, *Natural Law in Judaism* (Cambridge: Cambridge University Press, 1998), 149–67. In the early modern period, see, e.g., John Selden, *De Successionibus in Bona Defuncti ad Leges Ebraerorum* (London: Richard Bishop, 1636).

points out that there are differences between the law of nature and the Decalogue. One of the most significant differences is that God reveals one to the
conscience and the other through the written law, the Torah.[24] Burgess does
not believe that the light of nature can sufficiently instruct people for proper
worship or provide knowledge sufficient for salvation. Nevertheless, the law
of nature provides reproof for evil conduct. "Doth not Nature," writes Burgess, "condemne lying, couzening in your trades, lusts, and uncleannesse?"
Burgess appeals to Cicero (106–43 BC) and his *On Obligations* to show that
unbelievers condemn deception and unlawful gain.[25]

At this point Burgess's explanation of common notions provides a robust
account of two of the Confession's uses of the term *light of nature*. The
Confession identifies the light of nature as one of the means by which Christians can determine whether or not their use of Christian liberty is moral or
immoral: "They, who upon pretence of Christian Liberty, shall oppose any
lawfull Power, or the lawfull exercise of it, whether it bee Civil or Ecclesiasti-
call, resist the Ordinance of God. And, for their publishing of such Opinions,
or maintaining of such Practices, as are contrary to the light of Nature, or to
the known Principles of Christianity" (20.4). The divines believed, therefore,
that a Christian should not use his Christ-bought liberty to violate the moral
law and that two guardrails against doing so were naturally revealed law and
supernaturally revealed law, or common notions and Scripture. Noteworthy
is that the divines appeal to 1 Corinthians 5:1: "It is reported commonly that
there is fornication among you, and such fornication as is not so much as
named among the Gentiles, that one should have his father's wife" (KJV).
In other words, not only did Scripture prohibit such sexual immorality (Lev.
18:8), but so did natural law, the common notions that pagans had by virtue
of the divinely heart-inscribed works of the law. The assembly's commentary
on Scripture explains the significance of Paul's statement and the Confession's
rationale for appealing to common notions: "The sin was incest, forbidden,
Levit. 18:8. *The nakedness of thy fathers wife shalt thou not uncover*; an
horrible crime, and such as the very Gentiles detested, and severely punished
in their laws, if any among them (which seldom fell out) defiled themselves
with any such unnatural contract, or abominable act."[26]

Such conclusions were common among Reformed theologians. French Reformed theologian Lambert Daneau (ca. 1535–ca. 1590), for example, appealed

---

24. Burgess, *Vindiciae Legis*, 65.

25. Burgess, *Vindiciae Legis*, 66; see, e.g., Cicero, *De Officiis* (*On Duties*), trans. Walter
Miller, Loeb Classical Library (Cambridge, MA: Harvard University Press, 1913), 1.10.33, p. 35.

26. *Annotations upon All the Books of the Old and New Testament*, 3rd ed. (London: Evan
Tyler, 1657), comm. 1 Cor. 5:1.

to the light of nature to explain why the Gentile sailors on Jonah's doomed voyage were fearful and cried out to their respective gods: "That men by the light of nature are taught sufficiently that there is a god, and that he is the governour of this world, and that he is the author & giver of life, and other good things unto us: but who he is they are ignorant, who have not learned it out of his word."[27] In Daneau's judgment, the light of nature included the "testimony or witness of conscience," which was present in both the believer and unbeliever and enabled them to discern the difference between good and evil.[28] Daneau offers a full-fledged explanation of the character and boundaries of the light of nature:

> For all men by the remnants of the light of nature which is in them, far generally knowe, that God is both just, and also merciful: that which his government of the worlde, and experience it selfe doeth prove: but yet all this notwithstanding they neither know the foundation, nor yet the force both of this justice, and also mercy of God, as namely being infidels, the which nevertheless the faithful far understand, being taught both by the word of God and also by the holy ghost. We have therefore seen before both in the mariners, and also in the Ninevites themselves, what manner of common knowledge there is in all men, yea, even in the infidels concerning the righteousness of God, to wit, that he is just, and a punisher of wickedness: so also this is a common principle engrafted in the hearts of all men, that God likewise is merciful and loving. But both these knowledges far far differ from that, which the godly and the faithful have concerning both these properties and virtues of God, out of his word, and by the feeling and sweetness of a true faith.[29]

The light of nature, therefore, includes common knowledge among believer and unbeliever that binds them to the same moral standards but leaves the unbeliever far short of true faith and saving knowledge.

That natural law was suitable for determining questions of morality even among unbelievers did not mean that it provided a foundation on which to construct a tower to heaven. The Westminster divines recognized that the light of nature was the means by which people might be "never so diligent to frame their lives" but that such moral conduct fell far short of the required

27. Lambert Daneau, *A Fruitfull Commentarie upon the Twelve Small Prophets* (Cambridge: University of Cambridge, 1594), comm. Jon. 1:5, p. 95. In general, see Daneau, *The Wonderfull Woorkmanship of the World: Wherein Is Conteined An Excellent Discourse of Christian Naturall Philosophie* (London: Andrew Maunsell, 1578).

28. Daneau, *Fruitfull Commentarie*, comm. Jon. 1:10, p. 102. So also Dudley Fenner, *The Sacred Doctrine of Divinitie* (London: Felix Kyngston, 1613), 10; William Twisse, *A Discovery of D. Jackson's Vanity* (Amsterdam, 1631), 455.

29. Daneau, *Fruitful Commentarie*, comm. Jon. 3:9, pp. 201–2.

supernatural regenerative work of the Spirit (10.4; cf. WLC q. 60). Burgess confirms this interpretation in his lectures when he acknowledges that the light of nature instigates and provokes people to morally good actions toward God and man. And in fact, pagans have written wholesome laws by means of the light of nature. In support of this claim Burgess cites Scripture and the testimony of pagan philosophers.[30] Burgess appeals to Scripture and the time when pagan Jethro advised Moses concerning the best and most sagacious way to rule Israel during the nation's journey in the wilderness. Burgess again cites Chrysostom to make his point: "*That great Man Moses (saith he) who was so potent in words and workes, who was the friend of God, which commanded the creatures, was helped in counsell by Jethro his father-in-law, an obscure man, and a Barbarian.*"[31] Burgess appeals to several pagan philosophers to prove his point, including Aristotle (384–322 BC), Plato (ca. 428–348 BC), and Seneca (4 BC–AD 65).[32]

Burgess appealed to Aristotle to prove that reason was a prisoner, bound by the chains of lust and sinful affections, which the peripatetic philosopher manifested in his own life. Aristotle knew what was good but nevertheless pursued pleasure or profit instead of virtue. Despite his pursuit of pleasure, Aristotle knew that the better part of the mind sought better things, that is, what was morally right. Plato similarly had knowledge of the one true God, argues Burgess, but he did not communicate it to the common person.[33] Burgess also appeals to Seneca through a citation of Augustine's (354–430) *City of God*, where Augustine explains that Seneca kept the truth in unrighteousness: "That liberty, in truth, which [Varro] wanted, so that he did not dare to censure that theology of the city . . . in part possessed by Annaeus Seneca. . . . It was in part possessed by him, I say, for he possessed it in writing, but not in living."[34] In particular, the reason Burgess cites Augustine's analysis of Seneca is because Seneca condemned idolatry: "They dedicate images of the sacred and inviolable immortals in most worthless and motionless

30. Burgess, *Vindiciae Legis*, 68–69.

31. Burgess, *Vindiciae Legis*, 68; see Chrysostom, *Homilies on Second Corinthians* 18 (NPNF[1] 12:366–67).

32. At this point in church history some believed Seneca corresponded with the apostle Paul; see Pseudo-Seneca, "The Correspondence of Paul and Seneca," in *The Apocryphal New Testament*, trans. M. R. Jones (Oxford: Clarendon, 1924).

33. Burgess, *Vindiciae Legis*, 68. Here Burgess likely employs a commonly used set of references to make his point, as the same citations to Plato, Augustine, and Seneca appear in John Flavel (ca. 1627–91), *The Method of Grace*, in *The Whole Works of the Reverend Mr. John Flavel*, 2 vols. (London: D. Midwinter et al., 1740), 1:408. It is also possible that Flavel relied on Burgess for his citations of the same authorities.

34. Augustine, *City of God* 6.10 (NPNF[1] 2:119).

matter. They give them the appearance of man, beasts, and fishes, and some make them of mixed sex, and heterogeneous bodies. They call them deities, when they are such that if they should get breath and should suddenly meet them, they would be held to be monsters."[35]

Burgess interacts with Augustine's quotation of Seneca because it applies to both pagan and "Popish" idolatry, but at the same time Burgess follows Augustine, who castigates the philosopher for his failure to follow his own counsel:

> But this man, who philosophy had made, as it were, free, nevertheless, because he was an illustrious senator of the Roman people, worshipped what he censured, did what he condemned, adored what he reproached, because, forsooth, philosophy had taught him something great—namely, not to be superstitious in the world, but, on account of the laws of cities and the customs of men, to be an actor, not on the stage, but in the temples—conduct the more to be condemned, that those things which he was deceitfully acting he so acted that the people thought he was acting sincerely.[36]

Burgess summarizes his point when he explains that the light of nature inclines the heart to what is objectively good and shows what it should desire, but he also adds: "Not that we have any strength naturally to what is good."[37]

Human Reason

Burgess places other ideas under the rubric of the light of nature. In particular, he devotes a considerable amount of space to explaining how the light of nature included human reason. Burgess is fully aware of the noetic effects of sin and recognizes that only a sovereign act of God's Spirit enables natural man to accept the things of God (1 Cor. 2:14). Natural man, according to Burgess, is not someone engaged in carnal or gross sin but rather a pagan such as Cicero or Aristotle. Burgess believes that three things obscure the light of nature: (1) poor education, (2) old customs and degeneration, and (3) God's just judgment (Rom. 1:24–32).[38] But that reason was corrupted by sin does not mean that reason should therefore be rejected. Burgess sees several functions of reason for unregenerate and regenerate humanity.

35. Augustine, *City of God* 6.10 (*NPNF*[1] 2:119).
36. Augustine, *City of God* 6.10 (*NPNF*[1] 2:120).
37. Burgess, *Vindiciae Legis*, 69–70.
38. Burgess, *Vindiciae Legis*, 71.

First, the light of nature renders people inexcusable before the divine bar, as Paul states in Romans 1:20.[39] This point aligns with the Confession's first reference to the light of nature in its opening statement: "Although the light of Nature . . . so farre manifest the Goodnesse, Wisdome, and Power of God, as to leave men unexcusable" (1.1). Second, Burgess believes that the light of nature, or reason, is of use to the regenerate when enlightened by God's word. "Lay aside Reason at first," writes Burgess, "and then receive truths by Faith; and afterwards improve them by Reason, and it will excellently help." Burgess echoes the ancient principle that goes back to Augustine, namely, faith seeking understanding.[40] Burgess likens reason to Hagar, Sarah's handmaid, and counsels his readers not to cast her out.[41] In fact, Burgess agrees with Roman Catholic Franciscan theologian Diego Estella (1524–78) and quotes him as saying, "It is with Faith and Reason, as with the mould that is at the root of the barren and fruitlesse tree; take the mould out, and throw in muck or other compost, and then put the mould in, it will much help the tree, which hindered it before."[42] When reason is sanctified by the Spirit, it becomes a useful tool for the better comprehension of Scripture.

But a third role for reason is in religious and moral matters—that is, in God's work of salvation. At first blush, such a role for reason might appear to overthrow all that Burgess has argued thus far. Yet Burgess is very precise in the way he accounts for the role of reason in salvation. Burgess argues that the light of nature is the "residue of the glorious image of God," and as such is absolutely necessary in two ways: (1) as a passive qualification for saving faith, and (2) as an instrument. Burgess explains these two uses of the light of nature in the following manner. Stones are incapable of reason and do not bear the image of God: "Therefore Reason, or the light of Nature, makes man in a passive capacity fit for grace; although he hath no active ability for it."[43] Burgess does not appeal to the category but likely has in mind the common threefold doctrine of faith, which consists of *notitia* (the facts), *assensus* (comprehension), and *fiducia* (trust).[44] Fallen human beings are incapable of

39. Burgess, *Vindiciae Legis*, 70.
40. Augustine, *Tractates on the Gospel of John*, Fathers of the Church 88 (Washington, DC: Catholic University of America Press, 1993), 29.6, pp. 17–19.
41. Burgess, *Vindiciae Legis*, 71. The use of Sarah and Hagar as faith and reason goes back at least to Clement of Alexandria; see his *Stromata* 1.5 (ANF 2:305–6).
42. Burgess, *Vindiciae Legis*, 71.
43. Burgess, *Vindiciae Legis*, 72.
44. See, e.g., Guillaume Bucanus, *Institutiones Theologicae* (Geneva: Jacob Stoer, 1625), 29.7, p. 276; Bucanus, *Body of Divinity, or Institutions of Christian Religion* (London: Daniel Pakeman et al., 1659), 328–30; Zacharias Ursinus, *Corpus Doctrinae Orthodoxae* (Heidelberg: Jonah Rodius, 1616), 108; Ursinus, *The Commentary of Dr. Zacharias Ursinus on the Heidelberg*

embracing Christ in a saving manner by the power of unaided reason. There is
no governing role for reason in accepting the person and work of Christ. On
the other hand, when someone presents the truth of the gospel, the recipient
must have a rational comprehension of the facts and what those facts mean. In
this sense, reason has a role in salvation. Burgess makes this very point when he
discusses the instrumental role of reason: "For we cannot beleeve, unlesse we
understand whether knowledge be an act ingredient into the essence of faith, or
whether it be prerequisite: all hold there must be an act of the understanding,
one way or other, going to beleeve. Hence knowledge is put for faith, and *Hebr.
11. By faith we understand.* Thus it is necessary as an instrument."[45] Or in the
words of Zacharias Ursinus (1534–83), "It is proper for us, therefore, to obtain
a knowledge of that in which we are to believe, before we exercise faith."[46]

Burgess is acutely aware of the potential for misunderstanding his claim
regarding the role of reason in salvation. He carefully demarcates the boundaries between the role of reason and the necessity of the Spirit's sovereign work
of regeneration, as does the Confession and its use of the light of nature (1.1;
10.4). Burgess notes, for example, that there are certain things known both
by reason and faith, but in different ways. The devils believe God is one, for
example, by "an evident intuitive knowledge of God, and feel it by experience;
not that they have faith, for that is a supernaturall gift wrought by God, and
hath accompanying it *pia affectio*, to him that speaketh, as the first truth."[47]
Burgess distinguishes his own view from the Lutherans, who diminish fallen
reason too much, and the Socinians, who attribute greater power to it than they
ought. Burgess gladly acknowledges that excellent men have demonstrated the
truth of Christianity by reason, and "we may by the same Reason prove that
the Christian Religion is the true one." But how can we compare bald reason
to faith? Burgess rejects, therefore, the views of Anglican theologian William
Chillingworth (1602–44), whom Burgess quotes as follows, "We therefore
receive the Scriptures to be the Word of God, because we have the greatest
Reason that this is the Word of God." Burgess rejects this idea as a form of
rationalism and warns that we must not confound the *instrument* with the
judge. That is, Scripture provides truth and reason hammers it for greater

---

Catechism (Columbus, 1852; repr., Grand Rapids: Eerdmans, 1954), 110–11; Francis Turre-
tin, *Institutio Theologiae Elencticae* (Geneva: Samuel de Tournes, 1688), 15.12.11; Turretin,
Institutes of Elenctic Theology, ed. James T. Dennison Jr., trans. George Musgrave Giger, 3
vols. (Phillipsburg, NJ: P&R, 1992–97); see Richard A. Muller, *Dictionary of Latin and Greek
Theological Terms: Drawn Principally from Protestant Scholastic Theology*, 2nd ed. (Grand
Rapids: Baker Academic, 2017), s.v. *notitia* (235), *assensus* (42–43), *fiducia* (123).
    45. Burgess, *Vindiciae Legis*, 72.
    46. Ursinus, *Commentary*, 110.
    47. Burgess, *Vindiciae Legis*, 73.

understanding: "As the Smith that takes that Golden plate, and beates it into what shape he pleaseth, his hammer doth not make it gold, but only gold of such a shape: And thus also Reason doth not make a truth divine, only holds it forth, and declareth it in such a way."[48] Burgess believes that reason still has an important role to play, but at the same time he carefully demarcates its boundaries: "Let us then follow the light of Nature no further than we ought; let her be an hand-maid, not a mistresse. And then we must take heed of going against her where she doth truly direct."[49]

Burgess is not alone in his understanding of the role and function of the light of nature, as similar views appear in another Westminster divine, John Arrowsmith (1602–59). In his *Armilla Catechetica* (1659), Arrowsmith explains that there are three types of knowledge of God: natural, literal, and spiritual.[50] The natural knowledge comes from the book of nature, which Arrowsmith describes in the following manner: "The Book of Scripture without doubt hath preeminence in worth by many degrees; but that of the creatures had the precedency, and was extant long before the written word." On this point, it is noteworthy that Arrowsmith appeals to Socrates (d. 399 BC) and Bernard of Clairvaux (1090–1153), who speak of the "book of all the creatures . . . to contemplate God in" and the ability to read nature, respectively.[51] Arrowsmith then delineates six ways by which people can know there is a God through the "natural light" available to them: by looking backward, forward, upward, downward, within, and without.[52]

Arrowsmith elaborates on these in the following manner, citing Scripture, pagan, and Christian authorities, including Ovid (43 BC–AD 17), Livy (59 BC–AD 17), Menander (342–290 BC), Plato, Galen (AD 129–210), Tertullian (ca. AD 155–ca. 240), Basil of Caesarea (AD 329–379), and Calvin (1509–64) to prove the legitimacy of each category:

Backward: By looking back to the creation of the world people can see and understand that God exists (Rom. 1:20).

Forward: By looking ahead to the final judgment and the rewards and punishments of the next world.

Upward: By looking up to the existence of angels and demons and tracing the effects back to the causes of evil mischief, especially.

48. Burgess, *Vindiciae Legis*, 73–74.
49. Burgess, *Vindiciae Legis*, 76.
50. John Arrowsmith, *Armilla Catechetica: A Chain of Principles* (Cambridge: John Field, 1659), 3.1, p. 111.
51. Arrowsmith, *Armilla Catechetica*, 3.1, p. 119.
52. Arrowsmith, *Armilla Catechetica*, 3.2, pp. 120–21.

Downward: By looking to things beneath humans, such as the elements, plants, and brute beasts (Ps. 19:1; Job 12:7–9).

Within: By looking within to human physiology (Ps. 139:14) as well as to the dictates of conscience.

Without: By looking around at the various events in the world, great deliverances and calamities (Ps. 9:16).[53]

In these six ways that humans can find God by the light of nature, Arrowsmith shows the wide and expansive scope of the book of creatures. Within the framework of these six ways, Arrowsmith also explains the means by which human reason can inquire after God: by way of causality (*via causalitatis*), elimination (*via remotionis*), and prominence (*via eminentiae*). But Arrowsmith clearly states that none of these ways can make a full discovery of God's essence.[54] Arrowsmith's and Burgess's understandings of the light of nature admit the same categories and have the same boundaries, and both encompass human reason, conscience (common notions), and the ability to discern the existence of God from the creation.

Conclusion

Burgess's lectures on the light of nature are more expansive than what this chapter has covered. He deals with many other related topics that merit further investigation. But this survey certainly invites the question, Why did Burgess have a greater conception of the light of nature than his twentieth-century counterparts do? There are several brief answers to this question. First, in the middle of the seventeenth century, philosophers such as John Locke (1632–1704) rejected the idea of common notions.[55] In the twentieth century, this rejection made its way to liberal and conservative Reformed theologians alike, including Karl Barth (1886–1968) and Cornelius Van Til (1895–1987).[56] Historians and theologians in the twentieth century believed that natural law was an unwanted post-Reformation cancerous wart that grew

53. Arrowsmith, *Armilla Catechetica*, 3.1–2, pp. 121–27.

54. Arrowsmith, *Armilla Catechetica*, 3.3, pp. 129–30.

55. John Locke, *Essays on the Law of Nature*, ed. W. von Leyden (Oxford: Clarendon, 2002), 137–45, 161–79; see also Arthur F. McGovern, "John Locke on Knowledge of the Natural Law" (master's thesis, Loyola University, 1958), 18–51.

56. Karl Barth, *Church Dogmatics*, ed. G. W. Bromiley and T. F. Torrance (Edinburgh: T&T Clark, 1988), IV/1:369–72; see also Rinse H. Reeling, *Karl Barth and Post-Reformation Orthodoxy* (London: Routledge, 2015), 88; Cornelius Van Til, *The Defense of the Faith*, 3rd ed. (Phillipsburg, NJ: P&R, 1967), 160–78, esp. 168–69.

on the otherwise beautiful face of Reformed theology. In this vein, a number of twentieth-century theologians tried to pit Calvin against the so-called Calvinists by arguing that natural law was an outlier in the Genevan's theology that his disciples wrongly exaggerated and employed.[57] Recent scholarship has ably dismantled this fictional narrative.[58] The later chapter on Calvin delves into these matters in greater detail.

Second, twentieth-century theologians ceased to recognize natural revelation as an ontological aspect of anthropology and more or less located it strictly in the created world. While Burgess would heartily agree that God reveals himself in the world, he at the same time believed that common notions, or the light of nature, were a remnant of God's image: "The image of God did primarily consist in righteousness and true holinesse; yet secondarily it did also comprehend the powers and faculties of the reasonable soule in the acts thereof."[59] On this point, Burgess appealed to Romans 1, especially 1:19–20, and the fact that Paul acknowledges that fallen humanity possesses the truth.[60]

Third, twentieth-century Reformed theologians and philosophers identified common notions (or the light of nature) and the use of reason in theology with Roman Catholicism. Such is the case with August Lang's essay on the Reformation and natural law, Herman Dooyeweerd's (1894–1977) assessment of Reformed scholastic theology, and Van Til's evaluation of common notions, as we will see in subsequent chapters. In their efforts to saw off a perceived diseased branch, they also cut off the perch on which Burgess and the Westminster Confession sat. What these scholars believed was rotten Roman Catholic theology was instead part of the common catholic heritage that stretched back through Aquinas to Augustine and the apostle Paul. This is evident by Burgess's positive quotation of Aquinas. Paul wrote of the Gentiles who did by nature what the law required because they had the works of the law written on their hearts, and Reformed theologians like Burgess and others confirmed their exegetical conclusions when they explored the works of pagan philosophers such as Plato, Aristotle, Seneca, and Cicero. But as classical learning fell under the scorn of historians and theologians, they ceased to cite these ancient authorities. Theologians removed foundation stones that eventually caused the wall of natural law and reason to collapse.

57. See, e.g., August Lang, "The Reformation and Natural Law," in *Calvin and the Reformation*, trans. J. Gresham Machen (New York: Revell, 1927), 56–98.

58. See David VanDrunen, *Natural Law and the Two Kingdoms: A Study in the Development of Reformed Social Thought* (Grand Rapids: Eerdmans, 2010), 67–115; Stephen J. Grabill, *Rediscovering the Natural Law in Reformed Theological Ethics* (Grand Rapids: Eerdmans, 2006), 70–97.

59. Burgess, *Vindiciae Legis*, 67.

60. Burgess, *Vindiciae Legis*, 68.

Twentieth-century commentators on the Confession, therefore, ignore or reject what Reformed theologians once thought was an integral part of their system of doctrine.

In the end, this brief exploration of Burgess's lectures demonstrates that the light of nature was more than the revelatory testimony of the created world. Moreover, the light of nature had a greater function than merely rendering fallen humanity inexcusable before the divine bar of judgment. The light of nature certainly incorporates these two elements but also includes the subjects of natural law and human reason. Natural law is a vital part of the image of God, even though it has been ravaged by the noetic effects of sin. Reason also had a role to play in a person's salvation, albeit a passive role, but a role nonetheless. When our eyes pass over the term *light of nature* in the Westminster Confession, we should recognize that more is present than first meets the eye. We must also not automatically assume that contemporary expositions of the Westminster Confession accurately or exhaustively unpack its teachings. The church must patiently revisit the works of the early modern period so that the fresh breeze of the centuries reminds us of forgotten truth, which allows us to refine and expand our own understanding of the Westminster Confession of Faith. With a better understanding of the light of nature, we reacquire an important tool for our apologetics toolbox. But we must first explore the topic of common notions in greater detail so that we have a better understanding of how this concept functioned in early modern Reformed theology. By retrieving the idea of common notions, we add yet another useful tool to our defense of the faith. We rediscover the importance of the book of nature and its utility in our interaction with the unbelieving world.

2

COMMON NOTIONS

For when the Gentiles, which have not the law, do by nature the things contained
in the law, these, having not the law, are a law unto themselves: Which shew
the work of the law written in their hearts, their conscience also bearing witness, and their thoughts the mean while accusing or else excusing one another.

Romans 2:14–15 KJV

There is, to be sure, a certain light of nature remaining in man after the fall,
by virtue of which he retains some notions about God, natural things, and the
difference between what is moral and immoral, and demonstrates a certain
eagerness for virtue and for good outward behavior. But this light of nature
is far from enabling man to come to a saving knowledge of God and conversion to him—so far, in fact, that man does not use it rightly even in matters of
nature and society. Instead, in various ways he completely distorts this light,
whatever its precise character, and suppresses it in unrighteousness. In doing
so he renders himself without excuse before God.

Canons of Dordt, III/IV art. 4

In his highly esteemed series of lectures on the law, *Vindiciae Legis*, Anthony
Burgess spills a great deal of ink exegeting and exploring the theological implications of Romans 2:14–15, quoted above. Burgess's treatment covers five
lectures and forty-seven pages.[1] He exegetes Romans 2:14–15 because, within

---

1. Anthony Burgess, *Vindiciae Legis: A Vindication of the Morall Law and Covenants*
(London: Thomas Underhill, 1647), 57–104.

his understanding of the moral law, the law of nature constitutes one of two legal pillars in his doctrine of the covenant of works: the law of nature and God's positive command (Gen. 1:27). This chapter focuses on the concept of *common notions* for several reasons. First, Burgess provides a useful definition and discussion of the concept. Second, he cites authorities in support of his definition, a move that reveals the catholic nature of his claims. Third, Burgess's discussion reveals more information regarding the phrase *light of nature* when it appears in the Westminster Standards. Fourth, understanding common notions provides Christians with important information regarding the point of contact they share with unbelievers, which they can employ as they evangelize. Hence, this chapter unpacks Burgess's discussion of common notions and then compares his understanding with other Reformed theologians to demonstrate that his use of the concept was nearly universally accepted within early modern Reformed theology. It was not until late orthodoxy and beyond that Enlightenment rationalists scuttled the concept. The chapter then concludes with some observations about the role of common notions and their utility for defending the faith.

Burgess on Common Notions

Exegetical Prolegomena

Burgess opens his first lecture on Romans 2:14–15 by explaining who Paul has in mind when he states that the Gentiles have the works of the law written upon their hearts. Burgess explains that Paul refers to those who do not have the law of Moses, that is, those peoples who were not a party to the Mosaic covenant in which God explicitly revealed the moral law. Burgess was aware of other possible interpretations, namely, that Paul has Gentile Christian converts in view, a probable opinion argued by Chrysostom (ca. 349–407) and Roman Catholic theologian Guilielmus Estius (1542–1613).[2] But as probable as such an opinion might be, Burgess interprets the term as a reference to non-Jews who did not receive the explicitly revealed law at Sinai. This is because Paul states they are "'without a law, and a law to themselves' which could not be true of Gentiles converted."[3] Burgess also rejects the Pelagian interpretation of

---

2. Cf. Chrysostom, *Homilies on Romans* 5 (NPNF[1] 11:364–66); Guilielmus Estius, *Commentarius Epistolae ad Romanos*, in *Commentariorum in Epistolas Apostolicas*, 11 vols. (Louvain: J. P. G. Michel, 1778), 1:94–102. On Chrysostom's views on Rom. 2:14–15, see Matthew Levering, "Christians and Natural Law," in *Natural Law: A Jewish, Christian, and Islamic Trialogue*, ed. Anver M. Emon, Matthew Levering, and David Novak (Oxford: Oxford University Press, 2014), 86–91.

3. Burgess, *Vindiciae Legis*, 59.

this term, which argues that Paul has in view the prophecy of Jeremiah 31:33, "I will put my law in their inward parts, and write it in their hearts" (KJV).[4] Pelagian theologians, according to Burgess, argue that God wrote the law on Gentile hearts and thus enabled them to fulfill it unto salvation. In other words, Pelagians believed that the Bible taught works-salvation, a claim that according to Burgess runs contrary to the doctrine of grace and the gospel.[5]

As Burgess moves through the text he asks, What does Paul mean by *nature*? What, precisely, is in view when Paul says that the Gentiles "do by nature the things contained in the law"? Burgess quickly acknowledges that not all unbelievers perform the things of the law, as is evident from Paul's statements in Romans 1:18–32. Neither does Paul claim that they perform the things universally contained in the law. Rather, they perform some "external acts" as Aristides (530–468 BC) and Socrates (d. 399 BC) explain.[6] That Burgess cites these two ancient authorities is important because he begins to unveil the classical sources of his understanding of the law of nature, or common notions. By *nature*, therefore, Burgess understands "that naturall light of conscience, whereby they judged and performed some externall acts, though these were done by the help of God."[7]

Burgess then turns to the question of how God writes the law on human hearts. In his response, Burgess distinguishes this Pauline text from the prophecy of Jeremiah and refutes what he considers the erroneous exegesis of Augustine (354–430), who correlates the two texts.[8] But Burgess avers that there is a twofold writing of the law. The first consists of knowledge and judgment whereby God enables people to know the difference between good and evil. The second affects the will and affections, by which redeemed sinners have a propensity and delight to act on what they know to be good. According to Burgess, Jeremiah's prophecy deals with this second inscription of the law on the heart, which is a benefit of the covenant of grace and union with Christ. Whereas the first inscription deals with matters Paul addresses in Romans 1:19,

4. Pelagius, *Pelagius's Commentary on St. Paul's Epistle to the Romans*, trans. Theodore de Bruyn (Oxford: Clarendon, 1998), 72–73; see also Levering, "Christians and Natural Law," 96–99.

5. Burgess, *Vindiciae Legis*, 59.

6. John M. Rist, *Human Value: A Study in Ancient Ethics* (Leiden: Brill, 1997), 18. Medieval theologians employed the distinction between internal conditions and external acts, which continued into the early modern period; see, e.g., Thomas Aquinas, *Summa Theologica* (repr., Allen, TX: Christian Classics, 1948), Ia-IIae q. 20. By this point in the historical discussion, however, Burgess may simply be repeating common names and concepts rather than directly citing these ancient texts; cf., e.g., Zacharias Ursinus, *The Commentary of Zacharias Ursinus on the Heidelberg Catechism*, trans. G. W. Williard (1852; repr., Phillipsburg, NJ: P&R, n.d.), 68.

7. Burgess, *Vindiciae Legis*, 59–60.

8. Augustine, *On the Spirit and the Letter* 43–48, esp. 46 (NPNF[1] 5:101–3); Levering, "Christians and Natural Law," 99–104.

namely, "That which may be known of God is manifest in them; for God hath shewed it unto them" (KJV). God declares his laws in two ways: externally and internally. By the former, he creates good and wholesome laws to govern human beings. And internally, God also declares these laws by writing them upon the conscience, which either brings fear or comfort to people because they either heed or disregard the testimony of conscience.[9] Burgess therefore concludes that God writes his law on the hearts of all people, which leads him to the specific subject of the law of nature, and it is here that he turns to the subject of common notions.

Common Notions

What are common notions? The previous chapter touched on this concept in Burgess's lectures, but it will be helpful to review briefly his main definitions and claims. Burgess describes common notions thus: "The Law of Nature consists in those common notions which are ingrafted in all men's hearts," some of which include the existence of God as well as a general knowledge of the difference between good and evil. Burgess positively invokes Thomas Aquinas's (1225–74) treatment of natural law and common notions to substantiate his point.[10] In agreement with Aquinas, Burgess believes common notions do not require proof because they are self-evident.

How do common notions function before and after the fall? Burgess acknowledges that there are certainly prefall and postfall differences in how common notions function. In the prefall context, these laws were perfectly implanted in Adam's heart, but now, in a postfall world, human beings have only residual fragments.[11] But at the same time, even though Burgess uses negative language to describe the postfall state of common notions, that does not mean he completely eradicated the idea from his postfall anthropology, which stands in contrast to the views of the Lutheran theologian Matthias Flacius Illyricus (1520–75). Illyricus argued for God's de novo infusion of common notions into human beings when he regenerates them. Illyricus's views were rejected by the Lutheran churches in the Formula of Concord (1577).[12] Burgess therefore rejects the idea that the fall completely obliterated common notions from the human heart.

9. Burgess, *Vindiciae Legis*, 60.
10. Burgess, *Vindiciae Legis*, 62; see also Aquinas, *Summa Theologica*, Ia-IIae q. 94 art. 2.
11. Burgess, *Vindiciae Legis*, 62.
12. Matthias Flacius Illyricus, *De Peccati Originalis aut Veteris Adami Appellationibus et Essentia*, in *Clavis Scripturae S. seu Sermone Sacrarum* (Basil: Eusebius Episcopius, 1580), 370; see also Robert C. Schultz, "Original Sin: Accident or Substance—the Paradoxical Significance of FC I, 53–62 in Historical Context," in *Discord, Dialogue, and Concord: Studies*

Recall that Burgess acknowledges the difficulty in determining the precise boundaries of the law of nature. He identifies four opinions on where these boundaries lie:

1. *The general principles in which man and beast agree, such as self-defense and the desire for life.* Burgess rejects this version because it excludes ethical categories such as honesty and righteousness. Beasts are incapable of sin and obligation to the law.
2. *The general custom of the nations, or* ius Gentium. Burgess rejects this claim because not all people agree on what, precisely, constitutes a vice or a virtue.
3. *The reason in every person.* This too is uncertain because people disagree on many ethical questions.
4. *The will of God declared to Noah in seven precepts and later to Moses in the Decalogue.* Burgess objects because the law of nature thus extends from first principles to deduced conclusions.[13]

Instead of these four opinions, Burgess identified the law of nature as it is revealed in the moral law delivered by Moses at Sinai. Yet he quickly points out that there are differences between the law of nature and the Decalogue. One of the primary differences is that God reveals one to the conscience and the other through the written law, the Torah.[14] Burgess does not believe that the light of nature can sufficiently instruct people for proper worship or provide knowledge sufficient for salvation.

Comparative Analysis

To what degree are Burgess's views similar to other historic sources on common notions? And how conventional were his views among his Reformed peers? This section explores these questions by first surveying the ancient and medieval pedigree of the concept and then tracing its reception among ancient authorities, medieval thinkers, and early modern theologians and confessions. It shows that Burgess's views were of ancient and medieval origins and were held by the overwhelming majority within the early modern Reformed tradition.

---

in the Lutheran Reformation's Formula of Concord, ed. Lewis W. Spitz and Wenzel Lohff (Philadelphia: Fortress, 1977), 38–57.

13. Burgess, *Vindiciae Legis*, 62–63.

14. Burgess, *Vindiciae Legis*, 65.

Ancient Origins

Any early modern Reformed theologian would heartily acknowledge that God is the ultimate source of common notions, and they would do so typically based on Romans 2:14–15, among other texts. The ultimate source, therefore, of common notions is God, but the proximate source of the concept is the ancient philosophers—Socrates, Plato (ca. 428–348 BC), and Aristotle (384–322 BC) among others. However, the one who developed the concept of common notions most explicitly is the ancient mathematician Euclid (fl. 300 BC), who proposed what he called five *koinai ennoiai*, or common notions:

1. Things equal to the same thing are also equal to one another.
2. If equal things are added to equal things, then the wholes are equal.
3. If equal things are subtracted from equal things, then the remainders are equal.
4. Things that coincide with one another are equal to one another.
5. The whole is greater than the part.[15]

Euclid's main point is that these mathematical principles are self-evident and known by all, so they should not require proof. Ancient philosophers also employed a version of the concept but applied it to the commonly shared knowledge that all people possess. Olympiodorus, for example, wrote a commentary on Plato's *Gorgias* around AD 550, in which he describes the *common notions* as the God-given foundations for right moral conduct.[16]

Thomas Aquinas

Theologians such as Augustine acknowledged that God wrote his law on the hearts of all people, and others, such as Boethius (ca. 480–524), observed that people universally recognize certain propositions. Although Boethius does not invoke his name, he nevertheless refers to Euclid's common notions: "If you take equals away from two equals, the remainders are equal."[17] Aquinas also explored these concepts and eventually included them in his own understanding of natural law.[18] In addition to the principles he culls

15. Euclid, *The Thirteen Books of The Elements*, trans. Thomas L. Heath, 2nd ed. (1956; New York: Dover, 2016), 1:155.

16. A. A. Long, *Epictetus: A Stoic and Socratic Guide to Life* (Oxford: Clarendon, 2002), 95.

17. Thomas Aquinas, *An Exposition of "On the Hebdomads" of Boethius* (Washington, DC: Catholic University of America Press, 2001), 1.20, p. 3.

18. Aquinas, *Summa Theologica*, Ia-IIae q. 94 art. 2. For an overview of Aquinas on natural law, see Michael Baur, "Law and Natural Law," *The Oxford Handbook of Aquinas*, ed. Brian

from Boethius, Aquinas includes other self-evident concepts such as the law of noncontradiction, that the same thing cannot be affirmed and denied at the same time, which he bases on Aristotle's concepts of being and nonbeing. From these and other considerations, Aquinas identifies the first precept of law: people should pursue good and avoid evil.[19] He affirms with Isidore that natural law is common to all nations.[20] But he then drills down into the subject and explains how natural law functions, namely, how reason moves from the common to the proper, as Aristotle argues.[21] In this particular case, Aquinas invokes the categories of speculative and practical reason. Speculative reason deals with indemonstrable principles, and practical reason deals with contingent matters.[22] Recall that these are the same categories that Burgess invoked in his own explanation of common notions, thus demonstrating the Thomistic character of his concept of natural law.[23]

Nevertheless, Aquinas writes, "In speculative matters truth is the same in all men, both as to principles and as to conclusions: although the truth is not known to all as regards the conclusions, but only as regards the principles which are called common notions."[24] This statement constitutes a classic formulation of the concept of common notions, one that Reformed theologians repeatedly invoke in their own discussions of the subject. In fact, there is little variation between Aquinas and later Reformed theologians on this point. Even though some Reformed theologians claim that Aquinas believed the fall had no effect on human reason, Aquinas nevertheless clearly states the contrary:

> We must say that the natural law, as to general principles, is the same for all, both as to rectitude and as to knowledge. But as to certain matters of detail, which are conclusions, as it were, of those general principles, it is the same for all in the majority of cases, both as to rectitude and as to knowledge; and yet in some few cases it may fail, both as to rectitude, by reason of certain obstacles,

---

Davies and Eleonore Stump (Oxford: Oxford University Press, 2012), 238–54; Clifford G. Kossel, "Natural Law and Human Law (Ia IIae, qq. 90–97)," in *The Ethics of Aquinas*, ed. Stephen J. Pope (Washington, DC: Georgetown University Press, 2002), 169–93.

19. Aquinas, *Summa Theologica*, Ia-IIae q. 94 art. 2; see Aristotle, *Metaphysics*, in *The Basic Works of Aristotle*, ed. Richard McKeon (New York: Random House, 1941), 4.6, p. 749.

20. Aquinas, *Summa Theologica*, Ia-IIae q. 94 art. 4; see Isidore, *The Etymologies of Isidore of Seville*, trans. Stephen A. Barney et al. (Cambridge: Cambridge University Press, 2006), 5.4, p. 117.

21. Aquinas, *Summa Theologica*, Ia-IIae q. 94 art. 4; see Aristotle, *Physics*, in *The Basic Works of Aristotle*, ed. Richard McKeon (New York: Random House, 1941), 1, pp. 218–36.

22. Aquinas, *Summa Theologica*, Ia-IIae q. 94 art. 4.

23. Burgess, *Vindiciae Legis*, 62.

24. Aquinas, *Summa Theologica*, Ia-IIae q. 94 art. 4.

... and as to knowledge, since in some the reason is perverted by passion, or evil habit, or an evil disposition of nature.[25]

In other words, Aquinas distinguishes between principles and conclusions. He acknowledges that the principles of natural law are the same in all people, but given the noetic effects of sin, people draw erroneous conclusions from these common principles.[26] Early Reformed theologians embraced these same categories and distinctions but arguably placed greater emphasis on the noetic effects of sin. They did not, however, in any way reject Aquinas's categories or the validity of common notions.

Philip Melanchthon and John Calvin

One of the first Protestant theologians to introduce natural law to the burgeoning tradition was Philip Melanchthon (1497–1560). Melanchthon reflected on Romans 1 and 2 and incorporated natural law into his theological system. He also recognized common notions by tracing them back to the shared mathematical principles elaborated by Euclid.[27] Other Protestant Reformers, such as Reformed theologian John Calvin (1509–64), also affirmed natural law. In his comments on Romans 1:19, Calvin argues that "which may be known of God" comes from the knowledge written by God upon human hearts.[28] In his comments on Romans 2:14–15, Calvin refers to common notions:

> Since then all nations, of themselves and without a monitor, are disposed to make laws for themselves, it is beyond all question evident that they have some notions of justice and rectitude, which the Greeks call preconceptions, *prolēpseis*, and which are implanted by nature in the hearts of men. They have then a law, though they are without law: for though they have not a written law, they are yet by no means wholly destitute of the knowledge of

25. Aquinas, *Summa Theologica*, Ia-IIae q. 94 art. 4; see also Arvin Vos, *Aquinas, Calvin, and Contemporary Protestant Thought: A Critique of Protestant Views of Thomas Aquinas* (Washington, DC: Christian University Press, 1985), 137–38.

26. For Aquinas's exegetical basis for his claims in the *Summa* on natural law, see Thomas Aquinas, *Commentary on the Letter of Saint Paul to the Romans*, ed. J. Mortensen and E. Alarcòn, trans. F. R. Larcher, Latin/English Edition of the Works of St. Thomas Aquinas 37 (Lander, WY: Aquinas Institute for the Study of Sacred Doctrine, 2012), comm. Rom. 2:14–15, §§215–23, pp. 75–77; see also Eugene F. Rogers Jr., "The Narrative of Natural Law in Aquinas's Commentary on Romans 1," *Theological Studies* 59 (1998): 254–76.

27. John Platt, *Reformed Thought and Scholasticism: The Arguments for the Existence of God in Dutch Theology, 1575–1650* (Leiden: Brill, 1982), 10–26.

28. John Calvin, *Romans*, trans. John Owen (Edinburgh: Calvin Translation Society, 1849), comm. Rom. 1:19, p. 70.

what is right and just; as they could not otherwise distinguish between vice and virtue.[29]

For Calvin, this was neither a slip of the quill nor a moment in which he inconsistently reverted to his former Roman Catholic ways. This was Calvin's careful reflection on Paul's text.[30] His comments not only anticipate Burgess's later exegesis of the same texts but are also similar to those of Aquinas. The next chapter investigates the parallels between Calvin and Aquinas in greater detail.

Girolamo Zanchi

One of the significant contributors to the early modern Reformed development of natural law was Girolamo Zanchi (1516–90), who was trained in Thomism by a fellow reformer, Peter Martyr Vermigli (1499–1562).[31] Zanchi thus included a wealth of medieval knowledge in his distinctively Reformed system of theology. In fact, in his massive theological corpus, Zanchi presented the Reformed equivalent of Aquinas's *Treatise on Law*, which was imbedded in his *Summa Theologica*.[32] Aquinas's fingerprints appear throughout Zanchi's treatise, but this does not mean that Zanchi uncritically adopted the medieval doctor's views. In fact, while Zanchi agreed with Aquinas that God inscribed his law on human hearts, in contrast to Aquinas, he argued that Paul's statements in Romans 2:14–15 mean that natural law is not a marred relic in the postfall image of God. Rather, God reinscribed the law on human minds after the fall to ensure its continued testimony.[33] "Natural law," writes Zanchi, "is a common principle and, therefore, a distinct rule put into the hearts and minds of human beings by God himself, warning them what they should do and what they should avoid."[34] According to Zanchi natural law has three functions: (1) to teach the difference between good and evil, (2) to obligate human beings to good and protect them from evil, and (3) to condemn and

29. Calvin, *Romans*, comm. Rom. 2:14–15, pp. 96–97.
30. See R. Scott Clark, "Calvin on the *Lex Naturalis*," *Stulos Theological Journal* 6, nos. 1–2 (1998): 1–22; David VanDrunen, *Natural Law and the Two Kingdoms: A Study in the Development of Reformed Social Thought* (Grand Rapids: Eerdmans, 2010), 67–115; Stephen J. Grabill, *Rediscovering the Natural Law in Reformed Theological Ethics* (Grand Rapids: Eerdmans, 2006), 70–97.
31. On Vermigli's Thomism, see John Patrick Donnelly, *Calvinism and Scholasticism in Vermigli's Doctrine of Man and Grace* (Leiden: Brill, 1976).
32. Stephen Grabill, introduction to *On the Law in General*, by Girolamo Zanchi, trans. Jeffrey J. Veenstra (Grand Rapids: Christian's Library, 2012), xxv.
33. Grabill, "Introduction," xxvii; Zanchi, *On the Law*, thesis 8, p. 15.
34. Zanchi, *On the Law*, thesis 8, p. 13.

convict people when they violate its principles.[35] Not only does the Decalogue
testify to the truths of natural law, but the Gentiles also possessed knowledge
about God evident from the apostle's sermon at Mars Hill (Acts 17:22).[36]

Francis Junius

Francis Junius (1545–1602) expounds natural law in his treatise on *The
Mosaic Polity*, which is a work devoted to the exposition of moral law. Within
his treatise, he deals with natural law and presents the following thesis: "The
natural law is that which is innate to creatures endowed with reason and
informs them with common notions of nature, that is, with principles and
conclusions adumbrating the eternal law by a certain participation."[37] It is
immediately apparent that Junius echoes Aquinas's understanding of law
and participation, namely, that creatures participate in the divine by means
of the eternal law.[38] Junius identifies the proximate source of common notions
to be the ancient philosophers.[39] And as Burgess after him, Junius speaks of
speculative and practical reason and states that all people, just and unjust
alike, possess these common notions so that they can pursue good and avoid
evil.[40] Junius divides common notions into two categories, namely, principles
and conclusions. Burgess and Junius echo what were the standard elements of
common notions. The principles are those things known in themselves and
are immutable and indemonstrable, such as God's existence. Conclusions,
on the other hand, are those things that are deductions from the principles,
such as that God must be worshiped.[41]

Junius's understanding of common notions, therefore, bears strong Thomist
accents, evident not only by his repetition of the categories of principles and
conclusions, but also from his emphasis on natural law serving as the shadow
of the eternal law by which human beings participate in the divine.[42] Junius
also writes with Thomist inflections when he discusses Adam's prefall nature.
Natural law, according to Junius, deals strictly with natural things. Since "no
human being living according to pure nature either would have known supernatural life and grace (which leads to life) by natural law, or would even gain

---

35. Zanchi, *On the Law*, thesis 8, p. 17.

36. Zanchi, *On the Law*, theses 8, 11, pp. 19–20, 24.

37. Francis Junius, *The Mosaic Polity*, trans. Todd M. Rester, ed. Andrew M. McGinnis
(Grand Rapids: CLP Academic, 2015), thesis 4, p. 44.

38. Cf. Aquinas, *Summa Theologica*, Ia-IIae qq. 90–97.

39. Junius, *Mosaic Polity*, thesis 4, p. 45.

40. Junius, *Mosaic Polity*, thesis 4, p. 45.

41. Junius, *Mosaic Polity*, thesis 4, p. 46.

42. Junius, *Mosaic Polity*, thesis 4, p. 47.

it naturally, it was necessary that a law superior to nature be added by the grace of God."[43] Hence, even though Adam was unfallen and free from sin, the perfect common notions written on his heart were insufficient for him to have knowledge of eternal life. Junius does not invoke the term, but he has in mind the *donum superadditum*, or the superadded gift of grace. According to Thomas, in a state of pure nature Adam was incapable of attaining or even conceiving of eternal life; thus Adam required an infusion of God's grace in the prefall state.[44] Junius adopts a similar understanding of Adam's prefall state and incorporates it into his own doctrine of the covenant of works. The fact that Reformed theologians adopted large portions of Thomas's formulation of common notions does not mean that they all did so to the same degree. Some adopted more than others. In other words, Reformed theologians varied in the extent to which they employed the concept of common notions as a part of their formulations of the covenant of works.

The Leiden Synopsis

The Leiden Synopsis, a theological work written by three professors who served as delegates to the Synod of Dordt (1618–19), was a collection of theological disputations from the University of Leiden.[45] The professors' intention was to publish the cycle of disputations that ran through *loci* of theology to codify post-Dordt orthodox theology, given the rise of heterodox Remonstrant theology. The disputation on the law in the Leiden Synopsis addresses the subject of common notions, which it places under the category of natural law (*lex naturalis*). The Synopsis defines natural law as "the light and direction of sound reason in the intellect informing man with common notions to distinguish right from wrong, and honorable from shameful—so that he may understand what he should do or shun."[46] So like Burgess, the Synopsis locates common notions under the category of the law of nature and bases this on Romans 2:14–15. In a fashion similar to Burgess, the Synopsis divides the law of nature into two categories, namely, external and internal testimony. The external testimony is the law that the Gentiles themselves establish (Rom. 2:14), and the internal testimony is the witness of conscience, by which the Gentiles deliberate between right and wrong based on the authority of the law written on their

43. Junius, *Mosaic Polity*, thesis 4, p. 48.
44. See, e.g., Aquinas, *Summa Theologica*, Ia-IIae q. 109 art. 4 rep. obj. 3.
45. Donald Sinnema and Henk van den Belt, "The *Synopsis Purioris Theologiae* (1625) as a Disputation Cycle," *Church History and Religious Culture* 92, no. 4 (2012): 505–37.
46. *Synopsis Purioris Theologiae / Synopsis of a Purer Theology*, ed. Dolf te Velde et al., trans. Riemer A. Faber, 2 vols. (Leiden: Brill, 2014), disp. 18.13, 1:436–37.

hearts (Rom. 2:15).[47] And like Burgess, the Synopsis connects the law of nature with the Decalogue, which is a summary of the moral law.[48] In the exposition of the law of nature, all pronouncements must conform to the exemplar of the Decalogue. If there is a conflict, then God's law takes precedence.[49]

There is a slight difference between Burgess and the Synopsis, however, since the latter employs a distinction between the practical principles (*principia practica*), which are the primary principles of common notions, and the conclusions from those principles (*conclusiones ex principiis*), which are the secondary principles. Prior to the fall the primary and secondary principles functioned in perfect harmony in concert with the will to carry out the commands of the will in Adam's affections. After the fall, however, the primary notions remain unchanged and clearly shine forth (*perspicue relucent*), but the "secondary notions stagger with wretched hesitation whenever one goes from general things to particular ones, and they deviate from the sound rule of equity, as is shown by the examples of the very unfair laws and overly corrupt customs that are found in the histories of the gentile peoples." After the fall, therefore, the noetic effects of sin obscured and nearly wiped out the common notions, though little sparks of these notions do remain to convict and condemn people of sin.[50]

At this point the authors of the Synopsis reflect not only their own convictions but also those of the Synod of Dordt, which codified the concept:

> There is, to be sure, a certain light of nature remaining in man after the fall, by virtue of which he retains some notions about God, natural things, and the difference between what is moral and immoral, and demonstrates a certain eagerness for virtue and for good outward behavior. But this light of nature is far from enabling man to come to a saving knowledge of God and conversion to him—so far, in fact, that man does not use it rightly even in matters of nature and society. Instead, in various ways he completely distorts this light, whatever its precise character, and suppresses it in unrighteousness. In doing so he renders himself without excuse before God.[51]

The Canons refer to the "light of nature" and "notions about God, natural things, and the difference between what is moral and immoral," which are common notions. This statement also reflects the distinction between primary

---

47. *Synopsis Purioris Theologiae*, disp. 18.19–26, 1:438–39.
48. *Synopsis Purioris Theologiae*, disp. 18.31, 1:440–41.
49. *Synopsis Purioris Theologiae*, disp. 18.29, 1:440–41.
50. *Synopsis Purioris Theologiae*, disp. 18.14–17, 1:436–37.
51. Canons of Dordt, III/IV art. 4. See also Theodore Haak, *The Dutch Annotations upon the Whole Bible* (1637; London: Henry Hills, 1657), comm. Rom. 2:14–15.

and secondary (corrupt) principles. It is important to note that the Synod limits the function of common notions: they are nonsaving.

Westminster Standards

When we examine the Westminster Standards, we must first account for a slight terminological difference between these documents and others of the period. Without doubt, the Standards do not employ the terms *common notions* or *natural law*. The Standards employ other terms that denote the same concepts, however, as these two terms. First, the Confession speaks of the "law of nature that, in general, a due proportion of time be set apart, for the Worship of God; so, in his word, by a positive, Moral, and perpetuall Commandment, binding all men, in all Ages, he hath particularly appointed One Day in Seven, for a Sabbath" (21.7). The Confession uses the term *law of nature* in parallel with a similar term *light of nature* (21.1). Theologians of the period used this phrase *light of nature* as a synonym or approximation for *common notions*. John Downame (1571–1652), for example, writes, "But the combat of conscience doth begin oftentimes long before conversion, even as soone as we have the use of reason and understanding, receiving common notions from the light of Nature."[52] Here Downame writes of the common notions *and* the light of nature, but elsewhere he speaks of the "common notions of the light of Nature."[53] Similar terminology appears in Pierre Du Moulin (1568–1658), who connects common notions with "natural light" and a "generall knowledge of the law."[54] Hence, the connection between common notions and the light of nature opens a vista to see how the divines used common notions in the Standards.

The term *light of nature* occurs nine times throughout the Standards and closely parallels the concepts exposited in other, fuller treatments of the subject, such as those in Burgess's *Vindiciae Legis*. The light of nature

1. manifests "the Goodnesse, Wisdome, and Power of God, as to leave men unexcusable, yet are they not sufficient to give that knowledge of God and of his Will, which is necessary unto salvation" (1.1; Rom. 2:14–15; 1:19–20; Ps. 19:1–3; Rom. 1:32 with 2:1; cf. WLC q. 2; Rom. 1:19–20; Ps. 19:1–3; Acts 17:28);[55]

---

52. John Downame, *The Christian Warfare against the Devill, World and Flesh Wherein Is Described Their Nature, the Maner of Their Fight and Meanes to Obtaine Victorye* (London: William Stansby, 1634), 2.8.9, p. 1107.

53. Downame, *Christian Warfare*, 2.9.6, p. 1110.

54. Pierre Du Moulin, *The Anatomy of Arminianisme* (London: Nathaniel Newbery, 1620), 26.13, p. 215.

55. Burgess, *Vindiciae Legis*, 70. The Assembly commissioned a number of divines to write a commentary on the whole Bible: *Annotations upon All the Books of the Old and New Testament*,

2. assists in determining matters related to worship with "circumstances concerning the Worship of God, and Government of the Church, common to human actions and Societies" (1.6; 1 Cor. 11:13–14; 14:26, 40);[56]

3. is the means by which people might be "never so diligent to frame their lives" (10.4; cf. WLC q. 60; 1 Cor. 1:20–24), which refers to their moral conduct that nevertheless falls short of the supernatural work of the Spirit required for salvation;[57]

4. provides Christians with one of two pillars to determine whether or not they publish or practice sinful things (20.4);

5. "sheweth that there is a God, who hath Lordship and Sovereignty over all, is good, and doth good unto all, and is therefore to bee feared, praised, called upon, trusted in, and served" (21.1; Rom. 1:20; Acts 17:24; Ps. 119:68; Jer. 10:7; Pss. 31:23; 18:3; Rom. 10:12; Ps. 62:8; John 24:14; Mark 12:33);[58]

6. appears less clearly in the fourth commandment (WLC q. 121);

7. helps Christians determine when certain sins are of a more serious nature than others (WLC q. 151; Rom. 1:26–27).

There is nothing in the Standards to indicate that Burgess's views were in any way out of accord with the mainstream opinion regarding the use of common notions within early modern Reformed theology. In fact, the parallels between Burgess and the Standards reveal that the Standards largely codify in summary form what appears more expansively in Burgess's lectures.[59] Moreover, in statements scattered throughout the Standards, the Westminster divines substantively affirmed the same points concerning common notions that were codified in the Canons of Dordt and other Reformed confessions, such as the Second Helvetic Confession (1563).[60]

In fact, the Westminster divines were well educated and knew both the origins of common notions and their widespread use within the Reformed

---

3rd ed. (London: Evan Tyler, 1657). Note that the *Annotations*, comm. Rom. 1:19–20, states, "Partly by the light of nature in their consciences, partly by the consideration of the creature of God, whereby his attributes are evidently noticed, and after a sort tasted and felt." Also see *Annotations*, comm. Rom. 2:14–15, which states, "They have the law of nature imprinted in their souls."

56. Cf. Burgess, *Vindiciae Legis*, 74.

57. Cf. Burgess, *Vindiciae Legis*, 68–70.

58. Cf. Burgess, *Vindiciae Legis*, 76.

59. Stephen J. Casselli, *Divine Rule Maintained: Anthony Burgess, Covenant Theology, and the Place of the Law in Reformed Scholasticism* (Grand Rapids: Reformation Heritage Books, 2015), 13, 31–37.

60. Second Helvetic Confession §12.

tradition. George Gillespie (1613–48), one of the Scottish divines, affirmed the "*Natura duce* [guidance of nature] . . . by such common notions, as God hath imprinted in the Nature of all men."[61] Gillespie devoted an entire chapter to the subject of the law of nature because this was contested territory between Roman Catholic and Reformed theologians regarding worship. Roman Catholic theologians appealed to the law of nature to justify some of their practices, whereas the Reformed argued that, yes, some worship principles were derived from the law of nature, or common notions, but that "the acceptable way of Worshiping the true God, is instituted by himselfe, and so limited by his own revealed Will, that he may not bee Worshipped . . . any other way not prescribed in the holy Scripture" (21.1). These differences between Roman and Reformed theologians did not, however, lead Gillespie to throw out the baby with the bathwater. That is, Roman Catholic theologians' transgressing the legitimate boundaries for common notions in worship was no reason to reject the right use of the concept.

In his defense of the proper use of common notions, Gillespie appeals to a number of authorities, both ancient and contemporary, including Aquinas, the Leiden Synopsis, Zanchi, Roman Catholic exegete Diego de Estella (1524–78), Augustine, David Pareus (1548–1622), and Junius. He also alludes to the apostle Paul (Rom. 2:14–15; 1 Cor. 11:13–14).[62] On common notions, Gillespie believed that the Reformed tradition and Aquinas were in general agreement: "The Law of Nature cannot direct us unto a supernatural end, as is acknowledged not only by our Divines, but by *Aquinas* also."[63] Other divines such as Anthony Tuckney (1599–1670) held a similar opinion. Tuckney was the chief author of the Larger Catechism's exposition of the Decalogue, and in his own understanding of natural law he positively cited Roman Catholics such as Aquinas, Domingo Soto (1494–1560), Bartolome de Medina (1528–80), Francisco de Toledo (1532–96), Francisco Suarez (1548–1617), Robert Bellarmine

61. George Gillespie, *A Dispute against the English-Popish Ceremonies Obtruded upon the Church of Scotland* (Edinburgh, 1660), 3.9, p. 319. The phrase *duce natura* is pure Cicero, *De natura deorum* 1.1, and elsewhere; see David Craig Noe, "*Oikeiosis, Ratio*, and *Natura*: The Stoic Challenge to Cicero's Academism in *De Finibus* and *Natura Deorum*" (PhD diss., University of Iowa, 2003), 142–45. My thanks to David Noe for alerting me to this connection.

62. Gillespie, *Dispute*, 3.9, pp. 319–20; see also, e.g., *Synopsis Purioris Theologiae*, disp. 18.26; Aquinas, *Summa Theologica*, Ia-IIae q. 94 art. 4; Diego de Estella, *In Sanctum Iesu Christi Evangelium Secundum Lucam Doctissima Pariter & Piissima Commentaria* (Verdussen, 1655), comm. Luke 6:31, p. 1:298; Augustine, *Confessions*, trans. Henry Chadwick (Oxford: Oxford University Press, 1991), 2.4, pp. 28–29; David Pareus, *In Divinam ad Romanos S. Pauli ap. Epistolam Commentarius* (Frankfort, 1608), comm. Rom. 1:19, cols. 91–94; Junius, *Mosaic Polity*, thesis 4, pp. 44–48; Girolamo Zanchi, *Omnium Operum Theologicorum*, vol. 4 (Geneva: Joannis Tornaesij, 1649), theses 8–10, cols. 188–94.

63. Gillespie, *Dispute*, 3.9, p. 316.

(1542–1621), and Gabriel Vasquez (1549–1604).[64] Whatever polemical ire they had for erroneous Roman Catholic doctrine, Gillespie and Tuckney did not include common notions among the topics of dispute. Common notions were part of a shared catholic doctrinal heritage. Moreover, theologians of the period were not ashamed of the pagan origins of this concept. In his commentary on the Heidelberg Catechism, Petrus de Witte (1622–69) explains that all nations know of the final judgment: "The common notions of all Nations teach this: *Aristotle, Tully, Seneca, Plato, Philosophers, Orators* are witnesses of this."[65] Early modern Reformed theologians acknowledged pagan authorities because they confirmed the teaching of the apostle Paul (Rom. 1:19; 2:14–15). In other words, these are some of the authorities that Paul likely had in mind when he wrote of the Gentiles who had the knowledge and law of God inscribed on their hearts.[66] But this did not mean that these theologians allowed these authorities to go unchecked. Reformed legal scholar Johannes Althusius (1557–1638), for example, meticulously collated the Decalogue, Jewish law, Roman law, and European customary law in his effort to demonstrate their parallels while yet acknowledging the regulative function of the Decalogue.[67]

Francis Turretin

At the height of Reformed Orthodoxy, Francis Turretin (1623–87) continued to advocate common notions in his formulation and use of natural law in his wider system of theology.[68] Like Burgess, he divides law into natural and positive categories, namely, that which God inscribes on the heart and that which he commands, such as the command not to eat from the tree of knowledge. Natural law reflects God's nature whereas positive laws come solely from

64. Anthony Tuckney, *Praelectiones Theologicae* (London: Stephen Swart, 1679), pars secunda, q. 25; Alexander Gordon, "Tuckney, Anthony," in *Dictionary of National Biography* (London: Smith, Elder, & Co., 1885–1900), 57:286. See also Chad Van Dixhoorn, ed., *Minutes and Papers of the Westminster Assembly*, 5 vols. (Oxford: Oxford University Press, 2012), 1:140.

65. Petrus de Witte, *Catechizing upon the Heidelbergh Catechisme* (Amsterdam: Gillis Joosten Saeghman, 1664), Lord's Day 25, q. 57, p. 439.

66. See, e.g., Burgess, *Vindiciae Legis*, 69.

67. Stephen J. Grabill, "Althusius in Context: A Biographical and Historical Introduction," in *On Law and Power*, by Johannes Althusius, trans. Jeffrey J. Veenstra (Grand Rapids: Christian's Library, 2013), xxiv; see also Johannes Althusius, *Dicaeologicae Libri Tres*, 2nd ed. (Frankfurt: Corvinus, 1649); John Witte Jr., "A Demonstrative Theory of Natural Law: The Original Contribution of Johannes Althusius," in *Public Theology for a Global Society*, ed. Deirdre King Hainsworth and Scott R. Paeth (Grand Rapids: Eerdmans, 2010), 21–36; Grabill, *Natural Law*, 122–50.

68. Grabill, *Natural Law*, 151–74.

his will.[69] In concert with Burgess, he rejects the Jewish notion that natural law finds its origins in the seven precepts God gave to Adam and Noah: six prohibitions—(1) idolatry, (2) blasphemy, (3) theft, (4) incest, (5) murder, and (6) consuming a living animal—and a seventh dealing with the appointment of judges and magistrates.[70] Neither is natural law those principles common to human beings and animals, as Justinian teaches in his *Institutes*. Rather, like Burgess, Turretin argues that natural law pertains only to rational creatures.[71] He describes this aspect of natural law as follows: "It is rightly by common practical notions, or the light and dictation of conscience (which God has engraven by nature upon every individual, to distinguish between virtue and vice, and to know the things to be avoided and the things to be done)."[72]

Like the authors of the Leiden Synopsis, Turretin distinguishes common notions into two categories: primary (principles) and secondary (conclusions). The principles are immutable and self-evident. The principles can be immediate, "for the first dictation of nature (which are proximately gathered from the principles and consequence and with greater difficulty are deduced from the principles)." Or they are mediate, which means people deduce conclusions from the principles. Immediate principles admit no variety, but the noetic effects of sin due to the fall corrupt mediate principles. Nevertheless, Turretin argues that even though sinful reason corrupts conclusions, "still this does not prevent its always remaining the same among all, as to its first principles and the immediate conclusions thence deduced."[73]

Turretin bases the legitimacy of common notions on six different arguments, which begin with Scripture and end with the testimony of heathen philosophers:[74]

1. Romans 2:14–15, "the Gentiles which have not the law," that is, the written law of Moses (Rom. 1:19). Here Turretin closely parallels Burgess's exegesis of these two texts.
2. The consent of the nations.
3. Every person's conscience, which informs them of the difference between good and evil. The conscience produces distress in the face of sin and

69. Francis Turretin, *Institutes of Elenctic Theology*, ed. James T. Dennison Jr., trans. George Musgrave Giger, 3 vols. (Phillipsburg, NJ: P&R, 1992–97), 11.1.4.

70. Turretin, *Institutes*, 11.1.8.

71. A point also made by Francisco Suarez, *Tractatus de Legibus ac Deo Legislatore* (London: J. Dunmore, 1679), 2.6, pp. 68–74. My thanks to David Sytsma for drawing my attention to this source.

72. Turretin, *Institutes*, 11.1.10.

73. Turretin, *Institutes*, 11.1.11.

74. Turretin, *Institutes*, 11.1.12–17.

a sense of fear of divine judgment. As evidence, like Burgess, Turretin appeals to Cicero: "The wicked are punished, not so much by judgment, as by anguish of conscience and the torment of crime."[75]

4. God's rule and government of humanity.

5. If there were no common notions, then people would be entirely autonomous and thus free to hate or love God, to kill or honor parents, because each person's will would be decisive in matters of ethics and morality.

6. The testimony of the heathen philosophers, such as Socrates, Plato, Aristotle, and the Stoics, who bravely opposed those who rejected the concept of common notions. Turretin cites Cicero again: "We are born to justice, and that right is not established by opinion, but by nature."[76] In this regard, Turretin's quotation of Plato illustrates his point: "In all times and nations this universal law must forever reign, eternal and imperishable. It is the sovereign master and emperor of all beings. God himself is its author, its promulgator, its enforcer. And he who does not obey it flies from himself, and does violence to the very nature of man."[77]

Turretin, however, was keen to explore further the impact of the noetic effects of sin to round out his treatment of common notions.

When people cauterize their consciences (1 Tim. 4:2) or give themselves over to all sorts of uncleanness (Eph. 4:19), they certainly suppress the second act or exercise of common notions, that is, conclusions. They do not, however, extinguish or destroy the first principle.[78] Even if nations enact wicked laws that promote practices repugnant to natural law, such as idolatry, human sacrifice, theft, rape, homicide, or incest, this does not prove that they never received common notions from God. At this point, Turretin disagrees with Westminster divine John Selden (1584–1654), who made just such an argument. Rather than disprove the existence of common notions, the fact that they engage in such wicked conduct confirms that they have abused and striven against the light of nature they have received.[79] Just because sin obscures

75. Cicero, *Laws*, in *De Republica, De Legibus*, trans. Clinton Walker Keyes, Loeb Classical Library (Cambridge, MA: Harvard University Press, 1928), 1.14.40, pp. 340–41.

76. Cicero, *Laws* 1.10.28, pp. 328–39.

77. Lactantius, *The Divine Institutes: Books I–VII*, trans. Mary Francis McDonald, Fathers of the Church 49 (Washington, DC: Catholic University of America Press, 1964), 6.8, pp. 412–13.

78. Turretin, *Institutes*, 11.1.18.

79. Turretin, *Institutes*, 11.1.19; John Selden, *De Iure Naturali & Gentium, Iuxta Disciplinam Ebraeorum, Libri Septem* (London: Richard Bishop, 1640), 75–94. See also Van Dixhoorn, *Minutes and Papers*, 1:136. On Selden's views, see David Sytsma, general introduction to *Of the Law of Nature*, by Matthew Hale, ed. David Sytsma (Grand Rapids: CLP Academic, 2015),

common notions does not at all entail their complete destruction, much less that they never existed.[80]

Turretin employs the moral law (the Decalogue) as the guardrail to delineate where the natural and moral law overlap. He explains that natural law "agrees as to substance and with regard to principles, but differs as to accidents and with regard to conclusions." Our duties toward God and neighbor, for example, also appear in natural law. The difference, however, between the natural and moral law pertains to the mode of delivery. God delivered the moral law clearly and distinctly, whereas sin obscures natural law. God engraved the natural law on human hearts, whereas he wrote the moral law on stone tablets. Natural law pertains universally to all people, whereas the moral law so delivered at Sinai only pertains to those called by the word. And natural law only addresses matters regarding morality, whereas the moral law also details ceremonies that pertain to redemption.[81]

As to why God delivered the moral law at Sinai, Turretin argues that God added new brushstrokes to the sin-stained portrait of humanity. God republished the moral law to five ends: (1) to reconfirm the teaching of natural law, (2) to correct human misunderstandings of the law because of sin, (3) to supplement the lack of human knowledge where sin obliterated it, (4) so that humans would see their need of a mediator (Rom. 3:20; 8:3; 10:4), and (5) to separate Israel from the rest of the nations (Deut. 4:6–7; Ps. 147:19–20; Rom. 9:4).[82] Noteworthy here is that Turretin appeals to Romans 10:4, "For Christ is the end of the law for righteousness to every one that believeth," which comes from the same context as Paul's quotation of Leviticus 18:5 (Rom. 10:5). In other words, he does not explicitly raise the subject here, but he nevertheless implicitly links common notions to the covenant of works. Only Christ brings an end to the consequences of the violated covenant of works, which has the natural law as one of its main ingredients. In his treatment of the covenant of works, Turretin makes the connection explicit when he invokes the distinction between the twofold law God gave to Adam: the natural and symbolic. God gave Adam general knowledge by inscribing it on his heart (Rom. 2:14–15) and

---

ix–lvi, esp. xxix, xxxv, xlix; G. J. Toomer, *John Selden: A Life in Scholarship*, 2 vols. (Oxford: Oxford University Press, 2009), 2:490–594; John Witte and Harold J. Berman, "The Integrative Jurisprudence of John Selden," in *Great Christian Jurists in English History*, ed. Mark Hill QC and R. H. Helmholz (Cambridge: Cambridge University Press, 2017), 139–61; and J. P. Somerville, "Selden, Grotius, and the Seventeenth-Century Intellectual Revolution in Moral and Political Theory," in *Rhetoric and Law in Early Modern Europe*, ed. Victoria Kahn and Lorna Hutson (New Haven: Yale University Press, 2001), 318–44.

80. Turretin, *Institutes*, 11.1.20.
81. Turretin, *Institutes*, 11.1.21–22.
82. Turretin, *Institutes*, 11.1.23.

specific knowledge through the positive command not to eat from the tree of knowledge.[83] These are the same two categories that Burgess employs in his own doctrine of the covenant of works vis-à-vis common notions.

Conclusion

At the very least, common notions were a noncontroversial feature of early modern Reformed theology. The entire tradition—from the early Reformers, such as Melanchthon and Calvin, all the way through the High Orthodox theology of Turretin—was shot through with this concept. Even with the dawn of the Enlightenment and the twilight of Reformed High Orthodoxy, Reformed theologians such as Herman Witsius (1636–1708), Benedict Pictet (1655–1724), Richard Baxter (1615–91), and Bernardinus de Moor (1709–80) still maintained the concept.[84] There were, of course, some dissenting voices, such as Lutheran theologian Illyricus or John Selden, who believed that the fall eradicated common notions. But the overwhelming majority of those within the early modern Reformed tradition accepted common notions, evidenced by the confessional codification of the concept in the Canons of Dordt and the Westminster Standards. It was not until René Descartes (1596–1650) and John Locke (1632–1704) that the use of common notions began to wane.[85] Locke completely rejected them, and Descartes believed that they could not be conclusively proved and should thus be set aside. In fact, common notions were a point of contention between Descartes and Gisbert Voetius (1589–1676), a noted stalwart of Reformed Orthodoxy.[86]

Despite the waning acceptance of the idea, there were notable exceptions to the trend. Adherents to classic early modern Reformed theology, such as Charles Hodge (1797–1878), appealed to the idea of common notions in their exegesis of Romans 1:19 and 2:14–15. Hodge writes regarding Romans

83. Turretin, *Institutes*, 8.3.12.

84. Benedict Pictet, *Christian Theology*, trans. Frederick Reyroux (London: L. B. Seeley & Sons, 1834), 1.2, p. 6; Richard Baxter, *More Reasons for the Christian Religion and No Reason against It* (London: Nevill Simmons, 1672), 119; Herman Witsius, *An Essay on the Use and Abuse of Reason in Matters of Religion* (Norwich: Crouse, Stevenson & Matchett, 1795), §11, p. 11; Bernardinus de Moor, *Continuous Commentary of Johannes Marckius' Didactico-Elenctic Compendium of Christian Theology*, trans. Steven Dilday (Culpeper, VA: L&G Reformation Translation Center, 2014), 12, pp. 1:116–23.

85. John Locke, *Essays on the Law of Nature*, ed. W. von Leyden (Oxford: Clarendon, 2002), 137–45, 161–79.

86. René Descartes, "Letter to Voetius, May 1643," in *The Philosophical Writings of Descartes*, trans. John Cottingham et al., 3 vols. (Cambridge: Cambridge University Press, 1991), 3:220–24.

1:19, "The knowledge of God does not mean simply a knowledge that there is a God, but, as appears from what follows, a knowledge of his nature and attributes, his eternal power and Godhead." Hodge follows Beza's explanation when he notes that this knowledge of God is *in them*, in the Gentiles: "It is not of a mere external revelation of which the apostle is speaking, but of that evidence of the being and perfections of God which every man has in the constitution of his own nature, and in virtue of which he is competent to apprehend the manifestations of God in his works." Hodge also cites Calvin to the same effect.[87] Hodge presents similar comments in his exegesis of Romans 2:14–15. The "Gentiles," according to his exegesis of the text, refers to those who "have in their own nature a rule of duty; a knowledge of what is right, and a sense of obligation." Paul refers to the "inward operations of their moral nature" when he mentions the works of the law inscribed on the heart. "The *syneidēsis*," writes Hodge, "is the *conscientia consequens*, the inward judge, whose acts are described in the following clause: *Their thoughts alternately accusing or even excusing.*"[88]

In the later nineteenth century and early twentieth century, Herman Bavinck (1854–1921) employed common notions in his own theology.[89] Bavinck found the concept in Aquinas and the Reformed Orthodox, such as Voetius, and he connected them with the "commonsense way of 'the natural light of reason,'" which he gleaned from the likes of Amandus Polanus (1561–1610) and Zanchi.[90] Karl Barth (1886–1968), however, had a different opinion and especially sought to expunge all natural theology from theology and to rest solely and exclusively on Christ.[91] Barth specifically saw the Leiden Synopsis and its defense of common notions as an example of an incipient rationalism that had to be torn out by the roots.[92] But despite this general twentieth-century antipathy toward common notions, there are four important observations about the practices of earlier Reformed theologians:

1. By drawing the concept of common notions chiefly from Romans 1:19 and 2:14–15, they were following the teaching of Scripture and

87. Charles Hodge, *Romans* (1835; repr., Edinburgh: Banner of Truth, 1989), 36. I am grateful to David Sytsma for pointing me to these references.

88. Hodge, *Romans*, 55.

89. Herman Bavinck, *Reformed Dogmatics*, ed. John Bolt, trans. John Vriend, 4 vols. (Grand Rapids: Baker Academic, 2003–8), 1:207–33, esp. 223–33; 2:53–91.

90. Bavinck, *Reformed Dogmatics*, 1:225, 232.

91. VanDrunen, *Natural Law and the Two Kingdoms*, 316–47; Grabill, *Natural Law*, 21–53.

92. Karl Barth, *Church Dogmatics*, ed. G. W. Bromiley and T. F. Torrance (Edinburgh: T&T Clark, 1988), IV/1:369–72; see also Rinse H. Reeling, *Karl Barth and Post-Reformation Orthodoxy* (London: Routledge, 2015), 88.

specifically the apostle Paul's claims regarding the works of the law divinely inscribed on the heart.

2. Although positively citing pagan authorities as examples of those who rightly explained the law of nature inscribed on their hearts, they distinguished between principles and conclusions. The principles of common notions are present in all, but given the noetic effects of sin, unbelievers can and do draw false conclusions.

3. They cited Aquinas and other Roman Catholic theologians positively because even though they had significant disagreements over matters of soteriology, worship, and polity, they nevertheless believed that Aquinas rightly explained common notions.

4. They believed that common notions were not a neutral territory but rather part of the image of God, which was within the context of the covenant of works. Common notions, a subset of natural law, formed one of the key pillars of the covenant of works as well as one part of the greater general revelatory testimony of the book of nature.

These four points present important historical and exegetical data for the recovery of the concept of common notions for defending the faith.

Contrary to the claims of Barth, for example, who argued that there is no point of contact between the believer and unbeliever, classic Reformed theology maintains that believers and unbelievers have the image of God in common.[93] More specifically, common notions about moral right and wrong and the existence of God enable believers to appeal to this divinely inscribed knowledge in the process of defending the faith. The believer can appeal to both the books of nature and Scripture and know that they will speak with one voice. Only the sovereign work of the Spirit, however, will correct the fallen human mind to enable it to use both books aright and draw correct conclusions. But before we can engage some of the philosophical and theological objections to the recovery of common notions, we must deal with the claim that Calvin rejected all forms of natural theology or that it was only incidental to his theology. In other words, is Calvin a theological island in contrast with the rest of the Reformed tradition? Did the Reformed tradition soil the pristine, biblically oriented theology of Calvin? Did they trade their inheritance in Christ for the bowl of Aristotelian and scholastic lentils?

---

93. Karl Barth, *Church Dogmatics*, ed. T. F. Torrance (Edinburgh: T&T Clark, 1936–68), I/1:236–37; Emil Brunner and Karl Barth, *Natural Theology: Comprising "Nature and Grace" by Professor Dr. Emil Brunner and the Reply "No!" by Dr. Karl Barth* (1946; repr., Eugene, OR: Wipf & Stock, 2002), 127.

3

CALVIN

For since men are imbued by nature with some knowledge of God, they draw true principles from that source.

John Calvin

Calvin . . . did not bring out with sufficient clearness at all times that the natural man is as blind as a mole with respect to natural things as well as with respect to spiritual things.

Cornelius Van Til

Among the popular legends of the Reformation is that John Calvin (1509–64) was a biblically faithful expositor of Scripture, but his followers distorted his theological legacy through the reintroduction of medieval categories, most notably, scholasticism. This narrative at one time was virtually unquestioned in Calvin scholarship, but recent decades have overturned the problematic thesis of Calvin versus the Calvinists.[1] In short, some historians created a Calvin of

1. See, e.g., Heiko A. Oberman, *The Dawn of the Reformation: Essays in Late Medieval and Early Reformation Thought* (Edinburgh: T&T Clark, 1986); David Steinmetz, *Calvin in Context*, 2nd ed. (Oxford: Oxford University Press, 2010); Richard A. Muller, *The Unaccommodated Calvin: Studies in the Foundation of a Theological Tradition* (Oxford: Oxford University Press, 2000); R. Scott Clark and Carl R. Trueman, eds., *Protestant Scholasticism: Essays in Reassessment* (Carlisle, UK: Paternoster, 1999); Willem J. van Asselt and Eef Dekker, *Reformation and Scholasticism: An Ecumenical Enterprise* (Grand Rapids: Baker Academic, 2001).

faith, who served as a forerunner for different twentieth-century theologians and movements. This chapter aims to revisit some of the particular claims regarding Calvin's stance toward scholasticism, natural law and common notions, and traditional arguments for the existence of God to demonstrate that Calvin stands in continuity with the early modern Reformed tradition and its use of the book of nature.

After briefly examining some of the claims regarding Calvin's views, this chapter presents evidence from Calvin's own work on these three subjects to demonstrate continuities with the medieval past, in particular with the formulations of Thomas Aquinas (1225–74). My intent is to prove that contemporary Reformed theologians cannot claim that Calvin based his theology on Christ as the uncontested starting point for all knowledge of God. The chapter then concludes with some general observations about the contemporary misunderstandings of Calvin. This chapter explores Calvin's views on these subjects, not because he is normative for the Reformed tradition, but because contemporary theologians frequently appeal to him and his supposed rejection of the book of nature in his defense of the faith, and we must test their claims. The aim of this chapter, therefore, is to demonstrate that Calvin stands in general continuity with his medieval past and the theologians of early modern Reformed Orthodoxy.

Calvin the Christocentric Theologian?

German church historian August Lang wrote an essay on natural law and the Protestant Reformation. Lang argued that Philip Melanchthon (1497–1560) introduced natural law into the Reformation and that this was an instance of creative genius on his part but ultimately a compromise with fallen autonomous reason.[2] Lang further argued that Calvin was no friend of natural law. Even though Calvin opens his *Institutes* with the concept of humanity's natural knowledge of God, this knowledge was rendered "completely corrupted and stifled" due to the fall.[3] Lang concludes that Calvin attributed "almost no importance at all" to the concept of natural law.[4] In contrast to Calvin, later Calvinists developed natural-law theories and employed them as weapons in the theological conflicts of the time.[5] Lang attributes the rise of the Enlighten-

2. August Lang, "The Reformation and Natural Law," in *Calvin and the Reformation: Four Studies*, trans. J. Gresham Machen (New York: Revell, 1909), 59, 62.
3. Lang, "Reformation and Natural Law," 69.
4. Lang, "Reformation and Natural Law," 72.
5. Lang, "Reformation and Natural Law," 72.

ment to the Reformed failure to heed Calvin's low estimation of natural law. Rather than follow Calvin's lead, Calvinists failed to purge their theology of the medieval Roman Catholic teachings on natural law.[6] Lang expresses his own surprise at this turn of events: "If natural law has its roots in medieval Catholicism, that only brings the chief question, How could doctrines that were Catholic in spirit be appropriated in Reformation territory at such an early time with so little hesitation?"[7] Lang believes that Calvin's peers and successors did not sufficiently filter their theology and simply resorted to traditional Catholic answers to various theological questions.[8]

In his famous debate with Emil Brunner (1889–1966), Karl Barth (1886–1968) gave his emphatic "No!" to the question of natural theology. As a part of his negative answer, Barth claimed that Calvin rejected natural theology: "The possibility of a real knowledge by natural man of the true God, derived from creation, is, according to Calvin, a possibility in principle, but not in fact, not a possibility to be realized by us."[9] Barth believed that the chief representative of natural theology was Aquinas because he posited the idea that grace perfects nature.[10] Calvin escaped this theological trap, but subsequent Reformed theologians did not.[11] According to Barth, Calvin rejected the idea of a "point of contact" between natural man and God: "There is no relation, nothing common, and hence no inner connection."[12] Like Lang, Barth believed that Melanchthon's influence poisoned Calvin's heritage, and others such as Zacharias Ursinus (1534–83) and Caspar Olevianus (1536–87) recklessly employed the tainted doctrine.[13] In contrast to the idea that nature constitutes a legitimate starting point for the knowledge of God, Barth held that all knowledge of God had to begin exclusively with Christ. Subsequent Reformed theologians would have avoided the dreaded scholastic nature-grace dualism if they "determined to know the eternal and therefore the only basis of the divine work in the work itself, in its temporal occurrence, to know the

6. Lang, "Reformation and Natural Law," 88.

7. Lang, "Reformation and Natural Law," 93.

8. Lang, "Reformation and Natural Law," 94, 97.

9. Barth, "No!," in Emil Brunner and Karl Barth, *Natural Theology: Comprising "Nature and Grace" by Professor Dr. Emil Brunner and the Reply "No!" by Dr. Karl Barth* (1946; repr., Eugene, OR: Wipf & Stock, 2002), 106. For a more comprehensive bibliography of scholars who argue that Calvin rejected natural law and natural theology, see David VanDrunen, *Natural Law and the Two Kingdoms: A Study in the Development of Reformed Social Thought* (Grand Rapids: Eerdmans, 2010), 94n88.

10. Barth, "No!," 100–101.

11. Barth, "No!," 102–5.

12. Barth, "No!," 107.

13. Karl Barth, *Church Dogmatics*, ed. G. W. Bromiley and T. F. Torrance (Edinburgh: T&T Clark, 1936–68), IV/1:58–59.

eternal divine Logos in His incarnation."[14] For Barth, Christology is both the starting and ending point of all theology—there is no place for natural theology.[15]

Cornelius Van Til made similar claims regarding Calvin's stance toward natural theology and scholasticism. According to Van Til, the opening words of Calvin's *Institutes* constitute "a complete break with scholastic theology."[16] Van Til also argued that he was following Calvin in his own apologetic program when he rejected the Roman Catholic concept of common notions.[17] Van Til believed that Reformed theology needed to outgrow scholasticism's conceptions of natural theology and natural ethics.[18] Since Calvin completely broke with scholasticism, Reformed theologians needed to follow his lead.[19] Van Til acknowledged that Calvin admitted natural knowledge in his theological system and even approvingly quoted pagan authorities in the process.[20] But according to Van Til, this natural knowledge was solely for the purpose of rendering sinners inexcusable, though Van Til does not adequately explain how this natural knowledge functions to bring about their inexcusability.[21] But Van Til believed that Calvin was inconsistent in his explanations of fallen humanity's natural knowledge.[22] Despite Calvin's "break" with medieval theology and his heroic efforts to destroy the "scholastic monstrosity," Val Til laments that subsequent Calvinists did not follow his program: "But after Calvin the everlasting temptation besetting all Christians, especially sophisticated Christians, to make friends with those that are of Cain's lineage proved too much for many Lutheran and even Reformed theologians and so Lutheran and Reformed Scholasticism were begotten and born."[23]

Herman Dooyeweerd had an equally negative assessment of scholasticism in contrast to Calvin's supposed unsullied theology. Dooyeweerd believed that medieval scholastic theologians like Aquinas constructed their theology on the foundation of an unholy alliance between Greek philosophy and biblical

14. Barth, *Church Dogmatics*, IV/1:66.

15. Myron B. Penner, "Calvin, Barth, and the Subject of Atonement," in *Calvin, Barth, and Reformed Theology*, ed. Neil B. MacDonald and Carl R. Trueman (Milton Keynes, UK: Paternoster, 2008), 138.

16. Cornelius Van Til, *Christianity in Conflict*, 3 vols. (1962; Glenside, PA: Westminster Campus Bookstore, 1996), 3:27.

17. Cornelius Van Til, *Defense of the Faith*, 3rd ed. (Phillipsburg, NJ: P&R, 1967), 210.

18. Cornelius Van Til, *Common Grace and the Gospel* (Phillipsburg, NJ: P&R, 1972), 93–94.

19. Van Til, *Common Grace*, 191.

20. Cornelius Van Til, *Introduction to Systematic Theology* (Phillipsburg, NJ: P&R, 1974), 82–83.

21. Van Til, *Introduction to Systematic Theology*, 59.

22. Van Til, *Introduction to Systematic Theology*, 82.

23. Cornelius Van Til, *Herman Dooyeweerd and Reformed Apologetics*, 3 parts (Philadelphia: Westminster Theological Seminary, 1972), 3:17.

doctrine.[24] Reformed Orthodox theologians drew from this poisoned well and corrupted Calvin's pristine theology. Like Lang, Dooyeweerd laid the blame at Melanchthon's feet, though he also included Theodore Beza (1519–1605) as an accomplice.[25] According to Dooyeweerd, Calvin had the proper starting point for all knowledge, not merely theology: we must begin with God and his self-disclosure in Scripture.[26] At this point Dooyeweerd, though not himself Barthian, parallels Barth's Christocentrism; Barth and Dooyeweerd employ the same idealist methodology in their theology. Subsequent chapters will address this subject in greater detail.

Scholasticism

According to some theologians, Calvin was radically opposed to scholasticism. This particular claim rests on two faulty assumptions regarding scholasticism: (1) it entails specific theological beliefs, and (2) it is ultimately speculative, rationalistic, and unbiblical. Hence these claims create the supposed wedge between Calvin and later Reformed theologians who employed scholasticism in their theology. A number of twentieth-century theologians have identified scholasticism with specific theological and philosophical commitments. Brian Armstrong has offered one of the clearest summaries of the supposed content of scholasticism. He identifies four defining characteristics: (1) it asserts religious truth on the basis of deductive reasoning from given assumptions or principles, most notably through syllogistic argumentation; (2) reason has equal standing with faith in theology, which means that scholastic theologians jettison the authority of revelation; (3) it presents truth in terms of definitive statement, which thus creates a means by which to measure one's orthodoxy; and (4) it has great interest in metaphysical speculation, especially regarding the doctrine of God.[27] According to Armstrong, there is a striking absence of these features in Calvin's theological program, especially in his *Institutes*.[28]

Despite the popularity of such descriptions and definitions of scholasticism, more recent scholarship has proved that scholasticism is primarily a method of

---

24. Herman Dooyeweerd, *In the Twilight of Western Thought*, ed. D. F. M. Strauss, Collected Works, Series B 16 (Grand Rapids: Paideia, 2012), 90; Dooyeweerd, *Reformation and Scholasticism in Philosophy*, ed. D. F. M. Strauss, trans. Ray Togtmann, 3 vols., Collected Works, Series A 5–7 (Grand Rapids: Paideia, 2012), 1:3.

25. Dooyeweerd, *Western Thought*, 108; Dooyeweerd, *Reformation and Scholasticism*, 1:16; 2:13–15.

26. Dooyeweerd, *Western Thought*, 116; Dooyeweerd, *Reformation and Scholasticism*, 1:15.

27. Brian Armstrong, *Calvinism and the Amyraut Heresy: Protestant Scholasticism in Seventeenth-Century France* (1969; repr., Eugene, OR: Wipf & Stock, 2004), 32.

28. Armstrong, *Calvinism*, 32–33.

doing theology and does not predetermine specific doctrinal outcomes or dictate preestablished roles for reason and revelation.[29] The scholastic method finds its roots in the medieval organization of education. There were three parts of a common medieval educational model: lecture (*lectio*), where a teacher read and commented on an authoritative text; reflection (*meditatio*), where the student meditated on the lecture; and inquiry (*quaestio*), where the student could pose questions. As medieval education developed, the *quaestio* became the most important part of instruction and gradually was the chief method of studying authoritative texts. In addition to the *quaestio*, medieval teachers conducted scholarly discussions, or *disputationes*. The teacher (*magister*) would assign a topic (*quaestio*) for debate (*disputatio*), and to facilitate this process the teacher would draw up a number of theses. The assigned student would then respond to a number of objections throughout the course of the disputation.[30] *Disputatio* and *quaestio* lie at the heart of the scholastic method. This method does not require any specific philosophical or theological commitments but simply sets the parameters for the orderly discussion of a doctrinal topic. Thus it is common to Roman Catholic, Reformed, Lutheran, and Arminian theologians.

This description of the scholastic method has several implications for the second claim regarding Calvin, namely, his supposed rejection of scholasticism because of its rationalistic and unbiblical nature. Calvin's use of the scholastic method stands out when compared to the scholastic argumentation of Aquinas. In his *Summa Theologica* Aquinas asks, Is God the object of sacred doctrine? He then presents a scholastic dissection of the question in the following manner:

Objection 1. It seems that God is not the object of this science because in every science its object is presupposed. But this science cannot presuppose the essence of God.

Objection 2. Whatever conclusions are reached in any science must be comprehended under the object of the science. But through Scripture we reach conclusions about God and many other things, hence God is not the object of this science.

On the contrary [*sed contra*]. God is the object of this science, as it is mainly about God and hence is called theology.

29. Willem J. Van Asselt, "Introduction: What Is Reformed Scholasticism?," in *Introduction to Reformed Scholasticism*, ed. Willem J. Van Asselt et al., trans. Albert Gootjes (Grand Rapids: Reformation Heritage Books, 2011), 1; Richard A. Muller, *Scholasticism and Orthodoxy in the Reformed Tradition: An Attempt at Definition* (Grand Rapids: Calvin Theological Seminary, 1995), 3–4.

30. Pieter L. Rouwendal, "The Method of the Schools: Medieval Scholasticism," in *Introduction to Reformed Scholasticism*, 59–60; Richard A. Muller, *After Calvin: Studies in the Development of a Theological Tradition* (Oxford: Oxford University Press, 2003), 27–28.

I answer [*respondeo*] that God is the object of this science. The relationship between a science and its object is like that between a habit or faculty and its object.

Reply to Objection 1 [*ad primum*]. Although we cannot know God's essence, nevertheless we can make use of its effects.

Reply to Objection 2 [*ad secundum*]. Whatever conclusions we might draw from this sacred science, they are comprehended under God as in some way related to him.[31]

Aquinas tirelessly repeats this pattern throughout his *Summa*; in line with scholastic educational methods, it centers around the *quaestio* and bears the marks of the *disputatio*. Aquinas responds to the question, engages objections, and provides his own answer.

A close reading of the *Institutes* reveals that many chapters follow the form of scholastic disputation, which presents an initial statement, identifies objections, and then responds to them. One of the reasons why some nineteenth- and twentieth-century readers overlook these features is because modern editions of Calvin's works obscure his scholastic patterns of argumentation.[32] Sixteenth-century editions of Calvin's work drew attention to the scholastic nature of his arguments through the creation of a textual apparatus that modern editions typically do not include.[33] Nevertheless, even without the sixteenth-century textual apparatus to act as a road map to Calvin's argumentation, one can still observe the scholastic pattern in his *Institutes*. In *Institutes* 2.12 Calvin presents the following arguments:[34]

Sections 1–3: Four reasons why the Mediator was both divine and human

1. Necessary by divine decree
2. Had to convert the heirs of hell into children of God
3. That in our flesh he would present a perfect obedience
4. Consolation and confirmation of the whole church

31. Thomas Aquinas, *Summa Theologica* (New York: Benzinger Brothers, 1948), Ia q. 1 art. 7; Rouwendal, "Method of the Schools," 69–70.

32. Muller, *Unaccommodated Calvin*, 45.

33. Muller, *Unaccommodated Calvin*, 62–78.

34. Muller, *Unaccommodated Calvin*, 46. Compare *Institutes* 2.12.1–7 in both the Beveridge and the Battles editions. Beveridge presents an outline of the arguments that mirrors the older sixteenth-century textual apparatus, a feature not included in the Battles edition (John Calvin, *Institutes of the Christian Religion*, trans. Henry Beveridge [Grand Rapids: Eerdmans, 1957]; Calvin, *Institutes of the Christian Religion*, ed. John T. McNeill, trans. Ford Lewis Battles [Philadelphia: Westminster, 1960]). Unless otherwise noted, all English quotations from Calvin's *Institutes* come from the Beveridge translation.

Sections 4–7: A series of twelve objections and answers, which then concludes with a summary of the orthodox doctrine

Calvin employs the scholastic method here through the statement of his four
reasons and then his presentation of objections with their corresponding re-
sponses. The pattern reflects the methods associated with Aquinas's *Summa*.
But Calvin's continuity with medieval scholasticism goes beyond the structure
of his arguments.

In addition to scholastic argumentation, Calvin regularly employed common scholastic terminological distinctions.[35] Unfortunately, some English
translations obscure this terminology. In his explanation of how the bones
of Christ were and were not subject to breaking, Calvin writes:

Calvin's Institutes 1.16.9

Beveridge translation	Battles translation
Hence again, we see that there was good ground for the distinction which the school-men made between necessity, *secundum quid,* and necessity absolute, also between necessity *of consequent* and *of consequence.*	Whence again we see that distinctions concerning relative necessity and absolute necessity, likewise of consequent and conse-quence, were not recklessly invented in the schools.

The English reader has a greater ability to see Calvin's use of technical terms
in the Beveridge translation given that it leaves one Latin term untranslated
and italicizes others, which is less evident in the Battles translation. What lies
beneath the English translation are the technical terms *secundum quid* (with
respect to), *necessitas consequentiae* (necessity of the consequence, or hypo-
thetical necessity), and *necessitas consequentis* (necessity of the consequent,
or absolute necessity).[36] To its credit, the Battles edition footnotes the use of
the same terms in Aquinas's *Summa Theologica*.[37] In short, while there are
certainly differences between Calvin's *Institutes* and Aquinas's *Summa Theologica*, they both employ scholastic methodology and terminology. Therefore
one cannot easily pit Calvin against scholasticism, given that he employed
identical methodology and terminology in his own theology.[38]

---

35. Muller, *Unaccommodated Calvin*, 46.

36. Richard A. Muller, *Dictionary of Latin and Greek Theological Terms: Drawn Principally from Protestant Scholastic Theology*, 2nd ed. (Grand Rapids: Baker Academic, 2017),
s.v. *secundum quid* (328–29), *necessitas consequentiae* (229–30), *necessitas consequentis*
(230).

37. Aquinas, *Summa Theologica*, Ia q. 19 art. 3. See also Paul Helm, "Calvin (and Zwingli)
on Divine Providence," *Calvin Theological Journal* 29 (1994): 388–405, esp. 400–402.

38. David Steinmetz, "The Scholastic Calvin," in *Protestant Scholasticism*, ed. Clark and
Trueman, 16–30.

Natural Law and Common Notions

Despite the steady stream of twentieth-century claims that Calvin did not employ natural law in his theology, there is clear evidence to the contrary.[39] Two of the chief texts from which Calvin derives his doctrine of natural law are Romans 1:20 and 2:14–15. He appeals to Romans 2:14–15 when he echoes Paul's point that the "Gentiles have the righteousness of the law naturally / engraven on their minds" and hence "we certainly cannot say that they are altogether blind as to the rule of life."[40] People can access natural law, according to Calvin, either naturally by virtue of its inscription on the heart or through the two tables of the Decalogue: both avenues are legitimate means of access.[41] This parallels Aquinas, who makes the same point.[42] In Calvin's understanding of the natural knowledge of God, there is a link between God, the creation, and human beings. Although God is invisible, humans can know him in his works of creation: "they clearly demonstrate their Creator." The world is "a mirror or representation" (specula seu spectacula; Heb. 11:3).[43] Through God's works of creation, "He has so demonstrated His existence by His works as to make men see what they do not seek to know of their own accord, viz. that there is a God."[44] Calvin elsewhere explicitly connects the innate knowledge of God with the broader creation when he writes, "There is a certaine agreement betweene the Law of God, and the order of nature, which is engrafted in all men."[45]

This broader canvas of the creation finds its microcosmic counterpart in humanity's divinely created constitution. The characterization of humanity as a microcosm is a Stoic idea mediated to the Western tradition by Cicero.[46] In

39. For a survey of the similarities between Calvin and Aquinas specifically on natural law, see David VanDrunen, "Medieval Natural Law and the Reformation: A Comparison of Aquinas and Calvin," American Catholic Philosophical Quarterly 80, no. 1 (2006): 77–98, esp. 81–90.

40. Calvin, Institutes, 2.2.22; see also 4.20.16.

41. Calvin, Institutes, 2.8.1.

42. Aquinas, Summa Theologica, Ia-IIae q. 94 art. 6; Stephen J. Grabill, Rediscovering the Natural Law in Reformed Theological Ethics (Grand Rapids: Eerdmans, 2006), 89.

43. John Calvin, Romans and Thessalonians, Calvin's New Testament Commentaries, ed. T. F. Torrance and David F. Torrance (1960; repr., Grand Rapids: Eerdmans, 1996), comm. Rom. 1:20, p. 31.

44. Calvin, Romans, comm. Rom. 1:21, p. 32.

45. John Calvin, Sermons on Timothy and Titus, trans. Arthur Golding (1579; repr., Edinburgh: Banner of Truth, 1983), serm. 38 on 1 Tim. 5:4–5, p. 458; Günther H. Haas, "Ethics and Church Discipline," in The Calvin Handbook, ed. Herman J. Selderhuis (Grand Rapids: Eerdmans, 2008), 336; Kirk M. Summers, Morality after Calvin: Theodore Beza's Christian Censor and Reformed Ethics (Oxford: Oxford University Press, 2017), 67–68; Ronald S. Wallace, Calvin's Doctrine of the Christian Life (Eugene, OR: Wipf & Stock, 1997), 141–69.

46. Calvin, Institutes, 1.5.3; see also Egil Grislis, "Calvin's Use of Cicero in the Institutes I:1–5: A Case Study in Theological Method," Archiv für Reformationsgeschichte / Archive for Reformation History 62, no. 1 (1971): 10.

his commentary on Romans 2:14–15, Calvin explains that the Gentiles prove that God has imprinted on their hearts the ability to discriminate between justice and injustice, honesty and dishonesty. Calvin explains:

> There is no nation so opposed to everything that is human that it does not keep within the confines of some laws. Since, therefore, all nations are disposed to make laws for themselves of their own accord, and without being instructed to do so, it is beyond all doubt that they have certain ideas of justice and rectitude, which the Greeks refer to as *prolēpseis*, and which are implanted by nature in the hearts of men. Therefore they have a law, without the law; for although they do not have the written law of Moses, they are by no means completely lacking in the knowledge of right and justice.[47]

In his exegesis, Calvin acknowledges the concept of *prolēpsis*, which is similar to the concept of common notions.[48] Ancient authors employed the terms *prolēpsis* and common notions (*ennoiai*), or universal ideas as preconceptions or apprehensions of what was right. This concept of *prolēpsis* originated with Stoic philosophers.[49] Calvin's use of the concept stands in continuity with Aquinas's use of common notions.[50] Others, such as Peter Martyr Vermigli (1499–1562), Martin Bucer (1491–1551), and Philip Melanchthon (1497–1560), appeal to the Stoic concept of *prolēpsis* in their commentaries on Romans.[51] In fact, one has to wonder if Calvin gleaned the concept from these peers in the composition of his own commentary on Romans, though a more likely scenario is that he picked up the concept from his reading of ancient authorities such as Cicero and Seneca.

Pagans would not, for example, institute religious rites unless they were convinced that God should be worshiped, nor would they be ashamed of adultery or theft if they did not regard both as evil.[52] Calvin explains:

47. Calvin, *Romans*, comm. Rom. 2:14, p. 48.

48. Cf. R. B. Todd, "The Stoic Common Notions: A Re-examination and Reinterpretation," *Symbolae Osloenses* 48, no. 1 (1973): 47–75, esp. 51–52, 62.

49. Maryanne Cline Horowitz, "The Stoic Synthesis of the Idea of Natural Law in Man: Four Themes," *Journal of the History of Ideas* 35, no. 1 (1974): 3–16, esp. 5; Peter J. Leithart, "Stoic Elements in Calvin's Doctrine of the Christian Life, Part I: Original Corruption, Natural Law, and the Order of the Soul," *Westminster Theological Journal* 55 (1993): 41; Irena Backus, "Calvin's Concept of Natural and Roman Law," *Calvin Theological Journal* 38 (2003): 8.

50. Aquinas, *Summa Theologica*, Ia-IIae q. 94 art. 2.

51. See, e.g., Peter Martyr Vermigli, *Nature and Grace*, in *Philosophical Works: On the Relation of Philosophy to Theology*, ed. Joseph C. McLelland, Peter Martyr Library 4 (Kirksville: MO: Sixteenth Century Essays & Studies, 1996), 20; Martin Bucer, *Metaphrases et Enarrationes in Epist. D. Pauli Apostoli ad Romanos* (Basel: Peter Perna, 1562), 56–58; Michael Sudduth, *The Reformed Objection to Natural Theology* (Burlington, VT: Ashgate, 2009), 11–12.

52. Calvin, *Romans*, comm. Rom. 2:15, p. 48.

This is evidenced by such facts as these, that all the Gentiles alike institute religious rites, make laws to punish adultery, theft, and murder, and commend good faith in commercial transactions and contracts. In this way they prove their knowledge that God is to be worshipped, that adultery, theft, and murder, are evils, and that honesty is to be esteemed. It is not to our purpose to inquire what sort of God they take Him to be, or how many gods they have devised. It is sufficient to know that they think that there is a God, and that honour and worship are due to Him.[53]

Calvin identifies this innate knowledge of God's natural law with the testimony of the conscience. Calvin's exegesis parallels the views of his contemporaries, such as the Reformed Thomist Vermigli.[54]

Calvin appeals to the concept of common notions in his exegesis of Paul's famous defense of the gospel at Mars Hill in Acts 17. Calvin explains the nature of the apostle's appeal to a pagan poet:

He quotes a half-verse from Aratus, not so much for the sake of an authority, as to make the Athenians ashamed, for such sentences of the past flowed from no other fountain than nature and universal reason. And it is indeed no wonder that Paul, who was speaking to men who were unbelievers and ignorant of true godliness, uses the testimony of a poet, in which there appeared the confession of that knowledge, which nature has put into human minds and engraved upon them.[55]

In his explanation of Paul's apologetic strategy, Calvin notes that Paul appeals to "nature and universal reason" (*natura et communi ratione*).[56] Calvin explains how this common reason works:

For since men are imbued by nature with some knowledge of God, they draw true principles from that source. But despite the fact that as soon as thought of God steals upon their minds, they are soon in the midst of improper fabrications and die away, and so the pure seed degenerates into corruptions, yet the first general knowledge of God [*generalis notitia Dei*] remains in them for a time.[57]

53. Calvin, *Romans*, comm. Rom. 2:15, p. 48.
54. Peter Martyr Vermigli, *Most Learned and Fruitfull Commentaries of D. Peter Martir Vermilius* (London: John Daye, 1568), comm. Rom. 2:14–15, fols. 43r–44v–r; see also Grabill, *Natural Law*, 98–121, esp. 116–20.
55. John Calvin, *Acts 14–28*, Calvin's New Testament Commentaries, ed. T. F. Torrance and David W. Torrance, (1960; repr., Grand Rapids: Eerdmans, 1996), comm. Acts 17:28, p. 120; see also Calvin, *Institutes*, 1.5.3.
56. John Calvin, *Commentarii Integri Acta Apostolorum* (Geneva: Nicolas Barbirius & Thomas Courteau, 1564), comm. Acts 17:28, p. 304.
57. Calvin, *Acts 14–28*, comm. Acts 17:28, p. 121.

Once again, the knowledge is true, common, and accessible, but often misused. These concepts (universal reason and common notions) overlap with other concepts such as the seed of religion (*semen religionis*), the sense of deity (*sensus divinitatis*), and the light of nature (*naturae lux*).[58]

Within the context of these comments on Paul's strategy, Calvin disagrees with the Roman Catholic use of common reason, but he does not reject its proper use. He claims that "the Papists" (*Papistarum*) are more dependent upon human testimonies than the oracles of God. They attribute too much weight to Jerome (347–420), Ambrose (340–97), and "the rotten opinions of their Popes, just as if God had spoken." Moreover, he believes they give too much authority to Aristotle and that the "apostles and prophets were silent in the schools [*in scholis*]."[59] While there are undoubtedly differences between Aquinas and Calvin, he most likely addresses these comments to his Roman Catholic peers. In many places Calvin inveighs against the *scholastics*, which is a reference to the Roman Catholic theologians of the Sorbonne.[60] Calvin's reference to the abuse of Aristotle in "the schools" likely refers, therefore, to sixteenth-century Roman Catholics rather than medieval theologians such as Aquinas.

Arguments for the Existence of God

A close examination reveals that Calvin made use of some of the traditional arguments for the existence of God and stands in continuity with the catholic tradition. At the beginning of his *Institutes*, Calvin has three chapters that discuss the natural knowledge of God before he introduces the topic of Scripture:

1.3: The knowledge of God naturally implanted in the human mind

1.4: The knowledge of God stifled or corrupted, ignorantly or maliciously

1.5: The knowledge of God conspicuous in the creation and continual government of the world

1.6: The need of Scripture, as a guide and teacher, in coming to God as a creator[61]

58. Calvin, *Institutes*, 1.4.1; 1.3.3; 1.4.2.
59. Calvin, *Acts 14–28*, comm. Acts 17:28, pp. 120–21; Calvin, *Acta Apostolorum*, 304.
60. Muller, *Unaccommodated Calvin*, 46–52, esp. 50–51.
61. Paul Helm, "Reprise: Calvin, the Natural Knowledge of God, and Confessionalism," *Helm's Deep: Philosophical Theology* (blog), November 13, 2015, http://paulhelmsdeep.blogspot.com/2015/11/reprise-calvin-natural-knowledge-of-god.html?m=1.

Within the context of these chapters Calvin makes reference to a number of classical authors, but most notably to Cicero (106–43 BC).[62] Within the context of Cicero's work, the Roman orator refers to common notions.[63] Hence, when Calvin writes of the heathen who say that there is no nation so barbarous as not to be imbued with the conviction that there is a God, he has Cicero in mind and, in part, the concept of common notions.[64]

Evidence of the connection between common notions and Cicero, for example, appears when Cicero writes the following:

> For the belief in gods has not been established by authority, custom, or law, but rests on the unanimous and abiding consensus of mankind: their existence is therefore a necessary inference, since we possess an instinctive or rather innate concept [innatas cognitiones] of them; but a belief which all men by nature share must necessarily be true; therefore it must be admitted that the gods exist.[65]

Cicero then links the innate concept of deity to the Stoic concept of prolēpsis. This is the category that Calvin invoked in his comments on Romans 2:14.[66] Cicero writes:

> And since this truth is almost universally accepted not only among philosophers but also among the unlearned, we must admit it as also being an accepted truth that we possess a "preconception" as I called it above, or a "prior notion," of the gods. (For we are bound to employ novel terms to denote novel ideas, just as Epicurus himself employed the word prolēpsis in a sense in which no one had ever used it before.) We have then a preconception of such a nature that we believe the gods to be blessed and immortal. For nature, which bestowed on us an idea of the gods themselves, also engraved on our minds the belief that they are eternal and blessed.[67]

Calvin's reference to preconceptions (prolēpsis) overlaps with the idea of common notions, as Cicero's comments attest. At its essence, the first chapters of Calvin's Institutes mirror his commentary on Romans 1 and 2,

---

62. Calvin, Institutes, 1.3.3; cf. Cicero, De natura deorum, trans. H. Rackham, Loeb Classical Library (Cambridge, MA: Harvard University Press, 1972), 1.23, pp. 60–63; see also Grislis, "Calvin's Use of Cicero," 5–37; Peter J. Leithart, "That Eminent Pagan: Calvin's Use of Cicero in Institutes 1:1–5," Westminster Theological Journal 52, no. 1 (1990): 1–12.

63. Cicero, De natura deorum 1.17, pp. 45–47.

64. Cf. Calvin, Institutes (Battles), 1:44n5.

65. Cicero, De natura deorum 1.17, pp. 45–47.

66. Calvin, Romans, comm. Rom. 2:14, p. 48.

67. Cicero, De natura deorum 1.17, pp. 45–47.

where he cites pagan authorities who corroborate Paul's claim that the Gentiles know God and have a knowledge of right and wrong written on their hearts.

Calvin's opening arguments in *Institutes* 1.3–6 move from the knowledge of God implanted in the mind and its corruption by sin to the knowledge of God in the creation, which requires the corrective lenses of Scripture. Calvin, however, presents the knowledge implanted in the mind, or common notions, as one piece of a greater whole connected with the natural knowledge of God in the creation. The internal and external knowledge of God work together as a unit:

> Since the perfection of blessedness consists in the knowledge of God, he has been pleased, in order that none might be excluded from the means of obtaining felicity, not only to deposit in our minds that seed of religion of which we have already spoken, but so to manifest his perfections in the whole structure of the universe, and daily place himself in our view, that we cannot open our eyes without being compelled to behold him.[68]

On the heels of this statement Calvin cites Psalm 104:2, in which the psalmist speaks of God robing himself with light, and Psalm 19:1, which explains that the knowledge of God is open and manifest to all.

In his comments on Psalm 19:1, Calvin invokes the argument from design: "As soon as we acknowledge God to be the supreme Architect, who has erected the beauteous fabric of the universe, our minds must necessarily be ravished with wonder at his infinite goodness, wisdom, and power."[69] He notes that philosophers understand these matters better than most.[70] As in his *Institutes*, Calvin draws a connection between the knowledge implanted in humanity and the knowledge of God in creation. He acknowledges that in the writings of "heathen authors" God has put a knowledge of justice and uprightness, though because of the noetic effects of sin there are only certain mutilated principles that remain amid obscurity and doubt.[71]

Similar comments appear in Calvin's exegesis of Psalm 104. Calvin believed there was a link between God's being and the very fabric of the creation: one

68. Calvin, *Institutes*, 1.5.1.

69. John Calvin, *Commentary on the Book of Psalms*, in *Calvin's Commentaries*, 22 vols. (repr., Grand Rapids: Baker, 1993), comm. Ps. 19:1, 4:309. The volume number refers to the specific volume in the 22-volume set. See also Aquinas, *Summa Theologica*, Ia q. 2 art. 3.

70. Calvin, *Psalms*, comm. Ps. 19:2, 4:310.

71. Calvin, *Psalms*, comm. Ps. 19:7, 4:319.

can follow a line from the effect (creation) back to the cause (God), which reflects the argument from causality.[72] In his *Institutes*, Calvin quotes positively a poem from Virgil (70–19 BC) to illustrate this cause-and-effect relationship between God and the creation:

> Know, first, that heaven, and earth's compacted frame,
> And flowing waters, and the starry flame,
> And both the radiant lights, one common soul
> Inspires and feeds—and animates the whole.
> This active mind, infused through all the space,
> Unites and mingles with the mighty mass:
> Hence, men and beasts the breath of life obtain,
> And birds of air, and monsters of the main.
> Th' ethereal vigour is in all the same,
> And every soul is filled with equal flame.[73]

On this idea Calvin comments that the "method of investigating the divine perfections, by tracing the lineaments of his countenance as shadowed forth in the firmament and on the earth, is common both to those within and to those without the pale of the Church."[74]

Given this admission, Calvin has no qualms about positively invoking Plato (ca. 428–348 BC):

> We continue to live, so long as he sustains us by his power; but no sooner does he withdraw his life-giving spirit than we die. Even Plato knew this, who so often teaches that, properly speaking, there is but one God, and that all things subsist, or have their being only in him. Nor do I doubt, that it was the will of God, by means of that heathen writer, to awaken all men to the knowledge, that they derive their life from another source than from themselves.[75]

These comments amount to a substantive agreement with two of the Thomistic proofs, the cosmological and teleological arguments. Calvin does not present the arguments in a philosophical manner as Aquinas does, but he nevertheless discursively appeals to the concept of tracing the effects of the creation back

72. Calvin, *Psalms*, comm. Ps. 104:3, 6:146; cf. Aquinas, *Summa Theologica*, Ia q. 2 art. 3.
73. Calvin, *Institutes*, 1.5.5; see Virgil, *Aeneid*, in *Eclogue, Georgics, Aeneid Books 1–6*, ed. G. P. Goold, Loeb Classical Library (Cambridge, MA: Harvard University Press, 1999), 6.724–30, pp. 556–57.
74. Calvin, *Institutes*, 1.5.6.
75. Calvin, *Psalms*, comm. Ps. 104:29, 6:167.

to their cause and even cites pagan authorities positively in the process.[76] As Richard Muller observes:

> If, then, the *Institutes* does not contain demonstrations of the existence of God, it certainly contains arguments to the point, several of which related to the traditional proofs. Both these less logically stated forms of the logical proofs and Calvin's rhetorical and hortatory arguments find, moreover, precise parallels in the Reformed orthodox systems, in which rhetorical arguments stand alongside the logical proofs and in which the logical proofs often take on rhetorical rather than purely demonstrative forms.[77]

In fact, with Aquinas, Calvin believed that only the philosophically learned could access this natural knowledge of God; this is something the common rabble could not do.[78]

But there are two important qualifications regarding Calvin's use of these simplified arguments. First, Calvin deals with the natural testimony and arguments for God's existence before he introduces the necessity of Scripture. In fact, even though Calvin raises the importance and necessity of Scripture after he introduces the natural knowledge of God, he nevertheless postpones his formal discussion of Scripture until book 2.[79] Contrary to the claims of some, Calvin does not begin with the Christ of Scripture but, in a fashion similar to Aquinas, he first starts with the knowledge of God available through the book of nature.[80] As Egil Grislis notes: "In further agreement with Cicero, Calvin is prepared to acknowledge the continuous and positive dynamic role which is played by nature in bringing the existence of God to the attention of sinful humanity."[81]

Second, Calvin acknowledges that the noetic effects of sin significantly hamper fallen humanity's ability to use this natural knowledge in a profitable way for their salvation.[82] In the end, the natural knowledge of God renders fallen humanity inexcusable before the divine bar. But how does natural knowledge render fallen humanity inexcusable? Based on Romans 2:14–15, Calvin argues that God has given all people the ability to "distinguish between

76. Richard A. Muller, *Post-Reformation Reformed Dogmatics*, 4 vols. (Grand Rapids: Baker Academic, 2003), 3:173; see also Sudduth, *Reformed Objection*, 61; Grislis, "Calvin's Use of Cicero," 14.

77. Muller, *Reformed Dogmatics*, 3:174.

78. Calvin, *Institutes*, 1.5.11.

79. See Calvin, *Institutes*, 1.6.1; 2.6.1; Grabill, *Natural Law*, 82–83.

80. Calvin, *Institutes*, 1.2.1; see also Barth, *Church Dogmatics*, IV/1:66; Dooyeweerd, *Western Thought*, 116; Dooyeweerd, *Reformation and Scholasticism*, 1:15.

81. Grislis, "Calvin's Use of Cicero," 21.

82. Calvin, *Institutes*, 1.5.5, 14; 1.4.1–4.

justice and injustice."[83] This knowledge, "indelibly engraven on the human heart . . . is not a doctrine which is first learned at school, but one as to which every man is, from the womb, his own master."[84] In a postfall world, God still enables sinners to distinguish sufficiently between right and wrong, and he uses human conscience to commend moral conduct or condemn immoral conduct.[85]

So the testimony of the innate knowledge of God is abundantly clear. The problem is not with this testimony but with the sinful suppression of this testimony. Calvin explains, "Themistius is more accurate in teaching that the intellect is very seldom mistaken in the general definition or essence of the matter; but that deception begins as it advances farther—namely, when it descends to particulars."[86] Calvin cites Themistius (317–87) to make the point that the problem does not lie with the innate knowledge of God but with how the unbeliever uses it. Unbelievers condemn evil in the abstract but then privately commit the same evil. This means that Christians and non-Christians share the same ontology and epistemological data regarding right and wrong by virtue of their creation in God's image and the innate knowledge of God. But only believers have the ability to evaluate this knowledge and make proper use of it. This distinction stands in continuity with Aquinas and other Reformed theologians who distinguish knowledge and judgment from readiness and willingness to do what is just and honest, or inscribed principles versus erroneous conclusions.[87] The former is the same in all people whereas the latter is not. The natural knowledge of God must function properly within fallen people; otherwise they would have an excuse for their sinful conduct. That unbelievers have this knowledge, know it aright, but suppress or ignore it renders them inexcusable. The same principle applies to the external knowledge of God in the creation. People see it, sufficiently know it aright, yet sinfully suppress and ignore it.

83. Calvin, *Institutes*, 1.5.5.

84. Calvin, *Institutes*, 1.3.3; cf. 2.2.22.

85. Calvin, *Institutes*, 2.2.22.

86. Calvin, *Institutes*, 2.2.23. Calvin (Stephanus 1559 ed.) cites Themistius, *De anima* 3.46, but Battles locates the passage in Themistius, *De anima paraphrasis*, ed. Richard Heinze (Berlin: George Reimerus, 1899), 112; Themistius, *Aristotle: On the Soul*, trans. Robert B. Todd (London: Bloomsbury, 2014), 3.6, p. 138.

87. Cf. Aquinas, *Summa Theologica*, Ia-IIae q. 94 art. 4; Vermigli, *Fruitfull Commentaries*, comm. Rom. 2:14–15, fol. 44r; Francis Junius, *The Mosaic Polity*, ed. Andrew M. McGinnis, trans. Todd M. Rester (Grand Rapids: CLP Academic, 2015), thesis 4, p. 44; *Synopsis Purioris Theologiae / Synopsis of a Purer Theology*, ed. Dolf te Velde et al., trans. Riemer A. Faber, 2 vols. (Leiden: Brill, 2014), disp. 18.14–17, 1:436–37; Francis Turretin, *Institutes of Elenctic Theology*, ed. James T. Dennison Jr., trans. George Musgrave Giger, 3 vols. (Phillipsburg, NJ: P&R, 1992–97), 11.1.11.

Calvin explains the difference between the shared knowledge of the believer and unbeliever by positing two types of intelligence, a concept he borrows from Augustine (354–430).[88] Calvin writes, "The distinction is, that we have one kind of intelligence of earthly things, and another of heavenly things."[89] Earthly things address the present life, which includes policy, economy, mechanical arts, and liberal studies. Heavenly things pertain to true righteousness and the mysteries of the heavenly kingdom. Calvin employs this distinction because he wants to preserve the doctrine of the noetic effects of sin but at the same time recognize that fallen human beings still have true knowledge, which has been "implanted in the breasts of all without a teacher or lawgiver."[90] Indeed, "to charge the intellect with perpetual blindness so as to leave it no intelligence of any description whatever, is repugnant not only to the Word of God, but to common experience."[91] In fact, Calvin believed that when Christians read "profane authors," they could still marvel at the many admirable gifts provided by their Creator in spite of their fallen condition.[92] But with regard to heavenly intelligence, the unbeliever is blinder than a mole.[93] Calvin's view parallels Martin Luther's (1483–1546) nearly identical distinction between earthly and heavenly knowledge.[94]

Some, such as Van Til, believed that Calvin's assessment regarding earthly and heavenly knowledge was inconsistent: "Even Calvin, though by his doctrine of 'common grace' he was in a much better position to do justice to the knowledge of the non-Christian science without succumbing to it than others were, did not bring out with sufficient clearness at all times that the natural man is as blind as a mole with respect to natural things as well as with respect to spiritual things."[95] Van Til believed that "Calvin by no means countenances the notion that the natural man does know even the physical world truly."[96] Van Til believed his analysis was correct because Calvin speaks of humanity's natural knowledge as "vanity." The problem with Van Til's analysis is that it contradicts Calvin's clear statements on the matter. Calvin unmistakably

88. Calvin, *Institutes*, 2.2.12; cf. Grabill, *Natural Law*, 71; VanDrunen, *Natural Law*, 107; Backus, "Calvin's Concept," 14.

89. Calvin, *Institutes*, 2.2.13.

90. Calvin, *Institutes*, 2.2.13.

91. Calvin, *Institutes*, 2.2.12.

92. Calvin, *Institutes*, 2.2.14.

93. Calvin, *Institutes*, 2.2.18.

94. Brian Gerrish, *Grace and Reason: A Study in the Theology of Luther* (Oxford: Clarendon, 1962), 10–27. My thanks to David Sytsma, who alerted me to this source.

95. Van Til, *Introduction to Systematic Theology*, 82.

96. Van Til, *Introduction to Systematic Theology*, 82.

states that unbelievers are blind with regard to heavenly knowledge but not blind to earthly knowledge.

Additionally, *pace* Van Til, using the distinction of the two intelligences, Calvin believed that Christians could profit from the "work and ministry of the ungodly in physics, dialectics, mathematics, and other similar sciences" because they were ultimately the gifts of God despite their proximate source.[97] Calvin buttresses his claims by citing two authorities, Peter Lombard (ca. 1096–1160) and Homer. Calvin first qualifies his claims by noting Augustine's reminder, namely, that all of humanity's natural learning ultimately comes to naught vis-à-vis God unless it has a solid foundation in truth. Calvin notes that Lombard and the "Schoolmen" were forced to acknowledge this point because when Adam lost his supernatural gifts, the remaining natural gifts were corrupted.[98] Second, Calvin appeals to Homer, who claimed that all people excel in genius, not only because Jupiter has given it to them, but because he leads them day by day.[99] Calvin cites Homer to make the point that the earthly intelligence that fallen humans possess is one of the means by which God governs the world and ensures its stability.

Conclusion

When we survey Calvin's exegesis and theological formulations, the overwhelming conclusion is clear: some contemporary theologians have created a Calvin of faith, one who was either hostile to or uninterested in scholastic method, natural law, and common notions, as well as the traditional arguments for God's existence. The Calvin of history, on the other hand, reveals different data. Within the framework of his twofold knowledge of God, Calvin posited three forms of knowledge: a corrupt, partial, and extrabiblical knowledge of God through the creation; a biblical knowledge of God as creator; and a knowledge of God through Christ as redeemer.[100] Others, such as Westminster divine John Arrowsmith (1602–59), advocate a similar threefold knowledge of God: natural, literal, and spiritual.[101] There are undoubtedly differences

97. Calvin, *Institutes*, 2.2.16.

98. Calvin, *Institutes*, 2.2.16; see Peter Lombard, *The Sentences*, trans. Giulio Silano, 4 vols. (Toronto: Pontifical Institute of Medieval Studies, 2007–10), 2.25.

99. Calvin, *Institutes*, 2.2.17; see Homer, *Odyssey*, trans. A. T. Murray, rev. George E. Dimock, Loeb Classical Library (Cambridge, MA: Harvard University Press, 1919), 18.137, 2:206.

100. Muller, *Reformed Dogmatics*, 1:290.

101. John Arrowsmith, *Armilla Catechetica: A Chain of Principles* (Cambridge: John Field, 1659), 3.1, p. 111.

between Calvin and Aquinas. Calvin, for example, places greater emphasis on the noetic effects of sin, stresses the role of the conscience more than the intellect, and does not characterize the law of God as the *lex aeterna* like Aquinas.[102] Other Reformed theologians, however, do embrace Aquinas's *lex aeterna* concept.[103] There are enough continuities, however, to substantiate the claim that Calvin stood in continuity with Aquinas regarding the place and function of the scholastic method, the place and function of natural law and common notions, and the arguments for the existence of God. The medieval Thomistic understanding of natural law and common notions was simply a part of Calvin's education, and there is no evidence that Calvin anywhere repudiated this general outlook.[104]

Calvin, therefore, stands in continuity with the catholic tradition on common notions and their connections to the order of nature and the Reformed Orthodox use of these concepts.[105] In fact, Calvin's role in the composition of the 1559 Gallican Confession testifies to the codification and widespread acceptance of the natural knowledge of God: "As such this God reveals himself to men; firstly, in his works, in their creation, as well as in their preservation and control. Secondly, and more clearly, in his Word, which was in the beginning revealed through oracles, and which was afterward committed to writing in the books which we call the Holy Scriptures" (II). Guido de Bres (1522–67) echoed these same points when he employed them in expanded form in the Belgic Confession (1561):

> We know God by two means: First, by the creation, preservation, and government of the universe, since that universe is before our eyes like a beautiful book in which all creatures, great and small, are as letters to make us ponder the invisible things of God: God's eternal power and divinity, as the apostle Paul says in Romans 1:20. All these things are enough to convict humans and to leave them without excuse. Second, God makes himself known to us more clearly by his holy and divine Word, as much as we need in this life, for God's glory and for our salvation. (II)

102. Grabill, *Natural Law*, 92–93; VanDrunen, *Natural Law*, 101, 105, 107; VanDrunen, "Comparison of Aquinas and Calvin," 90–97.

103. See Junius, *Mosaic Polity*, thesis 4, p. 42; Girolamo Zanchi, *On the Law in General*, trans. Jeffrey J. Veenstra (Grand Rapids: CLP Academic, 2012), 4; Turretin, *Institutes*, 11.2.16; Anthony Tuckney, *Praelectiones Theologicae* (London: Stephen Swart, 1679), pars secunda, q. 47, p. 317; Aquinas, *Summa Theologica*, I-IIae q. 91 art. 1 rep. obj. 2.

104. Paul Helm, *John Calvin's Ideas* (Oxford: Oxford University Press, 2004), 363–64, 367–78; VanDrunen, *Natural Law and the Two Kingdoms*, 95–99; Susan Schreiner, *Theater of His Glory: Nature and the Natural Order in the Thought of John Calvin* (Grand Rapids: Baker, 1995), 2–3; Grabill, *Natural Law*, 70–97; cf. Backus, "Calvin's Concept," 12, 25.

105. J. Todd Billings, "The Catholic Calvin," *Pro Ecclesia* 20, no. 2 (2011): 121, 126.

Far from being an aberration, or a medieval hangover, or forbidden fruit to sophisticated minds, the natural knowledge of God plays an integral role in Calvin's theology. Common notions and the broader creation are all part of the order of nature that give testimony to God's existence. Calvin, therefore, stands in continuity with the medieval past and Reformed Orthodoxy on the use of the scholastic method, natural law and common notions, and arguments for the existence of God.

4

THOMAS AQUINAS

The sole way to overcome an adversary of divine truth is from the authority of Scripture—an authority divinely confirmed by miracles. For that which is above the human reason we believe only because God has revealed it.

Thomas Aquinas

Part of the problem with Van Til's critique of Aquinas is the rarity of his citations of primary sources.

There is a greater degree of agreement between Van Til and Aquinas than Van Til recognizes.

John Frame

In the effort to recover the book of nature for defending the faith, one of the chief obstacles is the theological reputation of Thomas Aquinas (1225–74). As the previous chapters attest, some Reformed theologians and philosophers such as Karl Barth (1886–1968) and Herman Dooyeweerd (1894–1977) have identified Aquinas as chiefly responsible for introducing synthetic thought to the church more broadly, and to the Reformed tradition more narrowly.[1] Cornelius Van Til is among the theologians who have made this claim. Van

1. Barth, "No!," in Emil Brunner and Karl Barth, *Natural Theology: Comprising "Nature and Grace" by Professor Dr. Emil Brunner and the Reply "No!" by Dr. Karl Barth* (1946; repr., Eugene, OR: Wipf & Stock, 2002), 100–101; Herman Dooyeweerd, *In the Twilight of Western Thought*, ed. D. F. M. Strauss, Collected Works, Series B 16 (Grand Rapids: Paideia, 2012), 90;

Til accused many theologians of synthetic thinking in combining biblical and pagan thought, thus compromising the purity and integrity of biblical doctrine. In his efforts to identify chief synthesis thinkers and thus preserve the purity of the Reformed theological system, one of the names that regularly surfaces is Aquinas. Thomas, Van Til tells us, compromised the integrity of Christian doctrine by embracing elements of Aristotelian philosophy. Moreover, Van Til ultimately accused Aquinas of being a rationalist. On his reading, Aquinas constructed a theological system not on the authority of Scripture but on a foundation of autonomous human reason. Van Til's condemnation of Aquinas reverberated in the halls of Reformed theology for a generation, and other theologians devoted to Van Til's apologetic methodology have repeated the accusation. But a salient question arises: Is Van Til's critique accurate? The short answer is no. The remainder of this chapter provides a longer and more detailed answer with necessary and important qualifications.

Here I will argue that Van Til and many of his students have misread Aquinas on the relationship between faith and reason as well as his use of Aristotelian philosophy. The chapter therefore first sets forth Van Til's claims about Aquinas. Then it explores what Aquinas actually said. Third, it offers analysis as to why Van Til misreads Aquinas. Van Til's most serious error, I believe, is that he reads Aquinas largely through secondary sources rather than carefully engaging Aquinas's works. Such a methodology naturally skews his interpretation. Hence, this chapter focuses exclusively on Aquinas, not the subsequent Thomist tradition. What Van Til has to say about later Thomism and Roman Catholicism is not in view and would require a separate analysis to determine its accuracy. The chapter then concludes with some observations about Aquinas and Reformed theology and apologetics.

Recovering an accurate reading of Aquinas as a theologian is necessary because early modern Reformed thinkers routinely appeal to him to establish their arguments, and generally agree with his use of the book of nature. This is especially evident when they interact with common notions and their connection to the wider order of nature. If Van Til's critique of Aquinas is accurate, then there is a significant problem for the Reformed Orthodox who include Thomist elements in their theology. If, on the other hand, Van Til's critique is inaccurate, then these Thomist elements can happily coexist and even thrive within Reformed thought. This chapter argues that Van Til and Aquinas actually have more in common than most assume and that a right

---

Dooyeweerd, *Reformation and Scholasticism in Philosophy*, ed. D. F. M. Strauss, trans. Ray Togtmann, 3 vols., Collected Works, Series A 5–7 (Grand Rapids: Paideia, 2012), 1:3.

understanding of Aquinas provides yet another useful theological tool for one's apologetic toolbox.

Van Til on Aquinas

In his book *Christian Apologetics*, Van Til presents an overview of his pre-suppositional approach.[2] In this work he sets forth a Reformed apologetic over and against Roman Catholic, Arminian, and less-consistent Reformed methodologies. In his treatment of the Roman Catholic view, Van Til regularly invokes Aquinas's name as its chief representative.[3] At other times he simply describes the "Roman Catholic" view. On those occasions, one may presume that Aquinas is still in the crosshairs.[4] There are five main charges that Van Til levels at Thomas and the Roman Catholic position.

1. Aquinas follows Aristotle by speaking of being and then introducing the distinction between the divine and created beings. Aquinas does not begin with the doctrine of the ontological Trinity.[5]

2. Roman Catholics try to prove the existence of God by employing the method of Aristotle to show that God's existence is in accord with the principles of logic.[6]

3. By appealing to the common ground of reason, Roman Catholics arrive at the existence of a god through theistic proofs, and this god accords with the presuppositions of natural reason but not the God of the Bible.[7]

4. Natural humankind are said to possess natural revelation and to correctly interpret it; there is no need for supernatural revelation to correct natural humankind's (fallen) interpretation of natural revelation.[8]

5. There are two Aquinases: Thomas the theologian and Thomas the philosopher. Thomas the philosopher appeals to and employs autonomous reason, and Thomas the theologian appeals to Scripture, but Thomas "the theologian need not at all ask St. Thomas the autonomous philosopher to reverse his decisions on the fundamental question about the existence of God."[9]

2. Cornelius Van Til, *Christian Apologetics* (Phillipsburg, NJ: P&R, 1976).
3. Van Til, *Christian Apologetics*, 9, 46, 53, 59, 69–70, 87, 88–89.
4. Van Til, *Christian Apologetics*, 17, 27, 43, 45, 52, 72.
5. Van Til, *Christian Apologetics*, 9, 43.
6. Van Til, *Christian Apologetics*, 17.
7. Van Til, *Christian Apologetics*, 45.
8. Van Til, *Christian Apologetics*, 52–53, 72.
9. Van Til, *Christian Apologetics*, 87.

In summary, Van Til maintains that Aquinas has let the infection of Greek autonomous reason into the fortress of faith, and reason has taken over.[10] Reason is the foundation on which Aquinas tries to build his system of doctrine and thus his apologetic methodology.

Van Til composed this portrait of Aquinas and Roman Catholic apologetic methodology in general, and subsequent Van Tillians have embraced it. In his criticism of E. J. Carnell's (1919–67) apologetic method, Greg Bahnsen (1948–95), for example, explains that the former begins his arguments from the standpoint of reason rather than the authority of revelation: "This signifies a departure from the Augustinian position that faith leads to understanding and an *endorsement of the position of Aquinas* that faith must have a rational foundation or platform on which to stand."[11] Bahnsen repeats this claim in his criticisms of the methodology of Francis Schaeffer (1912–84), who supposedly elevated reason over revelation rather than having revelation serve as the presupposition of reason. Schaeffer departed from Augustine's faith seeking understanding and instead embraced the natural theology of Aquinas.[12] Hence, in Bahnsen's mind, Aquinas is a rationalist and does not embody Augustine's (354–430) principle of faith seeking understanding.

What Aquinas Really Said

Van Til and other Van Tillians have claimed that Aquinas constructs a rational foundation upon which he then builds his theological system. The system rests upon autonomous reason rather than special revelation, or Scripture. What, however, does Aquinas actually say? How, for example, do the so-called proofs for the existence of God actually function within Thomas's theology? At this point it is important to examine Thomas directly and set aside how the proofs have been used in subsequent theological systems. The chief question here is, Did the proofs ever serve as the primary ground for Thomas's system, a rational stepladder that begins with reason and then rises to revelation? Quite simply, the answer is no.

10. For places where Van Til makes similar claims, see Cornelius Van Til, *The Defense of the Faith*, 3rd ed. (1955; Phillipsburg, NJ: P&R, 1967), 56; Van Til, *Common Grace and the Gospel* (Phillipsburg, NJ: P&R, 1972), 190; Van Til, *Essays on Christian Education* (Phillipsburg, NJ: P&R, 1979), 117; Van Til, "Christian Philosophy of Life: Address Presented to the Association for the Advancement of Christian Scholarship" (March 29, 1968), 19; Van Til, *Christianity in Conflict*, 3 vols. (1962; Glenside, PA: Westminster Campus Bookstore, 1996), 2:26–27, 30, 41; Van Til, *A Christian Theory of Knowledge* (Phillipsburg, NJ: P&R, 1969), 160, 175, 188, 196, 278, 285.

11. Greg Bahnsen, *Presuppositional Apologetics: Stated and Defended*, ed. J. McDurmon (Nacogdoches, TX: Covenant Media, 2008), 232.

12. Bahnsen, *Presuppositional Apologetics*, 248.

The Function of the Proofs

Aquinas never advanced the proofs as a rational foundation for his system of theology. Rather, they served as confirmation that rational discourse about God was possible, and such a claim was ultimately for the sake and benefit of faith.[13] In other words, the proofs function only on the presupposition of faith and the authority of Scripture.[14] They do not function independently within Thomas's system. Van Til's notion of Thomas the philosopher versus Thomas the theologian is a modern interpretive imposition upon Aquinas's theology that owes more to post-Enlightenment quests to imagine a Thomist philosophy independent of revelation.[15] The first piece of evidence that confirms this claim is the immediate context where we find the proofs. Thomas does not begin his *Summa Theologica* with the proofs, but with a question about the nature of sacred doctrine.[16] For Aquinas, philosophical knowledge is inadequate in and of itself. "Scripture," writes Aquinas, "inspired of God, is no part of philosophical science, which has been built up by human reason." Aquinas explains this point in further detail:

It was necessary for man's salvation that there should be a knowledge revealed by God, besides philosophical science built up by human reason. Firstly, indeed, because man is directed to God, as to an end that surpasses the grasp of his reason: "The eye hath not seen, O God, besides Thee, what things Thou hast prepared for them that wait for Thee" (Isa. 64:4). But the end must first be known by men who are to direct their thoughts and actions to the end. *Hence it was necessary for the salvation of man that certain truths which exceed human reason should be made known to him by divine revelation.*[17]

This statement constitutes the foundation of Aquinas's *Summa* and clearly establishes that its contents are sacred doctrine based on divine revelation.[18]

13. Richard A. Muller, "The Dogmatic Function of St. Thomas' 'Proofs': A Protestant Appreciation," *Fides et Historia* 24 (1992): 17.

14. W. J. Hankey, *God in Himself: Aquinas's Doctrine of God as Expounded in the "Summa Theologiae"* (Oxford: Oxford University Press, 1987), 36–37; Lawrence Dewan, "Faith and Reason from St. Thomas Aquinas's Perspective," *Science et Esprit* 58, no. 2 (2006): 113–23.

15. Mark D. Jordan, *Rewritten Theology: Aquinas after His Readers* (Oxford: Blackwell, 2006), 60–88, esp. 60, 63, 87; Rudi A. te Velde, *Aquinas on God: The "Divine Science" of the "Summa Theologiae"* (Surrey, UK: Ashgate, 2006), 1–36; Brian Davies, *Thomas Aquinas's "Summa contra Gentiles": A Guide and Commentary* (Oxford: Oxford University Press, 2016), 8–16.

16. Muller, "Dogmatic Function," 18–19; Christopher T. Baglow, "Sacred Scripture and Sacred Doctrine in Saint Thomas Aquinas," in *Aquinas on Doctrine: A Critical Introduction*, ed. Thomas Weinandy, Daniel Keating, and John Yocum (London: T&T Clark, 2004), 1–24.

17. Thomas Aquinas, *Summa Theologica* (repr., Allen, TX: Christian Classics, 1948), Ia q. 1 art. 1 (emphasis added).

18. Muller, "Dogmatic Function," 19.

Faith, not reason, is Aquinas's fundamental presupposition here: "Although those things which are beyond man's knowledge may not be sought for by man through his reason, nevertheless, once they are revealed by God they must be accepted by faith."[19]

If Aquinas's system, therefore, rests upon the presupposition of Scripture and the necessity of faith, then what role do the proofs play? The proofs enter Thomas's *Summa* at the second question on the existence of God, but they have roots that extend back to the first. In the eighth article of question one, Aquinas asks whether sacred doctrine is a matter of argument. To answer this question, he first turns to Titus 1:9, "[The elder] must hold firm to the trustworthy word as taught, so that he may be able to give instruction in sound doctrine and also to rebuke those who contradict it." Thomas therefore concludes from his exegesis that sacred doctrine is argumentative. He explains that those in other sciences do not argue to prove their principles but rather argue from their principles to demonstrate truths. For example, a scientist employs reason to prove conclusions in physics. But theology is different: "This doctrine does not argue in proof of its principles, which are the articles of faith, but from them it goes on to prove something else; as the Apostle from the resurrection of Christ argues in proof of the general resurrection (1 Cor. 15)."[20] So then, sacred doctrine ultimately makes its case from faith, not reason.

How does sacred doctrine function apologetically? Aquinas assigns it two roles: (1) to defend the faith and (2) to clarify articles of faith. First, since Scripture has no science above it, we can use it to dispute with an opponent only if we admit that some of its truths are obtained through divine revelation. For example, we can argue with heretics in this manner because they accept some of the principles of Scripture. But if we argue against an atheist, someone who completely denies the teachings of Scripture, "there is no longer any means of proving the articles of faith by reasoning, but only of answering his objections—if he has any—against faith."[21] Apologetically, Christians can respond to objections, but this does not mean they have somehow proved what ultimately only faith can embrace. This is the apologetic function of a faith-informed and reasoned defense of sacred doctrine.

Second, Aquinas states, "Arguments from human reason cannot avail to prove what must be received on faith, nevertheless this doctrine argues from articles of faith to other truths."[22] He explicitly declares that a person argues

19. Aquinas, *Summa Theologica*, Ia q. 1 art. 1 rep. obj. 1.
20. Aquinas, *Summa Theologica*, Ia q. 1 art. 8.
21. Aquinas, *Summa Theologica*, Ia q. 1 art. 8.
22. Aquinas, *Summa Theologica*, Ia q. 1 art. 8 rep. obj. 1.

from faith, which rests on the authority of revelation. But this does not mean that faith is irrational. Rather, "sacred doctrine makes use even of human reason, not, indeed, to prove faith (for thereby the merit of faith would come to an end), but to make clear other things that are put forward in this doctrine." This is the clarifying role of reason: "Since therefore grace does not destroy nature, but perfects it, natural reason should minister to faith as the natural bent of the will ministers to charity."[23] Some Reformed readers might wince at Thomas's invocation of nature and grace; I will address this issue below.[24] For the moment, however, we must observe how reason functions: it is an assistant or handmaid (*ancilla*) to faith. Reason answers objections and clarifies revealed truths.

Aquinas appeals to Paul's methodology at Mars Hill in Acts 17: "Hence sacred doctrine makes use also of the authority of philosophers in those questions in which they were able to know the truth by natural reason." But even then,

> sacred doctrine makes use of these authorities as *extrinsic and probable arguments; but properly uses the authority of the canonical Scriptures as an incontrovertible proof*, and the authority of the doctors of the Church as one that may properly be used, yet merely as probable. For our faith rests upon the revelation made to the apostles and prophets, who wrote the canonical books, and not on the revelations (if any such there are) made to other doctors.[25]

Once again, invoking the authority of the doctors of the church undoubtedly raises concerns for some with Reformed convictions; I will address this concern below. We should not miss the point, however, that only the authority of Scripture provides "incontrovertible proof."

The Proofs

When we closely examine the proofs, Aquinas does not begin from raw reason but from a scriptural foundation. He quotes Romans 1:20 to support the claim that one can demonstrate God's existence: "For his invisible attributes, namely, his eternal power and divine nature, have been clearly perceived, ever since the creation of the world, in the things that have been made." Before

---

23. Aquinas, *Summa Theologica*, Ia q. 1 art. 8 rep. obj. 2.
24. See David Sytsma, "'As a Dwarfe Set upon a Gyants Shoulders': John Weems (ca. 1579–1636) on the Place of Philosophy and Scholasticism in Reformed Theology," in *Die Philosophie der Reformierten*, ed. Günter Frank and Herman Selderhuis, Melanchthon-Schriften der Stadt Bretten (Stuttgart: Frommann-Holzboog, 2012), 299–321.
25. Aquinas, *Summa Theologica*, Ia q. 1 art. 8 rep. obj. 2 (emphasis added).

he gives the five proofs, he explains that there are two ways that one may argue for God's existence: by examining the effects and tracing them back to their cause (*quia*, an a posteriori argument) or by arguing from the cause to the effect (*propter quid*, an a priori argument). Aquinas explains, "When an effect is better known to us than its cause, from the effect we proceed to the knowledge of the cause. And from every effect the existence of its proper cause can be demonstrated, so long as its effects are better known to us."[26] In other words, Aquinas believes that arguing from the effect back to the cause is the preferred method.[27]

He then offers two clarifications. First, God's existence, known to humanity by natural reason, is not an article of faith, but merely a preamble to it. Faith, argues Aquinas, presupposes natural knowledge.[28] This does not represent a contradiction in Aquinas's thought, namely, that faith rests upon reason. Rather, Aquinas argues that human beings cannot conceive of faith apart from natural knowledge because supernatural knowledge (special revelation) always comes to us within the context of general revelation.[29] Second, even though he believes that one can demonstrate God's existence by reasoning back from effect to cause, Aquinas also stipulates that the effects are not proportionate to the cause. This means that the effects can reveal the cause, but not perfectly, which means that the effects do not reveal God as he is in his essence.[30]

When Aquinas actually sets forth the five ways, he first turns to Scripture and quotes Exodus 3:14, "I AM WHO I AM."[31] He quotes this verse in reply to

26. Aquinas, *Summa Theologica*, editio altera Romana (Rome: Forzani et S., 1894), Ia q. 2 art. 2.

27. Cf. Thomas Aquinas, *Commentary on Aristotle's Posterior Analytics*, trans. Ralph McInerny (Notre Dame, IN: Dumb Ox Books, 2007), 104–7.

28. Denys Turner, *Faith, Reason and the Existence of God* (Cambridge: Cambridge University Press, 2005), 16, 43–47.

29. Aquinas, *Summa Theologica*, Ia q. 2 art. 2 rep. obj. 1. For Aquinas, faith logically presupposes the natural knowledge of God, though it is not faith's sufficient ground. On the role of the preambles of faith and the natural knowledge of God, see John F. Wippel, "Thomas Aquinas on Philosophy and the Preambles of Faith," in *The Science of Being as Being: Metaphysical Investigations*, ed. Gregory T. Doolan (Washington, DC: Catholic University of America Press, 2012), 196–220; Gaven Kerr, *Aquinas's Way to God: The Proof in "De Ente et Essentia"* (Oxford: Oxford University Press, 2015). Later Reformed Orthodox theologians admit the same basic point: "The special knowledge of true faith (by which believers please God and have access to him, of which Paul speaks [Rom. 1:20]) does not exclude, but supposes the general knowledge from nature." Francis Turretin, *Institutes of Elenctic Theology*, ed. James T. Dennison Jr., trans. George Musgrave Giger, 3 vols. (Phillipsburg, NJ: P&R, 1992–97), 1.3.10.

30. Aquinas, *Summa Theologica*, Ia q. 2 art. 2 rep. obj. 2; cf. Anna Bonta Moreland, *Known by Nature: Thomas Aquinas on Natural Knowledge of God* (New York: Herder & Herder, 2010), 54–55.

31. Turner, *Faith, Reason and the Existence of God*, 43; Matthew Levering, *Proofs of God: Classical Arguments from Tertullian to Barth* (Grand Rapids: Baker Academic, 2016), 69.

two denials that God actually exists. Hence, from a plainly scriptural basis, he sets forth the five ways:

1. *The argument from motion.* Whatever is in motion has been put into motion by another. Fire makes wood, which is potentially hot, to be actually hot. The wood goes from potentiality to actuality. But there cannot be an infinite regression of motion: there must be something that possesses actuality. We eventually must arrive at a First Mover, which everyone understands is God.

2. *The nature of efficient cause.* There is an order of efficient causes. If you examine an effect, there must be an efficient cause for that effect. There cannot be an infinite series of intermediate causes, since one will eventually arrive at the ultimate efficient cause, which everyone calls God.

3. *The nature of possibility and necessity.* Things naturally either are or are not. Everything that exists also has the possibility of not existing, which means that there is the possibility that at one time nothing existed. But if nothing existed, then it would be impossible for anything to have begun to exist, which is absurd. Hence, if everything is merely possible, there must be something that exists necessarily. Although all things are either caused or not caused by something else, it is impossible to have an infinite series of causes. Therefore, something must have its own self-existence by necessity, which all people know as God.

4. *The gradation found in things.* All things have something that is good, noble, and true about them, but these things are characterized by the predicates of "more" and "less." In other words, if something is hot, there is something that is hotter, and something that is hottest. Therefore, there must be something that is not merely true but also truest, best, and noblest. Consequently, there must be something that is the cause of the goodness in beings and every other perfection, which is God.

5. *The governance of the world.* Things in the world that lack intelligence nevertheless act in predictable ways, and they do not do so randomly but by design. Unintelligent things cannot move toward an end unless they are directed by a being endowed with knowledge and intelligence. That an arrow flies straight and strikes its target points back to an archer. God is the one who, therefore, directs all natural things to an end.

So the five ways for demonstrating the existence of God are from motion, efficient causality, possibility and necessity, gradation, and design.

We should observe what these arguments are and what they are not. Given what Aquinas has argued thus far, we should remember that they are probable demonstrations rather than incontrovertible proofs.[32] Aquinas has also started from a scriptural foundation. Moreover, Thomas's arguments do not end here. He does not offer his five proofs and then close the book on who God is. In other words, we have not yet arrived at a proper understanding of God.[33] These arguments merely get the ball rolling and serve to answer objections and offer clarifications: he does not intend them to serve as a rational foundation for faith. Rather, Aquinas offers these proofs to demonstrate that the claims of Christianity are rational and even demonstrable, which means that Christians and non-Christians can enter into a genuine dialogue about God's existence.[34] In other words, by setting reason upon a foundation of faith, Aquinas has demonstrated that faith and reason alike point to the one God who is the object of sacred doctrine. Christianity is at once both biblical and rational. This conclusion means that theological discourse, even with unbelievers, is possible.[35]

Further evidence that Aquinas did not build his system on a foundation of reason but on faith comes from his immediate historical context. Dante Alighieri's (1265–1321) famous *Divine Comedy* makes reference to Aquinas's methodology for demonstrating the existence of God. In *Puragtorio*, canto 3, Dante writes:

> Foolish is he who hopes our intellect
> can reach the end of that unending road
> only one Substance in three Persons follows.
>
> Confine yourselves, o humans, to the *quia*;
> had you been able to see all, there would
> have been no need for Mary to give birth.[36]

Within the context of canto 3 the Roman poet Virgil (70–19 BC) leads Dante through purgatory and on the journey rebukes the foolish people who believe that they can reach God by means of reason alone. Virgil warns them to confine themselves to the *quia*, to employ a posteriori arguments, to reason from the effect back to the cause. The *propter quid* argument, arguing from the cause

32. Aquinas, *Summa Theologica*, Ia q. 1 art. 8 rep. obj. 2.
33. Brian Davies, *The Thought of Thomas Aquinas* (Oxford: Clarendon, 1992), 26–27.
34. Muller, "Dogmatic Function," 22.
35. Muller, "Dogmatic Function," 24.
36. Dante Alighieri, *The Divine Comedy: Inferno, Purgatorio, Paradiso*, trans. Allen Mandelbaum (1980; New York: Knopf, 1995), Purgatorio, canto 3.34–39, p. 226.

to the effect, an a priori argument, is the fool's errand, according to Dante. We cannot know God's essence as an a priori. Moreover, Virgil ends his warning with a reference to divine revelation: the incarnation. In other words, if humanity had been capable of scaling the heights of heaven by the power of reason alone, then there would have been no need for the incarnation or divine revelation. All of this shows that Aquinas's arguments were not restricted to academic disputations but rather flowed into popular literature. Moreover, even their dissemination in popular literature showed that the *quia* arguments were not a form of rationalism but ultimately rested on divine revelation.

Analysis

Van Til's accusations clash with Thomas Aquinas's testimony about the function and nature of the proofs for God's existence within his *Summa*. What accounts for the disparity? There are three chief reasons: (1) reading Thomas in the light of postmedieval developments, particularly a post-Enlightenment reading; (2) trying to divide Aquinas the philosopher from Aquinas the theologian; and (3) failing, ultimately, to examine closely the primary sources.

Reading Thomas through the Enlightenment

In the wake of the Reformation, Protestant theologians moved Thomas's proofs from being treated under the doctrine of God to the doctrine of creation.[37] Philip Melanchthon (1497–1560) did this presumably because he believed that under the doctrine of creation the proofs painted a clearer portrait of the connections between the creation and the Creator.[38] According to Melanchthon, the proofs confirmed correct ideas in the minds of believers and proved the doctrine of providence.[39] But under the doctrine of creation, the proofs no longer served the same function as they did in Aquinas's system. This move obscured the original function of the proofs. When later theologians, such as Zacharias Ursinus (1534–83), moved the proofs back to the doctrine of God, they did so without the antecedent explanation of the instrumental

37. For what follows, see Muller, "Dogmatic Function," 24–25. For an overview of the use of the arguments for the existence of God in Reformed theology, see John Platt, *Reformed Thought and Scholasticism: The Arguments for the Existence of God in Dutch Theology, 1575–1650* (Leiden: Brill, 1982).

38. Philip Melanchthon, *The Chief Theological Topics: Loci Praecipui Theologici 1559*, trans. J. A. O. Preus, 2nd ed. (St. Louis: Concordia, 2011), 43–45; Melanchthon, *Commentary on Romans*, trans. Fred Kramer (St. Louis: Concordia, 1992), comm. Rom. 1:20, pp. 76–79.

39. Melanchthon, *Chief Theological Topics*, 43, 45.

function of reason.[40] The proofs were a form of rational argumentation that functioned within sacred theology. Ursinus mentions only a series of arguments common to philosophy and theology that prove God's existence.[41]

In the eighteenth century, theologians employed the proofs as a rational foundation to establish the existence of God and to serve a larger system of natural theology, where it gives the same access to God as special revelation.[42] Further Enlightenment developments only exacerbated the problem. Immanuel Kant (1724–1804), for example, did not directly engage Thomas's proofs but instead addressed Enlightenment versions of them originating from Gottfried Leibniz (1646–1716). Leibniz converted the proofs from the *quia* (a posteriori) to *propter quid* (a priori) arguments, completely inverting their function. Leibniz offers a purely rational argument, one severed from any consideration of scriptural authority.[43]

Christian Wolff (1679–1754) followed Leibniz and maintained that reliable knowledge of something could only be established on a *principle of sufficient reason* (PSR), and that a PSR was a self-evident, or axiomatic, principle of human thought.[44] The PSR was the one concept or idea that explained a system of thought, why something had to exist.[45] In the hands of Leibniz and Wolff, the Thomistic proofs took on an entirely different rationalistic cast. In other words, Leibniz and Wolff did not heed Dante's warning to embrace the *quia*.

Thus in the twentieth century most Protestant theologians assumed that the proofs were a rationalist foundation for natural theology or saw them as taking on water and sinking due to Kant's intellectual torpedoes against the proofs. Yet Kant never engaged Aquinas directly but seems only to have made use of Enlightenment versions of Thomas's arguments.[46]

40. Zacharias Ursinus, *The Commentary of Dr. Zacharias Ursinus on the Heidelberg Catechism* (Columbus, 1852; repr., Grand Rapids: Eerdmans, 1954), q. 25, pp. 120–23.

41. Ursinus, *Commentary*, q. 25, p. 121.

42. Cf., e.g., Jean-Alphonse Turretin, *Dissertations on Natural Theology* (Belfast: James Magee, 1777); Martin I. Klauber, *Between Reformed Scholasticism and Pan-Protestantism: Jean-Alphonse Turretin (1671–1737) and Enlightened Orthodoxy at the Academy of Geneva* (Selinsgrove, PA: Susquehanna University Press, 1996); Richard A. Muller, *Post-Reformation Reformed Dogmatics*, 4 vols. (Grand Rapids: Baker Academic, 2003), 1:305–10.

43. G. W. Leibniz, "On the Ultimate Origination of Things," in *Discourse on Metaphysics and Other Essays*, trans. Daniel Garber and Roger Ariew (Indianapolis: Hackett, 1991), 41–48.

44. Matt Hettche, "Christian Wolff," *Stanford Encyclopedia of Philosophy*, ed. Edward N. Zalta, Winter 2014 ed. (last revised November 11, 2014), §8.3, http://plato.stanford.edu/archives/win2014/entries/wolff-christian/.

45. Christian Wolff, *Philosophia Prima, sive Ontologia, Methodo Scientifica Pertractata qua Omnis Cognitionis Humanae Principia Continentur*, 9th ed. (Frankfurt: Officinia Libraria Rengeriana, 1736), §§53, 56, 69, 70, pp. 36, 39–40, 46–49. See Alexander R. Pruss, *The Principle of Sufficient Reason: A Reassessment* (Cambridge: Cambridge University Press, 1960).

46. Muller, "Dogmatic Function," 25.

Kant specifically critiques the Leibniz-Wolffian idea of a PSR, evident in his description of basing an argument on a rational presupposition:

> In spite of its urgent need to presuppose something that the understanding could take as the complete ground for the thoroughgoing determination of its concepts, reason notices the ideal and merely fictive character of such a presupposition much too easily to allow itself to be persuaded by this alone straightway to assume a mere creature of its own thinking to be an actual being.[47]

Kant rejects the rationalistic proofs, such as the cosmological argument, because they are based on pure principles of reason.[48] Kant differentiates between *cosmotheology*, the transcendental arguments of Leibniz and Wolff, and *ontotheology*, which is based on revelation. Leibniz and Wolff argue purely from reason to prove the existence of God, which stands in marked contrast to Aquinas's revelation-based theology.[49] Kant describes these rational arguments in the following manner:

> Nature theology infers the properties and existence of an author of the world from the constitution, the order and unity, that are found in this world, in which two kinds of causality and its rules have to be assumed, namely, nature and freedom. Hence it ascends from this world to the highest intelligence, either as the principle of all natural or all moral order and perfection.[50]

This description bears similarities to Thomas's proofs but also exhibits significant dissimilarities. Kant mentions nothing of the authority of Scripture and the role of faith, key presuppositions in Aquinas's understanding of the dogmatic function of the proofs within his *Summa*. Hence, Kant does not fully engage Aquinas's version of the proofs. This is a problem that continues in the evaluations and rejection of Thomas's arguments by theologians like Barth.[51]

Related to post-Enlightenment versions of his arguments are the function and role of reason within Aquinas's system. One of the regular mantras that appear in rejections of Thomas's proofs is that, even if he places Scripture at the foundation of his system, he still reaches illegitimate conclusions

47. Immanuel Kant, *Critique of Pure Reason*, trans. Paul Guyer and Allen W. Wood (Cambridge: Cambridge University Press, 1998), pt. 2, div. 2, bk. 2, chap. 3, §3, pp. 559–60.

48. Kant, *Critique of Pure Reason*, pt. 2, div. 2, bk. 2, chap. 3, §5, pp. 569ff.

49. Fergus Kerr, *After Aquinas: Versions of Thomism* (Oxford: Blackwell, 2002), 52–72, esp. 56.

50. Kant, *Critique of Pure Reason*, pt. 2, div. 2, bk. 2, chap. 3, §7, p. 584.

51. Thomas Joseph White, "How Barth Got Aquinas Wrong: A Reply to Archie J. Spencer on Causality and Christocentrism," *Nova et Vetera* 7, no. 1 (2009): 241–70. See also Paul Jersild, "Natural Theology and the Doctrine of God in Albrecht Ritschl and Karl Barth," *Lutheran Quarterly* 14, no. 3 (1962): 239–57.

because he does not account for the noetic effects of sin and attributes too much power to unaided, fallen human reason. Some characterize Thomas's view as presupposing the nature-grace dualism. Van Til, for example, argues that Thomas believed that in the fall humanity lost the *donum superadditum* (additional gift [of grace]) and all the supernatural gifts, but all the natural gifts, including reason, remained and were thus unharmed and unaffected by the fall. This supposedly leaves reason intact and capable of discerning theological truth by means of natural revelation.[52] Once again postmedieval readings of Thomas play a role in this contemporary reception.

Aquinas specifically states that human nature was damaged as a result of the fall:

> As a result of original justice, the reason had perfect hold over the lower parts of the soul, while reason itself was perfected by God and was subject to Him. Now this same original justice was forfeited through the sin of our first parent, as already stated (q. 81, a. 2); so that all the powers of the soul are left, as it were, destitute of their proper order, whereby they are naturally directed to virtue; which destitution is called a wounding of nature.[53]

So according to Aquinas, the fall wounds human nature; due to the loss of original righteousness, reason no longer controls the lower parts of the soul. Four wounds are inflicted on the soul due to the fall: disordered reason, malice, weakness, and concupiscence.[54] In fact, Aquinas believed that the greatest spiritual penalty of the fall was the frailty of reason: "From this it happens that man with difficulty arrives at knowledge of the truth; that with ease he falls into error; and that he cannot entirely overcome his beastly appetites, but is over and over again beclouded by them."[55] Aquinas believed that original justice is the glue that holds the powers of the soul intact and ensures that (1) reason remains in subjection to God, (2) the moral will remains in subjection to reason, and (3) the body remains in subjection to the soul, which consists of the faculties of reason and will. Aquinas writes, "Now the cause of this corrupt disposition that is called original sin, is one only, viz. the privation of original justice, *removing the subjection of man's mind to*

52. Van Til, *Christian Apologetics*, 52–53.

53. Aquinas, *Summa Theologica*, Ia-IIae q. 85 art. 3. For analysis on the effects of the fall in Aquinas, see Arvin Vos, *Aquinas, Calvin, and Contemporary Protestant Thought: A Critique of Protestant Views on the Thought of Thomas Aquinas* (Washington, DC: Christian University Press, 1985), 136–47.

54. Aquinas, *Summa Theologica*, Ia-IIae q. 85 art. 3.

55. Thomas Aquinas, *Summa contra Gentiles*, trans. Anton C. Pegis, 5 vols. (Notre Dame, IN: University of Notre Dame Press, 1975), 4.52.1.

God."[56] Human reason is not completely destroyed, but Thomas clearly states that the fall has damaged reason sufficiently that God's grace is necessary.[57]

This leads to a second observation: it appears that Van Til largely engaged Aquinas on these subjects through secondary sources: "The great textbook of Evangelical apologetics is Bishop Butler's famous *Analogy.* . . . Suffice it to point out that its argument is closely similar to that which is found, for instance, in the *Summa contra Gentiles* of Thomas Aquinas."[58] Van Til regularly refers to the "Aquinas-Butler" method.[59] In general, Joseph Butler (1692–1752) argued that, based on observing human practices and convention, we could extrapolate conclusions about the nature and being of God. Butler writes: "But it must be allowed just, to join abstract reasonings with the observation of facts, and argue from such facts as are known, to others that are like them; from that part of the divine government over intelligent creatures, which comes under our view, to that larger and more general government over them, which is beyond it."[60] This argument is decidedly different from Aquinas's. Butler argues from general observation, whereas Aquinas begins with Scripture and faith in his *Summa* and also regularly invokes Scripture in his *Summa contra Gentiles*.[61] In addition to this, there is a philosophical and metaphysical ocean between the two theologians, namely, the Enlightenment and the different concepts of knowledge and causality, for example.[62] Van Til incorrectly blurred the lines between Aquinas and Butler.

The difference between Butler and Aquinas clearly emerges when one compares Butler's *Analogy* with Aquinas's *Summa contra Gentiles* (*SCG*). Van

56. Thomas Aquinas, *Commentary on the Letter of St. Paul to the Romans,* ed. J. Mortensen and E. Alarcòn, Latin/English Edition of the Works of St. Thomas Aquinas 37 (Lander, WY: Aquinas Institute for the Study of Sacred Doctrine, 2010), lect. 3, §416, p. 141, emphasis added.

57. Bernhard Blankenhorn, *The Mystery of Union with God: Dionysian Mysticism in Albert the Great and Thomas Aquinas* (Washington, DC: Catholic University of America Press, 2015), 215–48, esp. 200–221.

58. Van Til, *Christian Apologetics,* 46; see also 69–70.

59. See, e.g., Van Til, *Defense of the Faith,* 4, 202, 203; Van Til, "Response by C. Van Til to G. R. Lewis," in *Jerusalem and Athens,* ed. E. R. Geehan ([Nutley, NJ]: P&R, 1971), 366; Van Til, *Christian Theory of Knowledge,* 72, 216, 289; Van Til, "Letter to Francis Schaeffer," Philadelphia, PA, March 11, 1969, 6–7; Van Til, introduction to *The Inspiration and Authority of the Bible,* by B. B. Warfield (Phillipsburg, NJ: P&R, 1948), 21, 25.

60. Joseph Butler, *Analogy of Religion, Natural and Revealed to the Constitution and Course of Nature* (New York: Harper & Brothers, 1860), 86–87.

61. See, e.g., Aquinas, *SCG,* 3.1–7.7, 1:63–75.

62. See, e.g., Brian W. Ogilvie, "Natural History, Ethics, and Physico-Theology," in *Historia: Empiricism and Erudition in Early Modern Europe,* ed. Gianna Pomata and Nancy G. Siraisi (Cambridge, MA: MIT Press, 2005), 75–103; Wolfgang Philipp, "Physicotheology in the Age of Enlightenment: Appearance and History," in *Studies on Voltaire and the Eighteenth Century* 57, ed. Theodore Besterman (Banbury, UK: Voltaire Foundation, 1967): 1233–67. I am grateful to David Sytsma for alerting me to these sources.

Til argues that the two works are "closely similar." Butler begins his book with observations about the difference between probable and demonstrative evidence. Probability, not certainty, is the basis on which people make numerous decisions in their lives.[63] He then proposes that on the basis of analogical reasoning, we can arrive at knowledge of God.[64] Then, based on observations of the law of nature, Butler observes that we can deduce that there is an afterlife.[65] The first part of Butler's *Analogy* proceeds along these lines, drawing arguments from various aspects of the law of nature. Aquinas does not appeal to the law of nature in this fashion; *pace* Van Til, this is not the way that Aquinas's *SCG* proceeds.

In one sense, there is broad similarity between Butler and Aquinas: both present natural arguments and then proceed to revealed theology, and Van Til likely has these parallels in mind. But on closer examination, there are some significant differences between Butler and Aquinas. Butler begins with reason whereas Aquinas, unlike Butler, invokes the authority of Scripture at the outset of his *SCG*. The very opening words of the *SCG* are a quotation from Proverbs 8:7, "My mouth shall meditate truth, and my lips shall hate impiety."[66] In contrast to Butler, Aquinas's opening chapters of the *SCG* are replete with quotations and citations of Scripture. Aquinas acknowledges that some truths are beyond reason (such as the doctrine of the Trinity) and other truths are available to natural fallen reason (such as God's existence).[67] But he stipulates, "If the only way open to us for the knowledge of God were solely that of the reason, the human race would remain in the blackest shadows of ignorance."[68]

Hence Aquinas writes, "That is why it was necessary that the unshakeable certitude and pure truth concerning divine things should be presented to men by way of faith." In support of this conclusion, he cites two passages of Scripture: "Henceforward you walk not as also the Gentiles walk in the vanity of their mind, having their understanding darkened" (Eph. 4:17–18). "All thy children shall be taught of the Lord" (Isa. 54:13).[69] On the necessity of

---

63. Butler, *Analogy of Religion*, 84–85. Butler, unlike Aquinas, employs probability, which has more to do with mathematic conceptions of causality than do Aquinas's Aristotelian conceptions. See Barbara J. Shapiro, *Probability and Certainty in Seventeenth Century England: A Study of the Relationships between Natural Science, Religion, History, Law, and Literature* (Princeton: Princeton University Press, 1985). I am grateful to David Sytsma for alerting me to this source.

64. Butler, *Analogy of Religion*, 86.

65. Butler, *Analogy of Religion*, 91–106.

66. Aquinas, *SCG*, 1, 1:59.

67. Aquinas, *SCG*, 1.2.3; 1.3.2, 1:62–63.

68. Aquinas, *SCG*, 1.2.4, 1:67.

69. Aquinas, *SCG*, 1.4.5–7, 1:68.

Scripture in the apologetic task, Aquinas is explicit: "The sole way to overcome an adversary of divine truth is from the authority of Scripture—an authority divinely confirmed by miracles. For that which is above the human reason we believe only because God has revealed it."[70] Much like Van Til, Aquinas argues from the presupposition of faith: "We shall first seek to make known that truth which faith professes and reason investigates."[71] Based on this evidence, Butler and Aquinas may be similar in the structure of their arguments in the same way a horse is similar to a zebra, but upon closer examination we quickly discover that the horse and zebra are two different animals.

Aquinas the Philosopher versus Aquinas the Theologian

One of the criticisms that Van Til raises against Aquinas is that as a theologian he engages Scripture, but as a philosopher he abandons its authority.[72] On the one hand, Van Til operates within a context where Roman Catholic philosophers tried to present Aquinas as a philosopher. Etienne Gilson (1884–1978), one of Van Til's regular theological foils, presents a philosophical portrait of Aquinas, notable in the title of his book *The Christian Philosophy of St. Thomas Aquinas*.[73] Gilson writes:

> The personality of St. Thomas lies outside the compass of our work. The saint belongs properly to the field of hagiography. The theologian requires a highly specialized treatment and should by rights be given first place in an exhaustive study of St. Thomas. The mystic and his interior life are to a large extent quite beyond our reach. *It is only the philosophical activity which he puts to the service of theology that directly concerns us.*[74]

While such a study may be legitimate and warranted, numerous historians and theologians have noted that, if pressed too far, such a portrait rends what is inseparable in Aquinas.[75]

---

70. Aquinas, *SCG*, 1.9.2, 1:77.
71. Aquinas, *SCG*, 1.9.3, 1:78; see also Reinhard Hütter, *Dust Bound for Heaven: Explorations in the Theology of Thomas Aquinas* (Grand Rapids: Eerdmans, 2012), 188–89.
72. Van Til, *A Christian Theory of Knowledge*, 174–75; Van Til, *Christian Apologetics*, 88.
73. Etienne Gilson, *The Christian Philosophy of St. Thomas Aquinas* (Notre Dame, IN: University of Notre Dame Press, 1956); see, e.g., Cornelius Van Til, *Introduction to Systematic Theology* (Phillipsburg, NJ: P&R, 1974), 216–17; Van Til, *Common Grace and the Gospel*, 51; Van Til, *Christian Apologetics*, 88.
74. Gilson, *Christian Philosophy*, 3 (emphasis added). I am grateful to Richard Muller for alerting me to this reference.
75. Jordan, *Rewritten Theology*, 60–88, esp. 60, 63, 87; te Velde, *Aquinas on God*, 1–36; Davies, *Aquinas's "Summa contra Gentiles,"* 8–16.

As Brian Davies explains, if one were to approach Aquinas and tell him he was a philosopher, he would automatically reject the claim because this was a title reserved for pagan thinkers, such as Aristotle or Plato. Aquinas never formally taught philosophy and never describes his work in these terms. Aquinas was first a commentator on Holy Scripture and second a theologian.[76] As one Aquinas scholar declares: "When one interprets Thomas as a rationalist philosopher or theologian, one misses the burning heart of everything he wrote. Aquinas was a saint deeply in love with Jesus Christ, and the image of Christ pervades the entire edifice that is his philosophical, theological, and scriptural work."[77] The fact that we must recognize the inseparability of Aquinas's theological and philosophical thought does not automatically legitimize everything that he claims about the use of reason and the book of nature. It does, however, press the question of how Aquinas supported his claims about these things. And in this case, one must recognize that his commitment to faith seeking understanding is fundamental to his theology.

Scant Primary-Source Analysis

Given what Van Til says about Aquinas, one might conclude that Van Til did not read Aquinas. Van Til did read him but rarely engaged in a close primary-source analysis. In fact, John Frame has made this same observation: "Part of the problem with Van Til's critique of Aquinas is the rarity of his citations of primary sources."[78] In one of the few places that he does engage Aquinas, Van Til touches on the text for only a moment and draws inaccurate conclusions. In his analysis, Van Til claims that Aquinas begins both his *Summa Theologica* and *SCG* "by means of the natural reason." In other words, human reason can prove God's existence, and this controls everything that he says in the rest of his work.[79] Van Til then quotes a statement from the beginning of Aquinas's *SCG*: "Now, in considering the divine substance, we should especially make use of the method of remotion.[80] For, by its immensity, the divine substance surpasses every form that our intellect reaches. Thus we are unable to apprehend it by knowing what it is."[81] Van Til objects to employing remotion because this method

76. Davies, *Aquinas's "Summa contra Gentiles,"* 6.
77. Robert Barron, *Thomas Aquinas: Spiritual Master* (New York: Crossroad, 1996), 13.
78. John Frame, *Cornelius Van Til: An Analysis of His Thought* (Phillipsburg, NJ: P&R, 1995), 356.
79. Van Til, *Christian Theory of Knowledge*, 169.
80. The process of remotion, or elimination, seeks to define an object by eliminating all that is extraneous to it. For example, one can define God by what he is not, using words such as immortal (i.e., not mortal), immaterial (not material), and invisible (not visible).
81. Van Til, *Christian Theory of Knowledge*, 169; cf. Aquinas, *SCG*, 1.14.2, 1:96.

does not account for the "self-attesting Christ speaking in the Scriptures."[82] Westminster divines such as John Arrowsmith (1602–59) employed this argument to demonstrate God's existence,[83] but Van Til nevertheless criticizes Aquinas for arguing that some truths about God can be known by reason and others by faith. He claims that Aquinas never considers the meaning of cause and effect according to a Christian rather than a non-Christian construction, which vitiates his argument.[84] According to Van Til, the fundamental flaw in Thomas's methodology is that he combines pagan Greek philosophy with his Christian theology, although they are ultimately incompatible.[85]

The problem with Van Til's analysis is that he hardly interacts with what Aquinas actually states, and in particular he does not factor in Aquinas's doctrine of Scripture and its role within his apologetic methodology. For example, when Van Til cites Aquinas to the effect that there are some truths known by reason and others by revelation, Van Til does not engage Aquinas's supporting exegesis of Scripture.[86] In the context, Aquinas appeals to Job 11:7 in support of his argument: "Peradventure thou wilt comprehend the steps of God, and wilt find out the Almighty perfectly?" He also cites Job 36:26, "Behold, God is great, exceeding our knowledge," and the apostle Paul, "We know in part" (1 Cor. 13:9).[87] In his commentary on Job, Aquinas explains the significance of 11:7:

> Footprints are signs of someone walking on a road. So the works of God are called his road and the production of creatures is understood as a kind of procession of God in creatures, as the divine good which exists in him simply and in the highest sense proceeds from him by degrees to effects derived from him when higher things are understood to be better than lower things. Therefore, the footprints of God are certain signs found in creatures from which God can be known in a certain sense through his creatures. But as the human mind cannot totally and perfectly understand creatures in themselves, much less can it have a perfect idea about the Creator in himself.[88]

In this case, Aquinas believes that Scripture teaches that humans can reason their way back to God by tracing the effects back to their cause, but that such

82. Van Til, *Christian Theory of Knowledge*, 170.
83. John Arrowsmith, *Armilla Catechetica: A Chain of Principles* (Cambridge: John Field, 1659), 3.3, p. 130.
84. Van Til, *Christian Theory of Knowledge*, 173.
85. Van Til, *Christian Theory of Knowledge*, 174–75.
86. Van Til, *Christian Theory of Knowledge*, 170; cf. Aquinas, *SCG*, 1.3.2, 1:63.
87. Aquinas, *SCG*, 1.3.7, 1:65–66.
88. Thomas Aquinas, *Commentary on the Book of Job*, trans. Brian Thomas Becket Mullady, Latin/English Edition of the Works of St. Thomas Aquinas 32 (Lander, WY: Aquinas Institute for the Study of Sacred Doctrine, 2016), chap. 11, lect. 1, pp. 143–44.

reasoning is limited. Aquinas's comments on Job 11:7 parallel those from his commentary on Romans 1:20.[89] In the simplest terms, Aquinas believes reason can discover God because the Bible says so.[90]

Faith Seeking Understanding

To rightly understand Aquinas, we must know his historical context and the subsequent philosophical and theological changes that occurred in the Enlightenment. A fundamental conviction in Aquinas's day was *fides quaerens intellectum* (faith seeking understanding). Theologians of the Middle Ages, such as Aquinas and Anselm of Canterbury (ca. 1033–1109), believed they were following in Augustine's (354–430) footsteps regarding the relationship between faith and reason. Augustine writes: "Understanding is the reward of faith. Therefore do not seek to understand in order to know, but believe in order that you may understand."[91] Anselm famously took up this principle in his *Proslogion*: "I do not try, Lord, to attain Your lofty heights, because my understanding is in no way equal to it. But I do desire to understand Your truth a little, that truth that my heart believes and loves. For I do not seek to understand so that I may believe; but I believe so that I may understand. For I believe this also, that 'unless I believe, I shall not understand' [Isa. 7:9]."

There are two noteworthy observations about Anselm's statement. First, he based this Augustinian idea on the Vulgate translation of Isaiah 7:9.[92] Anselm believed that he was following a scriptural principle. Second, this statement appears in the opening pages of the *Proslogion*, where Anselm sets forth his so-called ontological argument for the existence of God. Anselm famously argues that God is a being greater than which cannot be conceived. The subsequent reception of this argument has been mixed, with the first objection coming from Guanilo of Marmoutier Abbey in Tours (eleventh century), whose response Anselm included with the *Proslogion*. Aquinas also objected to the argument,[93] and Van Til's criticism reveals his objections to the argument:

89. Aquinas, *Romans*, chap. 1, lect. 6.116–22, pp. 40–42.

90. Contra Cornelius Van Til, *The Reformed Pastor and Modern Thought* (Phillipsburg, NJ: P&R, 1980), 9.

91. Augustine, *Tractates on the Gospel of John, 28–54*, Fathers of the Church 88 (Washington, DC: Catholic University of America Press, 1993), 29.6.

92. The church fathers also appealed to Isa. 7:9 in this manner. See, e.g., Clement of Alexandria, *Stromata* 1.1; 2.2; 4.21 (*ANF* 2:301, 349, 434); Tertullian, *Against Marcion* 4.20, 25; 5.11 (*ANF* 3:380, 389, 453).

93. Aquinas, *Summa Theologica*, Ia q. 2 art. 1.

We should be careful when we say that God is the being than whom nothing higher can be thought. If we talk of the highest being of which we can think, in the sense of *have a concept of*, and attribute to it actual existence, we do not have the biblical notion of God. God is not the reality that corresponds to the highest concept that man, considered as an independent being, can think. Man cannot think an absolute self-contained being; that is, he cannot have a concept of it in the ordinary sense of the term. God is infinitely higher than the highest being of which man can form a concept.[94]

As with his analysis of Aquinas, Van Til presents Anselm's argument as if it were a purely rational and autonomous attempt to establish God's existence. Van Til never acknowledges that Anselm begins his argument from the presupposition of faith seeking understanding.

Further, Van Til does not discuss the nature and historical context of Anselm's argument. *Proslogion* is a Latin term adapted from the Greek, which literally means "a word to another" but also connotes *prayer*. Anselm's *Proslogion* is a prayer to God.[95] Anselm originally wrote the *Proslogion* for his fellow Benedictine monks, who devoted themselves to lives of hymns, prayers, vows of silence, and the study of theology.[96] Anselm is quite explicit on this point, claiming it as a meditation written for believers: "I have written the following short tract dealing with this question as well as several others, from the point of view of one trying to raise his mind to contemplate God and *seeking to understand what he believes.*"[97] In fact, Anselm never titled the work "the ontological argument for the existence of God." This was a title that Immanuel Kant gave it, and Kant did not directly engage Anselm but rather versions offered by René Descartes (1596–1650) and Leibniz.[98] Anselm titled it the *Proslogion*, or "Faith in the Quest of Understanding."[99]

94. Van Til, *Introduction to Systematic Theology*, 206.

95. Marilyn McCord Adams, "Praying the *Proslogion*: Anselm's Theological Method," in *The Rationality of Belief and the Plurality of Faith*, ed. Thomas D. Senor (Ithaca, NY: Cornell University Press, 1995), 14.

96. Jean Leclercq, *The Love of Learning and the Desire for God: A Study in Monastic Culture*, trans. Catharine Misrahi (New York: Fordham University Press, 1961), 197, 215; Giovanni Miccoli, "Monks," in *Medieval Callings*, ed. Jacques Le Goff, trans. Lydia G. Cochrane (Chicago: University of Chicago Press, 1987), 64; Ulrich G. Leinsle, *Introduction to Scholastic Theology*, trans. Michael J. Miller (Washington, DC: Catholic University of America Press, 2010), 111–15.

97. Anselm, *Proslogion*, preface in *Anselm of Canterbury: The Major Works*, ed. Brian Davies and G. R. Evans (Oxford: Oxford University Press, 1998), 83 (emphasis added).

98. Kant, *Critique of Pure Reason*, pt. 2, div. 3, bk. 2, chap. 3, §4, pp. 563–69.

99. Anselm, *Proslogion*, preface, p. 83.

There is a significant difference between Anselm's and Descartes's versions of the so-called ontological argument. Descartes writes:

> Clearly the idea of God, that is, the idea of a supremely perfect being, is one I discover to be no less within me than the idea of any figure or number. And that it belongs to God's nature that he always exists is something I understand no less clearly and distinctly than is the case when I demonstrate in regard to some figure or number that something also belongs to the nature of a figure or number. . . . It is obvious to anyone who pays close attention that existence can no more be separated from God's essence than its having three angles equal to two right angles can be separated from the essence of a triangle, or than that the idea of a valley can be separated from the idea of a mountain. Thus it is no less contradictory to think of God (that is, a supremely perfect being) lacking existence (that is, lacking some perfection) than it is to think of a mountain without a valley.[100]

Descartes offers an argument devoid of Scripture, which is quite different from Anselm's argument. And as such, Van Til's criticisms against a Cartesian version of the argument squarely hit the target. But in Anselm's hands, the argument takes on a decidedly different cast, since it is actually a meditation written for believers in the form of a prayer to God.

In fact, prayer-filled cries to God punctuate the *Proslogion*.[101] In the very opening of the work, Anselm implores, "Teach me to seek You, and reveal Yourself to me as I seek, because I can neither seek You if you do not teach me how, nor find You unless You reveal Yourself. Let me seek You in desiring You; let me desire You in seeking You; let me find You in loving You; let me love You in finding You."[102] In another place Anselm prays: "Lord my God, You who have formed and reformed me, tell my desiring soul what You are besides what it has seen so that it may see clearly that which it desires."[103] And within these cries Anselm repeatedly invokes Scripture: "Help me 'because of Your goodness, Lord' [Ps. 25:7]. 'I sought Your countenance, Your countenance I will seek, O Lord; do not turn Your face away from me' [Ps. 27:8–9]. Raise me up from my own self to You. Purify, heal, make sharp, 'illuminate' the eye of my soul so that it may see You [Ps. 13:3]. Let my soul gather its strength again and with all its understanding strive once more towards You, Lord."[104] These prayer-cries appear repeatedly and in a sense never cease; they

---

100. René Descartes, *Meditations on First Philosophy*, 3rd ed. (New York: Hackett, 1993), §§65–66, pp. 43–44.

101. Adams, "Praying the Proslogion," 16.

102. Anselm, *Proslogion*, §1, p. 86.

103. Anselm, *Proslogion*, §14, p. 98.

104. Anselm, *Proslogion*, §18, pp. 97–98.

appear in chapters 1, 14–18, and 24–25.[105] Moreover, in these prayers Anselm explicitly admits that he cannot ascend to an understanding of God by the power of raw reason: "I do not try, Lord, to attain Your lofty heights, because my understanding is in no way equal to it. But I do desire to understand Your truth a little, that truth that my heart believes and loves."[106]

How can Van Til characterize Anselm's argument as an example of autonomous reason creating a notion of God divorced from revelation when it was written as a prayer for believers, quotes Scripture, was originally titled "faith seeking understanding," admits the impotence of reason to ascend to God's knowledge apart from God's mercy, and contains persistent cries to God for divine assistance? Van Til never explains why he holds that Anselm's appeals to Scripture are invalid. Perhaps he was more focused on Enlightenment versions of the argument?[107] Nevertheless, this is another example of Van Til's engagement of medieval theology divorced from its historical context and mediated through the Enlightenment's secondary sources. He fails to account for the overall commitment of faith seeking understanding. This was the context and conviction for Anselm just as for Aquinas.[108] Aquinas writes: "Someone may err by making reason precede faith when it comes to matters of faith rather than making faith precede reason, as when someone is willing to believe only what that person is able to discover by reason. It should in fact be just the other way around."[109]

Reforming Thomas and Correcting Van Til

Just because Van Til misread Aquinas does not mean that we must embrace everything that Thomas said.[110] Conversely, it does not mean that everything Van Til said on these matters is categorically wrong. Rather, the truth lies somewhere in the middle: Aquinas and Van Til actually share many common convictions regarding the relationship between faith and reason and the function of the proofs for the existence of God. Frame makes this very point: "There is a greater degree of agreement between Van Til and Aquinas than Van Til recognizes."[111] Both approach these matters from the vantage point of

105. Adams, "Praying the *Proslogion*," 16.
106. Anselm, *Proslogion*, §1, p. 87.
107. E.g., Van Til, *Common Grace and the Gospel*, 191.
108. Davies, *Thought of Thomas Aquinas*, 21–22.
109. Thomas Aquinas, *De Trinitate*, as quoted in Davies, *Aquinas's "Summa contra Gentiles,"* 6.
110. Others have come to similar conclusions; see, e.g., Vos, *Aquinas, Calvin, and Contemporary Protestant Thought*, 161–74.
111. Frame, *Van Til*, 267.

faith seeking understanding. One need not embrace every detail of Aquinas's theology in order to recognize that it has broad similarities to Van Til's. There is a better way than Aquinas's to account for prefall and postfall humanity; his understanding of nature and grace and the *donum superadditum* obscures righteousness as something native to man's originally created nature apart from the necessity of divine grace. A better rubric for understanding grace in a postfall context is that grace redeems and consummates nature.[112]

Aquinas assigns Scripture the chief place of authority in doctrine but assigns its authoritative interpretation to the church. Protestants generally and the Reformed in particular rightly reject the idea that church authority is equal to the Scriptures. But we need not scuttle Aquinas's entire argument simply because he invokes the authority of the church in an illegitimate fashion. Rather, we can excise the problematic element and affirm with classic Reformed theology the supremacy of Scripture in the doctrine and life of the church. Scripture is "the supreme judge by which all controversies of religion are determined" (WCF 1.10).

Another area that requires refinement is Aquinas's understanding of the noetic effects of sin. He clearly maintains that the fall damaged human reason, but his understanding rests on his nature-grace model of prefall anthropology. The *donum superadditum* (original justice) held reason in check, but in the fall people engaged in concupiscence and vice rather than virtue due to the loss of supernatural grace. To be clear, the fall involves more than the loss of supernatural grace; it also includes the consequential presence of corruption.[113] But for Thomas, the loss of original righteousness is the formal element of original sin.[114] Is the nature-grace model the best way to account for prefall and postfall anthropology vis-à-vis the noetic effects of sin? Historically, the Reformed tradition has answered this question in the negative,[115] but this does not mean that Aquinas's proofs for the existence of God are rationalistic and therefore false. Unlike Van Til, who treated Aquinas like a seamless robe, early modern Reformed theologians employed parts of Aquinas's system while discarding the incompatible elements.[116] They could adopt Aquinas's views

---

112. Cf. David VanDrunen, *Divine Covenants and Moral Order: A Biblical Theology of Natural Law* (Grand Rapids: Eerdmans, 2014), 34–36; Michael Horton, *Lord and Servant: A Covenant Christology* (Louisville: Westminster John Knox, 2005), 3–21; Turretin, *Institutes*, 1.9.5.

113. Aquinas, *Summa Theologica*, Ia-IIae q. 83 art. 2.

114. Aquinas, *Summa Theologica*, Ia-IIae q. 82 art. 3.

115. On the Reformed scholastic critical engagement with medieval theologians on these issues, see Sebastian Rehnman, "Alleged Rationalism: Francis Turretin on Reason," *Calvin Theological Journal* 37 (2002): 255–69, esp. 260–62; Christopher Cleveland, *Thomism in John Owen* (Surrey, UK: Ashgate, 2010).

116. See similar comments in Frame, *Van Til*, 268.

on natural law and argue from the creation back to its creator to prove God's existence but at the same time lay greater stress on the noetic effects of sin.

Conversely, Van Til misread elements of the medieval tradition. Although he erroneously evaluated Aquinas's views, this does not invalidate all of Van Til's insights about the problematic nature of autonomous reason. What Van Til has to say about Enlightenment rationalism is true, and Aquinas would likely agree with his assessment.[117] Moreover, contrary to popular perceptions about Van Til's supposed objection to the use of evidence in apologetics, Van Til believed that evidence was important and necessary. But he also believed that the evidence had to rest on the proper authority, Scripture. Hence, he believed that the various proofs for the existence of God were useful when properly formulated.[118]

The problem is that many Van Tillians have read Van Til's rejection of the proofs for the existence of God and therefore reject Aquinas. Van Til states: "We would not say that these arguments, as they have been historically formulated even by non-Christians, are valid to a point. We do not hesitate to affirm that they are invalid."[119] But then Van Til qualifies his rejection: "If the Christian forms the proofs theistically correctly, they are, to be sure, a weapon in his hand with which he may confirm himself and ward off the attack of the enemy. But then this defense and confirmation is on the ground that he has the truth and that his opponents trust in a lie."[120] Properly framed, Van Til was in favor of using the theistic proofs. Van Til's mistake lies in his belief that Aquinas promoted a rationalist view of the proofs.[121] The truth of the matter is that Van Til's qualified description of an acceptable form of the proofs fits Aquinas's own view. Van Til and Aquinas would not agree on everything, but they both employ a methodology that rests upon the principle of faith seeking understanding. *Pace* Van Til, Aquinas does not embrace reason seeking faith; he is not a rationalist.[122]

Conclusion

The Reformed Orthodox appeal to Aquinas does not constitute an obstacle to recovering the book of nature for defending the Christian faith. In fact,

117. See, e.g., Thomas Joseph White, *Wisdom in the Face of Modernity: A Study in Thomistic Natural Theology*, 2nd ed. (Ave Maria, FL: Sapientia, 2016).
118. Van Til, *Christian Apologetics*, 2; Van Til, *Introduction to Systematic Theology*, 16–17, 104–5, 146; cf. Thom Notaro, *Van Til and the Use of Evidence* (Phillipsburg, NJ: P&R, 1980).
119. Van Til, *Introduction to Systematic Theology*, 198.
120. Van Til, *Introduction to Systematic Theology*, 199.
121. Van Til, *Christian Apologetics*, 44–45.
122. Contra Van Til, *Introduction to Systematic Theology*, 205.

rather than an obstacle, Aquinas proves to be another useful tool in the apologetics toolbox. The fact that Aquinas argued from a foundation of Holy Scripture should cause us to reevaluate his appeals to the book of nature, reason, common notions, and the arguments for the existence of God. It is true that from a Reformed standpoint there are a number of problematic elements in Aquinas's soteriology and ecclesiology. But these errors did not prevent Reformed Orthodox theologians from routinely appealing to him in their own use of the book of nature. Even Aquinas's employment of Aristotle cannot be automatically dismissed on the grounds that it is synthetic thinking. Aquinas cited Paul's example at Mars Hill and believed that he was following suit. Aquinas's claims must be judged at the bar of Scripture, and he should be given a fair hearing, one that accounts for the discontinuities between his theology and later Enlightenment developments that radically altered the perception of his thought.

Therefore, as Herman Bavinck (1854–1921) once observed,

> Irenaeus, Augustine, and Thomas do not belong exclusively to Rome; they are Fathers and Doctors to whom the whole Christian church has obligations. Even the post-Reformation Roman Catholic theology is not overlooked. In general, Protestants know far too little about what we have in common with Rome and what divides us. Thanks to the revival of Roman Catholic theology under the auspices of Thomas, it is now doubly incumbent on Protestants to provide a conscious and clear account of their relationship to Rome.[123]

Aquinas and other theologians of the Middle Ages and patristic period belong equally to Protestants. They have insights to offer, and we have much to learn from them regarding theology and, perhaps especially, apologetics.

---

123. Herman Bavinck, "Foreword to the First Edition (Volume 1) of the *Gereformeerde Dogmatiek*," trans. John Bolt, *Calvin Theological Journal* 45 (2010): 9–10.

5

WORLDVIEW

We must really do what Karl Barth has insisted that we must do but has not
done, namely, start our interpretation of the whole of life *von oben* [from above].
We must begin our mediation upon any fact in the world in the light of the Son
of God, the light which is as the light of the sun, the source of all other light.

Cornelius Van Til

Despite Van Til's affirmation of the ambiguity of the unbeliever's position
under common grace, he nevertheless writes as though the unbeliever knows
and affirms no truth at all and thus is not at all affected by common grace.

John Frame

The effort to recover the book of nature requires the skill of an Olympian
hurdler, because there are a number of obstacles that stand in the way. The
first comes in the form of *worldview*. As common as the term and concept
are within Reformed theology, few have investigated its origins. But what is a
worldview? According to Abraham Kuyper (1837–1920), a worldview offers
a comprehensive explanation of humanity's relationships to God, their fellow humans, and the world to such an extent that no department of human
knowledge goes untouched.[1] To be sure, there are some who define worldview
quite loosely. N. T. Wright, for example, characterizes a worldview as the way

---

1. Abraham Kuyper, *Lectures on Calvinism* (1898; Grand Rapids: Eerdmans, 1931), 11, 19.

in which people view reality, with worldviews typically providing answers to life's key questions: Who are we, where are we, what is wrong with the world, and what is the solution?[2] Dennis Johnson presents a similar definition of worldview when he describes it as a means by which people and groups construct paradigms to make sense of experience and the world in which they live.[3] These uses of the term and concept are benign. All people have ways of looking at the world, and the same holds true for various philosophies and religions. There are, for example, and speaking very generally, Christian, Buddhist, Muslim, and atheist ways of looking at the world. So if this concept is true and legitimate, how does the idea of worldview constitute a hurdle to the recovery of the book of nature for defending the faith?

According to those who have investigated its origins, historic worldview theory (HWT) is a very distinct idea that begins with nineteenth-century German idealism and includes the following characteristics: (1) the rejection of a common doctrine of humanity, (2) a single principle from which one deduces a worldview, (3) an exhaustive systematic explanation of reality, and (4) the incommensurability of competing worldviews. These aspects of HWT create an inhospitable environment for the historic Reformed appeal to the book of nature. The increased use of HWT is inversely proportional to the decreased use of the book of nature.

This chapter argues that HWT is contrary to the teaching of the Scriptures because it rejects a common doctrine of humanity. The Bible clearly teaches that all people bear the image of God; all people by virtue of their creation in God's image have common notions. Also problematic is the claim that a worldview must present an exhaustive explanation of the world. The Bible does not provide an exhaustive view of reality. The Bible certainly addresses the key elements of God, humanity, and the world, and thus has implications for all of life, but it does not address all things. In line with the historic Reformed faith, I maintain that the Bible principally teaches what humanity is to believe concerning God and the duties that are required of them. I purposefully echo the third question of the Westminster Shorter Catechism here. The catechism does not stress the exhaustive nature of the Scriptures but explains that the Bible gives only principles for life in general. If the Bible provides an exhaustive view of everything, then as some worldview advocates argue, the Christian worldview must stand in complete antithesis to all other

---

2. N. T. Wright, *The New Testament and the People of God*, vol. 1 of *Christian Origins and the Question of God* (Minneapolis: Fortress, 1992), 124.

3. Dennis Johnson, "Between Two Wor(l)ds: Worldview and Observation in the Use of General Revelation to Interpret Scripture, and Vice Versa," *Journal of the Evangelical Theological Society* 41, no. 1 (1998): 70.

worldviews. There would then be a unique Christian view on everything because the Bible exhaustively explains all reality, and it is morally incumbent
on Christians to follow its teachings. The Bible must be the only foundation
for *all* knowledge. The Bible, however, presents a very different picture. It
explains that Christians and non-Christians possess a shared knowledge of
the world and even God's existence; they share God-given common notions.

To prove this chapter's thesis, I first trace the origins of HWT from German
nineteenth-century idealism and its adoption to varying degrees by James Orr
(1844–1913), Kuyper, and Cornelius Van Til. Second, I demonstrate how Van
Til rejected the catholic and Reformed concept of common notions because
he believed they were tainted by pagan philosophy. I believe that Van Til
rejected common notions because at points in his apologetics he employed
HWT. But what Van Til took away with the left hand he reintroduced with
the right. Even though he rejected common notions, he nevertheless employed
the same concept, appealed to the same passages of Scripture, and used the
same doctrines but under a different term, namely, "common ground." Van Til
tried to mix the proverbial oil of HWT with the water of historic Reformed
theology, and their incompatibility produced tensions within his thought and
needlessly distanced Van Til and the twentieth-century Reformed community
from the book of nature. Despite his protestations, Van Til actually agrees
with the historic Reformed tradition in its use of common notions.

Third, I explore the impact of Van Til's use of HWT on the Reformed
community and the idea that Scripture is the source for all knowledge. As
important as Scripture is, to argue that it alone is the foundation for all
knowledge diminishes God's good and necessary book of nature. Fourth,
not wanting to rest merely on the precedent of the Reformed tradition's use
of the book of nature, I set forth a brief scriptural case for common notions
with a survey of the similarities between the Code of Hammurabi and the
Covenant Code, Paul's apologetic address at Mars Hill, and echoes of Aristotle in Romans 2:14–15. Fifth, I provide arguments and evidence against
the claims that the Bible offers an exhaustive view of the world. Such ideas
run counter to the Scripture's own clear teaching that it has not provided an
exhaustive view of things.

I believe that Christians have drawn unbiblical ideas from the well of
Enlightenment confidence by uncritically adopting HWT. They press the
Bible into saying things that it does not really say and have unintentionally
marginalized the book of nature. Christians undoubtedly stand in antithesis
to non-Christians, but not at every point of their existence. There is a place
for common notions, not because we capitulate to sinful human autonomy,
but because we rightly recognize that God has created all human beings in

his image. This means that we can engage unbelievers in dialogue and have genuine communication with them because we share a common divinely given image and because, even in spite of sin and its noetic effects on human reason, we share common notions about God, the world, and even God's law. These common notions do not sideline the absolute necessity of the Spirit's sovereign work of grace in regeneration, the only means by which fallen human beings will ever accept the special revelation of the gospel of Christ. But these common notions mean that we do not stand in antithesis at every point of interaction with the unbeliever. In order to improve the church's apologetics arsenal, we must recover common notions, or in Kuyperian terms, we must recognize the importance, utility, and necessity of common grace.[4]

Origins of Historic Worldview Theory

The term *worldview* is quite common in evangelical and Reformed circles likely due to the popular and influential nature of Kuyper's 1898 Stone Lectures at Princeton Seminary, where he advocated the need for Christians to develop a holistic life and worldview.[5] But seldom has anyone questioned the historical origins of the term and concept. Proponents of the worldview concept acknowledge that the term originated with nineteenth-century German philosophy and the term *Weltanschauung*, but few drill down below the surface and explore its specific philosophical content. Recent research has traced the first use of the term *Weltanschauung* to Immanuel Kant (1724–1804). In his *Critique of Judgment* (1790), Kant put forth the idea that people need to dig beneath the substrate underlying the world's appearance and our worldview: "For only by means of this power and its idea do we, in a pure intellectual estimation of magnitude, comprehend the infinite in the world of sense *entirely under* a concept, even though in a mathematical estimation of magnitude *by means of numerical concepts* we can never think it in its entirety."[6] Kant

4. See, e.g., Abraham Kuyper, *Common Grace: God's Gifts for a Fallen World*, 2 vols. (Bellingham, WA: Lexham, 2016).

5. See, e.g., J. P. Moreland and William Lane Craig, *Philosophical Foundations for a Christian Worldview* (Downers Grove, IL: IVP Academic, 2003); James W. Sire, *Naming the Elephant: Worldview as a Concept* (Downers Grove, IL: IVP Academic, 2015); Albert M. Wolters, *Creation Regained: Biblical Basics for a Reformational Worldview* (Grand Rapids: Eerdmans, 1985); Michael W. Goheen, *Living at the Crossroads: An Introduction to Christian Worldview* (Grand Rapids: Baker Academic, 2008).

6. Immanuel Kant, *Critique of Judgment: Including the First Introduction*, trans. Werner S. Pluhar (1790; repr., Indianapolis: Hackett, 1987), 111–12; see also David K. Naugle, *Worldview: The History of a Concept* (Grand Rapids: Eerdmans, 2002), 58–59.

identifies a worldview as a perch from which someone views the totality of the world and subsumes it under a concept, an organizing principle. This idea resonated with a number of nineteenth-century philosophers, including G. W. F. Hegel (1770–1831), Søren Kierkegaard (1813–55), Friedrich Nietzsche (1844–1900), and Wilhelm Dilthey (1833–1911).[7] Dilthey offers one of the more sustained explorations of the concept, so we can focus attention on his view. He has been described as the father of HWT because he first presented a systematic treatment of the subject.[8]

Dilthey looked at nineteenth-century Germany and saw chaos in the competing claims of different philosophies, religions, and scientific theories. He observed that these different systems of thought could not all be true.[9] Dilthey believed that the ultimate root of any worldview was life itself.[10] The riddle of existence posed three key questions: Where do I come from? Why do I exist? What will become of me?[11] The only way to calm the intellectual tempest was to rise above the chaos and offer a metaphilosophy of worldview, a philosophy of philosophy.[12] According to Western ideals, "There was but one type of man, endowed with a particular nature. A similar notion of a universal type was at the root of Christian teachings of the first and second Adam and the Son of Man. Even the natural philosophy of the sixteenth century retained the same premise."[13] Evolutionary theory razed the concept of the universal man.[14] Instead of discovering the meaning of the universe in one particular religion or philosophy, claims had to be evaluated in terms of how they interpret the world. Answers lie, therefore, not in the physical world, but in man and his life experience.[15] "The essence of our inductions," writes Dilthey, "the very sum of our knowledge rests on these presuppositions which, in turn, are founded on our empirical consciousness."[16] Worldviews, therefore, try to solve the riddle of life.[17]

---

7. Naugle, *Worldview*, 68–107. Others concur that Dilthey is the one who developed the concept of worldview. See Frederick C. Beiser, *After Hegel: German Philosophy, 1840–1900* (Princeton: Princeton University Press, 2014), 48–51.

8. Naugle, *Worldview*, 84.

9. Wilhelm Dilthey, *The Types of World Views and Their Unfoldment within the Metaphysical Systems*, in *Dilthey's Philosophy of Existence: Introduction to Weltanschauungslehre*, trans. and ed. William Kluback and Martin Weinbaum (New York: Bookman Associates, 1957), 17.

10. Dilthey, *World Views*, 21.

11. Naugle, *Worldview*, 83.

12. Naugle, *Worldview*, 84.

13. Dilthey, *World Views*, 19.

14. Dilthey, *World Views*, 20.

15. Dilthey, *World Views*, 20.

16. Dilthey, *World Views*, 23.

17. Naugle, *Worldview*, 86; Dilthey, *World Views*, 23–24.

Dilthey sets forth the formative laws and structures of worldviews. Regarding laws, Dilthey claims that people shape their worldviews from the source material of their life experiences. In this manner, life experience produces universal attitudes, which Dilthey comprehensively describes as optimism and pessimism.[18] In terms of structure, Dilthey identifies three key features: (1) the cosmic picture, (2) determining the effectual value of life, and (3) upper-level consciousness.[19] Dilthey explains how these different elements coalesce: "In these preliminary phases the spirit gained in stability and freedom, but it completes its dominion over reality in the region of judgments and concepts, where finally the relatedness and true being of reality are adequately and uniformly comprehended. When a world view evolves fully, the process regularly begins in these phases of the cognition of reality."[20]

Beyond matters of structure, Dilthey identifies three different types of worldviews: (1) naturalism, (2) idealism of freedom, and (3) objective realism. In naturalism, human beings are determined by nature; in idealism of freedom, life-forming ideas do not originate in the physical world but in the mind; and objective realism tries to combine naturalism and subjective idealism.[21] These different worldviews always compete against one another and can never corner the market on knowing reality.[22] Nevertheless, Dilthey recognizes that worldviews seek to rise to the level of "universally valid knowledge."[23]

Dilthey and a host of other German philosophers and theologians embraced the worldview concept in the nineteenth century, and the idea traveled throughout Europe and landed in the lap of one United Presbyterian theologian. James Orr delivered a series of lectures in 1893, which were published as *The Christian View of God and the World*.[24] In his opening lecture, Orr professed to his audience that his consumption of German philosophy gave him repeated exposure to the term *Weltanschauung*, leading him to believe that the concept was important. He adopted the concept and consequently wanted to set forth a "Christian view of the world."[25] Rather than deal with elements of Christian theology, he wanted to address the entire Christian system of thought. Orr believed that he could employ the Christian system of thought apologetically. By comparing competing worldviews, Orr explains,

18. Dilthey, *World Views*, 25.
19. Naugle, *Worldview*, 87.
20. Dilthey, *World Views*, 26.
21. Naugle, *Worldview*, 92–97.
22. Naugle, *Worldview*, 97.
23. Dilthey, *World Views*, 39.
24. James Orr, *The Christian View of God and the World as Centering in the Incarnation* (1893; Edinburgh: Andrew Elliot, 1907).
25. Orr, *Christian View of God*, 3.

"it is no longer an opposition of detail, but of principle. This circumstance necessitates an equal extension of the line of the defence."[26] Orr was well aware of the origins of this idea and traced it back to Kant.

Like Kant and Dilthey, Orr believed that a worldview offered a comprehensive view of reality.[27] And like Dilthey, he maintained that a worldview sought to answer life's biggest questions: What principles should guide one's life? What is the goal of one's existence? What rational justification does one offer for one's beliefs?[28] Orr pointed to Christianity as the one worldview that could do justice to all of these questions, a worldview centered on the incarnation of Christ. All of the truth scattered throughout the world's philosophies and religions had a home in Christianity. Truth was no longer dismembered and strewn about the intellectual landscape but was unified in the Christian worldview.[29] Orr was also acutely aware of the antagonism between the Christian and non-Christian worldviews,[30] recognized the mutually exclusive claims of Christianity and other worldviews, and concluded that they were incompatible. Orr writes:

> There is a definite Christian view of things, which has a character, coherence, and unity of its own, and stands in sharp contrast with counter theories and speculations, and . . . this world-view has the stamp of reason and reality upon itself, and can amply justify itself at the bar both of history and experience. I shall endeavor to show that the Christian view of things forms a logical whole which cannot be infringed on, or accepted or rejected piecemeal, but stands or falls in its integrity, and can only suffer from attempts at amalgamation or compromise with theories which rest on totally distinct bases.[31]

Orr believed that Christian and non-Christian worldviews were incompatible and consequently stood in antithetical relationship to one another.

Orr appears to have both embraced and rejected key elements of HWT, though it is not clear whether this was intentional. Orr embraced the idea that a worldview provided an exhaustive answer to life's key questions, but he disagreed regarding the source of the knowledge. Dilthey locates the origin of knowledge in man, whereas Orr places it in revelation. Moreover, Orr had confidence that Christianity could be king of the hill because of its divine origins. But it appears that Orr uncritically used a key element of HWT,

26. Orr, *Christian View of God*, 4.
27. Orr, *Christian View of God*, 4–5.
28. Orr, *Christian View of God*, 7.
29. Orr, *Christian View of God*, 12.
30. Orr, *Christian View of God*, 9.
31. Orr, *Christian View of God*, 16.

namely, the scuttling of a universal view of man. Dilthey rejected natural law and on this basis claimed that the various worldviews were hopelessly incompatible because of no commonly shared assumptions. Dilthey believed that the various worldviews stood in irreconcilable antithesis to each other. Orr offered the same conviction in different garb, declaring that Christian and non-Christian worldviews stand in antithesis: "The Christian view of things forms a logical whole which cannot be infringed on, or accepted or rejected piecemeal, but stands or falls in its integrity, and can only suffer from attempts at amalgamation or compromise with theories which rest on totally distinct bases."[32] Orr embraced the HWT tenet of the incommensurability of worldviews.

Orr employed the idealist concept that one single principle explains a worldview, which gives a holistic, systematic, and exhaustive explanation of the world.[33] And in Orr's judgment, the one single principle that explained the Christian worldview was Christ. This is evident in the subtitle of his book, *The Christian View of God and the World: As Centering in the Incarnation.* Orr was convinced that Christology was the central dogma of Christianity and held this view in agreement with D. F. Strauss (1808–74) and Ludwig Feuerbach (1804–72).[34] In fact, Orr believed that Johann Gottlieb Fichte (1762–1814), Friedrich Wilhelm Joseph Schelling (1775–1854), and George Wilhelm Friedrich Hegel "rendered an essential service to theology in overcoming the shallow rationalism of the preceding period, and in restoring to its place of honour in the Christian system the doctrine of Christ's Person, which it had become customary to put in the background."[35] Noteworthy at this point are Orr's references to Isaac Dorner (1809–84), one of the theologians who advanced principial versus soteriological Christocentrism.[36] That is, rather than saying that Christ is central to salvation (soteriological Christocentrism), as with the doctrine of the Reformers, Christology is the one doctrine from which one deduces an entire system (principial Christocentrism).[37] Orr insisted on the

32. Orr, *Christian View of God*, 16.

33. Paul W. Franks, *All or Nothing: Systematicity, Transcendental Arguments, and Skepticism in German Idealism* (Cambridge, MA: Harvard University Press, 2005), 17, 61, 85–86, 146–47.

34. Orr, *Christian View of God*, 40; cf. David Friedrich Strauss, *Der alte und der neue Glaube: Ein Bekenntniss* (Bonn: Emil Strauss, 1895); Ludwig Feuerbach, *Das Wesen des Christenthums* (Leipzig: Otto Bigand, 1841).

35. Orr, *Christian View of God*, 41.

36. Orr, *Christian View of God*, 9, 119, 323; cf. Isaac Dorner, *A System of Christian Doctrine*, 4 vols. (Edinburgh: T&T Clark, 1888), 1:169–70; Richard A. Muller, "Emmanuel V. Gerhart on the 'Christ-Idea' as Fundamental Principle," *Westminster Theological Journal* 48 (1986): 102.

37. On this distinction, see Richard A. Muller, "A Note on 'Christocentrism' and the Imprudent Use of Such Terminology," *Westminster Theological Journal* 68 (2006): 253–60.

centrality of Christ to the Christian worldview as the all-controlling doctrine.[38] Orr was dubious about the proposal that other doctrines, such as the kingdom of God, could adequately serve as the central doctrine.[39] Notable in Orr's commitment to principial Christocentrism is the diminished role of natural theology: "Christ's doctrine of the Father is, indeed, entirely unmetaphysical. We meet with no terms such as absolute, infinite, unconditioned, first cause, etc., with which the student of philosophy is familiar."[40]

Kuyper on Worldview

The trail from Kant to Dilthey and Orr leads to Kuyper's 1898 Stone Lectures at Princeton Theological Seminary.[41] When Kuyper wrote his lectures he turned to Orr's *The Christian View of God and the World* to glean information.[42] Kuyper was well aware of the European intellectual climate and the popularity of the worldview concept, but he also looked to Orr for inspiration. Kuyper even cited Orr's lectures as he sought to define the term *worldview*.[43] Peter Heslam notes the parallels between Kuyper's and Orr's formulations and definitions.[44] Kuyper, for example, states, "Two *life systems* are wrestling with one another, in mortal combat. . . . [Since] in Modernism the vast energy of an all-embracing *life-system* assails us, then also it must be understood that we have to take our stand in a life-system of equally comprehensive and far-reaching power."[45] Like Orr, and even echoing Dilthey to a certain extent, Kuyper argues that a worldview must address our relations to (1) God, (2) humans, and (3) the world.[46] The similarities are significant: both Kuyper and Orr believe that the Christian worldview offers an exhaustive explanation of the world, stands in antithesis to other worldviews, and is a life-system that finds its source in Christianity.

There are three key differences, however, between Orr and Kuyper's formulations. First, unlike Orr, Kuyper believed that Calvinism was the purest

38. Orr, *Christian View of God*, 4, 11, 33, 35, 39–41, 77, 120, 213, 347, 351.

39. Orr, *Christian View of God*, 352.

40. Orr, *Christian View of God*, 77.

41. James D. Bratt, "Abraham Kuyper: Puritan, Victorian, Modern," in *Kuyper Reconsidered: Aspects of His Life and Work*, ed. Cornelis van der Kooi and Jan de Bruijn, VU Studies on Protestant History (Amsterdam: VU Uitgeverij, 1999), 63.

42. Peter S. Heslam, *Creating a Christian Worldview: Abraham Kuyper's Lectures on Calvinism* (Grand Rapids: Eerdmans, 1998), 93; also Naugle, *Worldview*, 7.

43. Kuyper, *Lectures on Calvinism*, 11n1.

44. Heslam, *Christian Worldview*, 93–95.

45. Kuyper, *Lectures on Calvinism*, 11.

46. Kuyper, *Lectures on Calvinism*, 19.

expression and form of Christianity.[47] Orr contended merely for Christianity. Second, Kuyper's rhetoric of antithesis sounded very much like Orr, but he made allowances for agreement between different worldviews. In his larger corpus, especially his writings on common grace, Kuyper acknowledges that there are areas of shared knowledge and even praises non-Christian philosophers for their insights.[48] This means that Kuyper did not always posit a strict antithesis between the Christian and non-Christian worldviews. Worldviews are not incommensurable. Third, and I believe this point is significant, Kuyper does not mention the origins of the worldview concept. Orr delved into its origins in Kant and other Continental philosophers, such as Auguste Comte (1798–1857), but he also explained that the idea substantively originated in ancient Greek philosophy.[49] When Kuyper presented the worldview concept, he wiped it clean of its philosophical origins and presented a relatively untraceable idea for popular consumption and adoption.

Van Til on Worldview

Christ as the Starting Point for Knowledge

Van Til sought to advance the science of apologetics by employing Kuyper's insights, acknowledging that he was following in Kuyper's footsteps.[50] During his time as a theology student, Van Til devoured Kuyper's works.[51] Van Til embraced Kuyper's overall worldview program.[52] Van Til writes: "The Christian life and world view . . . presents the *only true* interpretation of human experience."[53] He pressed Kuyper's insights into service but made some significant changes. Like Kuyper, Van Til acknowledged the category of common grace, but he more forcefully stressed the principle of antithesis.[54] Van Til believed that as insightful as Kuyper was, Kuyper did not press

47. Kuyper, *Lectures on Calvinism*, 15, 17.

48. David VanDrunen, *Natural Law and the Two Kingdoms: A Study in the Development of Reformed Social Thought* (Grand Rapids: Eerdmans, 2010), 278–89.

49. Orr, *Christian View of God*, 5.

50. Van Til was very familiar with Kuyper's *Lectures on Calvinism* as he quoted pages and pages of Kuyper's lectures in his "Christian Philosophy of Life" (address presented to the Association for the Advancement of Christian Scholarship, Philadelphia, March 29, 1968), 8–15.

51. John R. Muether, *Cornelius Van Til: Reformed Apologist and Churchman* (Phillipsburg, NJ: P&R, 2008), 46; John Frame, "Cornelius Van Til," in *Handbook of Evangelical Theologians*, ed. Walter Elwell (Grand Rapids: Baker, 1993), 156–67.

52. See, e.g., Cornelius Van Til, *A Christian Theory of Knowledge* (Phillipsburg, NJ: P&R, 1969), 301.

53. Cornelius Van Til, *Christian Apologetics* (Phillipsburg, NJ: P&R, 1976), 38.

54. VanDrunen, *Natural Law and the Two Kingdoms*, 393.

antithesis as strongly as he should have. He criticized Kuyper and Herman Bavinck (1854–1921) for promoting "abstract thinking," which Van Til defines as removing theological thought from the context of its origin within a particular worldview.[55] To employ abstract thinking was to fall into scholasticism.[56] In other words, one cannot selectively take elements of a system of thought because they inevitably bring philosophical and theological baggage that hinders the Christian worldview. In line with the idealist elements within HWT, Van Til took an "all or nothing approach."[57]

Van Til accused Kuyper and Bavinck of having a synthetic epistemology, which combines incompatible elements from competing worldviews. This is Rome's chief problem with its "semi-Aristotelian epistemology."[58] In line with the criticisms of Herman Dooyeweerd (1894–1977), Van Til believed that Kuyper uncritically employed modern philosophy's understanding of the universal and particular.[59] Van Til writes: "Kuyper has a weakness in the foundation of his epistemology. He did not start unequivocally from the presupposition of the ontological Trinity. He has, to some extent, allowed himself to formulate his problems after the pattern of a modernized Platonism."[60] In Van Til's opinion, all synthesis thinking must be banished from the Christian worldview. Like Dooyeweerd, Van Til sought a purely biblical starting point for one's epistemology.[61] Hence, Van Til proposed an alternative to the synthetic epistemology of scholasticism, Rome, Kuyper, and Bavinck: "The ontological trinity will be our interpretative concept everywhere. God is our concrete universal; in Him thought and being are coterminous, in Him the problem of knowledge is solved."[62]

55. Cornelius Van Til, *Common Grace and the Gospel* (Phillipsburg, NJ: P&R, 1972), 34; see also 38–39, 41–42, 45–49, 51, 52, 57, 228. Van Til expressed his criticism of Kuyper and Bavinck in a number of places. See Cornelius Van Til, *Introduction to Systematic Theology* (Phillipsburg, NJ: P&R, 1974), 47–48, 265, 285, 289–90, 294, 295; Van Til, "Response of Van Til to G. C. Berkouwer" and "Response to D. Gaffin," in *Jerusalem and Athens: Critical Discussions on the Theology and Apologetics of Cornelius Van Til,* ed. E. R. Geehan ([Nutley, NJ]: P&R, 1971), 203–4, 239, 242–43; Van Til, *The New Synthesis Theology of the Netherlands* (Phillipsburg, NJ: P&R, 1976), 30, 43; Van Til, *Christian Theory of Knowledge,* 20, 301.

56. Van Til, *Common Grace,* 43.

57. John Frame, *Cornelius Van Til: An Analysis of His Thought* (Phillipsburg, NJ: P&R, 1995), 266.

58. Van Til, *Common Grace,* 34.

59. Van Til, *Common Grace,* 35.

60. Van Til, *Common Grace,* 38.

61. See, e.g., Herman Dooyeweerd, *In the Twilight of Western Thought,* ed. D. F. M. Strauss, Collected Works, Series B 16 (Grand Rapids: Paideia, 2012).

62. Van Til, *Common Grace,* 64; see also Van Til, *Christianity and Idealism* (Philadelphia: P&R, 1955), 85, 90.

For Van Til, beginning with the ontological Trinity means that God, first and foremost, interprets all of reality, every fact. The only way to perceive reality aright is to think God's thoughts after him. Hence, only the Christian worldview provides the comprehensive starting point for one's epistemology. In his later works, Van Til stresses the self-attesting Christ of Scripture as his starting point.[63] Like Orr, Van Til believed that he had to begin from an overarching principle that explained everything. Van Til writes: "In epistemology we must begin 'from above.' That is, we must presuppose God."[64] Van Til uses the same methodology as Orr when he explains that Christ is the touchstone for all knowledge: "No valid interpretation of any fact can be carried on except upon the basis of the authoritative thought communication to man of God's final purposes in Scripture, as this Scripture sets forth in final form the redemptive work of Christ. Every fact must be interpreted Christologically."[65] In fact, in what might be a surprise to some, Van Til registered his agreement with Karl Barth (1886–1968) on this point: "We must really do what Karl Barth has insisted that we must do but has not done, namely, start our interpretation of the whole of life *von oben* [from above]. We must begin our meditation upon any fact in the world in the light of the Son of God, the light which is as the light of the sun, the source of all other light."[66]

This quotation does not mean that Van Til was a Barthian. Rather, Van Til and Barth were part of a larger nineteenth- and twentieth-century theological movement that adopted tenets of German idealism. Theologians implemented the idealist method of deducing a system of doctrine from a single concept, and they maintained that Christology was this starting point.[67] Note, for

63. Cornelius Van Til, "My Credo," in *Jerusalem and Athens: Critical Discussions on the Theology and Apologetics of Cornelius Van Til*, ed. E. R. Geehan ([Nutley, NJ]: P&R, 1971), 3, 19, 21.

64. Van Til, *Christianity and Idealism*, 85.

65. Cornelius Van Til, *The Reformed Pastor and Modern Thought* (Phillipsburg, NJ: P&R, 1980), 98.

66. Van Til, *Reformed Pastor*, 196; cf. Frame, *Cornelius Van Til*, 173, 175.

67. Theologians committed to principial Christocentrism include the following: Philip Schaff, *Theological Propaedeutic: A General Introduction to the Study of Theology* (New York: Charles Scribner's Sons, 1893), 362; Emanuel V. Gerhart, *Institutes of the Christian Religion*, 2 vols. (New York: Armstrong & Son, 1891), 1:15–16; Charles A. Briggs, *The Bible, the Church, and the Reason: The Three Great Fountains of Divine Authority*, 2nd ed. (New York: Charles Scribner's Sons, 1893), 55; Henry Boynton Smith, *System of Christian Theology* (New York: Armstrong & Son, 1884), 91–105; cf. Richard A. Muller, "Henry Boynton Smith: Christocentric Theologian," *Journal of Presbyterian History* 61, no. 4 (1983): 429–44; Richard A. Muller, "Emanuel V. Gerhart on the 'Christ Idea' as Fundamental Principle," *Westminster Theological Journal* 48, no. 1 (1986): 97–117; Annette G. Aubert, *The German Roots of Nineteenth-Century American Theology* (Oxford: Oxford University Press, 2013), 71–72, 136–38.

example, the similarities between Orr, Van Til, and the earlier statements of Emanuel Gerhart (1817–1904):

> Christ glorified is the one primordial and unchangeable source of divine knowledge. This source He is to His people not by the exertion of external influences, nor merely by verbal teaching, but by mystical union with them; a union begotten by the Holy Spirit and made effectual through personal faith. The transcendent Christ becomes an immanent vital principal, from which is developed a Christian ethical life and a Christian consciousness.[68]

Gerhart's statement comes from the very same historical milieu in which Orr constructed and presented his lectures on worldview. In fact, Van Til agreed with Orr that idealism allowed theologians to present the claims of Christianity in a new and more effective way. Van Til writes, "This is the significance of Kant's 'Copernican Revolution.' It is only in our day that there can therefore be anything like a fully consistent presentation of one system of interpretation over against the other. For the first time in history the stage is set for a head-on collision. There is now a clear-cut antithesis between the two positions."[69] According to Van Til, Kant began with humanity as the ultimate reference point, and Van Til began with the self-attesting Christ of Scripture. These were two mutually exclusive starting points, one from below and the other from above. Van Til, therefore, did not advocate a loose understanding of worldview, one that offered a basic outlook on life, but instead adopted key elements of HWT.

Common Notions versus Common Ground?

Van Til's starting point of the self-attesting Christ of Scripture, like Orr's, resulted in a diminished view and role for any form of natural theology in his system. But at this point we enter one of the more complex and ambiguous aspects of Van Til's thought, namely, the question of knowledge shared between believer and unbeliever. To be clear, Van Til acknowledges that believers and unbelievers have shared knowledge, but there are many contradictory statements in his writings on this point. John Frame has made this same observation: "An important problem, however, emerges at this point. Despite Van Til's affirmation of the ambiguity of the unbeliever's position under common grace, he nevertheless writes as though the unbeliever knows

---

68. Gerhart, *Institutes*, 1:48.
69. Cornelius Van Til, introduction to *The Inspiration and Authority of the Bible*, by Benjamin B. Warfield, ed. Samuel G. Craig (repr., Phillipsburg, NJ: P&R, 1948), 23–24.

and affirms no truth at all and thus is not at all affected by common grace."[70] Frame lists multiple instances from Van Til's writings. For example, taken at face value, the following statement allows for no point of contact between believer and unbeliever: "That all men have all things in common metaphysically and psychologically, was definitely asserted, and further, that the natural man has epistemologically nothing in common with the Christian."[71] But as Frame notes, Van Til admits that believers know something of God and the truth, "after a fashion."[72]

Where things become problematic, however, is when Van Til rejects common notions. Van Til was well aware of the Thomist appeal to and use of common notions. He rejected the historic Reformed concept of common notions because he believed it was an example of synthetic thinking. Van Til chided Bavinck, for example, for his adoption of the Thomistic common notions: "He should have begun boldly by setting off the consistent Christian position over against Greek speculation and over against the half-Christian, half-Greek speculation of Thomas."[73] Such a view, in Van Til's estimation, "leads away from Calvin and back to Thomas Aquinas."[74] Van Til felt that Roman Catholic natural theology crept into Reformed theology through the belief that the natural man has "the power of interpreting some aspect of the world without basic error."[75] In saying this, Van Til undoubtedly had Bavinck and Kuyper in mind but also Reformed Orthodox theologians, those who embraced scholasticism in their theology.[76] With his rejection of common notions, Van Til departs from the catholic and Reformed faith.

It is ironic that what Van Til takes away with the left hand he reintroduces with the right. Early in his career, Van Til rejected common notions and introduced his own version of the concept: "We must not make our appeal to the 'common notions' of unbelievers and believers but to the 'common notions'

---

70. John Frame, "Van Til on Antithesis," in *John Frame's Selected Shorter Writings* (Phillipsburg, NJ: P&R, 2015), 2:272. See also Frame, "Cornelius Van Til," in *John Frame's Selected Shorter Writings*, 2:217–19.

71. Van Til, *Defense of the Faith*, 3rd ed. (1955; Phillipsburg, NJ: P&R, 1967), 169. Cf. VanDrunen, *Natural Law and the Two Kingdoms*, 392–99.

72. Frame, "Van Til on Antithesis," 273.

73. Van Til, *Introduction to Systematic Theology*, 47–48, 195–96. Also see the following for similar comments regarding rejecting common notions: Cornelius Van Til, *The Defense of the Faith*, 168–75, 210, 298; Van Til, *Common Grace and the Gospel*, 51–58, 142–43, 169; Van Til, "My Credo," 21; Van Til, *Essays on Christian Education* (Phillipsburg, NJ: P&R, 1979), 91; Van Til, *Christian Apologetics*, 45, 51.

74. Van Til, *Defense of the Faith*, 175.

75. Van Til, *Common Grace and the Gospel*, 143.

76. Van Til, *Common Grace and the Gospel*, 285, 289–90; also, Van Til, *The New Synthesis Theology of the Netherlands* (Phillipsburg, NJ: P&R, 1976), 12.

that, by virtue of creation in God's image, men as men all have in common."[77]
Later in his career, when Van Til made this same point, he altered it to set
apart his own view: "That we no longer make an appeal to 'common notions'
which Christian and non-Christian agree on, but to the 'common ground'
which they actually have because man and his world are what the Scripture
says they are."[78] What, according to Van Til, is this "common ground"? Van
Til argues that it means appealing to the unbeliever in terms of the image of
God, his status as a covenant breaker, his conscience involuntarily approving
or disapproving of his conduct, the law implanted in him at his creation, and
his sense of deity.[79] Van Til writes, "We should therefore rather speak of the
innate knowledge of God in man as the revelation thought-content that arises
with his self-consciousness, inasmuch as his own constitution is revelation
of God. Calvin asserts that consciousness of self and consciousness of God
are involved in one another."[80]

Van Til appeals to the same categories that Reformed Orthodox theologians invoked when they promoted the concept of common notions. According to Anthony Burgess (d. 1664), for example, common notions are a part
of the image of God and a constituent element of the law of God revealed
through nature, and thus constitute the innate knowledge of God.[81] In other
words, it is difficult to tell the difference between the historic catholic and
Reformed appeal to common notions and Van Til's common ground. Van
Til needlessly rejected the catholic and Reformed concept of common notions. Why did Van Til do this? There are several reasons: (1) Van Til had an
erroneous understanding of scholasticism, which he believed was an unholy
synthesis of pagan and Christian thought; (2) he wanted to distance himself
as much as possible from all forms of Roman Catholicism; (3) he believed
that Aquinas began from below, from Aristotelian principles of autonomous
human reason, and Van Til wanted to start from above; (4) he believed that
Aquinas was a seamless robe: to use one part of his thought was to embrace
it all; and (5) he allowed his use of HWT to affect his theology. The degree
to which he pressed the idea of starting from a single point and deducing a
system, one antithetical to all others, is the degree to which he emphasized the

77. Cornelius Van Til, *The Defense of the Faith* (Philadelphia: P&R, 1955), 396. The same
unaltered statement appears in the third edition: Van Til, *Defense of the Faith*, 3rd ed., 298.

78. Van Til, "My Credo," in *Jerusalem and Athens*, 21.

79. Van Til, "My Credo," in *Jerusalem and Athens*, 21; Van Til, *Introduction to Systematic
Theology*, 94; Van Til, *Defense of the Faith*, 200; Van Til, *Common Grace and the Gospel*, 70;
Van Til, *Christian Apologetics*, 15, 57, 61.

80. Van Til, *Introduction to Systematic Theology*, 196.

81. Anthony Burgess, *Vindiciae Legis: A Vindication of the Morall Law and Covenants*
(London: Thomas Underhill, 1647), 57–104, esp., e.g., 59–60, 62, 113.

incommensurability of Christian and non-Christian knowledge. A repeated theme in Van Til's thought is the antithetical *principles* at work in Christian and non-Christian worldviews.[82] His emphasis on *principles*, starting points, reflects his agreement with an idealist-influenced methodology.

Van Til argued that non-Christians had to set aside their principle of autonomous epistemology and embrace the principle of the authority of Scripture: "Unless one accepts the Bible for what true Protestantism says it is, the authoritative interpretation of human life and experience as a whole, it will be impossible to find meaning in anything."[83] Echoing Orr, Van Til believed that the Christian worldview could not be set forth in piecemeal fashion but only as a systemic whole.[84] Hence, Scripture plays the chief role in epistemology:

> Thus the Bible, as the infallibly inspired revelation of God to sinful man, stands before us as that light in terms of which all the facts of the created universe must be interpreted. All of finite existence, natural and redemptive, functions in relation to one all-inclusive plan that is in the mind of God. Whatever insight man is to have into this pattern of the activity of God he must attain by looking at all his objects of research in the light of Scripture.[85]

Van Til also made an additional qualification: not only is Scripture the necessary starting point and presupposition of all knowledge, but so too is the internal testimony of the Holy Spirit:

> Christian theism maintains that the subject of knowledge owes its existence to God. Accordingly, all its interpretive powers are from God and must therefore be reinterpretive powers. In the second place, when the subject of knowledge is to come into contact with the object of knowledge, the connection is possible only because God has laid it there. In other words, the subject-object relation has its validity via God. Theologically expressed, we say that the validity of human knowledge in general rests upon the *testimonium Spiritus Sancti*. In addition to this, Christian theism maintains that since sin has come into the world, no subject of knowledge can really come into contact with any object of knowledge, in the sense of interpreting it properly, unless the Scripture give the required light and unless the regeneration by the Spirit give a new power of sight.[86]

82. See, e.g., Van Til, *Introduction to Systematic Theology*, 26, 29; Van Til, *Defense of the Faith*, 169, 201; Van Til, *Common Grace and the Gospel*, 166; Van Til, *Essays on Christian Education*, 83.
83. Van Til, *Defense of the Faith*, 150.
84. Van Til, *Defense of the Faith*, 115.
85. Van Til, *Defense of the Faith*, 107.
86. Cornelius Van Til, *A Survey of Christian Epistemology*, In Defense of Biblical Christianity 2 (Phillipsburg, NJ: P&R, 1969), 184.

For Van Til, the Christian worldview stands in utter antithesis to all other worldviews.[87] Only when the Holy Spirit regenerates persons can they rightly refract all reality through the interpretive lens of Scripture and think God's thoughts after him.

Van Til's Influence and Impact

Van Til's version of the apologetic implications of a truly Christian worldview struck a chord with many in the conservative Reformed community. Van Til inspired a generation of Christians to press his insights into service by advocating a distinctly Reformed approach to numerous areas of life.[88] Inspired by Van Til, Theonomists (literally, "God's law") rejected the idea of natural law and argued that God's law is the only standard by which one can live.[89] Others stimulated by Van Til argued that there must be a unique Christian philosophy and metaphysics with its own exclusive methodology.[90] Some within the Christian counseling movement eschewed the non-Christian worldview that undergirded psychology and espoused nouthetic counseling, which recognized that most psychological disorders were ultimately due to sinful conduct and that Scripture offered the solution to these so-called maladies.[91]

Others have pressed Van Til's insights to "redeem" science and mathematics.[92] Some have also promoted the idea of a decidedly Christian view of scholarship in the academy, and Christian views of history as an academic discipline.[93] Still others claim that there must be a unique Christian approach

87. Notably, Karl Barth argued along similar lines and claimed that no point of contact existed. Richard E. Burnett, "Point of Contact," in *The Westminster Handbook to Karl Barth*, ed. Richard E. Burnett (Louisville: Westminster John Knox, 2013), 165–67.

88. Frame, *Cornelius Van Til*, 394.

89. Greg L. Bahnsen, *Theonomy in Christian Ethics* (Nacogdoches, TX: Covenant Media, 2002), 387, 521. Not all Van Tillians followed this school of thought; see William S. Barker and W. Robert Godfrey, eds., *Theonomy: A Reformed Critique* (Grand Rapids: Zondervan, 1991).

90. Henry Van Til, *The Calvinistic Concept of Culture* (1959; Grand Rapids: Baker Academic, 2001), 56.

91. Jay E. Adams, *Competent to Counsel: Introduction to Nouthetic Counseling* (Grand Rapids: Zondervan, 1986), xxi.

92. Vern S. Poythress, *Redeeming Mathematics: A God-Centered Approach* (Wheaton: Crossway, 2015), 26; Poythress, *Redeeming Science: A God-Centered Approach* (Wheaton: Crossway, 2006), 27–28.

93. D. G. Hart, "Christian Scholars, Secular Universities, and the Problem with the Antithesis," *Christian Scholar's Review* 30, no. 4 (2001): 382–402; William C. Davis, "Contra Hart: Christian Scholars Should Not Throw in the Towel," *Christian Scholar's Review* 34, no. 2 (2005): 187–200; John M. Frame, "In Defense of Something Close to Biblicism: Reflections on *Sola Scriptura* and History in Theological Method," *Westminster Theological Journal* 59 (1997): 269–91; David F. Wells, "On Being Framed," *Westminster Theological Journal* 59 (1997):

to art, politics, and all spheres of human existence.[94] Those sympathetic with Kuyper's broader project have made similar arguments concerning the use and implications of worldviews.[95] By claiming that only by the testimony of the Holy Spirit and regeneration can people rightly access general human knowledge, Van Til created a minority report within the historic Reformed tradition. Van Til blurred the distinction between general and special revelation and the general and special operations of the Holy Spirit.[96]

As noted in earlier chapters, the Reformed tradition has acknowledged the existence of natural law, common notions, and the light of nature. Reformed theologians recognized that common notions appeared in Greek philosophy, such as in Aristotle's *Nicomachean Ethics*, but they ultimately acknowledged the validity of the concept because Scripture taught it. Zacharias Ursinus (1534–83), the primary author and chief expositor of the Heidelberg Catechism, for example, writes:

> The conceptions or notions of general principles which are natural to us, as the difference between things proper and improper, &c., cannot be the result of mere chance, or proceed from an irrational nature, but must necessarily be naturally engraven upon our hearts by some intelligent cause, which is God. "The Gentiles show the work of the law written in their hearts," &c. (Rom. 2:15).[97]

Westminster divines Burgess and Thomas Goodwin (1600–1680) also offer similar exegesis of Romans 2:14–15. Burgess argues for a twofold writing of the law upon the hearts of all people.[98] Goodwin maintains the doctrine of common notions and explains them in the following manner:

> In having at first a glimmering light and common, yet obscure principles and glimpses of the notions of things sown in the mind by nature, which then by observation and laying things together, and so gathering one thing from another,

---

293–300; Richard A. Muller, "Historiography in the Service of Theology and Worship: Toward Dialogue with John Frame," *Westminster Theological Journal* 59 (1997): 301–10; John M. Frame, "Reply to Richard Muller and David Wells," *Westminster Theological Journal* 59 (1997): 311–18.

94. H. Van Til, *Calvinistic Concept of Culture*, 56.

95. George M. Marsden, *The Outrageous Idea of Christian Scholarship* (Oxford: Oxford University Press, 1998); Mark A. Noll, *The Scandal of the Evangelical Mind* (Grand Rapids: Eerdmans, 1994); Cornelius Plantinga, *Engaging God's World: A Christian Vision of Faith, Learning, and Living* (Grand Rapids: Eerdmans, 2002).

96. David S. Sytsma, "Herman Bavinck's Thomistic Epistemology: The Argument and Sources of His *Principia* of Science," in *Five Studies in the Thought of Herman Bavinck, A Creator of Modern Dutch Theology*, ed. John Bolt (Lewiston, NY: Edwin Mellen, 2011), 18, 43.

97. Zacharias Ursinus, *The Commentary of Dr. Zacharias Ursinus on the Heidelberg Catechism* (Columbus, 1852; repr., Grand Rapids: Eerdmans, 1954), 121.

98. Burgess, *Vindiciae Legis*, 57–104, esp. 60.

the mind improveth and enlargeth, till it arise to a particular, clear, distinct, and perfect knowledge of those things which it seeks to know. This is the natural way of man's understanding in both estates, both of innocent and corrupt nature; and that in all things that are known by him either of these estates wherein common principles (as that the whole is greater than its parts, &tc), *koinai ennoiai* [common notions], as the Grecians call them, hints, glimpses, as I call them, many of which are even in the minds of children.[99]

These opinions were not peculiar to Ursinus, Burgess, or Goodwin, as the previous chapters demonstrate.

But despite the Reformed tradition's regular use of common notions, Van Tillians have sought only to fortify their position. Some Van Tillians argue, for example, that Bavinck's epistemology is inconsistent and has pagan elements within it because he employs a form of Thomistic realism. Scott Oliphint, for example, claims that Bavinck has an infection or bug in his system.[100] Like Van Til, Oliphint opposes Bavinck and contends that there can be only one foundation for theology and other science, namely, Scripture.[101] Oliphint maintains that *sola scriptura* is the "ground and foundation for our epistemology."[102] Other Van Tillians, such as John Frame, have made similar claims under Van Til's influence.[103] Such a commitment may be true to Van Til, but it conflicts with the historic Reformed early modern consensus.

Oliphint claims that a key element of the Reformation was a renewed focus on Scripture "as our only foundation for knowing, for believing, and for reasoning properly."[104] Oliphint appeals to Richard Muller's analysis to support his claim: "*This view of the problem of knowledge [during the Reformation] is the single most important contribution of the early Reformed writers to the theological prolegomena of orthodox Protestantism.* Indeed, it is the doctrinal issue that most forcibly presses the Protestant scholastics toward the modification of the medieval models for theological prolegomena."[105] Oliphint, however,

---

99. Thomas Goodwin, *Of the Creatures and the Condition of Their State by Creation*, in *The Works of Thomas Goodwin*, vol. 7 (Edinburgh: James Nichol, 1863), 2.5, pp. 45–46.

100. K. Scott Oliphint, "Bavinck's Realism, the Logos Principle, and *Sola Scriptura*," *Westminster Theological Journal* 72 (2010): 359–90.

101. Oliphint, "Bavinck's Realism," 360–61.

102. Oliphint, "Bavinck's Realism," 390; also Oliphint, "Prolegomena Principle: Frame and Bavinck," in *Speaking the Truth in Love: The Theology of John Frame*, ed. John J. Hughes (Phillipsburg, NJ: P&R, 2009), 201–32.

103. Frame, "Something Close to Biblicism," 274; Frame, "Reply to Richard Muller," 312, 314.

104. K. Scott Oliphint, *Covenantal Apologetics: Principles and Practice in Defense of Our Faith* (Wheaton: Crossway, 2013), 129.

105. Oliphint, *Covenantal Apologetics*, 129n7, emphasis original; see also Richard A. Muller, *Post-Reformation Reformed Dogmatics*, 4 vols. (Grand Rapids: Baker Academic, 2003), 1:108. For

misunderstands Muller's point. Muller does not address the subject of general epistemology, or revelational epistemology, but the knowledge of God.[106]

Elsewhere Oliphint tries to support the idea of Scripture as the only source for all knowledge by appealing to Edward Leigh (1602–71).[107] Oliphint sees statements in Leigh's theology that, at first glance, seem to support his appeal: "The holy Scriptures are that Divine instrument and means, by which we are taught to believe what we ought touching God, and ourselves, and all creatures, and how to please God in all things unto eternal life." If Scripture is the instrument by which God teaches about all creatures, then should not *sola scriptura* have the greatest significance for general epistemology? While Oliphint might try to make such a claim, there are three important counterobservations. First, Oliphint does not account for what Leigh says regarding prolegomena; Leigh does not address general epistemology in his doctrine of Scripture. Regarding general epistemology, Leigh distinguishes natural and supernatural principles of knowledge. When he addresses Scripture, he does so under "the principles of Religion," not general epistemology.[108]

Leigh's claim about Scripture giving us knowledge of all creatures is actually a quotation from John Robinson (ca. 1575–1625), indicated by the following citation immediately following Leigh's statement: "*Robins. Essayes 8th Observ.*"[109] Robinson's statement comes from the context of reflecting on the doctrine of Scripture and its relationship to faith, not knowledge in general:

> The holy Scriptures are that divine Instrument and means, by which we are taught to beleeve what wee ought touching God, and our selves, and all creatures, and how to please God in all things unto eternal Life. I speak of *beleeving* things, seeing *Faith comes by hearing*: for else, we know things touching God by that which we *see, feele,* and *discerne* in, and by his *workes.*[110]

Robinson's point is that the word instructs believers for unity in the church, obedience, and worship.[111] In context, Robinson acknowledges the use of the light of nature:

what follows, I am grateful for Richard Muller's assistance in identifying sources and checking presented arguments.

106. On his revelational epistemology, see K. Scott Oliphint, *Reasons for Faith: Philosophy in the Service of Theology* (Phillipsburg, NJ: P&R, 2006), 341.

107. See, e.g., *Covenantal Apologetics*, 23.

108. Edward Leigh, *A Systeme or Body of Divinity* (London, 1654), prolegomena.

109. Leigh, *Systeme or Body of Divinity*, 1.2, p. 7.

110. John Robinson, *Essayes, or Observations Divine and Morall: Collected out of Holy Scriptures, Ancient and Modern Writers, Both Divine and Human* (London: I. Bellame, 1638), 93–94.

111. Robinson, *Essayes*, 95, 99, 102.

> When wee avow *the Scriptures* perfection, wee exclude not from men common
> sense, and the light of nature, by which we are both subjects capable of under-
> standing them, and directed in sundry manners of doing the things commanded
> in them: yea, besides other humane helps, wee both acknowledge, and begge
> of God as most needful for their fruitfull understanding, the light of his holy
> Spirit: onley wee account, and avow them as a most perfect rule neither crooked
> any way, nor short in any thing requisite. This their sufficiency and perfection is
> not to be restrained to matters simply necessarie to Salvation: For who can say,
> how many, or few, and no more nor lesse, they are? But to matters necessarie to
> obedience, that we may *please God* in all things, great, or small.[112]

According to Robinson, the Scriptures are not the starting point for all knowledge. Rather, in line with the historic Reformed tradition, there are two sources
of knowledge, nature and Scripture, but the Scriptures have applicability to
all of life to enable Christians to please God.

Robinson's views were in the mainstream of historic, early modern Reformed theology on the relationship between general knowledge and the
Scriptures. William Whitaker (1548–95), the theologian who wrote the definitive refutation of the Roman Catholic doctrine of Scripture and codified
the Reformed understanding of the same, explains:

> Assuredly, this is the difference between theology and philosophy: since it is
> only the external light of nature that is required to learn thoroughly the arts
> of philosophy; but to understand theology aright, there is need of the internal
> light of the Holy Spirit, because the things of faith are not subject to the teach-
> ing of mere human reason. We may, in a certain manner, be acquainted with
> the doctrines of scripture, and obtain an historical faith by the ministry of the
> word, so as to know all the articles of faith, and deem them to be true, and
> all without the inward light of the Spirit, as many impious men and devils do;
> but we cannot have the πληροφορία [*plērophoria*], that is, a certain, solid, and
> saving knowledge, without the Holy Spirit internally illuminating our minds.
> And this internal clearness it is, which wholly flows from the Holy Ghost.[113]

Whitaker clearly identifies reason as the means by which people understand
philosophy and the regeneration of the Spirit as the means by which they grasp
theology. He even allows that unbelievers may understand the Scriptures to
a certain degree but that saving knowledge, what he calls *plērophoria* (full
assurance), comes only through the regenerative work of the Spirit.

112. Robinson, *Essayes*, 100–101.
113. William Whitaker, *A Disputation on Holy Scripture* (Cambridge: Cambridge University
Press, 1849), 364.

Robinson identifies the Scriptures as "a most perfect rule," which is a common phrase in early modern Reformed theology. A version of the phrase appears, for example, in the Westminster Shorter Catechism: "What rule hath God given to direct us how we may glorifie and enjoy him [God]? A. The Word of God . . . is the only rule to direct us how we may glorifie and enjoy him" (q. 2). Anthony Burgess, one of the Westminster divines, explains what a *rule* is.[114] Anticipating the Shorter Catechism, Burgess writes: "The Word is the onely rule and principle in matters of Religion and Reformation."[115] The word, therefore, is a rule to guide Christians in glorifying God, but Burgess immediately stipulates:

> When we say its a rule, it must be extended to that end for which it is a rule; for as the Scripture is not a rule to Physicians or Mathematicians in their proper arts, so neither doth it particularly tend to this, or that individuall action for all essentials it is a rule, and a generall rule for circumstantials. Nor doth this detract from the perfection of Scripture, that it doth not command every circumstance because then a thing is imperfect, when it wants some perfection that is due to it: It is not an imperfection in the body, that its not every where, because this is not requisite to the body, so neither is it to be expected from the Scripture, that all circumstantials must be by name commanded.[116]

In other words, the Scriptures do not address everything, and this is OK. This is where the book of nature enters the picture. The next question in the Shorter Catechism confirms this conclusion when it defines the principal teaching of Scripture as what man should believe concerning God and the duties God requires of man (q. 3).

Burgess was not alone in this opinion, as other Westminster divines such as Samuel Rutherford (1600–1661) argued the same point:

> Scripture is our Rule, but 1. not in miraculous things. 2. Not in things temporarie, as Communitie of Goods. 3. Not in things Literally exponed, as to cut off our hands and feet. 4. Not in things of Art and Science, as to speake Latine, to demonstrate conclusions of Astronomie. 5. It is not properly our Rule in Circumstances, which are but naturall conveniences of time, place, and person, and such like.[117]

114. Anthony Burgess, *The Difficulty of and the Encouragements to a Reformation: A Sermon Preached before the Honourable House of Commons at the Publik Fast, Septem. 27, 1643* (London: Thomas Underhill, 1643).

115. Burgess, *Difficulty and Encouragements*, 3.

116. Burgess, *Difficulty and Encouragements*, 8.

117. Samuel Rutherford, *A Dispute Touching Scandall and Christian Libertie*, in *The Divine Right of Church-Government and Excommunication* (London: John Field, 1646), 99.

Rutherford clearly sets boundaries for the Scriptures because they chiefly address theological and moral issues, not temporal matters, science, or education, such as learning Latin. When Rutherford argues that Scripture is not a rule for *circumstances*, he appeals to a principle that the Westminster divines codified in the Confession: "There are some circumstances concerning the worship of God, and government of the church, common to human actions and societies, which are to be ordered by the light of nature, and Christian prudence, according to the general rules of the Word, which are always to be observed" (WCF 1.6). In other words, in the Confession's doctrine of Scripture the divines acknowledge that there are some things Scripture does not address, which requires the use of the light of nature (the use of God's other book, the book of nature), to determine matters, even those pertaining to worship.

Oliphint elsewhere cites another early modern theologian to support his claim that some early modern Reformed theologians have argued that Scripture is the source of all knowledge. Oliphint quotes Philippe du Plessis-Mornay (1549–1623): "For if every science has its *principles*, which it is not lawful to remove, be it ever so little: much more reason is it that it should be so with that thing which hath the ground of all *principles* as its *principle*."[118] Oliphint takes this quote and claims: "The *principium* of Scripture is meant to ground anything else that we affirm in theology *and in any other discipline*."[119] Oliphint misunderstands du Plessis-Mornay's statement. He does not say, *pace* Oliphint, that Scripture is the principium for any other discipline. The surrounding context from which Oliphint draws his quote says something quite different. Du Plessis-Mornay writes:

> Surely unto him that treateth of Religion, it ought to be granted as an unviolable Principle, *That there is a God*; and all men ought to be forbidden to call it into question, upon paine of not being men any more. *For if every Science have its Principles, which is not lawfull to remove, be it never so little: much more reason is it that it should be so, with that thing which hath the ground of all Principles for his Principle.* Neverthelesse, let us with the leave of all good men, bestow this Chapter upon the wickedness of this our age: and if there bee any which by forgetting God, have in very deede forgotten their owne shape, and mistaken their owne nature: let them learne thereby to reknowledge themselves againe.[120]

118. K. Scott Oliphint, "Covenant Model," in *Four Views on Christianity and Philosophy*, ed. Paul M. Gould and Richard Brian Davis (Grand Rapids: Zondervan, 2016), 74; see Philippe du Plessis-Mornay, *A Worke concerning the Trunesse of Christian Religion*, trans. Philip Sidney Knight and Arthur Golding (London: George Potter, 1604), 2.

119. Oliphint, "Covenant Model," 81, emphases added.

120. Du Plessis-Mornay, *Christian Religion*, 2.

Du Plessis-Mornay bookends Oliphint's quote (italicized above) with references to God, not Scripture, as the ground of all principles.

Oliphint's claim that Scripture is the principal source of knowledge works well with the methods of German idealism and singular starting points from which one deduces an exhaustive worldview. But it conflicts with early modern Reformed theology and its acknowledgment of two sources of knowledge: the books of nature and Scripture. This is not to say that the early modern Reformed tradition is perfectly monolithic on these points but rather that idealist-influenced claims about singular starting points do not appear. To claim that Scripture is the only ground for all knowledge ignores what the early modern Reformed tradition says about the book of nature. It also, as we will see below, conflicts with what we find in Scripture.

Scripture and Common Notions

Plain and simple, the alleged total incommensurability of worldviews does not fit with the claims of Scripture chiefly because the Bible teaches that all people bear God's image. This means that all people work with the same information, but quite obviously, to different ends. The Bible does not portray fallen humanity as existing in complete epistemological antithesis with believers at every point. To be sure, we have an antithetical relationship with the unbelieving world every time they sinfully suppress the truth in unrighteousness, whether that truth is revealed through general or special revelation. But this antithesis does not automatically eradicate common notions. Or, stated in Kuyperian terms, the antithesis does not eradicate common grace. I do not present a full-fledged case for common notions here, since others have ably done this, especially as it pertains, for example, to natural law.[121] Moreover, I agree with the exegesis offered by the theologians surveyed in the previous chapters regarding Psalms 19 and 104 (e.g., Calvin) and Romans 1:19–20 and 2:14–15 by Burgess and others.[122] I nevertheless raise three biblical examples that specifically challenge the claim that worldviews are incommensurable: the commonality between the Code of Hammurabi and the Mosaic law, Paul at Mars Hill, and Romans 2:14–15. In these three examples, inspired writers of Scripture arguably incorporate and appeal to commonly shared knowledge.

121. See David VanDrunen, *Divine Covenants and Moral Order: A Biblical Theology of Natural Law* (Grand Rapids: Eerdmans, 2014); VanDrunen, *A Biblical Case for Natural Law* (Grand Rapids: Acton Institute, 2012).

122. See also Andrew Willett, *A Six-Fold Commentary upon the Most Divine Epistle of the Holy Apostle S. Paul to the Romans* (Cambridge: Leonard Greene, 1620), comm. Rom. 1:18–19, 2:14, pp. 57, 59, 101.

Moses and Hammurabi

The first example comes from the Covenant Code, which appears in Exodus 20:22–23:33. The Code of Hammurabi was a Babylonian legal code that dates back to the eighteenth century BC. If the Mosaic Covenant Code originated in the fifteenth century BC, then the Code of Hammurabi predates the biblical Covenant Code by roughly three hundred years. The seniority of the Code of Hammurabi becomes especially relevant when we take into account the significant parallels between the two codes. There are numerous parallels, but the laws concerning ox goring illustrate the similarities:[123]

Code of Hammurabi (§§ 250–52)	Covenant Code (Exod. 21:28–32)
If a bull, when passing through the street, gore a man and bring about his death, this case has no penalty.	When an ox gores a man or a woman to death, the ox shall be stoned, and its flesh shall not be eaten, but the owner of the ox shall not be liable.
If a man's bull have been wont to gore and they have made known to him his habit of goring, and he have not protected his horns or have not tied him up, and that bull gore the son of a man and bring about his death, he shall pay one-half mina of silver.	But if the ox has been accustomed to gore in the past, and its owner has been warned but has not kept it in, and it kills a man or a woman, the ox shall be stoned, and its owner also shall be put to death. If a ransom is imposed on him, then he shall give for the redemption of his life whatever is imposed on him. If it gores a man's son or daughter, he shall be dealt with according to this same rule.
If it be the servant of a man, he shall pay one-third mina of silver.	If the ox gores a slave, male or female, the owner shall give to their master thirty shekels of silver, and the ox shall be stoned.

The two sections are very similar, though there are some differences. That both codes address ox goring is the first point of agreement and presents a clear case of one of two possibilities: either (a) Moses and Hammurabi share common information, or (b) Moses borrows from Hammurabi under divine inspiration. Second, both codes state that, in the case of an accidental goring, there is no penalty for the owner. Third, if the owner knew that his ox was dangerous and took no precautions for public safety, there is a penalty: a fine according to Hammurabi, death in the Covenant Code. Fourth, if the ox gores a servant or slave, then the penalty is equivalent, a third of a mina or thirty shekels of silver.[124] These parallels might not be all that significant if the

123. Robert Francis Harper, *The Code of Hammurabi: King of Babylon, about 2250 BC* (Eugene, OR: Wipf & Stock, 2007). For an overview of the similarities and differences between Hammurabi and the Covenant Code, see VanDrunen, *Divine Covenants*, 288–301.
124. David P. Wright, *Inventing God's Law: How the Covenant Code of the Bible Used and Revised the Laws of Hammurabi* (Oxford: Oxford University Press, 2009), 7.

Covenant Code predated Hammurabi (as a case of Van Til's borrowed capital) and Hammurabi borrowed from Moses. But the opposite might be true: Moses may have borrowed from Hammurabi. Has Moses borrowed capital from Hammurabi? Is he guilty of synthesis thinking? Has Moses compromised the Christian worldview by failing to recognize that there is no epistemological point of contact? Or, at minimum, do both legislators share common notions about law? If so, this still presents challenges to Van Til's claims about the absence of a point of contact. If Van Til's understanding of worldview and antithesis is correct, then these are vexing and troubling questions. If, on the other hand, believer and nonbeliever share common notions by virtue of being created in the image of God, then there are no problems. Both Hammurabi and Moses codify the law of God written on the heart, and as such, Moses may freely borrow from Hammurabi because he ultimately taps into God's natural law. In other words, all ideas ontologically originate from God, but this does not mean they all first come through Israel. We should not conflate ontology and epistemology.

Paul at Mars Hill

The second example comes from Paul's interaction with the Greek philosophers at Mars Hill. When Paul entered Athens, he was distraught over the rampant idolatry that confronted him everywhere (Acts 17:16). He immediately engaged in preaching and an apologetic presentation of the gospel, as he reasoned with "the Jews and the devout persons" "in the synagogue" (Acts 17:17). Paul's apologetic approach was based on special revelation: he was speaking with those who were familiar with the Old Testament. Hence, as in Amphipolis and Apollonia, Paul engaged the Jews of the local synagogue, and he "reasoned with them from the Scriptures, explaining and proving that it was necessary for the Christ to suffer and to rise from the dead" (Acts 17:2–3). But he did not take the same approach when he addressed the Epicurean and Stoic philosophers, who were unfamiliar with the Old Testament (Acts 17:18).[125]

Rather than begin with special revelation and the Scriptures, Paul appealed to an inscription he encountered while in Athens, "To the unknown god" (Acts 17:23). Paul explained that this unknown god was the God of the Bible, who made everything, created all humanity, and sovereignly determined their place

---

125. On Paul's philosophical context, see N. T. Wright, *Paul and the Faithfulness of God*, vol. 4 of *Christian Origins and the Question of God* (Minneapolis: Fortress, 2013), 197–245. Paul arguably follows the pattern of the Old Testament prophets when they engaged and condemned the Gentiles. The prophets appealed to violations of natural law rather than the Torah. See VanDrunen, *Divine Covenants*, 164–208.

in history (Acts 17:24–28). But instead of capping his address with an appeal to the Old Testament, he appealed to two of their own philosophers. The first quotation, "In him we live and move and have our being" (Acts 17:28a), comes from Epimenides (ca. 600 BC), which appeared in his poem *Cretica*:

> They fashioned a tomb for thee, O holy and high one—
> The Cretans, always liars, evil beasts, idle bellies!
> But thou art not dead; thou livest and abidest forever,
> For in thee we live and move and have our being.[126]

The second quotation, "For we are indeed his offspring" (Acts 17:28b), comes from the Cilician poet Aratus (ca. 315–240 BC) and his poem *Phaenomena*: "It is with Zeus that every one of us in every way has to do, for we are also his offspring."[127] There is a similar statement in a *Hymn to Zeus* by Cleanthes.[128] The thrust and purpose of these quotations is to confirm in the minds of his audience that these statements are true, but that they point not to Zeus or another false deity but to the one true and living God.

If HWT is correct, then, Paul erroneously appeals to elements within the Greek worldview to confirm the veracity of the Christian worldview. The two systems are supposedly mutually exclusive and have no shared knowledge. Without doubt, Paul presents the antithetical message of the gospel: he appeals to the one true God and the one man by whom God "will judge the world in righteousness" (Acts 17:30–31). Interestingly enough, he does not name Jesus, though he tells them that God raised him from the dead, another idea antithetical to the tenets of Greek philosophy (Acts 17:32). But Paul's address at Mars Hill nevertheless identifies points of contact with his audience. To be sure, Paul took the information (the unknown god, that we are all his children, and that in him we live and move and have our being) and purified it through the filter of special revelation. But he did not say, "Your knowledge is utterly false or different from the knowledge I now give you." According to Romans 1, they knew the truth but suppressed it in unrighteousness, and Paul challenged them based on their own convictions. Believers and nonbelievers have commonly shared knowledge, which makes communication and dialogue possible. The non-Christian's problem is not primarily epistemological but ethical. The epistemological problem arises as a consequence of ethics: he suppresses the truth in unrighteousness. His unethical grasp of the truth may eventually lead to epistemological chaos, but this is not universally true.

126. As quoted in Richard N. Longenecker, *Acts*, EBC (Grand Rapids: Zondervan, 1995), 272.
127. As quoted in Longenecker, *Acts*, 272.
128. C. K. Barrett, *Acts*, 2 vols., ICC (Edinburgh: T&T Clark, 1998), 848.

In one of Van Til's few exegetical works, he explains Acts 17 and the nature of Paul's address at Mars Hill.[129] Van Til rightly identifies the numerous points where Paul presents the antithesis of the gospel.[130] But at several points Van Til's comments contradict the passage. Van Til first introduces Paul's encounter with the citizens of Lystra: "The Apostle Paul was fully determined never to have his message subtly interwoven with that of those who worshiped and served the creature." Van Til offers this comment on Paul's reaction to being called a god by the citizens of Lystra (Acts 14:8–20): Paul "would rather be stoned to death than flattered. He would rend his clothes and call on men not to confuse his message with that of the priests of Jupiter, with the highest being of Plato, or the 'thought thinking itself' of Aristotle."[131] In this case, Van Til is correct, but we should also observe that Paul was rejecting their idolatry. They were clearly transgressing God's law: they were trying to worship the creature rather than the Creator. Therefore, Paul applies the full weight of gospel antithesis against their idolatry.

However, Van Til then takes the outcome at Lystra and wrongly applies it to the events at Mars Hill:

> Would Paul for a moment attach himself to what Stoics meant when they spoke of man as the offspring of God? No more than he would attach himself to what they meant who had built the altar to the unknown God. If he attached himself to the one he could also attach himself to the other. But he could not and did not attach himself to either. Both were involved in one another, and if Paul had attached himself to either he could no longer have preached Jesus and the resurrection.[132]

Van Til concludes: "Paul did virtually the same thing that he had done in Lystra; he challenged the wisdom of the world."[133] If Van Til's explanation is correct, then why did Paul say: "I found also an altar with this inscription, 'To the unknown god.' What therefore you worship as unknown, this I proclaim to you" (Acts 17:23)? Paul explicitly connects their unknown god to the one true God. Moreover, if Van Til is correct and Paul did not for a moment attach himself to the Stoic idea that we are all God's children, then what was the point of raising the quotations? I believe the HWT principle of

129. Cornelius Van Til, *Paul at Athens* (Phillipsburg, NJ: P&R, n.d.). This edition is not paginated; for ease of reference, I have assigned page numbers by counting from the first page of his address.

130. E.g., Van Til, *Paul at Athens*, 13–14.

131. Van Til, *Paul at Athens*, 3.

132. Van Til, *Paul at Athens*, 12.

133. Van Til, *Paul at Athens*, 13.

worldview incommensurability drives Van Til to say that Paul never attached himself to Stoic knowledge.

Van Til incorrectly concludes, therefore, that Paul acted identically in Lystra and Athens. In both cases Paul unquestionably challenged the wisdom of the world: he presented the antithesis of the gospel, most notably evident when the philosophers rejected the doctrine of the resurrection. But in Athens, Paul specifically identified elements of truth within his audience's collective knowledge and was free to do so because he was appealing to the truth they possessed by virtue of their creation in God's image and also what they could know from that creation. Paul neither embraced nor endorsed Stoic cosmology wholesale but merely identified some of the true elements within it so that he might correct the Athenian philosophers and thereby clear a path for the gospel. In this vein, J. Gresham Machen (1881–1937) rightly explains:

> One of the clearest instances of the broader use of the figure of fatherhood is found in the speech of Paul at Athens, Acts xvii.28: "For we are also His offspring." Here it is plainly the relation in which God stands to all men, whether Christians or not, which is in mind. But the words form part of an hexameter line and are taken from a pagan poet; they are not represented as part of the gospel, but merely as belonging to the common meeting ground which Paul discovered in speaking to his pagan hearers.[134]

Paul appealed to his pagan audience in terms of common notions, but he removed the erroneous elements that were obscuring their view of the truth. In the terms of earlier Reformed tradition, Paul appealed to the *principle* of common notions but challenged his audience's erroneous *conclusions*. Moreover, Paul began from below; he did not begin with the idealist perch "from above," with the self-attesting Christ of Scripture. He did not remain below, however, but brought his audience to Christ above.

Romans 2:14–15

The third example illustrating commonly shared knowledge is Paul's explanation in Romans 2:14–15, "For when Gentiles, who do not have the law, by nature do what the law requires, they are a law to themselves, even though they do not have the law. They show that the work of the law is written on their hearts, while their conscience also bears witness, and their conflicting thoughts accuse or even excuse them." I agree with Burgess's exegesis of

134. J. Gresham Machen, *Christianity and Liberalism* (1923; repr., Grand Rapids: Eerdmans, 1999), 61.

this text, which he presents in his *Vindiciae Legis*, but I want to add further
evidence that corroborates his exegesis. Recent research has argued that Paul
drew statements in these verses from the works of Aristotle. In technical exegetical terms, Paul echoes Aristotle.[135] There are three key phrases in Paul's
text that first appear in Aristotle:[136]

Romans 2:14–15	Aristotle
They are a law to them-selves [*heautois eisin nomos*].	The refined and free man will have this manner, being, as it were, *a law to himself* [*hoion nomos ōn heautō*] (*Nicomachean Ethics* 4.8.10 [1128a]).
The work of the law [*to ergon tou nomou*]	First, that justice is real and beneficial, but not that which (only) appears (to be just); nor the written law either, for it does not do *the work of the law* [*ergon to tou nomou*]. . . . And that it be-longs to the better man to use and abide by the unwritten rather than the written (laws) (*Art of Rhetoric* 1.15.7–8 [1375b]).
accuse or even excuse [*katēgorountōn hē kai apologoumenōn*]	First, then, let us speak of the laws, how one must use (them) when persuading and dissuading, and accusing and excusing [*katēgorountai kai apologoumenōn*] (*Rhetoric* 1.15.3 [1375a]).

These three phrases occur in both Aristotle and Paul, and notably, there
are no analogues in the Septuagint. The absence of these phrases from the
Septuagint is significant, because it means that Paul was not drawing on the
Old Testament when he employed them in Romans. It does not conclusively
prove he was dependent on Aristotle, but at a minimum it does point to the
fact that he was using extrabiblical data. But there are important considerations that support the claim that Paul echoed Aristotle.

Upon examination of the original context in Aristotle's writings, it appears
that Paul employed them in a way consistent with their original intent. This
does not mean that Paul was expounding the philosophy of Aristotle, but he
nevertheless found ready-made phrases to express his meaning; this was prob-
ably due to his rabbinic training, an education that exposed him to philosophy
and theology. In short, there are good reasons to believe that Paul employed
these phrases because they expressed common truths etched upon humans'
hearts by virtue of their creation in God's image. Therefore, Paul could appeal to these statements to show that what the Israelites received on Mount
Sinai through the revelation of the law, Gentiles also knew because God had
written the work of the law upon the hearts of all humanity.[137] Moreover, there
are other instances where Paul employed concepts from Greek philosophy,

135. C. John Collins, "Echoes of Aristotle in Romans 2:14–15: Or, Maybe Abimelech Was
Not So Bad after All," *Journal of Markets and Morality* 13, no. 1 (2010): 124.
136. Collins, "Echoes of Aristotle," 129–30.
137. Collins, "Echoes of Aristotle," 132–43.

such as in Galatians 5:23 and 1 Corinthians 11:14–15a.[138] In the former Paul states, "Against such things there is no law," which appears to echo sentiments from Aristotle's *Politics* (3.8.2): "But there can be no law dealing with such men." In the latter Paul echoes a phrase from Aristotle, "Does not nature itself teach you?" An identical paraphrase is in *Poetics* 24.12 (1460a): "Nature itself teaches the meter to be chosen that fits it."[139] Since Paul lived among Greek philosophers, he was bound to encounter their thought and expressions and, as at Mars Hill, employ their language and concepts insofar as they accorded with God-given common notions.[140] When and if they conflicted with special revelation, Paul always presented the antithesis of the gospel.

Exhaustive Epistemology or the Wisdom of Scripture?

The second chief problem with HWT is the claim that a worldview gives an exhaustive explanation of reality. It is one thing to claim that the Bible explains God, humans, and the world and as such has implications for every facet of life. It is another to claim that it is exhaustively comprehensive and is the source of all knowledge. Nineteenth-century idealists regularly make the claim that worldviews are systemic explanations of reality. The same trend appears with some Christian advocates of worldview, though in slightly muted form. Kuyper made similar claims in his Stone Lectures, evidenced by his addresses on religion, politics, science, and art. Kuyper believed that Calvinism was the "completed evolution of Protestantism, resulting in a both higher and richer stage of human development."[141] And as the highest evolved form of Protestantism, Calvinism "created a *life-* and *world-view*, and such a one as was, and still is able to fit itself to the needs of every stage of human development, in every department of life."[142] Kuyper compared Calvinism, for

---

138. Collins, "Echoes of Aristotle," 147–48. There are many other passages of Scripture that merit the same attention regarding natural law. For these passages, see VanDrunen, *Divine Covenants*, passim; Jonathan Burnside, *God, Justice, and Society: Aspects of Law and Legality in the Bible* (Oxford: Oxford University Press, 2011), 67–102; David Novak, *Natural Law in Judaism* (Cambridge: Cambridge University Press, 1998).

139. Collins, "Echoes of Aristotle," 147–48.

140. I do not agree with all of the arguments presented in the following essays from *Paul and the Philosophers*, ed. Ward Blanton and Hent de Vries (New York: Fordham University Press, 2013), 41–86, but they are worth noting because they explore the degree to which Paul may have employed Greek philosophical categories in his epistles: Hans Conzelmann, "The Address of Paul on the Areopagus"; Paul A. Holloway, "Paul as Hellenistic Philosopher: The Evidence of Philippians"; and Emma Wasserman, "Paul among the Ancient Philosophers: The Case of Romans 7."

141. Kuyper, *Lectures on Calvinism*, 41.

142. Kuyper, *Lectures on Calvinism*, 171.

example, to Lutheranism. Kuyper believed that Calvinism branched out into every area of life, whereas Lutheranism compartmentalized life into sacred and secular. Van Til offered similar opinions: "The Christian life and world view . . . presents itself as an *absolutely comprehensive* interpretation of human experience."[143] The same type of claim appears in popular explanations of worldview theory.[144] Hence, some Reformed theologians have tried to make the claim that there is a distinct Christian view of everything, which means that the church must always stand in antithesis to the world.

If the church always stands in antithesis to the world, then why would Moses echo or incorporate the Code of Hammurabi into the Covenant Code? This action defies the claims of a unique Christian view on matters of law. Rather, the Bible has a number of things in common with other cultures. We should not forget the significant differences: Hammurabi, for example, claimed that he was the source of the laws and that they revealed his wisdom.[145] The church acknowledges that God is the source of these laws by virtue of humankind's creation in the image of God. But acknowledging the differences should not cause us to eliminate the commonalities. Historically, the Reformed church has understood the limited scope and purpose of the Scriptures. The First Helvetic Confession, for example, states, "The entire biblical Scripture [*scopus Scripturae*] is solely concerned that man understand that God is kind and gracious to him and that he has publicly exhibited and demonstrated this his kindness to the whole human race through Christ his Son" (§5).[146] This statement shows that Christ rests at the doctrinal center of the Bible; it does not mean that Christ is the touchstone of every doctrine but that all doctrine, in one way or another, points to Christ.[147] As Thomas Watson (ca. 1620–86) explains: "What is the main scope and end of Scripture? Answ[er]. To chalk out a way to salvation: It makes a clear discovery of Christ."[148]

The Bible is not a comprehensive survey of world history: the vast majority of the world's history lies outside the pages of Holy Writ. The Bible explicitly states that many things are beyond humanity's knowledge, not just about God, but also about creation. In Job's dialogue with God, the Creator fired a flurry of questions at him, and Job stood silent with his hand over his mouth (Job 40:4). We should not fail to notice that biblical scholars place the

143. Van Til, *Christian Apologetics*, 38.
144. Philip Graham Ryken, *What Is the Christian Worldview?* (Phillipsburg, NJ: P&R, 2006), 7.
145. VanDrunen, *Divine Covenants*, 295.
146. As quoted in Richard A. Muller, *Post-Reformation Reformed Dogmatics*, 2:82.
147. Muller, *Post-Reformation Reformed Dogmatics*, 2:212.
148. Thomas Watson, *A Body of Practical Divinity* (London: Thomas Parkhurst, 1692), 15.

book of Job within the category of Wisdom literature.[149] God gives his law, but he also calls people to use wisdom. There are many circumstances in life that the Bible does not address, and these situations call for wisdom. Do you answer a fool according to his folly, lest he be wise in his own eyes? Or do you not answer a fool according to his folly, lest you become like the fool (Prov. 26:4–5)? To say that there is one definitive Christian view on how to answer a fool rides roughshod over the Bible's call to wisdom. The same themes and preponderance of unanswered questions also color the book of Ecclesiastes.[150] The Preacher sounds nothing like worldview theory proponents who offer a comprehensive view of reality.

If we say that the Bible provides an exhaustive view of the world, then we must affirm that there is a unique Christian view of everything. There can be no shared knowledge with the unbelieving world because the Scriptures alone hold all truth. If, on the other hand, we acknowledge that the Bible is entirely true yet does not provide an exhaustive view of the world, then we must exercise humility: we must affirm that knowledge rests in the two books that God has written, the books of nature and Scripture. As the Belgic Confession states:

> We know God by two means: First, by the creation, preservation, and govern-ment of the universe, since that universe is before our eyes like a beautiful book in which all creatures, great and small, are as letters to make us ponder the invisible things of God: God's eternal power and divinity, as the apostle Paul says in Romans 1:20. All these things are enough to convict humans and to leave them without excuse. Second, God makes himself known to us more clearly by his holy and divine Word, as much as we need in this life, for God's glory and for our salvation. (II)

Not only do we have the book of nature, but the Bible gives us only as much knowledge of God "as we need in this life, for God's glory and for our salva-tion." The stated scope is limited and not exhaustive, unlike that claimed by worldview theory.

The Bible does not provide principles of art, medicine, history, or math-ematics. The Bible does establish a number of firewalls that Christians must always factor into their various vocations. The Bible says that God immedi-ately created the universe out of nothing (Gen. 1; Heb. 11:3); matter is not

---

149. E.g., David J. A. Clines, *Job 1–20*, WBC (Dallas: Word, 1989), lx–lxii; Roland E. Murphy, *The Tree of Life: An Exploration of Biblical Wisdom Literature* (Grand Rapids: Eerdmans, 1990), 33–49.

150. Murphy, *Tree of Life*, 50–51.

eternal. But as the dialogue between Job and God reminds us, it does not reveal precisely how God created. The Bible tells us to think on whatever is lovely, commendable, and excellent (Phil. 4:8), but it does not proscribe certain types of art. I prefer realistic paintings to impressionistic art, but that is my personal preference, not a biblically mandated ethical choice. This is a point that Kuyper himself acknowledged. As much as he touted the antithesis between the Calvinistic and modern worldviews, he believed that antithesis played little if any role in the realm of the arts.[151] Kuyper believed that common grace emancipated art from being the exclusive property of the regenerate. In fact, Kuyper believed that if true art were restricted to the regenerate, then it would be solely a product of particular grace. This conclusion would be erroneous: Kuyper believed that the best artistic instincts were natural gifts that prospered by virtue of common grace.[152] In his Stone Lectures, for example, Kuyper does not talk of two types of art as he does two types of science.[153]

How does one evaluate certain artistic expressions when Scripture does not give any specific instruction on the subject, claims of the exhaustive nature of the Christian worldview notwithstanding? Russian novelist Leo Tolstoy (1828–1910), for example, believed that artistic expression appealing to sensual and decadent tastes should not be counted as true expressions of art. He therefore dismissed the works of German musical composer Richard Wagner (1813–83) and Italian painter Michelangelo (1475–1564).[154] How does one determine, on the basis of biblical exegesis, whether Wagner's "Flight of the Valkyries" or Michelangelo's *Doni Tondo* is too sensual? Tolstoy believed that most of Ludwig van Beethoven's (1770–1827) music failed to hit the mark of true art; according to Tolstoy it was utter gibberish, even Beethoven's famous Ninth Symphony.[155] One can legitimately reject any images or paintings of Christ as art on the basis of the prohibitions of the second commandment, but to determine sensuality in instrumental music is a highly subjective and exegetically impossible task. On what exegetical basis can one determine whether Beethoven's Ninth is true or false art? How exhaustive, then, can a Christian worldview be if it has gaping holes in its evaluation of artistic expression in music, literature, painting, poetry, or drama?

151. Heslam, *Creating a Christian Worldview*, 222.
152. Heslam, *Creating a Christian Worldview*, 215.
153. Heslam, *Creating a Christian Worldview*, 216.
154. Leo Tolstoy, *What Is Art?* (New York: Penguin Books, 1996), 77–79, 96–97, 101–3, 109, 111, 136; see Heslam, *Creating a Christian Worldview*, 200.
155. Tolstoy, *What Is Art?*, 97, 116, 136–37.

Similar problems attend other areas of life. The Bible tells us to preserve life, but it does not instruct us whether to conduct brain surgery or administer medication to heal a patient. The Bible tells us that its narratives are historically true, but it does not tell us how to write history and what methodologies we should employ.[156] The Bible tells us that God is a God of order (1 Cor. 14:40), but it does not give us specific theories of mathematics. The Bible does not tell us that a triangle consists of 180 degrees, nor does it indicate a preference for the metric versus imperial system of measurement. The Bible leaves these things to wisdom and natural revelation, both of which originate from God.

I believe one of the key problems with HWT is that it seeks to deduce an exhaustive understanding of reality from one principle. Such a methodology was pursued by much of nineteenth-century philosophy. Peter Heslam reports that the monist views of J. H. Scholten (1811–85) influenced and drove Kuyper's desire for coherence, system, and principle in his theology.[157] Philosophical monism famously infected historical-theological studies on Calvin and the Reformed tradition with the erroneous dogmatic assumption that so-called Calvinists deduced an entire system of theology from the doctrine of predestination. Such a methodology was foreign to early modern Reformed theology but was commonplace in the nineteenth century.[158] Nevertheless, this is precisely the manner in which Kuyper sought to employ Calvin's theology in his worldview. Kuyper spoke of Calvinism as a "mother principle" and "unity of starting point," which he identified with Calvin's "principle of the sovereignty of God."[159] While one might say that the sovereignty of God was a chief element in Calvin's theology, it was not the mother principle from which he constructed an exhaustive view of life and the world. Kuyper's advocacy of common grace mitigated the monistic tendencies in his worldview theory, but when others turned exclusively to antithesis, Scripture became the sole principle at the expense of other important principles. Scripture is certainly central, but not at the expense of the doctrines of creation, general revelation (in terms of common notions), and humankind (in terms of the *imago Dei*). Historically, the Reformed Orthodox argue that each *scientia* has its own distinct *principia*. Hence, natural philosophy has nature and reason as its distinct *principia*, whereas theology has Scripture and faith as its *principia*.

156. So Frame, "Reply to Richard Muller," 311–15; cf. criticism of Frame in Muller, "Historiography," 301–6.

157. Heslam, *Creating a Christian Worldview*, 240.

158. For critique and bibliography, see Richard A. Muller, *After Calvin: Studies in the Development of a Theological Tradition* (Oxford: Oxford University Press, 2003), 63–65, 94–98.

159. Kuyper, *Lectures on Calvinism*, 15, 19, 22; cf. Heslam, *Creating a Christian Worldview*, 93.

To claim that we must deduce all knowledge from one *principium* confuses general and special revelation.[160]

Conclusion

The problem with HWT is that it was forged on the anvil of human autonomous thinking: it was born under the dark star of Enlightenment rationalism, a mind-set committed to eradicating the concept of common human knowledge. We must reject HWT, not because of its origins, questionable as those are, but because of its claims to offer an exhaustive explanation of reality. We cannot reject common notions without denying key elements of the doctrines of humankind, creation, and revelation. With this shared knowledge, we can confidently carry on true, meaningful, and genuine dialogue with non-Christians and can even learn from them. Such dialogues mean not that we have capitulated to human autonomy but rather that we bear the same image and have the same Creator.

We can learn from the non-Christian about many things in the world because God has given humanity many tremendous gifts and insights. Calvin once explained that these were gifts of the Spirit liberally dispensed to humanity.[161] Calvin's lengthy observation is worth quoting in full:

> Shall we deny the light of truth to the ancient lawyers, who have delivered such just principles of civil order and polity? Shall we say that the philosophers were blind in their exquisite contemplation and in their scientific description of nature? Shall we say that those, who by the art of logic have taught us to speak in a manner consistent with reason, were destitute of understanding themselves? Shall we accuse those of insanity, who by the study of medicine have been exercising their industry for our advantage? What shall we say of all the mathematics? Shall we esteem them the delirious ravings of madmen? On the contrary, we shall not be able even to read the writings of the ancients on these subjects without great admiration; we shall admire them, because we shall be constrained to acknowledge them to be truly excellent. And shall we esteem any thing laudable or excellent, which we do not recognize as proceeding from God? Let us, then, be ashamed of such great ingratitude, which was not to be charged on the heathen poets, who confessed that philosophy, and legislation, and useful arts, were the inventions of their gods. Therefore,

160. See, e.g., Lucas Trelcatius, *A Brief Institution of the Common Places of Sacred Divinity* (London: Francis Burton, 1610), 1.1, p. 9; cf. Muller, *Post-Reformation Reformed Dogmatics*, 1:431–37.

161. John Calvin, *Institutes of the Christian Religion*, trans. John Allen (Grand Rapids: Eerdmans, 1948), 2.2.16.

since it appears that those whom the Scripture styles "natural men," [*psychi-kous*], have discovered such acuteness and perspicacity in the investigation of sublunary things, let us learn from such examples, how many good qualities the Lord has left to the nature of man, since it has been despoiled of what is truly good.[162]

We can stand in awe of the learning and acumen of unbelievers and work alongside them in many endeavors. Because of our mutually shared image of God, even in a fallen world, we can learn much from non-Christians. The Southern author Flannery O'Connor once observed that all literature is Christian literature because, like it or not, all authors write about this world, the world that God has created. Hence, at some level, intentionally or unintentionally, they write about themes inherent in fallen human existence and therefore ultimately write about revelational themes, whether general or special revelation.[163] Once again, when unbelievers write on such themes, they reflect on the true but at times distorted knowledge they glean from general revelation.

Historic worldview theory is also problematic because when German philosophers created it, they breathed the life of Enlightenment confidence into its nostrils. They believed that nothing was beyond humanity's reach, and hence a worldview offered an exhaustive explanation of reality. Christians have uncritically drunk from this well of confidence and to a certain extent have become inebriated with its spirit of certainty. Saying with Van Til that only Christians truly know and that the Bible is our only foundation for all knowledge places us on an unnecessary collision course with the world on *every* point and presses the Bible into service of tasks for which it was never intended. If we force the Bible to tell us more than what we are to believe concerning God and our duty to him, we undoubtedly add to it and denigrate God's good book of nature, regardless of our noble intentions.

Instead of advocating an exhaustive Christian view of life and the world, we must recognize that God has created the world as a wonderfully diverse place and given human beings many gifts of knowledge and insight. There may be many different ways to do things and no specifically Christian ways. Such diversity is not a capitulation to autonomy but instead echoes the depths of God's wisdom. No one person or ethnicity can exhaustively reflect God's infinite being. Moreover, by this shared knowledge we can communicate with unbelievers and even point out commonly held truths, but we will always do

162. Calvin, *Institutes*, 2.2.15.

163. Rosemary M. Magee, ed., *Conversations with Flannery O'Connor* (Jackson: University Press of Mississippi, 1987), 15; see also Flannery O'Connor, *Mystery and Manners: Occasional Prose* (New York: Farrar, Straus, & Giroux, 1970), 154–209.

so aware of the fact that unbelievers will undoubtedly suppress the truth in unrighteousness. This effort to hide behind a few intellectual fig leaves means that we must always be prepared to challenge the so-called wisdom of the world. With Paul, we can proclaim that we know who the unknown God is, and by the power of the Spirit, we can pray that God will remove the scales from unbelieving eyes and replace hearts of stone with hearts of flesh so that non-Christians may seek shelter in Christ (1 Cor. 2:14–16).

6

TRANSCENDENTAL ARGUMENTS

Neither shall I waste time at this stage by discussing in what sense it is permissible to speak of "proof" of so transcendent a reality as the Divine existence. We remember there the saying of [Friedrich Heinrich] Jacobi, that a God capable of proof would be no God at all.

James Orr

There is no reason to assume, as Van Til does, that anyone who uses an argument from design or causality is presupposing a nontheistic epistemology.

John Frame

Whether we like it or not, criticism can touch the essence of our religion, because religion has become incarnate, and for our sakes had to become incarnate and make itself vulnerable in historic form. As the Son of God while on the earth had to expose Himself to the unbelief and scorn of men, so the word of the Gospel could not be what it is for us unless it were subject to the same humiliation.

Geerhardus Vos

According to early modern Reformed theology, two of the chief components of the book of nature are the innate and acquired natural knowledge of God. The innate knowledge of God, common notions, is but one part of a greater whole. Francis Turretin (1623–87) explains this connection: "The orthodox, on the contrary, uniformly teach that there is a natural theology, partly innate (derived from the book of conscience by means of common notions [*koinas ennoias*]) and partly acquired (drawn from the book of creatures discursively)."[1] Turretin believed that the divinely implanted common notions corresponded to and functioned in concert with the created order. Common notions and the created order were connected, and thus these innate ideas pointed back to the existence of the Creator, which could be confirmed by the testimony from creation. People can trace the effects back to the cause.[2] Turretin believed his opinions on these matters were uniformly taught among the orthodox, but the same cannot be said about the book of nature in the post-Enlightenment context with the rise of the transcendental argument for the existence of God (TAG).

Greg Bahnsen (1948–95) believed that Cornelius Van Til brought a Copernican revolution to apologetics because he introduced the TAG as the chief apologetic means of argumentation.[3] Rather than beginning from below and arguing from effects back to the cause, Van Til believed that one had to begin from above and argue from the cause to the effects. Only by seeking to explain all reality in the light of the self-attesting Christ of Scripture could one present the best argument for the existence of God.[4] Therefore, instead of seeking to prove the existence of God, apologists are supposed to presuppose God's existence and argue from this presupposition. Van Til compared his TAG with the so-called traditional apologetic method, which argued in block-like manner, seeking to build one argument upon the other until the apologist completed the efforts to prove the existence of God. In his famous illustration, Van Til likened the traditional method to small-arms fire and his own TAG to a nuclear bomb: only the latter could effectively rout autonomous arguments against the claims of Christianity.[5] The TAG, therefore, is a superior and inherently more biblical form of apologetic methodology, according to Van Til and his disciples.[6]

1. Francis Turretin, *Institutes of Elenctic Theology*, ed. James T. Dennison Jr., trans. George Musgrave Giger, 3 vols. (Phillipsburg, NJ: P&R, 1992–97), 1.3.4.

2. David Sytsma, "The Use of Reason in Francis Turretin's Arguments for God's Existence," *Stromata* 47 (2006): 25.

3. Greg Bahnsen, *Van Til's Apologetic: Readings and Analysis* (Phillipsburg, NJ: P&R, 1998), 515.

4. See, e.g., Cornelius Van Til, "My Credo," and "Response to Herman Dooyeweerd," in *Jerusalem and Athens: Critical Discussions on the Theology and Apologetics of Cornelius Van Til*, ed. E. R. Geehan ([Nutley, NJ]: P&R, 1971), 3, 98; Van Til, *The Reformed Pastor and Modern Thought* (Phillipsburg, NJ: P&R, 1980), 76, 98, 196; Van Til, *The Protestant Doctrine of Scripture*, In Defense of Biblical Christianity 1 ([Philadelphia]: Den Dulk Christian Foundation, 1967), 12, 16.

5. Cornelius Van Til, *Christian Apologetics* (Phillipsburg, NJ: P&R, 1976), 61–65, 72–78; Van Til, *Defense of the Faith*, 3rd ed. (Phillipsburg, NJ: P&R, 1967), 114–22.

6. "The Recommended Curriculum for Ministerial Preparation in the Orthodox Presbyterian Church," in *The Book of Church Order of the Orthodox Presbyterian Church* (Willow Grove, PA: Committee on Christian Education of the Orthodox Presbyterian Church, 2015), 216.

This chapter argues that the TAG is a useful tool within the apologist's toolbox but is neither a silver-bullet argument nor the most biblically pure form of Reformed apologetics. This particular point has been raised among Van Til's disciples. John Frame has noted that Van Til's TAG gives the impression that "all the arduous labors of past apologists, proving this or that, can now be bypassed. Now, it seems, we only have to prove one thing, that universal intelligibility presupposes God." Van Til "had found a 'magic bullet,' a simple, straightforward argument that would destroy all unbelief in one fell swoop."[7] The degree to which apologists employ the TAG apart from the use of the book of nature is inversely proportional to the degree to which they depart from the historic Reformed faith. Van Til did not believe that evidence was unnecessary; he even maintained that, properly framed, one could employ the traditional proofs for the existence of God.[8] But some Van Tillians have not always acknowledged Van Til's positive use of evidence and have thus contributed to the diminished use of the book of nature within the contemporary Reformed community.

This chapter's thesis, therefore, is that the TAG can be a useful argument but not at the expense of the book of nature. Christians can employ the connection between the innate and acquired natural knowledge of God in the defense of the faith. In order to demonstrate the thesis regarding the necessity of appealing to the book of nature and the acquired natural knowledge of God, this chapter first explores the origins of the TAG, an argument originating with Immanuel Kant (1724–1804) and his idealist philosophy. This section reveals the connections between Kantian idealism, historic worldview theory (HWT), and how James Orr (1868–1940) employed these categories in his apologetics but with a significantly diminished use of evidence. Orr leaned away from the book of nature, and other apologists who employed his transcendental method outright rejected the appeal to evidence. Van Til allowed the use of evidence in his apologetics, but with the perception of the invincibility of the TAG, some Van Tillians erroneously assume that evidence is no longer needed. Second, the chapter briefly examines Van Til's use of the TAG to identify its idealist elements. As critical as Van Til was of Kant, this does not mean he completely rejected all things Kantian.

Third, the chapter deals with three issues, namely, whether (1) Van Til engages in synthetic thinking; (2) some overemphasize the coherence theory of truth at the expense of the correspondence theory; and (3) the TAG is wedded to

7. John Frame, *Cornelius Van Til: An Analysis of His Thought* (Phillipsburg, NJ: P&R, 1995), 316–17.

8. See, e.g., Cornelius Van Til, *Defense of the Faith*, 197; Van Til, *Introduction to Systematic Theology* (Phillipsburg, NJ: P&R, 1974), 104–5, 199.

outdated philosophical trends. Van Til accused Thomas Aquinas (1225–74) of employing synthetic thinking, combining pagan and Christian thought in order to defend the faith. But although Van Til rejected Aquinas's methodology, in truth his own TAG is similar. Both Aquinas and Van Til employed the dominant philosophies of their day in order to build an intellectual bridge to unbelievers; Aquinas and Van Til spoke with Aristotelian and Kantian accents, respectively.

The other two issues pertain to the TAG's emphasis on the coherence theory of truth. It is important for truth to present a coherent picture of reality, and the correspondence theory helps Christians understand the nature of truth. We determine the veracity or falsity of a statement based on the degree to which it corresponds to the world around us. Do our statements accurately describe the phenomena around us? In theological terms, does our understanding of reality correspond to God's understanding and the world he created? In apologetic terms, do our claims about the God of the Bible correspond to the world? Do the books of nature and Scripture speak with one voice in our defense of the gospel? In defending the gospel, apologists ought not to be inflexibly wedded to one philosophical trend, in this case, Kantian idealism.

The chapter concludes with some observations about employing the connections between the innate and acquired natural knowledge of God and the importance of the book of nature and evidence in apologetics.

Origins of Transcendental Arguments

Transcendental arguments originate with Immanuel Kant. Van Tillians and others such as John Frame, Greg Bahnsen, Don Collett, and Timothy Mc-Connel recognize this fact.[9] But given that some characterize the TAG as the most consistently biblical apologetic argument, it will prove beneficial to trace its Kantian origins. Tracing its origins will assist in assessing the continuities and discontinuities between Kant's and Van Til's versions of the TAG. It will also facilitate the critical analysis that follows below.

Kant developed the transcendental argument to refute Cartesian skepticism, which maintained that objects outside of us are doubtful and indemonstrable.[10]

9. John Frame, "Transcendental Arguments," in *New Dictionary of Christian Apologetics*, ed. W. C. Campbell-Jack and Gavin J. McGrath (Downers Grove, IL: InterVarsity, 2006), 716; Bahnsen, *Van Til's Apologetic*, 497; Don Collett, "Van Til and Transcendental Argument," *Westminster Theological Journal* 65 (2003): 295–96; Timothy McConnel, "The Influence of Idealism on the Apologetics of Cornelius Van Til," *Journal of the Evangelical Theological Society* 48, no. 3 (2005): 558–62.

10. Immanuel Kant, *Critique of Pure Reason*, trans. Paul Guyer and Allen Wood (Cambridge: Cambridge University Press, 1997), B274.

In response to Descartes, Kant begins with the skeptic's presupposition: we have mental experiences that have a temporal order. These experiences would not be possible unless we had a genuine experience of things outside us, which means that we can possess knowledge of the outside world. The argument may be summarized as follows:[11]

1. You are aware of your mental states as having a temporal order: the sensation of pain temporally follows the sensation of pleasure.

2. To perceive temporal order, you must be aware of the transition from pleasure to pain.

3. To have the possibility of an awareness of permanence, you cannot have awareness of yourself because no permanent self is revealed to your inner sense.

4. The permanence of which you are aware must be something other than yourself, which means that there is something outside of you in the external world.

5. Hence, you are aware of the external world because your subjective impressions are not possible without the external world. Thus your awareness of the external world arises from a genuine external objective world.

Stated in simpler terms, transcendental arguments make a specific claim, namely, that X is necessary for Y to exist. If Y exists, then it logically follows that X must also be true.[12] In other words, a transcendental argument argues by way of presupposition.

Historic worldview theory goes hand in hand with the TAG. James Orr embraced HWT in his defense of Christianity because he believed it was necessary to set forth Christianity as an entire system of thought rather than defend the faith in piecemeal fashion.[13] Robert Knudsen (1924–2000), professor of apologetics at Westminster Theological Seminary and colleague of Van Til, described Orr's approach as transcendental. Knudsen commented that one had to begin with the true starting point, namely, Christ.[14] Orr demonstrated

11. Robert Stern, "Transcendental Arguments," *Stanford Encyclopedia of Philosophy*, ed. Edward N. Zalta, Summer 2013 ed. (last revised February 25, 2011), §1, http://plato.stanford.edu/archives/sum2013/entries/transcendental-arguments/; see also Kant, *Critique of Pure Reason*, B275–79.

12. Stern, "Transcendental Arguments," §1.

13. E.g., James Orr, *The Christian View of God and the World: As Centering in the Incarnation* (Grand Rapids: Eerdmans, 1947), 13.

14. Robert D. Knudsen, "The Transcendental Perspective of Westminster's Apologetic," *Westminster Theological Journal* 48 (1986): 223–39.

this principle by rejecting the form of argumentation that lies behind the traditional proofs for the existence of God: "Proof in Theism certainly does not consist in deducing God's existence as a lower from a higher; but rather in showing that God's existence is itself the last postulate of reason—the ultimate basis on which all other knowledge, all other belief rests."[15] Orr even decries speaking of proving God's existence: "Neither shall I waste time at this stage by discussing in what sense it is permissible to speak of 'proof' of so transcendent a reality as the Divine existence. We remember there the saying of [Friedrich Heinrich] Jacobi, that a God capable of proof would be no God at all."[16]

Those who adopted transcendental arguments took Orr's statements as warrant to reject the use of evidence in apologetics. The Reformed philosopher and theologian Gordon Clark's (1902–85) biographer notes, "Clark took from Orr all three of these elements: a rejection of the proofs for God's existence, the necessity of an internally consistent worldview, and the ultimate distinctiveness of the Christian worldview."[17] Even though Van Til acknowledges the legitimacy of evidence, at points he nevertheless sounds very much like Orr, as when he writes the following:

> Of course Reformed believers do not seek to prove the existence of their God. To seek to prove or to disprove the existence of this God would be to seek to deny him. To seek to prove or disprove this God presupposes that man can identify himself and discover facts in relation to laws in the universe without reference to God. A God whose existence is "proved" is not the God of Scripture.[18]

Statements like these from Orr and Van Til have led some to argue that the use of the TAG precludes the use of evidence. Some critics have consequently concluded that Van Til was against the use of evidence.[19] Frame notes that this, in part, was Van Til's fault because "he did not give his students much instruction in the actual, detailed evidences of Christianity" and was more interested in large-scale philosophical issues rather than a detailed defense of the Bible.[20] To remedy this perceived weakness and lack of clarity, Thom

15. Orr, *Christian View of God*, 94.

16. Orr, *Christian View of God*, 94.

17. Douglas J. Douma, *The Presbyterian Philosopher: The Authorized Biography of Gordon H. Clark* (Eugene, OR: Wipf & Stock, 2017), 66.

18. Van Til, *Protestant Doctrine of Scripture*, 137.

19. See, e.g., C. Stephen Evans, *Faith beyond Reason: A Kierkegaardian Account* (Grand Rapids: Eerdmans, 1998), 19; Clark Pinnock, "The Philosophy of Christian Evidences," in *Jerusalem and Athens: Critical Discussions on the Theology and Apologetics of Cornelius Van Til*, ed. E. R. Geehan ([Nutley, NJ]: P&R, 1971), 421.

20. Frame, *Cornelius Van Til*, 182, 184.

Notaro published an entire book dedicated to proving that Van Til was willing to use evidence.[21] Nevertheless, the point still stands: there is a tendency to discount or diminish the use of evidence among some of those who employ the TAG. At this point some formulations of the TAG, therefore, are an obstacle to the recovery of the use of the book of nature in apologetics. This chapter explores some of these formulations in greater detail below. But the question of how Van Til specifically used the TAG is relevant and therefore requires exploration.

Van Til's Transcendental Argument

Early in Van Til's education, he grappled with idealism. He titled his doctoral dissertation "God and the Absolute," in which he argued that the God of Christian theism could not be identified with the Absolute of idealism.[22] Throughout his career, Van Til employed the language and terminology of idealism, though he redefined it and filled it with Christian content. In fact, early on, Van Til received significant criticism for employing idealist terminology in his apologetic works. In his over-the-top review of Van Til's work *Common Grace*, J. Oliver Buswell (1895–1977) accused Van Til of being "deeply mired in Hegelian idealistic pantheism."[23]

Despite the terminological similarities, Van Til never intended to repristinate idealism. Rather, he offered trenchant criticism.[24] He believed that Christianity and idealism had a number of formal similarities that allowed him to borrow elements from idealism to argue for the legitimacy of Christian theism.[25] The only way to argue for the existence of an absolute God was to do so by means of a transcendental rather than logical argument. He argued from the impossibility of the contrary.[26] In other words, only by presuppos-

21. Thom Notaro, *Van Til and the Use of Evidence* (Phillipsburg, NJ: P&R, 1980).

22. McConnel, "Influence of Idealism," 557. Van Til eventually published the core of his dissertation as a journal article: Cornelius Van Til, "God and the Absolute," *Evangelical Quarterly* 2, no. 4 (1930): 358–88. He later revised and expanded his dissertation, which he called, "The Metaphysics of Apologetics." This work was ultimately retitled and published as Cornelius Van Til, *A Survey of Christian Epistemology*, In Defense of Biblical Christianity 2 (Phillipsburg, NJ: P&R, 1969).

23. J. Oliver Buswell, "The Fountainhead of Presuppositionalism," *The Bible Today* 42, no. 2 (1948): 48; McConnel, "Influence of Idealism," 558.

24. See, e.g., Cornelius Van Til, *Immanuel Kant and Protestantism* (Philadelphia: Westminster Theological Seminary, [1960]); Van Til, *Christianity and Idealism* (Philadelphia: P&R, 1955).

25. McConnel, "Influence of Idealism," 565–66.

26. McConnel, "Influence of Idealism," 566.

ing the existence of God could a person explain the coherence of the world around him. Later in his apologetic writings, Van Til explains:

> The best and only possible proof for the existence of such a God is that his existence is required for the uniformity of nature and for the coherence of all things in the world. We cannot *prove* the existence of beams underneath a floor if by proof we mean that they must be ascertainable in the way that we can see the chairs and tables of the room. But the very idea of a floor as the support of tables and chairs requires the idea of beams that are underneath. But there would be no floor if no beams were underneath. Thus there is absolutely certain proof of the existence of God and the truth of Christian theism. Even non-Christians presuppose its truth while they verbally reject it. They need to presuppose the truth of Christian theism in order to account for their accomplishments.[27]

The similarities between Kant and Van Til stand out. Kant begins with the assumption, or presupposition, of the validity of human knowledge and then proceeds to employ reason to demonstrate the truthfulness of what those presuppositions imply. Van Til begins with the presupposition of theism and then seeks to demonstrate the implications of the truthfulness of that presupposition.[28] Yet we should notice that Van Til's argument is a subjective version of Aquinas's second and fifth arguments for the existence of God (from efficient causality and from the order and governance of the world).[29] In other words, Van Til argues from the effect (the chairs and table) back to the cause (the beams in the floor). But apart from objective referents, it represents only one person's sense of a need for coherence rather than an objective necessity.[30]

There are two additional similarities between Kant and Van Til. First, both focus on the issue of epistemology, the theory of how humans account for knowledge. Second, both employ a transcendental argument to account for their epistemology.[31] Of course, the primary difference between Kant and Van Til is that Kant's starting point is autonomous reason and Van Til's is the ontological Trinity.[32] Kant begins with man, and Van Til begins with God. Given their different starting points, they naturally arrive at different conclusions even though they employ the same type of transcendental argument.

27. Van Til, *Defense of the Faith*, 103.
28. McConnel, "Influence of Idealism," 568.
29. Cf. Thomas Aquinas, *Summa Theologica* (repr., Allen, TX: Christian Classics, 1948), Ia q. 2 art. 1.
30. I am grateful to Richard Muller for making this point to me in private correspondence.
31. McConnel, "Influence of Idealism," 577.
32. Van Til, *Christian Apologetics*, 13.

Analysis

In the following analysis, I address three questions related to the TAG: (1) Does Van Til engage in synthetic thinking because he employs the idealist TAG? (2) What is the importance and what is the necessity of acknowledging the correspondence theory of truth? (3) If apologists rigidly and inflexibly employ the TAG to the exclusion of other arguments, do they unnecessarily wed their apologetics to passing philosophical trends?

Synthesis Thinking?

Has Van Til violated his principles by engaging in synthesis thinking? According to Van Til, Aquinas was guilty of synthesis thinking because he based his theology on the non-Christian thought of Aristotle (384–322 BC). In fact, Van Til made the sweeping statement that all pre-Reformation medieval theology was synthetic thinking. Synthetic theology "was an edifice composed of two 'stories,' the first being that of the natural theology of the Greeks, and the second being the 'supernatural' theology of the Bible."[33] Van Til echoed the criticisms of Herman Dooyeweerd (1894–1977), who argued that philosophy and theology needed to seek a pure starting point.[34] Van Til writes:

> Rome's semi-Aristotelian epistemology influences, and accords with, its semi-Aristotelian ethics. Rome's notion of the common area of Reason between believers and non-believers controls its conception of the common cardinal virtues. So also what Kuyper and Bavinck think of the reprobate's knowledge of God will influence what they think of the reprobate's deeds before God. We shall seek to intimate, be it all too briefly, that in the epistemology of Kuyper, Bavinck, and Hepp there are remnants of an abstract way of thinking that we shall need to guard against in our common grace discussion.[35]

Van Til leveled the accusation of synthetic thinking against Aquinas and the Roman Catholic Church, and he also charged Abraham Kuyper (1837–1920), Herman Bavinck (1854–1921), and Valentine Hepp (1879–1950) with the same

33. Cornelius Van Til, *The New Synthesis Theology in the Netherlands* (Phillipsburg, NJ: P&R, 1975), 2.

34. Herman Dooyeweerd, *Transcendental Problems of Philosophic Thought: An Inquiry into the Transcendental Conditions of Philosophy* (Grand Rapids: Eerdmans, 1948), 59–77; see also Laurence O'Donnell, "Kees Van Til als Nederlandse-Amerikaanse, Neo-Calvinistisch-Presbyteriaan apologeticus: An Analysis of Cornelius Van Til's Presupposition of Reformed Dogmatics with Special Reference to Herman Bavinck's *Gereformeerde Dogmatiek*" (master's thesis, Calvin Theological Seminary, 2011), 102–3.

35. Cornelius Van Til, *Common Grace and the Gospel* (Phillipsburg, NJ: P&R, 1972), 34.

error. The implication here is that in all of church history, Van Til was one of the few theologians, Reformed or not, to begin with a pure starting point and present an uncompromised epistemology, which is reflected in his use of the TAG. Does Van Til's TAG truly represent a pure starting point? Is his claim correct regarding Aquinas, Kuyper, and Bavinck? Are they guilty of synthetic thinking?

There are two distinct issues here: whether Van Til is guilty of synthetic thinking and whether others such as Aquinas, Kuyper, and Bavinck are guilty of the same. Given the focus of this chapter, we will consider only the question of Van Til and synthetic thinking. There are clear connections between Van Til and idealism; he consciously drew on the arguments and terminology of this philosophical school of thought. Regarding vocabulary, for example, Van Til regularly employed the terms *concrete universal*, *limiting concept*, and God as the *Absolute*.[36] These terms originate in the idealist philosophy of Hegel and Kant, not the Scriptures. To be clear, Van Til did not employ these terms in a Kantian manner; he sought to fill them with Christian content.

According to G. W. F. Hegel (1770–1831), a concrete universal is distinct from an abstract universal. Abstract universals are ideas abstracted from observation. I see a table and therefore deduce that there is an abstract universal concept of the idea of table. Hegel objected to abstract universals and instead argued that universals had to be concrete; universals must posit an external reality.[37] Van Til argued, "God is our concrete universal."[38] Van Til's concrete universal is not a philosophical context; the Triune God is our philosophical context.

In *Critique of Pure Reason*, Kant employed the idea of a limiting concept, which guarded the distinction between the phenomenal and noumenal realms. We can know only phenomena; we cannot know what lies in the noumenal realm. This, in his mind, is a limiting concept.[39] Van Til embraced the notion of a limiting concept but defined it differently than Kant: "If we hold to a theology of the apparently paradoxical we must also hold, by consequence, to the Christian notion of a *limiting concept*." In Van Til's mind, Kant developed a non-Christian notion of a limiting concept, which rested on a non-Christian concept of mystery: "The non-Christian notion of the limiting concept is the

36. Van Til, *Common Grace*, vi, 26–27, 64; Van Til, *Defense of the Faith*, 23, 211; Van Til, "Response of Van Til to Knudsen," in *Jerusalem and Athens*, ed. Geehan, 302; Van Til, introduction to *The Inspiration and Authority of the Bible*, by Benjamin B. Warfield (Phillipsburg, NJ: P&R, 1948), 30, 31, 40; cf. McConnel, "Influence of Idealism," 579–81.

37. Charles Taylor, *Hegel* (Cambridge: Cambridge University Press, 1975), 112–14.

38. Van Til, *Common Grace*, 84.

39. Henry E. Allison, *Kant's Transcendental Idealism: An Interpretation and Defense* (New Haven: Yale University Press, 2004), 58–59; see also Kant, *Critique of Pure Reason*, B311.

product of would-be-autonomous man who seeks to legislate for all reality, but bows before the irrational as that which he has not yet rationalized." By contrast, "the Christian notion of the limiting concept is the product of the creature who seeks to set forth in systematic form something of the revelation of the Creator."[40] Autonomous reason underlies Kant's limiting concept, and revelation serves this role for Van Til.

In *Critique of Pure Reason*, Kant identifies the *absolute* with transcendental reality.[41] By contrast, Van Til identifies the absolute with God: "We must here truly face the Absolute. We must think His thoughts after Him. We must think analogically, rather than univocally."[42]

Hence, Van Til employs these idealist terms: concrete universal, limiting concept, and absolute. As noted above, Van Til received significant criticism for using these terms; critics believed that Van Til embraced idealist philosophy. Van Til responded to these criticisms by showing that his use of these terms was markedly different from their idealist counterparts.[43] The brief survey above clearly demonstrates that Van Til redefined these idealist terms. But why did he employ them? Van Til gives two reasons for his use of idealist terminology. First, Van Til believed that Christianity and idealism were cordially similar: "We have already noticed that formally there is much similarity between Theism and idealism."[44] Again, Van Til writes: "Throughout we have maintained that formally idealism and Theism are in cordial agreement."[45] Given the similarity and cordial agreement at the formal level, he believed he could employ idealist terminology, albeit redefined.[46]

Second, Van Til employed idealist terminology so he could build a bridge between Christianity and idealist philosophers:

After we answer, in preliminary fashion, the question as to *what* we believe as Reformed Christians, we face the problem how to get people interested

40. Van Til, *Common Grace*, 11.

41. Allison, *Kant's Transcendental Idealism*, 453n3; Kant, *Critique of Pure Reason*, B53.

42. Van Til, *Common Grace*, 28.

43. McConnel, "Influence of Idealism," 582.

44. Cornelius Van Til, "God and the Absolute" (PhD diss., Princeton University, 1927), 18, as cited in McConnel, "Influence of Idealism," 568.

45. Van Til, "God and the Absolute," 32–33, as quoted in McConnel, "Influence of Idealism," 569n47.

46. More work needs to be done to compare Van Til with nineteenth-century idealists such as Josiah Royce (1855–1916). One of Van Til's professors at Calvin College, W. Harry Jellema (1893–1932), studied under Royce while at Harvard University. Timothy I. McConnel, "The Historical Origins of the Presuppositional Apologetics of Cornelius Van Til" (PhD diss., Marquette University, 1999), 13, 110; cf. Josiah Royce, *Lectures on Modern Idealism* (New Haven: Yale University Press, 1919).

in our faith. Men in general do not use or even know our theological terms. But, to the extent that they are educated, they have had some training in secular philosophy. They have a non-Christian familiarity with the categories of God, man and the universe. If we are to speak to them and win them, it is necessary to learn their language. There is no possibility of avoiding this. We can make no contact with men unless we speak to them in their language.[47]

This seems like a commonsense approach: employ terms that idealist philosophers understand but correlate them with Christian theological content. When an idealist refers to the Absolute, you can tell him that the Absolute is the Triune God of the Scriptures.

In another sense, Van Til's reasons for using idealist nomenclature present inconsistencies for his apologetic methodology. Van Til repeatedly emphasizes that the Christian and non-Christian worldviews are in antithesis at every point. Van Til writes: "If the non-believer works according to the principles of the new man within him and the Christian works according to the principles of the new man within him then there is no interpretive content of any sort on which they can agree."[48] Yet in his interaction with idealism Van Til says, "We face the problem how to get people interested in our faith." His proposed solution is to speak to idealist philosophers in their terms, though he redefined them. Again, he clearly states: "We can make no contact with men unless we speak to them in their language."[49] Van Til seeks to build a bridge to idealist philosophers, not by means of appealing to their status as covenant breakers, but in terms of the cordial similarities between Christianity and idealism. He seeks to establish a point of contact through the similarities between Christianity and idealism and their own philosophical language. God is the absolute and concrete universal. Van Til seems to violate his stated principle regarding the necessary head-on collision. Van Til, of course, would likely claim that the head-on collision comes through his redefinition of the terms. But the question still stands: Why use the same terminology if there is no shared conception between the absolute or concrete universal and the God of Scripture? The concepts must be similar enough; otherwise there would be no point in employing the terms in the first place.

47. Van Til, *Defense of the Faith*, 23.
48. Van Til, "Introduction," 36, also 24. See also Van Til, *Christian Apologetics*, 38–58, 61; Van Til, *Introduction to Systematic Theology*, 26, 28, 29; Van Til, *Defense of the Faith*, 169, 212; Van Til, *Common Grace and the Gospel*, 151; Van Til, *Doctrine of Scripture*, 130; Van Til, *Essays on Christian Education* (Phillipsburg, NJ: P&R, 1979), 83, 187, 192–93.
49. Van Til, *Defense of the Faith*, 23.

Van Til would undoubtedly say that the similarities between Christianity and idealism are *formal*.[50] What, exactly, is formal agreement? In Frame's explanation of Van Til's use of the concept, formal agreement is when two people use the same words but with different meanings.[51] For example, when a person refers to Washington and intends the state but his friend thinks of the District of Columbia, there is a formal agreement between the two people: they use the same terms but with different meanings.[52] Yet, can we truly divorce formal from substantive agreement in a complete fashion? In the case of the formal agreement between the two uses of *Washington*, yes, one is a district and the other a state, but both are places where people live, both are in the United States, both have houses, cars, streets, public transportation, and the like. There is more than formal agreement: we are not merely dealing with a homonym. Van Til himself makes this very point. Van Til warns against the very thing he does when he adopts redefined idealist terminology.

In his defense of Christian education, he cautions against trying to use non-Christian methods to convey Christian information:

> We cannot afford to say that if only we place a different content before our pupils we need not worry about the form because the form is a neutral something. If a glass has contained carbolic acid you do not merely pour it out in order then to give your child a drink of water. How much more impossible will it be to take a spiritual content and pour it out of its form in order to use the latter for the pouring out of a definite Christian-theistic content? The connection between form and matter is too much like that of skin and flesh to allow for the easy removal of the one without taking something of the other for us not to be on our guard with respect to the educational methods of our opponents. We can never, strictly speaking, use their methods. We can use methods that appear similar to theirs, but never can we use methods that are the same as theirs.[53]

Given Van Til's warning, how successfully can one employ the terminology of idealism when form and content are so closely linked? To use the phrase of media ecologist Marshall McLuhan, the medium is the message.[54] If, as Van Til argues, form integrally relates to matter, then formal agreement involves more than the use of the same terms: it also includes some element of material

---

50. For more citations regarding the claim of *formal* agreement, see Frame, *Cornelius Van Til*, 195.

51. Frame, *Cornelius Van Til*, 195.

52. John Frame, "Cornelius Van Til," in *John Frame's Selected Shorter Writings* (Phillipsburg, NJ: P&R, 2015), 218.

53. Cornelius Van Til, *Essays on Christian Education* (Phillipsburg, NJ: P&R, 1979), 197.

54. Marshall McLuhan, *Understanding Media: The Extensions of Man*, ed. W. Terrence Gordon, critical ed. (1964; repr., Corte Madera, CA: Gingko, 1994), 17–36.

agreement. This means that worldviews overlap at certain points and cannot be entirely incommensurable.

This raises another inconsistency in Van Til's methodology. How does Van Til's method differ from Aquinas's? Aquinas famously employed Aristotelian terms and arguments for reasons very similar to Van Til's, though obviously in a different historical-theological context. Van Til sought to build a bridge to idealist philosophy, whereas Aquinas sought to establish dialogue with Muslim Aristotelians. Regarding Muslims, Aquinas writes, "The Mohammedans and the pagans, do not agree with us in accepting the authority of any Scripture, by which they may be convinced of their error. . . . We must, therefore, have recourse to the natural reason, to which all men are forced to give their assent. However, it is true, in divine matters the natural reason has its failings."[55] Aquinas, therefore, engaged Muslims in terms of their philosophical beliefs since they did not accept the authority of the Scriptures. He employed natural reason in his apologetics, though he acknowledged its shortcomings: "Now, while we are investigating some given truth, we shall also show what errors are set aside it; and we shall likewise show how the truth that we come to know by demonstration is in accord with the Christian religion."[56]

Broadly considered, Van Til and Aquinas employed a similar apologetic methodology. Both spoke to the philosophical trends of their day from the platform of the authority of Scripture: Aquinas spoke in an Aristotelian dialect and Van Til in an idealist one. Aquinas argued for the existence of God in terms of Aristotelian categories of causality, and Van Til in terms of Kantian transcendental argumentation. Scott Oliphint describes Van Til's methodology in the following manner:

> Van Til took that which was formally true in idealism (due to common grace) and transplanted it into the Reformed Christian faith and there he nurtured and watered it to fruition because only in Christian "soil" could these formally true ideas have their proper growing place. When he uses arguments, terms, and methods of idealism, therefore, we must see them as surgically removed and then transplanted into the light of scriptural truth.[57]

Van Til's idealism and Aquinas's Aristotelianism are extrascriptural and originate in natural, not special, revelation, though both rest on the authority of

55. Thomas Aquinas, *Summa contra Gentiles*, trans. Anton C. Pegis, 5 vols. (Notre Dame, IN: University of Notre Dame Press, 1955), 1.2.3, p. 1:62.

56. Aquinas, *SCG*, 1.2.4, 1:62–63.

57. K. Scott Oliphint, "The Consistency of Van Til's Methodology," *Westminster Theological Journal* 52 (1990): 34.

Scripture.[58] This is not to say that their respective methodologies are perfectly consonant. Nevertheless, others have also noted this consonance between Van Til and Aquinas.[59]

Van Til, for example, maintains the sole authority of Scripture, whereas Aquinas assumes in addition the authority of the church. Van Til employs the TAG as an idealist argument, which is distinct from Aquinas's realist epistemology, which undergirds his five proofs for the existence of God. Aquinas does assume the authority of the church, but he also argues that Scripture alone provides the necessary truths for theological knowledge. This stands in contrast to theological authorities who provide probabilities and philosophers who offer opinions. Van Til and Aquinas have their differences, but the broad outlines of their methodologies are similar. These facts cast doubt on Van Til's claims regarding the biblical purity of his own methodology as it pertains to the TAG and its idealist roots. By being the first to employ idealist transcendental argumentation for the purpose of Reformed apologetics, Van Til's approach was unique, but he was not the first to use philosophical categories to defend the Christian faith. Aquinas took the formal agreement between Aristotelian concepts and terminology and transplanted them into the soil of the Christian faith, nurtured them, and saw to their growth in the light of scriptural truth. But for some reason, Van Til took a weed whacker to Aquinas's Aristotelian garden and nurtured his Kantian one.

Coherence Theory of Truth

A second issue regarding the TAG is that some of its proponents use one theory of truth to excess. In terms of the TAG, the apologist makes the claim that the presupposition of the existence of the Triune God of the Bible best explains all reality—whether it is scientific experimentation, ethics, aesthetics, politics, philosophy, or anything else. This methodology rests on the coherence theory of truth. A classic definition of the coherence theory of truth runs thus: "Truth in its essential nature is that systematic coherence which is the character of a significant whole."[60] A similar definition appears in more recent coherence theories associated with British idealism: "A belief is true if and

---

58. Cf. Aquinas, *Summa Theologica*, Ia q. 1 arts. 1–10; Richard A. Muller, "The Dogmatic Function of St. Thomas' 'Proofs': A Protestant Appreciation," *Fides et Historia* 24 (1992): 15–29.

59. Frame, *Cornelius Van Til*, 267.

60. Harold H. Joachim, *The Nature of Truth* (Oxford: Clarendon, 1906), 76; see also Michael Glanzberg, "Truth," *Stanford Encyclopedia of Philosophy*, ed. Edward N. Zalta, Fall 2014 ed. (last revision January 22, 2013), §1.2, http://plato.stanford.edu/archives/fall2014/entries /truth/; Richard L. Kirkham, *Theories of Truth: A Critical Introduction* (Cambridge: MIT Press, 1992), 104–12.

only if it is part of a coherent system of beliefs."[61] Much of Van Til's interaction and engagement with idealism was through its British twentieth-century versions such as that presented in F. H. Bradley's (1846–1924) *Appearance and Reality*. Van Til was first exposed to Bradley during his undergraduate education at Calvin College and continued to interact with him throughout his career.[62] The coherence theory of truth certainly fits within Van Til's apologetic and theological system.[63] Van Til argues that the claims of Christianity best explain all reality.

Van Til's disciples have rigorously made this point in their own use of the TAG. Bahnsen, for example, illustrates how the TAG works:

> The apologist explains how rationality, communication, meaning, science, morality, and man's redemption and renewal are quite understandable, meaningful, coherent, or intelligible within the biblical worldview—within the framework of thinking God's thoughts after Him. The apologist then subjects the unbeliever's worldview to an internal critique to show that it is (1) arbitrary, and / or (2) inconsistent with itself, and / or (3) lacking the preconditions for the intelligibility of knowledge (language, logic, science, morality, redemption, etc.). . . . Thus the Christian has proved the rationality and necessity of His [*sic*] scripturally based worldview.[64]

Note that the effectiveness of the TAG rests upon the perceived (in)coherence of the contested worldviews. But something Bahnsen neither shows nor demonstrates is the necessity to employ evidence in conjunction with the TAG. At certain points, Bahnsen also gives the impression that the use of evidence is illegitimate, as we see in the title of one of his essays, "The Impropriety of Evidentially Arguing for the Resurrection."[65] Bahnsen, for example, writes:

> Scripture itself should be enough to dissuade a person from depending upon evidential arguments for Christ's resurrection. . . . The only tool an apologete needs is the word of God, for the sinner will either presuppose its truth and find Christianity to be coherent and convincing (given his spiritual condition and past experience) or he will reject it and never be able to come to a knowledge of the truth.

61. Glanzberg, "Truth," §1.2.
62. McConnel, "Influence of Idealism," 557; see F. H. Bradley, *Appearance and Reality: A Metaphysical Essay*, 6th ed. (1893; London: George Allen & Unwin, 1916).
63. Oliphint, "Van Til's Methodology," 34–35.
64. Greg Bahnsen, *Van Til's Apologetic: Readings and Analysis* (Phillipsburg, NJ: P&R, 1998), 513.
65. Greg Bahnsen, "The Impropriety of Evidentially Arguing for the Resurrection," *Synapse* 2 (1972), http://www.cmfnow.com/articles/PA003.htm. Subsequent citations come from this essay.

If the apologete uses evidence, he should never use it to prove Christianity but only to confirm it. Bahnsen's version of the TAG steers away from evidence.

Truth is not exhausted by whether it coheres as a system or worldview. In other words, a system might be internally coherent, but ultimately the system must address what is external to it, objective reality. A system of thought, such as Rudolf Bultmann's (1884–1976) understanding of a demythologized New Testament, has a systemic coherence.[66] If, as Bultmann argues, the doctrine of the resurrection is a myth, and people are raised from the dead when they existentially embrace Christ, then within Bultmann's system his claim is true.[67] But when it comes to determining the truth, the proposed answer must not only function within a coherent system but also correspond to reality.

A classic definition of the correspondence theory of truth is this: "What we believe or say is true if it corresponds to the way things actually are—to the facts."[68] In other words, knowledge represents the adequation of the mind to a thing. I have a true understanding of a horse if my mental conception of the horse is adequated to the reality of the horse outside my mind. "Truth," writes Bavinck, "is agreement between thought and reality and thus expresses a relation between the contents of our consciousness and the object of our knowledge."[69] The roots of the correspondence theory are quite old, going back at least as far as Plato.[70]

Neoclassical correspondence theory has also argued that at its core lies an ontological thesis: "A belief is true if there *exists* an appropriate entity—a fact—to which it corresponds. If there is no such entity, the belief is false."[71] In this vein, given that the bodily resurrection of Christ is a historical fact (an existing entity), then Bultmann's claims are false. Regardless of how well Bultmann's claims cohere within his system, they do not correspond to the way things actually are: his claims do not correspond to the historical fact of Christ's resurrection. To revisit briefly Bahnsen's objection regarding evidentially arguing for the resurrection, Christ not only provided his words to his disciples but also presented his physical body. He encouraged doubting Thomas to place his finger in his wounds, to look at his hands, and touch his side, and *then* Christ exhorted him to believe (John 20:27–29). Christ's

66. Rudolf Bultmann, "New Testament and Mythology: The Problem of Demythologizing the New Testament Proclamation," in *New Testament and Mythology and Other Basic Writings*, ed. Schubert M. Ogden (Philadelphia: Fortress, 1989), 1–43.

67. Bultmann, "New Testament and Mythology," 36–41.

68. Glanzberg, "Truth," §1.1.1.

69. Herman Bavinck, *The Certainty of Faith*, trans. Harry der Nederlanden (St. Catharines, ON: Paideia, 1980), 19.

70. Glanzberg, "Truth," §1.1.

71. Glanzberg, "Truth," §1.1.2.

truth-claims were coherent and corresponded to the reality of his resurrected body. Christ presented evidence to corroborate his claims. The apostles followed this pattern in their own presentation of the gospel. The apostle John writes, "That which was from the beginning, which we have heard, which we have seen with our eyes, which we looked upon and have touched with our hands, concerning the word of life—the life was made manifest, and we have seen it, and testify to it and proclaim to you the eternal life" (1 John 1:1–2). John could have appealed to Christ's authority alone or to his own apostolic authority, but he also appealed to the reality of Christ's incarnation—what he and the other apostles saw, touched, and heard. Luke's description of Christ's interaction with the disciples is relevant here: "He [Jesus] presented himself alive to them after his suffering by many proofs" (Acts 1:3).

As important as it is to demonstrate the coherence of claims about the existence of God, such as with the TAG, these claims must correspond to reality. Correspondence to reality lies at the heart of Aquinas's proofs for the existence of God.[72] Scripture speaks of the existence of God; Aquinas, for example, cites Exodus 3:14 and the name of God, I AM. But then he moves to demonstrate that the existing world points back to the God of Scripture.[73] This particular issue has been raised among Van Til's disciples, as noted in the introduction.[74] Some Van Tillians believe the TAG, in and of itself, is the one and only necessary argument to prove the validity of the Christian life and worldview.[75] This has been fostered, I believe, by Van Til himself: "Now the only argument for an absolute God that holds water is a transcendental argument."[76] Others, such as Van Til's longtime colleague Robert Knudsen, have argued that there is an inconsistency in Van Til's thought regarding the use of evidence that has contributed to its diminished presence in his apologetic system. Knudsen observes that in Van Til's use of the TAG, he regularly points away from evidence to its ground.

In other words, Van Til believed that one had to examine the foundation of evidence, which was more important than the evidence itself. Hence, Van Til focused on the vertical and gave too little attention to the horizontal.[77] Of particular relevance for the recovery of the book of nature are Knudsen's

---

72. Muller, "Dogmatic Function," 23–24. Also see Bruce D. Marshall, *Trinity and Truth* (Cambridge: Cambridge University Press, 2000), 217–82; William C. Placher, *Unapologetic Theology: A Christian Voice in a Pluralistic Conversation* (Louisville: Westminster John Knox, 1989), 123–37.

73. Aquinas, *Summa Theologica*, Ia q. 2 art. 3.

74. Frame, *Cornelius Van Til*, 316–17; McConnel, "Influence of Idealism," 578n78.

75. So, e.g., Bahnsen, *Van Til's Apologetic*, 500, 502–4.

76. Cornelius Van Til, *Survey of Christian Epistemology*, 11.

77. Knudsen, "Transcendental Perspective," 236.

comments regarding Van Til's (dis)use of the book of nature: "Because of this strain in his thinking, Van Til has had difficulty with the twin ideas of a created order and of a structure of creation. . . . One must *look away* from the idea of an order and structure within the creation."[78] This pattern emerges in one of the first biographies of Van Til by one of his students, William White Jr., when he claims that apologetics, "being more abstract, is considerably more difficult to put across than, say, church history, which deals with the concrete."[79] This description of Van Til's approach reveals the theoretical nature of his apologetics. In truth, if apologetics deals with theological claims about the world and the gospel's place within it, then it might at times be theoretical but should also be equally concrete. The books of nature and Scripture work in tandem.

As common as the diminished use of evidence might be among some Van Tillians, Frame has offered a welcome corrective:

> If Van Til's transcendental approach is to succeed, however, it must abandon the assumption that traditional arguments are necessarily autonomous and welcome the assistance of such arguments to complete the transcendental argument. The traditional arguments are in fact necessary to establish the existence of God as a transcendental conclusion. And there is no reason to assume, as Van Til does, that anyone who uses an argument from design or causality is presupposing a nontheistic epistemology.[80]

Frame's comments have been interpreted as negating Van Til's apologetic system, because Frame has removed its central feature, the TAG.[81] Nevertheless, such criticisms do not address the TAG's overemphasis on the coherence theory of truth. If God is the author and source of truth, then biblical claims most certainly have systematic coherence, but they must also correspond to the way things actually are.

Some might counter that the correspondence theory of truth posits autonomous reason as determining the validity or invalidity of all truth-claims. In other words, the objection may be that a correspondence theory of truth begins with autonomous reason rather than the ontological Trinity. Generally speaking, Aquinas believed that one's mental conceptions had to correspond to reality; in this he followed Aristotle.[82] But there are at least two other important factors to consider: was Aquinas an unreconstructed Aristotelian, or did

78. Knudsen, "Transcendental Perspective," 236–37.
79. William White Jr., *Van Til: Defender of the Faith* (Nashville: Nelson, 1979), 73.
80. Frame, "Transcendental Arguments," 717.
81. Bahnsen, *Van Til's Apologetic*, 500.
82. Marshall, *Trinity and Truth*, 217–23.

he invoke important theological truths?[83] Aquinas went far beyond Aristotle. Like Van Til in redefining idealist philosophical concepts, Aquinas believed that truth was ultimately related to God. Given that God created all things, to understand reality through truth-claims means aligning one's mind with God's mind. Aquinas writes: "Truth, therefore, is properly and primarily in the divine intellect. In the human intellect, it exists properly but secondarily."[84]

In other words, human beings must think God's thoughts after him if they are to have any conception of truth; human beings must submit their understanding of reality to the divine intellect.[85] In fact, Aquinas aligns truth not merely with a generic notion of God but specifically with Christ. In his comments on Colossians 2:3, "In [Christ] are hidden all the treasures of wisdom and knowledge," Aquinas writes: "Whatever is not according to Christ should be rejected."[86] According to Aquinas, we must participate in the Divine and receive illumination from him in order truly to grasp reality and understand truth.

Is there room to improve upon Aquinas's formulation? I believe there is. But for the time being, it is worth noting that Van Til was not the first to claim that we need to think God's thoughts after him in order to grasp the truth. Moreover, thinking God's thoughts after him not only means that this body of knowledge will have systemic coherence. It must also correspond to reality, to the world God created. The Reformed Orthodox recognized this and therefore generally agreed with Aquinas on the connection between innate and acquired natural knowledge. God has bound together common notions and the natural order in the pages of his book of nature. Just as we must be cautious regarding Greeks bearing gifts and giving too much credence to the abilities of human reason, we must conversely be leery of Germans bearing gifts lest we give too little consideration to the book of nature.

83. On the continuities and discontinuities between Aquinas and Aristotle, see Gilles Emery and Matthew Levering, ed., *Aristotle in Aquinas's Theology* (Oxford: Oxford University Press, 2015).

84. Thomas Aquinas, *The Disputed Questions on Truth*, trans. Robert W. Mulligan, 3 vols. (Chicago: Henry Regnery, 1952), q. I art. 4, 1:17.

85. Some might counter that Aquinas and Van Til have very different concepts of analogy, and hence their purported similarities are superficial. Contrary to this objection, Van Til's concept of analogy is actually Thomist. On this point, see Robert LaRocca, "Cornelius Van Til's Rejection and Appropriation of Thomist Metaphysics" (master's thesis, Westminster Theological Seminary, 2012).

86. Thomas Aquinas, *Commentary on the Letters of St. Paul to the Philippians, Colossians, Thessalonians, Timothy, Titus, and Philemon*, trans. F. R. Larcher, Latin/English Edition of the Works of St. Thomas Aquinas (Lander, WY: Aquinas Institute for the Study of Sacred Doctrine, 2012), §§95–96, pp. 108–9; Marshall, *Trinity and Truth*, 125. In fact, Marshall notes that Aquinas's view is basically the same as Martin Luther's: Bruce D. Marshall, "Faith and Reason Reconsidered: Aquinas and Luther on Deciding What Is True," *The Thomist* 63, no. 1 (1999): 1–48.

Passing Philosophical Trends?

The third and last observation regarding the TAG concerns its connections to Kantian thought. The TAG grew out of Kant's understanding of transcendental philosophy. Van Til adopted these Kantian ideas in an effort to build a point of contact with idealist philosophers. But in recent years there has been a balkanization of the philosophical landscape so that the hermeneutic of suspicion dominates many discussions, and people no longer accept the claims of metanarratives.[87] People now typically reject the Enlightenment confidence in reason, an objective understanding of reality, and the ability to transcend personal biases formed by one's racial or cultural context. Postmoderns, therefore, have an "incredulity toward metanarratives," that is, a disbelief in any ability to explain the big picture.[88] The present philosophical discussion has shifted from Kantian epistemological categories and moved to postmodern ones. Idealism is no longer a dominant conversation partner but rather one opinion among many other postmodern voices, such as Jacques Derrida (1930–2004), Jean-François Lyotard (1924–98), and Michel Foucault (1926–84). In fact, some within the Reformed tradition believe that the future of fruitful dialogue with culture lies with the postmodern insights of Derrida, Lyotard, and Foucault, rather than with Kant's idealism.[89]

One of the chief criticisms of Aquinas's arguments for the existence of God is that they have become passé given Enlightenment progress. In the wake of the Humean critique of causality and Kant's devastating dismantling of the various arguments for the existence of God, Aquinas is supposedly outdated.[90] If we accept such conclusions, then given the recent philosophical seismic shifts, one has to wonder how effective the TAG can be. If the apologist happens to be interacting with a person who is devoted to idealism, then the TAG is a useful tool, but an apologist who happens to be dialoguing with a postmodern who rejects the tenets of idealism would need to employ other tools. To claim that the TAG is the most biblical form of apologetics fails to recognize its

---

87. Brian Leiter, "The Hermeneutics of Suspicion: Recovering Marx, Nietzsche, and Freud," in *The Future for Philosophy*, ed. Brian Leiter (Oxford: Clarendon, 2004), 74–105; Jean-François Lyotard, *The Postmodern Condition: A Report on Knowledge* (Manchester, UK: Manchester University Press, 1984).

88. Lyotard, *Postmodern Condition*, xxiv.

89. James K. A. Smith, *Who's Afraid of Postmodernism? Taking Derrida, Lyotard, and Foucault to Church* (Grand Rapids: Baker Academic, 2006).

90. The opposite may be true: recent research argues that a version of a Thomist idea of causality is being reintroduced in scientific fields. See Michael J. Dodds, *Unlocking Divine Actions: Contemporary Science and Thomas Aquinas* (Washington, DC: Catholic University of America Press, 2012). More broadly, see Thomas Joseph White, *Wisdom in the Face of Modernity: A Study in Thomistic Natural Theology*, 2nd ed. (Ave Maria, FL: Sapientia, 2016).

philosophical origins. It needlessly attaches apologetic methodology to certain idealist concepts that are neither purely biblical nor even philosophically necessary. This is not to concede any legitimacy to the postmodern critique of Christianity but simply to acknowledge the inadvisability of attaching the claim of "most biblical approach" to something that is not necessarily biblical but rather philosophical. We must refuse to surrender what is biblical. But what if the "biblical" apologetic is not as biblical as once thought? Whoever claims to be purely biblical and free from human opinions might actually be the slave of a defunct philosopher or theologian.

Given the balkanized philosophical landscape, dogmatically adhering to one specific idealist-bound form of apologetic argumentation clearly hobbles the Christian apologist. The TAG and HWT go hand in hand, and if one seeks to evangelize a person who has a systematic worldview, then it can be quite useful. But what if the person has not a coherent worldview but only an eclectic, postmodern assortment of beliefs? The TAG is likely not as useful in such a case. Rather than claim that the TAG is the most biblical form of argumentation, Christians need to be fleet-footed and employ arguments that fit the occasion.

This is especially the case with the recent historical move to what some have described as neomedievalism.[91] Neomedievalism "embraces the fragmentation of sovereignty and seeks to reorient international relations ideas away from state centrism toward an unstructured system of overlapping authorities and allegiances to better comprehend world affairs."[92] In other words, institutions (nations, religions, or schools of philosophy) no longer have hegemonic presence or authority. Rather, we are making a turn back toward a feudal landscape where different pockets of religions, philosophical schools of thought, terrorist groups, drug cartels, and the like drive cultural, military, philosophical, and religious understanding. In such a context, Christians need to be flexible, able to meet a host of beliefs rather than inflexibly locked into one philosophical form of argumentation.

Conclusion

In a Thomist-like fashion, Van Til borrowed elements of idealist philosophy (which he considered formally true) and made necessary corrections to align them with Scripture. While Van Til may have been one of the first to employ a Kantian transcendental argument in defense of Christianity, his move is far

91. Sean McFate, *The Modern Mercenary: Private Armies and What They Mean for World Order* (Oxford: Oxford University Press, 2014), 72–89.
92. McFate, *Modern Mercenary*, 74.

from Copernican. His methodology bears a strong resemblance to Aquinas's use of Aristotelian categories to build a bridge to Muslim philosophers. Just because Van Til employed idealist thought does not automatically disqualify its utility. Rather, other theologians can lay claim to defending the faith through the instrumental use of reason. Van Til stands in a long line of theologians who have employed philosophy in this manner. Correlatively, adherents to the TAG should be cautious regarding the exclusive use of the coherence theory of truth. As important as systemic coherence is, truth-claims must ultimately correspond to reality. We must use the book of nature in conjunction with the book of Scripture. We can make transcendental claims and show their systematic coherence, but we should always be willing to demonstrate how those claims correspond to the world around us.

In a similar vein, Reformed theologians in the early twentieth century faced the trend of the growth of mystical pietism and the tendency of Christians to retreat from the use of evidence. The line from the early twentieth-century hymn *I Serve a Risen Savior* aptly captures the nature of the mind-set: "You ask me how I know He lives; He lives within my heart." If some advocates of the TAG look away from the evidence to its transcendental source, then the mystical pietists look within and away from the evidence. In an extended statement that is worth quoting in full, J. Gresham Machen (1881–1937) addressed this issue:

> How, then, shall God be known; how shall we become so acquainted with Him that personal fellowship may become possible? Some liberal preachers would say that we become acquainted with God only through Jesus. That assertion has an appearance of loyalty to our Lord, but in reality it is highly derogatory to Him. For Jesus Himself plainly recognized the validity of other ways of knowing God, and to reject those other ways is to reject the things that lay at the very center of Jesus' life. Jesus plainly found God's hand in nature; the lilies of the field revealed to Him the weaving of God. He found God also in the moral law; the law written in the hearts of men was God's law, which revealed His righteousness. Finally Jesus plainly found God revealed in the Scriptures. How profound was our Lord's use of the words of prophets and psalmists! To say that such revelation of God was invalid, or is useless to us today, is to despise things that lay closest to Jesus' mind and heart. But, as a matter of fact, when men say that we know God only as He is revealed in Jesus, they are denying all real knowledge of God whatever. For unless there be some idea of God independent of Jesus, the ascription of deity to Jesus has no meaning. To say, "Jesus is God," is meaningless unless the word "God" has an antecedent meaning attached to it. And the attaching of a meaning to the word "God" is accomplished by the means which have just been mentioned.[93]

93. J. Gresham Machen, *Christianity and Liberalism* (1923; repr., Grand Rapids: Eerdmans, 1999), 55–56.

Machen believed that the book of nature, therefore, was just as important as the book of Scripture. Both of God's books are indispensable.

Machen echoed convictions shared by his Princeton Theological Seminary colleague Geerhardus Vos (1862–1949). In similar fashion, Vos addressed the tendency among advocates of higher criticism to denigrate the facts of biblical history and elevate the value of mystical experience:

> To join in the outcry against dogma and fact means to lower the ideal of what the Christian consciousness ought normally to be to the level of the spiritual depression of our own day and generation. How much better that we should all strive to raise our drooping faith and to reënrich our depleted experience up to the standard of those blessed periods in the life of the Church, when the belief in Bible history and the religion of the heart went hand in hand and kept equal pace, when people were ready to lay down their lives for facts and doctrines, because facts and doctrines formed the daily spiritual nourishment of their souls. May God by His Spirit maintain among us, and through our instrumentality revive around us, that truly evangelical type of piety which not merely tolerates facts and doctrines, but draws from them its strength and inspiration in life and service, its only comfort and hope in the hour of death.[94]

Vos believed there was an inextricable and vital link between the facts of history and the experience of faith, or in other terms, the books of nature and Scripture.

Employing the Thomist distinction between mixed and pure articles, Vos believed one could argue from the effects of the creation back to its creator:

> *Articuli puri* [pure articles] are those that cannot be derived both from reason and from revelation but depend entirely on revelation. *Articuli mixti* [mixed articles] flow from both reason and revelation. The question then is whether creation can be proven by reason. That has been attempted by starting from the concept of God. God, one says, could not remain shut up within Himself. He needed a world in order to love it, etc. Such reasoning is not legitimate. As far as we can judge, had the creation remained non-existent, God would have been all-sufficient, as He is now. We can certainly reason from the world up to God, but we cannot by logic descend from God to the world.[95]

94. Geerhardus Vos, "Christian Faith and the Truthfulness of Bible History," *Princeton Theological Review* 4, no. 3 (1906): 304–5.

95. Geerhardus Vos, *Theology Proper*, vol. 1 of *Reformed Dogmatics*, ed. Richard B. Gaffin Jr. (Bellingham, WA: Lexham, 2012–14), 157. I am grateful to Richard Barcellos for pointing me to this statement. On mixed articles, see Aza Goudriaan, "Theology and Philosophy," in *A Companion to Reformed Orthodoxy*, ed. Herman J. Selderhuis (Leiden: Brill, 2013), 32; Richard A. Muller, *Post-Reformation Reformed Dogmatics*, 1:402–5.

Within the context of demonstrating creation ex nihilo, Vos rejected an argument from above, reasoning from God to the creation, but did accept the idea of arguing from below.

But Vos was sensitive to the concern that, if Christians appealed to the facts and sought to demonstrate the evidential veracity and historicity of the Scriptures, they might allow the unregenerate to sit in judgment over the Scriptures. This is something that Van Til and others wanted to avoid at all costs. Nevertheless, Vos astutely observes:

> Whether we like it or not, criticism can touch the essence of our religion, because religion has become incarnate, and for our sakes had to become incarnate and make itself vulnerable in historic form. As the Son of God while on the earth had to expose Himself to the unbelief and scorn of men, so the word of the Gospel could not be what it is for us unless it were subject to the same humiliation.[96]

In other words, we need not try to protect the Scriptures or the gospel from the scorn of the unregenerate. Rather, God has condescended into history and willingly subjected himself to ridicule and false judgment in order to redeem sinners. As much as he has every right to command belief solely on the basis of his authority, Christ nevertheless bids sinners to touch his side, look at his wounds, and behold his resurrected body through the pages of Holy Writ and the facts of history—the pages of the book of nature. So while Machen and Vos addressed the mystical trends in their own day, their words are nevertheless instructive regarding the importance of appealing to both of God's books, nature and Scripture. We can and should, therefore, employ the innate and acquired natural knowledge of God in our efforts to defend the faith.

96. Vos, "Christian Faith," 300.

7

DUALISMS

But after Calvin the everlasting temptation besetting all Christians, especially sophisticated Christians, to make friends with those that are of Cain's lineage proved too much for many Lutheran and even Reformed theologians and so Lutheran and Reformed Scholasticism were begotten and born.

Cornelius Van Til

And insofar as the influence of the Thomistic-Aristotelian metaphysics had even revealed itself in some formulations of the Reformed Confessions, especially in the Westminster Confession, this attack could be easily interpreted as a deviation from the Church's doctrine.

Herman Dooyeweerd

One of the criticisms routinely leveled against using natural theology is that it admits dualistic thinking into one's theology. A common accusation, for example, comes from Cornelius Van Til, who argues that the Roman Catholic nature-grace dualism compromises both the theological and the apologetic integrity of the scriptural teaching about epistemology. Van Til explains that Roman Catholic theologians posit a twofold relationship between (1) nature, man's lower powers and faculties, which include reason, and (2) the *donum superadditum*, the superadded gift of grace. First, before the fall Adam was created and given natural gifts as well as superadded gifts of righteousness and holiness. Second, in his fall Adam lost the *donum superadditum*, righteousness and holiness, but his lower natural gifts, including reason, largely remained intact and unharmed by the fall. Within Roman Catholic apologetic systems, the nature-grace dualism supposedly allows Christians to engage unbelievers on the basis of reason. Christian apologists can approach and dialogue with unbelievers on the basis of this neutral ground. But Van Til maintains that the nature-grace dualism is unscriptural, since it leaves a beachhead of autonomous reason, which makes fallen human beings the arbiters of truth.[1] Autonomous humans will never capitulate to the authority of revelation and God's sovereignty as long as they sit on the judge's bench and arbitrate truth-claims according to their own fallen reason. Van Til contends that Roman Catholic theology falls short of scriptural teaching because it rests on an Aristotelian starting point, a dualistic understanding of man. Hence, Christians must purge dualistic thought from their theology and begin from a pure scriptural starting point.

The complaint against dualistic thought is common among Van Tillian and neo-Calvinist theologians and philosophers. Henry Van Til (1906–91), the nephew of Cornelius Van Til, regularly criticized dualistic thought in his book *The Calvinistic Concept of Culture*:

> Thus Rome, which claims for itself the appellation "Catholic," has changed New Testament catholicity, which purifies and sanctifies as its proper domain the whole life, and has substituted in its place a dualism, which separates the supernatural from the natural. Salvation always remains beside or above the natural, but does not enter it to transform it; creation and re-creation remain two independent entities.[2]

According to Henry Van Til, the nature-grace dualism affects Roman Catholic theology more broadly. It colors both Rome's postfall epistemology and its broader understanding of the church's doctrine of salvation and its relationship to culture. Henry Van Til criticizes dualistic views that divide life into secular and sacred realms: the state looks after a person's natural needs and the church oversees one's spiritual needs.[3] Such a division of life surrenders both reason and culture to an autonomous neutral zone and fails to exercise Christ's lordship over the whole creation. This dualism breeds a sloth, therefore, toward the biblically mandated task of transforming culture

---

1. Cornelius Van Til, *The New Synthesis Theology in the Netherlands* (Phillipsburg, NJ: P&R, 1976), 1–6; Van Til, *Christian Apologetics* (Phillipsburg, NJ: P&R, 1976), 9.

2. Henry Van Til, *The Calvinistic Concept of Culture* (1972; repr., Grand Rapids: Baker Academic, 2001), 18–19.

3. H. Van Til, *Calvinistic Concept of Culture*, 86.

and bringing it all under the sovereign rule of Christ.[4] To embrace dualistic principles, claims Van Til, is to follow in the footsteps of scholastic theology.[5] As important as the Protestant Reformation was, many Reformers, such as Martin Luther (1483–1546), failed to escape the clutches of dualistic scholastic thought.[6]

In line with many neo-Calvinist theologians, Henry Van Til believed that the Reformed church needs to implement the insights of Abraham Kuyper, who maintained that the Scriptures declare that "every square inch" of the creation belongs to Christ, and therefore he cries out "Mine!" In other words, since no area of life lies beyond the rule of Christ, all dualistic thought must be excised. But even then, Henry Van Til believed that Kuyper still had remnants of synthetic, or dualistic, thought because he distinguished between common and special grace.[7] Therefore the Reformed church must continue to purify Reformed doctrine from dualistic thought. Henry Van Til repeats this claim apart from any citations or argumentation; by this point in the development and reception of neo-Calvinist theology, the critique against dualism is unquestioned.[8] Similar critiques are offered by other neo-Calvinist theologians, such as James K. A. Smith, Albert Wolters, Cornelius Plantinga Jr., and Brian Walsh and Richard Middleton.[9]

The dualism critique, therefore, plays an important role in debates over apologetic methodology and is one more hurdle to clear in order to recover the use of the book of nature. But whence does the dualism criticism originate? From those who believe that Roman Catholic theology is dualistic, the common line of argumentation runs as follows: Aquinas taught a nature-grace dualism, he was a scholastic, scholastic theology is dualistic, so any and all

4. H. Van Til, *Calvinistic Concept of Culture*, 103.

5. H. Van Til, *Calvinistic Concept of Culture*, 175.

6. H. Van Til, *Calvinistic Concept of Culture*, 20, 227.

7. H. Van Til, *Calvinistic Concept of Culture*, 118, 134–35.

8. Karl Barth also levels the same criticisms against classic Reformed theology, namely, that the covenant of works introduces a dualism, and the nature-grace construct is also dualistic. See Karl Barth, *Church Dogmatics*, ed. G. W. Bromiley and T. F. Torrance (Edinburgh: T&T Clark, 1988), IV/1:55–66; Barth, "No!," in *Natural Theology: Comprising "Nature and Grace" by Professor Dr. Emil Brunner and the Reply "No!" by Dr. Karl Barth* (1946; repr., Eugene, OR: Wipf & Stock, 2002), 100–101, 103.

9. James K. A. Smith, "Will the Real Plato Please Stand Up? Participation versus Incarnation," in *Radical Orthodoxy and the Reformed Tradition: Creation, Covenant, and Participation*, ed. James K. A. Smith and James H. Olthuis (Grand Rapids: Baker Academic, 2005), 62; Albert M. Wolters, *Creation Regained: Biblical Basics for a Reformational Worldview*, 2nd ed. (Grand Rapids: Eerdmans, 2005), 64–65; Cornelius Plantinga Jr., *Engaging God's World: A Reformed Vision of Faith, Learning, and Living* (Grand Rapids: Eerdmans, 2002), 17–44; Brian Walsh and Richard Middleton, *The Transforming Vision: Shaping a Christian Worldview* (Downers Grove, IL: InterVarsity, 1984), 93–116.

scholasticism is therefore dualistic and hence unscriptural. Another version of the same criticism posits that a natural realm of any sort relies on a dualism; dualisms radically separate the unified nature of creation and redemption, so therefore dualisms should be rejected. The problem with these claims is that they have become so common that they no longer require verification or documentation. They are supposedly self-evident claims, perhaps even brute facts.

Contrary to these claims, this chapter argues that the dualism critique rests on an inaccurate evaluation of the historical evidence. To invoke the claim of dualism may curry favor with neo-Calvinists, but there is little accurate historical-theological evidence to support the charges. In fact, many who level the dualism charge do so inaccurately: simply seeing two of something seems to warrant the charge of *dualism*. I believe there is a fourfold failure in most claims about dualisms: they separate what theologians merely distinguish, have little or no historical evidence to support them, ultimately rest on questionable philosophical claims rather than biblical exegesis, and employ the debunked hellenization thesis of Adolf von Harnack (1851–1930).

To prove that few Christian theologians actually advocate a true dualism, this chapter first surveys the three different types of dualisms: the classic dualism of Platonic philosophy, cosmic dualism, and the dualism of neo-Calvinist philosophy and theology. This chapter surveys the latter primarily through the claims of neo-Calvinist philosopher Herman Dooyeweerd (1894–1977), who has exercised a great degree of influence through his Reformational philosophy.[10] Second, the chapter analyzes and critiques the different claims about so-called dualistic thought and demonstrates that those accused of employing dualisms have been misrepresented. This caricature has largely arisen from a failure to read primary sources. Theologians such as Thomas Aquinas (1225–74) do not actually say what neo-Calvinists attribute to them.[11] And as common as the charge of scholasticism is, neo-Calvinist theologians fail to recognize that scholasticism is not a belief system but a methodology that does not predetermine theological conclusions.[12] The chapter concludes with observations about the dualist ghosts that supposedly haunt corners of the Reformed community.

10. David VanDrunen, *Divine Covenants and Moral Order: A Biblical Theology of Natural Law* (Grand Rapids: Eerdmans, 2014), 527–29.

11. Arvin Vos, *Aquinas, Calvin, and Contemporary Protestant Thought: A Critique of Protestant Views on the Thought of Thomas Aquinas* (Washington, DC: Christian University Press, 1985), 123–60.

12. Richard A. Muller, *Scholasticism and Orthodoxy in the Reformed Tradition: An Attempt at Definition; Inaugural Address, Calvin Seminary Chapel, September 7, 1995* (Grand Rapids: Calvin Theological Seminary, 1995).

Three Different Dualisms

Classic Platonic Dualism

Plato (ca. 428–348 BC) explains the relationship between the soul and body in terms of a dualism, and this in turn is fundamental to his epistemology. According to Plato, physical things are real, but they are ultimately shadows of immaterial, eternal forms. The chair I see before me is a poor copy of the eternal, immaterial concept of a chair.[13] According to Plato, the person's immortal soul resides in the body, and through the body it perceives the physical world, but ultimately the body and soul wage war against one another. Plato describes this conflicted relationship in terms of the body dragging the soul around to hear, touch, and smell physical realities in such a manner that "the soul itself strays and is confused and dizzy, as if it were drunk, insofar as it is in contact with that kind of thing."[14] In this respect, nature orders human existence in such a manner as to have the soul rule over the body.[15] The soul is like the divine—it is immortal, intelligible, uniform, and indissoluble. By contrast, the body is human, mortal, unintelligible, and inconsistent.[16]

Upon death, the body falls away and the soul makes its way "to the invisible, which is like itself, the divine and immortal and wise, and arriving there it can be happy, having rid itself of confusion, ignorance, fear, violent desires, and the other human ills."[17] The soul escapes the corrupting influence of the body, which sought to bewitch the soul with physical earthly pleasures.[18] The souls of those who carelessly practiced gluttony, violence, or drunkenness return and enter the bodies of donkeys or similar animals. By contrast, those who practiced virtue, denied themselves physical pleasures, and pursued justice and moderation may enter the bodies of gentle creatures, such as bees or wasps. But only those who have lived the purest of lives enter the company of the gods.[19] Plato writes:

> This is how the soul of a philosopher would reason: It would not think that while philosophy must free it, it should while being freed surrender itself to

13. Howard Robinson, "Dualism," *Stanford Encyclopedia of Philosophy*, ed. Edward N. Zalta, Winter 2012 ed. (last revised November 3, 2011), §1.2, http://plato.stanford.edu/archives /win2012/entries/dualism/.

14. Plato, *Phaedo*, in *Plato: Five Dialogues: Euthyphro, Apology, Crito, Meno, Phaedo*, trans. G. M. A. Grube and John M. Cooper, 2nd ed. (Indianapolis: Hackett, 2002), §79c.

15. Plato, *Phaedo* 80.

16. Plato, *Phaedo* 80b.

17. Plato, *Phaedo* 81.

18. Plato, *Phaedo* 81b.

19. Plato, *Phaedo* 82a–c.

pleasures and pains and imprison itself again, thus laboring in vain like Penelope at her web. The soul of the philosopher achieves a calm from such emotions; it follows reason and ever stays with it contemplating the true, the divine, which is not the object of opinion. Nurtured by this, it believes that one should live in this manner as long as one is alive and, after death, arrive at what is akin and of the same kind, and escape from human evils. After such nurture there is no danger . . . that one should fear that, on parting from the body, the soul would be scattered and dissipated by the winds and no longer be anything anywhere.[20]

Within this metaphysical structure, the body is the prison of the soul, and hence the soul of the philosophically enlightened one constantly seeks to escape the body.[21]

Plato's dualistic anthropology revolves around an irreconcilable conflict between the material and immaterial aspects of man. Humans consist of two elements that war against one another in a conflict that might find resolution in death should they possess the philosophical knowledge required to break out of the prison house of the body. In this dualism, the soul is superior to the body; matter is inherently inferior. Now, the assumption might be that Plato's views are characteristic of all ancient Greek philosophers, but this is incorrect.[22] Aristotle (384–322 BC) did not believe in the category of Platonic forms, which enabled him to argue that the soul is the form of the body. Aristotle did believe that the soul was immaterial since it did not have a bodily organ. If the soul was material and had a bodily organ, then its function would be restricted to the limitations of its organ. For example, an eye is restricted to the function of sight, and the ear to the function of sound. Bodily organs limit their function, whereas the soul has no such limitations and thus must be immaterial. Nevertheless, for Aristotle the soul is the form of the body, or the immaterial dispositions of a material body. In this case, the form is the substance of the body. In other words, Aristotle does not employ a Platonic dualism.[23] In fact, Aristotle believed that when a person died, the soul did not continue apart from the body. Form and matter are inseparable.[24] Notably, later medieval and Protestant theologians would employ the body-soul distinction but maintain that body and soul were only temporarily separable

20. Plato, *Phaedo* 84a–b.

21. Plato, *Phaedo* 82e–83.

22. Diogenes Allen, *Philosophy for Understanding Theology*, 2nd ed. (Atlanta: John Knox Press, 2007), 21–37, esp. 35–37.

23. Robinson, "Dualism," §1.2; see Aristotle, *De Anima*, trans. R. D. Hicks (Cambridge: Cambridge University Press, 1907), 3.4, 429a10–b9.

24. John W. Cooper, *Body, Soul, and Life Everlasting: Biblical Anthropology and the Monism-Dualism Debate* (Grand Rapids: Eerdmans, 2000), 71–72.

during the intermediate state—a very un-Aristotelian move. And they also maintained that upon the resurrection, body and soul were reunited—a very un-Platonic move.

Cosmic Dualism

A second type of dualism posits a perpetual conflict between two different but nevertheless equal powers in the universe. Some Eastern religions believe there is a cosmic struggle between the eternal principles of good and evil. Historically, one of the best-known versions of a dualism is Manichaeism. Augustine (354–430) famously polemicized against Manichaeism.[25] Gnostic sects promoted a dualistic understanding of the cosmos where an evil demiurge, identified with the God of the Old Testament, created the world and imprisoned eternal souls in material bodies. The path to salvation lies in discovering the true knowledge (*gnōsis*) of the cosmos and thus finding redemption from the material body.[26] The apocryphal *Acts of Andrew* (§6) speaks of human beings as immaterial and ultimately related to the uncreated, rational, heavenly, and pure powers above. The apocryphal *Acts of John* (§§ 97–102) presents a disembodied Jesus explaining that the creation originated from demons and that redemption consists in becoming just like the disembodied savior.[27] The greater cosmic dualism finds its counterpart in the microcosmic body-soul dualism, where the material body wages war against the imprisoned spirit.

Dooyeweerdian Dualism

Unlike the classic Platonic or cosmic dualisms, which posit an antithesis between spirit and matter, Dooyeweerd offers a slightly different understanding and definition of what constitutes a dualism. Dooyeweerd set out to establish a purely biblical conception of philosophy, one free of pagan notions. To accomplish his goal, he established Reformational philosophy. Within the broader structure of his philosophy, Dooyeweerd identifies the motivating factors in different philosophical schools of thought, theoretical attempts to account for a worldview. Dooyeweerd calls these motivating factors *ground motives*. In the big picture, there are two primary ground motives: biblical and apostate. Within the apostate category, Dooyeweerd identifies three different

25. Augustine, *Writings against the Manichaean Heresy* (NPNF[1] 4:3–368); Peter Brown, *Augustine of Hippo* (Oakland: University of California Press, 2013), 35–49.

26. Richard Bauckham, "Imaginative Literature," in *The Early Christian World*, ed. Philip F. Esler, 2 vols. (New York: Routledge, 2000), 791–815, esp. 809.

27. For these apocryphal texts, see Wilhelm Schneemelcher, ed., *New Testament Apocrypha*, 2 vols. (Louisville: Westminster John Knox, 1992), 2:101–51, 152–209.

subtypes: the Greek form-matter motive, the scholastic nature-grace motive, and the Enlightenment nature-freedom motive.[28] For the purposes of this chapter, we will focus on the Greek form-matter and scholastic nature-grace ground motives, contrasting them with Dooyeweerd's biblical ground motive.

Foundational to Dooyeweerd's understanding is the relationship between eternity and time. According to Dooyeweerd, we must distinguish between three different realms: the eternal, the created supratemporal, and the temporal realms. In his understanding, the two creation accounts (Gen. 1 and 2) are not about the same creation but are about the creation of the supratemporal and temporal realms respectively.[29] The supratemporal realm, the *aevum*, is an intermediate created reality between God's eternity and the temporal realm.[30] Humanity originates in the supratemporal *aevum* and enters the temporal realm. The center of a person's being is the heart, which originates in the *aevum* and has a peripheral extension within the temporal realm of the body. Dooyeweerd writes: "The all-sided temporal existence of man, *i.e.*, his 'body,' in the full Scriptural sense of the word, can only be understood from the supratemporal religious center, *i.e.*, the 'soul,' or the 'heart,' in its Scriptural meaning."[31] Dooyeweerd does not divide humans into soul and body, which in his judgment is dualistic and reflective of the Greek form-matter ground motive. Rather, he offers what he claims is a holistic view: humans originate in the supratemporal realm and have an inner and outer aspect of their holistic existence.[32]

In their creation, humans were supposed to redeem the entire temporal realm.[33] Dooyeweerd explains man's relationship to the temporal realm in terms of the biblical ground motive of creation, fall, and redemption in Christ.[34] Although other theologians may speak in terms of this linear narrative

---

28. J. Glenn Friesen, *Neo-Calvinism and Christian Theosophy: Franz von Baader, Abraham Kuyper, Herman Dooyeweerd* (Calgary: Aevum Books, 2015), 374–75.

29. Friesen, *Neo-Calvinism*, 439.

30. Friesen, *Neo-Calvinism*, 428.

31. Herman Dooyeweerd, *A New Critique of Theoretical Thought*, trans. David H. Freeman and H. de Jongste, 4 vols. (Phillipsburg, NJ: P&R, 1969), 3:784.

32. For others who try to argue for holistic anthropologies in contrast to the catholic body-soul distinction, see Bruce Reichenbach, *Is Man the Phoenix? A Study of Immortality* (Grand Rapids: Eerdmans, 1983); Murray J. Harris, "Resurrection and Immortality: Eight Theses," *Themelios* 1, no. 2 (1976): 50–55; Herman Ridderbos, *Paul: An Outline of His Theology* (Grand Rapids: Eerdmans, 1975), 497–508, 548–50; see also Cooper, *Body, Soul*, 159–60. For those who argue for a nonreductive physicalism, see Joel B. Green, "Scripture and the Human Person: Further Reflections," *Science and Christian Belief* 11 (1999): 51–63; Green, *Body, Soul, and Human Life: The Nature of Humanity in the Bible* (Grand Rapids: Baker Academic, 2008); Nancey Murphy, *Bodies and Souls, or Spirited Bodies?* (Cambridge: Cambridge University Press, 2006).

33. Friesen, *Neo-Calvinism*, 472.

34. Friesen, *Neo-Calvinism*, 410.

(creation-fall-redemption), unless they root it in the supratemporal *aevum*, they have not truly embraced the biblical ground motive. The supratemporal origin of humans, therefore, explains Dooyeweerd's anthropology and soteriology. One must begin with God and the supratemporal origin of humanity in order to arrive at a correct understanding of the human constitution and one's relationship to Christ and the broader world. Concerning humanity's creation, one's inner core originates in the *aevum* and is further clothed with a body in the temporal realm: "The human body is man himself in the structural whole of his temporal appearance. And the human soul, in its pregnant religious sense, is man himself in the radical unity of his spiritual existence, which transcends all temporal structures."[35] In this construction, a human being is an organic, nondualistic whole.[36]

Once humanity fell, this necessitated a new supratemporal root for humanity: Jesus Christ as the second Adam. The only way people can understand their existence is to be united with Christ:

> Christ as the fullness of God's Revelation is the Truth. Standing in the Truth, as the sharing in the fullness of meaning of the cosmos in Christ, is the indispensable pre-requisite for the insight into the full horizon of our experience. This means that we have once and for all given up the illusion of possessing the norm of truth in our own fallen selfhood. We have arrived at the self-knowledge that outside of the light of Divine Revelation we stand in falsehood.[37]

Once fallen human beings realize their need for Christ, they transcend the temporal earthly cosmos and participate in the transcendental root of the cosmos.[38] Fallen humanity obtains access to the transcendental root of the cosmos through union with Christ.[39] Dooyeweerd explains:

> The redemption by Jesus Christ and the communion of the Holy Spirit, which makes us into members of His body, has a central and radical sense. In Christ, mankind and the whole temporal world have received a new religious root in which the *imago Dei* is revealed in the fullness of its meaning. Thus the central theme of the Holy Scriptures, namely, that of creation, fall into sin, and redemption by Jesus Christ in the communion of the Holy Spirit, has a radical meaning, which is related to the central unity of our human existence. It effects the true knowledge of God and ourselves, if our heart is fully opened by the

35. Dooyeweerd, *New Critique*, 3:89.
36. Friesen, *Neo-Calvinism*, 461.
37. Dooyeweerd, *New Critique*, 2:564.
38. Dooyeweerd, *New Critique*, 2:593.
39. Friesen, *Neo-Calvinism*, 486–87.

Holy Spirit so that it finds itself in the grip of God's Word and has become the captive of Jesus Christ.[40]

This understanding of the biblical ground motive of creation-fall-redemption explains why Dooyeweerd rejects the so-called apostate ground motives. In contrast to the biblical ground motive, Dooyeweerd argues that all apostate ground motives absolutize the temporal, or immanent, realm. They idolize the temporal, which has the effect of creating antinomies, or a dialectic, between two different aspects of temporal reality. Any attempt to absolutize the temporal apart from the supratemporal center results in a dualism.[41]

Dooyeweerd rejects the Greek form-matter distinction because it is the way philosophers accounted for the immortal soul as the form of the material body. The form-matter distinction lies behind the scholastic nature-grace dualism. Dooyeweerd writes:

> This is why the traditional scholastic qualification of man as a rational-ethical being is unacceptable, as is the metaphysical dichotomistic view of body and soul, in which it is rooted. The unqualified act-structure of the human body is quite different from the traditional conception of a "rational soul," in the sense of an immortal spiritual subsistence which is the metaphysical "form" of the "material body." Nor is the human body to be conceived as a "material substance" distinct from the soul, or, in the genuine Aristotelian sense, as the "matter" of the "soul," which has only actuality through the soul as its "form." The human body is man himself in the structural whole of his temporal appearance. And the human soul, in its pregnant religious sense, is man himself in the radical unity of his spiritual existence, which transcends all temporal structures.[42]

In Dooyeweerd's analysis, the Greek philosophical failure to recognize the supratemporal origin of the human heart leads to absolutizing the temporal and thus creates an antithetical relationship between soul and body. Scholastic theologians inherited the same problem because they adopted the Greek philosophical anthropology.[43]

The failure to extirpate the Greek roots from Roman Catholic theology had significant negative side effects for Protestant theology. Dooyeweerd contends that the nature-grace dualism led to Luther's dialectical opposition of law and gospel. Behind the law-gospel dualism is Marcion's (AD 85–160) dialectical

40. Herman Dooyeweerd, *In the Twilight of Western Thought*, ed. D. F. M. Strauss, Collected Works, Series B 16 (1960; Grand Rapids: Paideia, 1999), 86.
41. Friesen, *Neo-Calvinism*, 375.
42. Dooyeweerd, *New Critique*, 3:89.
43. Dooyeweerd, *Twilight of Western Thought*, 32–33.

antithesis between the God of creation and the God of redemption, which was accompanied by a false antithesis between a legalistic view of the gospel and a "pseudo-Pauline emphasis on justification alone *at the expense of the law*."[44] Other dualisms include the division of life into sacred and secular realms, whether in government, science, philosophy, or education.[45] This dualistic infection spread far beyond Luther and well into Reformed theology.

According to Dooyeweerd, both Roman Catholic and Reformed scholastic theologians failed to uproot the apostate form-matter and nature-grace ground motives. The nature-grace dualism established a beachhead within Calvinistic thought and subsequently expressed itself in the polarities that were "characteristic of Lutheranism." "The Lutheran dualism of law and gospel," writes Dooyeweerd, "is foreign to the Reformed confession." Reformed scholasticism tries to build its doctrinal cathedral on the sand of Aquinas's nature-grace dualism and hence has the same foundational weaknesses.[46] But according to Dooyeweerd, Reformed scholasticism was not confined to the seventeenth century but also found expression even in Kuyper. Dooyeweerd believed that to posit two categories of grace (common and special) could "easily degenerate into a doctrine of two separate realms."[47] This led Dooyeweerd to speak of two Kuypers: the corrupted scholastic Kuyper and the biblically pure Kuyper.[48] James Smith even argues that Dooyeweerd is not really a Calvinist, saying, "Dooyeweerd's retrieval leaps over the scholastic contamination of Calvin in the seventeenth and eighteenth centuries and thus brings to life a Calvin not concerned with the order of the decrees, but rather the reformer concerned only with the 'knowledge of God and the knowledge of self'—an Augustinian, non-scholastic Calvin."[49]

Although Dooyeweerd's views seem complex, he simplifies his point in the following manner: "The central motive of the Holy Scripture is the common supra-scientific starting-point of a truly biblical theology and of a truly Christian philosophy. It is the key of knowledge of which Jesus spoke in his

44. Herman Dooyeweerd, *Reformation and Scholasticism in Philosophy*, ed. D. F. M. Strauss, 3 vols., Collected Works, Series A 5–7 (Grand Rapids: Paideia, 2012), 1:36–37. The same type of dualism claim persists among devotees of Norman Shepherd: see P. Andrew Sandlin, "Gospel or Law, or Gospel and Law," *Reformation and Revival Journal* 11, no. 2 (2002): 124–35.

45. Dooyeweerd, *Twilight of Western Thought*, 96–97.

46. Dooyeweerd, *Reformation and Scholasticism*, 1:38.

47. Dooyeweerd, *Reformation and Scholasticism*, 1:38; see also John Halsey Wood, *Going Dutch in the Modern Age: Abraham Kuyper's Struggle for a Free Church in the Netherlands* (Oxford: Oxford University Press, 2013), 144–48.

48. Herman Dooyeweerd, "Kuyper's Wetenschapsleer," *Philosophia Reformata* 4 (1939): 193–232.

49. James K. A. Smith, introduction to *Twilight of Western Thought*, by Dooyeweerd, xi; see also Smith, "Will the Real Plato Please Stand Up?," 65n20.

discussion with the Scribes and the lawyers. It is the religious presupposition of any theoretical thought, which may rightly claim a biblical foundation."[50] In other words, for a true understanding of the cosmos, one must begin with the proper starting point, the correct presupposition. In his view, the proper starting point is the biblical ground motive of creation-fall-redemption. Hence, Dooyeweerd rejected any view that did not embrace the biblical ground motive. Anything less inevitably led to antithetical dualisms because of the idolization of the temporal realm and the inability to account for supratemporal realities.

Before we turn to analysis, there are four important points related to Dooyeweerd's rejection of so-called dualistic thought. First, Dooyeweerd did not base his Reformational philosophy directly on the exegesis of the Scriptures. In fact, he criticized others, such as Van Til, for being rationalist in trying to extract propositional truth from the Bible.[51] In contrast, Dooyeweerd believed that the biblical ground motive was the only true starting point for philosophy, "But, as such, it [the Bible] can never become the theoretical object of theology—no more than God and the human I can become such an object."[52] Rather, Dooyeweerd maintained that philosophy should accord with Scripture but not be derived from it.[53] To rest philosophical claims on overly close exegesis of the Scriptures was supposedly the hallmark of scholasticism, and hence an improper method of doing philosophy.

Second, Dooyeweerd criticized some Reformed confessions of faith. In his view, the Westminster Confession (1647) was poisoned because of its dualistic anthropology. According to Dooyeweerd, the Westminster Confession presented its anthropology in terms of a dualistic Thomistic-Aristotelian conception: body and soul. Although Dooyeweerd claimed fidelity to the Three Forms of Unity,[54] his criticisms would also apply to the Heidelberg Catechism (1563).[55]

Third, Dooyeweerd did not hold to a traditional view of the relationship between philosophy and theology. Historically, Reformed theologians have believed that theology is the queen of the sciences, and hence philosophy is a

50. Dooyeweerd, *Twilight of Western Thought*, 86–87.

51. Friesen, *Neo-Calvinism*, 386; see also Herman Dooyeweerd, "Cornelius Van Til and the Transcendental Critique of Theoretical Thought," in *Jerusalem and Athens: Critical Discussions on the Theology and Apologetics of Cornelius Van Til*, ed. E. R. Geehan ([Nutley, NJ]: P&R, 1971), 74–88.

52. Dooyeweerd, *Twilight of Western Thought*, 87.

53. Dooyeweerd, "Cornelius Van Til," 86; Friesen, *Neo-Calvinism*, 397n11.

54. Recognized by many branches of the Reformed faith, the Three Forms of Unity are the Belgic Confession, the Heidelberg Catechism, and the Canons of Dordt.

55. Dooyeweerd, "Cornelius Van Til," 75; see WCF 4.2; G. C. Berkouwer, *Man: The Image of God* (Grand Rapids: Eerdmans, 1962), 256; Heidelberg Catechism, qq. 1, 11, 26, 34, 37, 57, 69, 109, 118, 121, esp. 57.

second-tier discipline, a handmaiden to theology.[56] In contrast, Dooyeweerd maintained that theology was based on philosophy.[57] His doctrine of Scripture, therefore, looks quite similar to his anthropology. Just as human beings have a supratemporal heart and temporal periphery, so do the Scriptures:

> When you see that, then it is no longer strange that Holy Scripture also has a center, a religious center and a periphery, which belong to each other in an unbreakable way. That center is the spiritual *dynamis*, the spiritual driving force that proceeds from God's Word in this central, all-inclusive motive of creation, revelation of the fall into sin, redemption through Jesus Christ in the fellowship of the Holy Spirit.[58]

Therefore, apart from recognizing the biblical ground motive, mere biblical exegesis is insufficient. As long as the Spirit has not opened a person's heart and given the "key of knowledge," the supratemporal origin of the heart, theological exegesis is ultimately doomed by a dualistic ground motive.[59] In other words, apart from the right presupposition, one cannot accurately exegete the Scriptures.

Fourth, while Dooyeweerd may be unknown to many in the broader Reformed church, especially within Presbyterian circles, he has been the most influential Dutch Reformed philosopher after Kuyper.[60] Van Til, for example, employs Dooyeweerd's three apostate ground motives in his evaluation of various theological systems, as does James Smith.[61] Van Til, like Dooyeweerd,

56. See, e.g., Richard A. Muller, *Post-Reformation Reformed Dogmatics*, 4 vols. (Grand Rapids: Baker Academic, 2003), 1:142, 360–405.

57. Friesen, *Neo-Calvinism*, 390.

58. Herman Dooyeweerd, "Centrum en Omtrek: De Wijsbegeerte der Wetsidee in een veranderende wereld," *Philosophia Reformata* 72 (2007): 1–20, as quoted in Friesen, *Neo-Calvinism*, 388.

59. Friesen, *Neo-Calvinism*, 389.

60. See, e.g., Berkouwer's significant interaction with Dooyeweerd: Berkouwer, *Man*, 94–95, 255–64. For Dooyeweerd's influence, see Michael J. McVicar, *Christian Reconstruction: Rousas J. Rushdoony and American Religious Conservatism* (Chapel Hill: University of North Carolina Press, 2015), 210; George M. Marsden, "Reformed and American," in *Reformed Theology in America: A History of Its Modern Development*, ed. David F. Wells (Grand Rapids: Baker, 1997), 9–10; Julie J. Ingersoll, *Building God's Kingdom: Inside the World of Christian Reconstruction* (Oxford: Oxford University Press, 2015), 14–16, 19–20; R. C. Sproul, John Gerstner, and Arthur J. Lindsley, *Classical Apologetics: A Rational Defense of the Christian Faith and a Critique of Presuppositional Apologetics* (Grand Rapids: Zondervan, 1984), 247–50; James K. A. Smith, *Desiring the Kingdom: Worship, Worldview, and Culture Formation* (Grand Rapids: Baker Academic, 2009), 24, 43; Smith, *Imagining the Kingdom: How Worship Works* (Grand Rapids: Baker Academic, 2013), 126n43; Smith, *Introducing Radical Orthodoxy: Mapping a Post-secular Theology* (Grand Rapids: Baker Academic, 2004), 26, 40, 42, 80.

61. Van Til, *New Synthesis Theology*, 5–6; Smith, *Introducing Radical Orthodoxy*, 147n15, 153–54.

also levels the same scholastic-infection accusation against Kuyper and Herman Bavinck (1854–1921).[62] For Van Til, there are two Kuypers and two Bavincks—the biblical versus scholastic theologians, pure versus poisoned by the Greek ground motive. Like Dooyeweerd, Van Til believed that Reformed theologians after Calvin drank from the contaminated well of scholasticism: "But after Calvin the everlasting temptation besetting all Christians, especially sophisticated Christians, to make friends with those that are of Cain's lineage proved too much for many Lutheran and even Reformed theologians and so Lutheran and Reformed Scholasticism were begotten and born."[63] Once the infection is diagnosed, Van Til believed, "the Reformed apologete is . . . better able than ever before to cut himself loose from every form of Scholasticism and Arminianism."[64] Smith offers similar observations regarding scholasticism.[65]

Analysis

If one adopts Dooyeweerd's views regarding the relationship between philosophy and theology, and especially exegesis and theology, it is impossible to argue with his conclusions. One must begin with his "biblical" ground motive and the supratemporal origins of humanity; otherwise all exegetical conclusions are false. Moreover, he labels as rationalistic any attempt to extract propositional truth from the Scriptures. Hence, on what basis can one argue with Dooyeweerd? He has nested himself on a philosophical perch, far out of reach even of the exegesis of the Scriptures—at least, that is what Dooyeweerd might want us to believe. The problem with Dooyeweerd's claims, however, is that he had to discover his "biblical" ground motive from the Scriptures. Where else did he learn of union with Christ and creation-fall-redemption? Dooyeweerd had to draw these philosophical points from Scripture; he rightly or wrongly *exegeted* them. Hence, the following analysis engages in counter-exegesis in addition to submitting Dooyeweerd's historical-theological claims to close scrutiny. The analysis proceeds along the following five points: (1) the historical-theological claims made by Dooyeweerd; (2) the inadequacies of his criticisms against so-called dualisms; (3) the Kantian nature of his Reformational theology; (4) his failure to recognize the differences between separations

62. Van Til, *New Synthesis Theology*, 30, 43, 56–57.

63. Cornelius Van Til, *Herman Dooyeweerd and Reformed Apologetics*, 3 parts (Philadelphia: Westminster Theological Seminary, 1972), 3:17.

64. Cornelius Van Til, "Herman Dooyeweerd (A Personal Tribute)," *Westminster Theological Journal* 39, no. 2 (1977): 319–27.

65. Smith, *Introducing Radical Orthodoxy*, 154nn34–35.

and distinctions; and (5) his reliance on the disproved hellenization thesis of von Harnack.

Historical-Theological Claims

Dooyeweerd claims that because Roman Catholic theology adopted the Greek philosophical form-matter dualism, its body-soul anthropology was infected and thus unbiblical. The nature-grace dualism only further compromised the Roman Catholic system of theology. Protestants drew from the same poisoned well during the Reformation, and the Reformed scholastics never escaped the grip of these dualistic ground motives. Such a narrative creates a convenient backdrop against which he offers his own ground motive, but in fact Dooyeweerd has constructed a mythological straw man. Thomas Aquinas unquestionably employs the Aristotelian categories of form and matter to describe the relationship between the body and the soul, but contrary to Dooyeweerd's claims, he does not hold to a dualistic construction. Aquinas has a view similar to that of Aristotle, not Plato. Aquinas is neither a dualist nor physicalist. Instead, he believes that humans are composite beings that are both spiritual and corporeal.[66]

Aquinas explains the relationship between body and soul in terms of the Aristotelian form-matter distinction. But it is important to note that for Aquinas, the soul is the *substantial* form of the body, not the *accidental* form.[67] In other words, we must not think in terms of Aquinas's substance-accidents distinction by which he explains the doctrine of transubstantiation. The soul is not an accidental form of the body. Rather, as the substantial form, the soul is the principle of life by which things have their essential features or characteristics.[68] In other words, Aquinas believes that human beings are not mere souls, and neither are they simply bodies, but they are both soul and body. Aquinas distinguishes between the soul and the body, but in the end they are ultimately inseparable.[69] Moreover, Aquinas takes issue with a dualistic understanding of the relationship between the body and the soul, the belief that a human is a soul imprisoned in the body. A person is not chiefly a soul but rather is both body and soul. Aquinas writes, "Some, however, tried

66. Brian Davies, *The Thought of Thomas Aquinas* (Oxford: Clarendon, 1993), 209.
67. Thomas Aquinas, *Summa Theologica* (repr., Allen, TX: Christian Classics, 1948), Ia q. 76 art. 8. Contemporary Roman Catholic theology still adheres to a Thomist anthropology; see *Catechism of the Catholic Church* (Mahwah, NJ: Paulist Press, 1994), §§362, 366. see also Edward Feser, *Scholastic Metaphysics: A Contemporary Introduction* (Piscataway, NJ: Editiones Scholasticae, 2014), 164–70.
68. Davies, *Thought of Thomas Aquinas*, 210.
69. Aquinas, *Summa Theologica*, Ia q. 75 art. 4.

to maintain that the intellect is united to the body as its motor. . . . This is, however, absurd."[70] Aquinas rejected the idea that the soul was merely the motivating impulse for the body; the soul was not simply the motor of the body.

Aquinas believed that by definition people are both body and soul: "To be united to the body belongs to the soul by reason of itself, as it belongs to a light body by reason of itself to be raised up. And as a light body remains light when removed from its proper place, retaining its proper place; so the human soul retains proper existence when separated from the body, having an aptitude and a natural inclination to be united to the body."[71] In other words, people who die are not complete human beings until they receive their resurrected bodies. Aquinas links the necessity of both body and soul to the resurrection of Christ. Whatever one postulates about humanity must also be said about Christ.[72] Contra Dooyeweerd, then, Aquinas does not have a dualistic anthropology, but this does not mean that there is no need for correction or refinement.

Dooyeweerd rightly identifies problems with Aquinas's use of the categories of nature and grace, but he fails to recognize that the Reformed theologians who came later rejected the nature-grace construct.[73] Aquinas believed that God created humans as body and soul, but in order to counterbalance our proclivity to favor the lower aspects of our being, God gave humans the superadded gift (*donum superadditum*) of original righteousness: "As a result of original justice, the reason had perfect hold over the lower parts of the soul, while reason itself was perfected by God, and was subject to Him."[74] Original righteousness, therefore, kept the lower parts of the soul in check.

We should note here, however, that Aquinas believed that the *donum superadditum* was part of humanity's original constitution at creation, not something added later, as in semi-Pelagian medieval formulations. Reformed scholastic theologian Francis Turretin (1623–87) specifically engages the question of nature and grace and rejects this later type of construct when he engages the views of Robert Bellarmine (1542–1621). Turretin, along with the "orthodox," indicates that original righteousness was not a superadded gift but was natural to man. Regarding the superadded gift, Turretin states: "No one of our divines asserts this."[75] Turretin believed that it was contrary to God's nature to create humanity in something less than an estate of righteousness.

---

70. Aquinas, *Summa Theologica*, Ia q. 76 art. 1.

71. Aquinas, *Summa Theologica*, Ia q. 76 art. 1 rep. obj. 6.

72. Davies, *Thought of Thomas Aquinas*, 218–19.

73. Dooyeweerd, *Reformation and Scholasticism*, 1:38.

74. Aquinas, *Summa Theologica*, Ia-IIae q. 85 art. 3.

75. Francis Turretin, *Institutes of Elenctic Theology*, ed. James T. Dennison Jr., trans. George Musgrave Giger, 3 vols. (Phillipsburg, NJ: P&R, 2002–7), 5.11.4.

For God to create humans in their natural state with a need for the superadded gift of righteousness would mean that in their original state, humans, even before the fall, were inherently defective.[76]

Instead, Turretin maintained that humankind's natural end, its successful probation in the garden, presupposes a natural means for obtaining it. This means that if eternal blessedness was the goal, then the natural means by which humanity would have obtained it was original righteousness.[77] Turretin then explains:

> Although original righteousness can properly be called "grace" or "a gratuitous gift" (and so not due on the part of God, just as the nature itself also, created by him), it does not follow that it is supernatural or not due to the perfection of the innocent nature. For although God owed nothing to man, yet it being posited that he willed to create man after his own image, he was bound to create him righteous and holy.[78]

Turretin highlights the gracious nature of humanity's endowment with righteousness, but he also quickly qualifies his remarks by placing this righteousness under the category of humanity's natural state, not one superadded by grace. In other words, contra Dooyeweerd's claim, Turretin and other Reformed theologians expressly rejected a nature-grace construct.

In some respects, Dooyeweerd correctly identifies problems with the nature-grace construct. (I say *construct* because, strictly speaking, it is not a true dualism: there is an imbalance between a human's lower and higher aspects of the soul, which the superadded gift addresses, but Aquinas does not hold to the inferiority of physical matter, as in Plato's anthropology.) But significant historical-theological errors hobble Dooyeweerd's claims concerning the supposed continued Reformed use of this category. Dooyeweerd's analysis falters on two counts: (1) he rarely, if ever, supports his claims with primary-source documentation; and (2) he erroneously defines *scholasticism*. Dooyeweerd attaches specific theological content to the term *scholasticism* instead of recognizing it as a method of doing theology common to academic settings in the Middle Ages and then in the late sixteenth and seventeenth centuries.[79] Dooyeweerd believed that, among the Reformers, Calvin alone escaped the clutches of scholasticism.[80] He therefore pitted Calvin against the "Calvinists."

76. Turretin, *Institutes*, 5.11.9.
77. Turretin, *Institutes*, 5.11.10.
78. Turretin, *Institutes*, 5.11.16.
79. Dooyeweerd, *Twilight of Western Thought*, 31–35, 47–48, 81–82, 96–97.
80. Dooyeweerd, *Twilight of Western Thought*, 116; Dooyeweerd, *Reformation and Scholasticism*, 1:15.

In one sense, Dooyeweerd's erroneous understanding of the relationship between Calvin and the rest of the Reformed tradition is a product of his age. But in the present day, the Calvin-versus-Calvinsts thesis has been dismantled by significant and trenchant critique.[81] Nevertheless, Dooyeweerd's erroneous claims persist among his contemporary disciples.[82] This was also the case with Van Til, who incorrectly identified scholasticism with rationalism. In fact, Dooyeweerd and Van Til repeatedly threw the epithet of *scholasticism* at one another, which was a way of accusing one another of rationalism.[83] Dooyeweerd's understanding of the nature-grace construct, as well as his broader understanding of scholasticism, casts significant doubt on his claims with respect to the supposed dualisms that underlie classic Reformed theology.

Additionally, for all of Calvin's supposed biblical purity, Dooyeweerd ignores two important elements of Calvin's thought. First, Calvin maintained a body-soul anthropology very similar to that of Aquinas. In fact, Calvin argues that Plato rightly identified the soul's immortal nature.[84] The "apostate ground motive" infection that Dooyeweerd attributes to later Reformed theologians is equally apparent in Calvin, though Dooyeweerd seems to have missed it. Nevertheless, Dooyeweerd still calls Calvin's theology "pure." Second, Dooyeweerd—and Van Til, for that matter—makes much of Calvin's epistemological starting point: one must begin with God in order to understand humans. Calvin notes that if we begin with a knowledge of ourselves, we would ultimately become displeased, given our ignorance, vanity, poverty, infirmity, depravity, and the like: "The knowledge of ourselves, therefore, is not only an incitement to seek after God, but likewise a considerable assistance toward finding him."[85] On the other hand, Calvin opines that no one can arrive at a true knowledge of self without first contemplating God's character and

81. See, e.g., Richard A. Muller, *Christ and the Decree: Christology and the Decree in Reformed Theology from Calvin to Perkins* (Grand Rapids: Baker Academic, 2008); Muller, *The Unaccommodated Calvin: Studies in the Foundations of a Theological Tradition* (Oxford: Oxford University Press, 2001); Muller, *After Calvin: Studies in the Development of a Theological Tradition* (Oxford: Oxford University Press, 2003); Muller, *Calvin and the Reformed Tradition: On the Work of Christ and the Order of Salvation* (Grand Rapids: Baker Academic, 2012).

82. E.g., James K. A. Smith, *Introducing Radical Orthodoxy*, 37; Smith, introduction to *Twilight of Western Thought*, by Dooyeweerd, xi; A. P. Bos and D. F. M. Strauss, "Greek Ontology and Biblical Cosmology: An Unbridgeable Gap," in *In the Phrygian Mode: Neo-Calvinism, Antiquity and the Lamentations of Reformed Philosophy*, ed. Robert Sweetman (Lanham, MD: University Press of America, 2007), 101–26.

83. See the exchange between Van Til and Dooyeweerd in E. R. Geehan, ed., *Jerusalem and Athens*, 74–128.

84. John Calvin, *Institutes of the Christian Religion*, trans. John Allen (Grand Rapids: Eerdmans, 1948), 1.15.6; Cooper, *Body, Soul*, 13.

85. Calvin, *Institutes*, 1.1.1.

then descending to consider one's own.[86] He opts for the latter approach as the "proper order of instruction," but unlike Dooyeweerd and Van Til, he does not vilify the other approach.[87] The Reformer does not characterize starting with man as pagan. Both Dooyeweerd and Van Til fail to note Calvin saying that one may begin with man and still arrive at the truth. Calvin's starting point is not as biblically pure nor as dogmatically necessary as Dooyeweerd or Van Til maintain, at least according to Calvin. If the chief authority in defining humanity and God is Scripture, then starting points are interchangeable as one inevitably leads to the other, regardless of whether one starts with humanity or with God. The *ordo docendi* (order of teaching) is not the same as the *ordo essendi* (order of being).

Criticisms against So-Called Dualisms

Dooyeweerd's misunderstanding of the nature-grace construct and scholasticism raises significant questions about his claims regarding dualisms. The bare accusation of a dualism has apparently been sufficient to sideline classic elements of Reformed theology. As noted above, Dooyeweerd believed that the Westminster Confession was faulty for embracing a scholastic, body-soul, dualistic anthropology: "And insofar as the influence of the Thomistic-Aristotelian metaphysics had even revealed itself in some formulations of the Reformed Confessions, especially in the Westminster Confession, this attack could be easily interpreted as a deviation from the Church's doctrine."[88] He leveled similar accusations against Kuyper's doctrines of common and particular grace and the distinction between law and gospel. Yet we should ask whether Dooyeweerd's accusations are accurate. Does the body-soul anthropology actually constitute a dualism? Does common grace, or correlatively natural law and common notions, impose a dualism on the creation? Do Reformed theologians actually understand justification in a dialectic and therefore dualistic manner by distinguishing between the functions of law and gospel?[89]

The answer to these questions depends on how one defines the concept of *dualism*. If Dooyeweerd's understanding of dualism is the benchmark, then body-soul, law-gospel, common-special grace, and natural and supernatural

86. Calvin, *Institutes*, 1.1.2.

87. Calvin, *Institutes*, 1.1.3.

88. Dooyeweerd, *Western Thought*, 38, 64, 108; Dooyeweerd, *Reformation and Scholasticism*, 1:37–38, 326–27; 2:90.

89. See Paul Jersild, "Natural Theology and the Doctrine of God in Albrecht Ritschl and Karl Barth," *Lutheran Quarterly* 14, no. 3 (1962): 239–57.

revelation are possibly dualistic. But Dooyeweerd's understanding of a dualism is considerably different from the classic gnostic or cosmic dualisms. In classic dualisms, there are two antithetical elements in perpetual irreconcilable conflict. Dualists pit the body against the soul, and soul seeks to overcome the negative influence of the body so it can escape its fleshly prison. In a cosmic dualism, good and evil perpetually yet unsuccessfully grapple for superiority. Westminster's doctrine of man advocates a catholic understanding of body and soul but does not pit the body against the soul. And the Confession (WCF 32) affirms the resurrection of the body, which is the very antithesis of a dualistic anthropology.

When Reformed theologians spoke in terms of law and gospel, like Luther, they did not create a dualism with two warring irreconcilable principles.[90] The law-gospel distinction is about recognizing that, in the point of justification, people are incapable of rendering perfect obedience to the law and require the imputed righteousness of Jesus, the covenant surety. Either Christ fulfills the law or the sinner tries to do it. Such an opposition comes straight from the apostle Paul: "But if it [God's election] is by grace, it is no longer on the basis of works" (Rom. 11:6). Paul also writes, "Now to the one who works, his wages are not counted as a gift but as his due. And to the one who does not work but believes in him who justifies the ungodly, his faith is counted as righteousness" (Rom. 4:4–5). In other words, either Christ's or the sinner's obedience justifies the sinner, not both. This is not a dualism but an either-or proposition. Moreover, even according to Dooyeweerd's idiosyncratic definition of a dualism (i.e., absolutizing one aspect over another) the purpose of the law-gospel distinction is to emphasize the sole place of Christ's obedience as that which secures the believer's redemption: "For by grace you have been saved through faith. And this is not your own doing; it is the gift of God, not a result of works, so that no one may boast" (Eph. 2:8–9). Classic early modern Reformed theology does not completely eliminate the law from the entirety of salvation, only from justification. The law fulfills a vital pedagogical function in driving the sinner to Christ, and normatively, it serves as a guide for the Christian life (WCF 19.6–7). Dooyeweerd does not

90. On law and gospel in Reformed theology, see, e.g., Zacharias Ursinus, *Larger Catechism*, in *An Introduction to the Heidelberg Catechism: Sources, History and Theology*, ed. Lyle D. Bierma et al. (Grand Rapids: Baker Academic, 2005), qq. 10, 31, p. 164; William Perkins, *A Commentarie or Exposition, upon the Five First Chapters of the Epistle to the Galatians* (Cambridge: John Legat, 1604), 292; Edward Fisher, *Marrow of Modern Divinity* (1645; repr., Edinburgh: John Boyd, 1778), 7; James Ussher, *Body of Divinitie* (London: Thomas Downes & George Badger, 1645), 159; Herman Bavinck, *Reformed Dogmatics*, ed. John Bolt, trans. John Vriend, 4 vols. (Grand Rapids: Baker Academic, 2003–8), 4:448–54; Louis Berkhof, *Systematic Theology: New Combined Edition* (1932; repr., Grand Rapids: Eerdmans, 1996), 612–15.

demonstrate that he has grasped these points and has instead painted with a very large brush: he seems to think that because there are two elements, law and gospel, these must constitute an unwarranted dualism.

The same holds true for Dooyeweerd's criticism of common grace and natural law. Common grace does not stand in antithesis to special grace; the former supports and undergirds the latter.[91] To borrow a scriptural narrative and adjust it for the sake of argument, common grace entails the preservation of Sodom for the sake of ten righteous people dwelling in it (Gen. 18:16–33). Common grace does not exist in an irreconcilable conflict with special grace; God is the author and source of both. The same holds true for natural law. God writes *his* laws and common notions on the hearts of all people (Rom. 2:14–15). Even in a fallen creation, people still know, follow, and employ them.[92] Reformed scholastic theologian Franciscus Junius (1545–1602), for example, specifically states that natural law originates from God: "The efficient cause of [natural law] is God the author of nature to whom belongs the care of the universe, but especially the cause of human beings."[93] Junius believed that God's law was infused into human nature. According to Junius, "*Infusing* is nothing other than that which is dispensed into us from the heavenly principle that is above us all and above our nature."[94] Natural law, therefore, is not a neutral zone: it is *God's* law. Junius, and other Reformed theologians, Calvin included, did not absolutize an element of temporal existence. They simply recognized that humans are created with God's law written on their hearts and that God used this law, even in a fallen world, to regulate their conduct. But unlike the perpetually unresolved tension of a cosmic dualism, common grace and natural law have a *telos* in view: they become unnecessary when Christ consummates history.

Therefore, what Dooyeweerd labels as dualistic is not so in reality. On Dooyeweerd's account, must we conclude that the catholic doctrine of Christ is a dualism because he has two natures? Must we conclude that anything with two elements constitutes a dualism? The answer to these questions is no. A classic dualism pits two principles against one another in an irreconcilable conflict.[95] Moreover, dualisms typically pit biblical truths against one another. Dualists characterize the body as evil, whereas Scripture says that it

91. For Kuyper's views on common grace, see, e.g., Abraham Kuyper, "Common Grace," in *Abraham Kuyper: A Centennial Reader*, ed. James D. Bratt (Grand Rapids: Eerdmans, 1998), 165–204.

92. VanDrunen, *Divine Covenants*, 209–62.

93. Francis Junius, *The Mosaic Polity*, trans. Todd Rester, ed. Andrew M. McGinnis (Grand Rapids: CLP Academic, 2015), thesis 4, p. 44.

94. Junius, *Mosaic Polity*, thesis 5, p. 48.

95. Berkouwer, *Man*, 211–13.

is good (Gen. 1:26–31). Cosmic dualisms claim that evil is eternal and equal in power to good, whereas Scripture says that evil is contingent and will eventually fall under God's eternal judgment. Dooyeweerd's error consists in creating an idiosyncratic definition of what constitutes a dualism and then applying it wherever it suits his system. And ironically, Dooyeweerd's admission that upon death a person's inner aspect separates from the outer aspect means that he ultimately holds to a dualistic anthropology, despite his claims to the contrary.[96]

The Kantian Nature of Dooyeweerd's Philosophy

The chief problem with Dooyeweerd's system is that, despite all his claims of biblical purity, his Reformational philosophy bears all the marks of Kantian transcendental thought.[97] As with transcendental arguments, one adopts a starting point and then deduces the rest of one's system from that starting point. The idea of a *central dogma*, which finds its origin in the thought of both Kant and Christian Wolff (1679–1754), colors a lot of nineteenth- and twentieth-century philosophy and theology. Kuyper's central dogma is the sovereignty of God; Van Til's central dogma is the ontological Trinity (or Scripture); and Dooyeweerd's central dogma is his biblical ground motive.[98] To characterize a proper starting point for knowledge and philosophy, Dooyeweerd invoked the Archimedean principle, "Give me a place to stand [*pou stō*], and I will move the world."[99] Dooyeweerd and other theologians and philosophers of the period looked for the one principle from which to deduce an entire system of thought, a procedure that bears the marks of German idealism.

Dooyeweerd writes, for example, "Standing in the Truth, as the sharing in the fullness of meaning of the cosmos in Christ, is the indispensable prerequisite for the insight into the full horizon of our experience."[100] For true knowledge, one must begin with Christ. Dooyeweerd defines his whole system in terms of his central dogma, his biblical ground motive. The problem is that the system of doctrine contained within the Scriptures cannot be distilled to one principle from which the whole is deduced or argued. Yes, the ontological Trinity is a key consideration and must feature prominently in

96. Berkouwer, *Man*, 255–56; Cooper, *Body, Soul*, 26–27.

97. Cooper, *Body, Soul*, 228–30.

98. Abraham Kuyper, *Lectures on Calvinism* (Grand Rapids: Eerdmans, 1931), 15, 19, 58–59; Cornelius Van Til, *Christian Apologetics* (Phillipsburg, NJ: P&R, 1976), 8, 13, 27.

99. Dooyeweerd, *New Critique*, 1:8–11.

100. Dooyeweerd, *New Critique*, 2:564.

any theological system, but we must also account for creation, revelation, eschatology, election, and so on. This is the problem with Dooyeweerd's ground motive as a central dogma. In many respects, he has a Barthian-like Christomonist central dogma; this is not, as some have pointed out, soteriological, but principial, Christocentrism.[101] That is, Christ is not merely at the center of soteriology; rather, Christ is the principle from which everything originates. If Dooyeweerd's ground motive is the central dogma, which centers on redemption through and union with Christ, then there is little or no place for preredemptive categories such as natural law, common notions, or the tension between this present evil age and the age to come, the inbreaking of the eschaton. Everything is eschatology, everything is special grace, everything centers on redemption.

Unlike central dogma-dominated systems, sixteenth- and seventeenth-century theological systems are superior because they employ the locus method.[102] Theologians did not look for one singular point from which to construct an entire system but instead recognized that there are multiple loci within theology, such as prolegomena, Scripture, the Triune God, Christology, soteriology, ecclesiology, and eschatology. Such a method acknowledges multiple doctrines and guards against allowing any one point to swallow the rest of the system. Dooyeweerd seems to be unaware of these things as he cites Calvin, and in particular Calvin's idea of the twofold knowledge of God, as a precursor to his own biblical ground motive. Yet Dooyeweerd strips the twofold knowledge of God out of Calvin's larger system and does not account for his body-soul anthropology or his endorsement of natural law, or of Plato, for that matter.[103] As much as Dooyeweerd may claim to be a descendant of Calvin, his Kantian idealism is worlds apart from Calvin's theological system. Moreover, Dooyeweerd does not really exegete the Scriptures but begins with a loosely biblical idea (his ground motive), whereas Calvin built his definitive 1559 *Institutes of the Christian Religion* on a lifetime of exegetical spadework.[104] Dooyeweerd's Reformational philosophy, therefore, is a scant shadow of Calvin's Reformed theology. Kant and the Enlightenment project loom large over Dooyeweerd's Reformational philosophy.

101. Richard A. Muller, "A Note on 'Christocentrism' and the Imprudent Use of Such Terminology," *Westminster Theological Journal* 68, no. 2 (2006): 256; also John Webster, "The Place of Christology in Systematic Theology," in *The Oxford Handbook of Christology* (Oxford: Oxford University Press, 2015), 611–28.

102. Cf. Muller, *Post-Reformation Reformed Dogmatics*, 1:123–46, 177–89.

103. For Calvin's views on natural law, see David VanDrunen, *Natural Law and the Two Kingdoms: A Study in the Development of Reformed Social Thought* (Grand Rapids: Eerdmans, 2010), 67–118.

104. See Muller, *Unaccommodated Calvin*, 99–117.

Separations versus Distinctions

One of the chief problems with the criticism against so-called dualisms is that Dooyeweerd and his disciples fail to recognize the difference between a true dichotomy (or separation) and a mere distinction. Dooyeweerd presents no primary-source evidence to validate his claims, for example, against the so-called body-soul dualism. He simply assumes that it is dualistic and therefore unbiblical. One finds the same type of inadequate analysis in his disciples. Smith writes:

> The Protestant fundamentalism of my early Christian formation was characterized by what I came to describe—following the wake of Kuyper and Dooyeweerd—as dualism. While dualism can refer to an oppositional bifurcation between sacred and secular, I have been particularly concerned with a (related) more docetic dualism that erects a hierarchical and oppositional bifurcation between the immaterial and material, the soul and the body, the invisible and visible.[105]

Smith cites no primary sources but refers only to other analyses that have come to similar conclusions. Albert Wolters never cites any sources but still inveighs against the supposed separation of sacred and secular.[106] If we actually examine the historical evidence, common dualism claims fail.

Among the Reformed, distinctions were a vital tool for proper theology. Johannes Maccovius (1588–1644), Reformed scholastic theologian and delegate to the Synod of Dordt (1618–19), wrote an entire work dedicated to distinctions: *A Hundredfold Most General Distinctions.*[107] Maccovius stood on the shoulders of his scholastic forebears because he believed that distinctions were necessary to determine agreement, difference, and perspicuity in theological discourse.[108] Such a methodology stretches back to the Middle Ages and was employed by theologians throughout their systems.

For example, John Duns Scotus (ca. 1266–1308) created two categories of distinctions, formal and real. A real distinction (*distinctio realis*) is a difference between two or more independent things, whereas a formal distinction

---

105. Smith, "Will the Real Plato Please Stand Up?," 62.

106. Wolters, *Creation Regained*, 11–12, 64–65. Another similar example of this claim, albeit with references to Plato, Aristotle, Augustine, and Thomas à Kempis, is Richard Middleton, *A New Heaven and Earth: Reclaiming Biblical Eschatology* (Grand Rapids: Baker Academic, 2014), 31–32, 246–48.

107. Johannes Maccovius, *A Hundredfold Most General Distinctions*, in *Scholastic Discourse: Johannes Maccovius (1588–1644) on Theological and Philosophical Distinctions and Rules*, ed. Willem J. van Asselt et al. (Apeldoorn: Instituut voor Reformatieonderzoek, 2009), 288–363.

108. Maccovius, *General Distinctions*, prolegomena, §3, p. 289.

(*distinctio formalis*) identifies formal aspects of a single thing, such as intellect and will, which are not separate but distinguishable.[109] Important to note here is that a formal distinction is not a real distinction.[110] In other words, a formal distinction merely observes aspects of a unified object; it does not separate them, because they are inseparable given their existence in a single object. In this respect, theologians were fond of the Latin phrase *distinctio sed non separatio* (a distinction but not a separation).

Theologians can *distinguish* between body and soul without separating them. Thomas Goodwin (1600–1680), for example, one of the framers of the Westminster Confession, makes this very point:

> As when you distinguish of a Man, that *quoad Animam*, according to his Soul he is the offspring of God; for God is the Father of Spirits: But *quoad Corpus*, according to his Body he is begotten by man, who are the Fathers of our Bodies: To say a Man is Mortal *quoad Corpus*, but immortal *quoad Animam:* Such a distinction were needless, if a Man had not both a Body, and a Soul: Or if that Body, and Soul, made not up one manner of Person: Or if the Soul were one Person, as an Angel is, and the Body another.[111]

Goodwin specifically distinguishes between body and soul, but he does not separate them, contra Dooyeweerd's analysis.

Other Reformed scholastics, such as Johannes Heidegger (1633–98), explicitly affirm the unity of human anthropology; they merely distinguish between body and soul. Heidegger writes: "God did not so create man's body and spirit as to be diverse *hyphistamena* [subsistences] but so as by the intimate union of both to make one man.—And each of them compounded and by God's will most straightly united constituted one man, one *hyphistamenon* [subsistence], one living, knowing, speaking person."[112] Heidegger rests his

---

109. Richard A. Muller, *Dictionary of Latin and Greek Theological Terms: Drawn Principally from Protestant Scholastic Theology*, 2nd ed. (Grand Rapids: Baker Academic, 2017), s.v. *distinctio* (94–96); also Maurice Grajewski, "The Formal Distinction of Duns Scotus and Its Philosophic Applications," *Proceedings of the American Catholic Philosophical Association* 20 (1945): 145–56.

110. Antonie Vos, *The Philosophy of John Duns Scotus* (Edinburgh: Edinburgh University Press, 2006), 259.

111. Thomas Goodwin, *Of the Knowledge of God the Father, and His Son Jesus Christ*, in *The Works of Thomas Goodwin*, vol. 4, ed. Thankfull Owen and James Barron (London: [Thomas Goodwin Jr.], 1683), 2.5, p. 86; see similar statements by Richard Baxter, *The Life of Faith in Three Parts*, in *The Practical Works of Mr. Richard Baxter, in Four Volumes* (1660; London: Thomas Parkhurst et al., 1707), 3.25, p. 656.

112. Johannes Heidegger, *Corpus Theologiae Christianae*, 2 vols. (Tiguri: ex Officina Heideggeriana, 1732), 6.91, pp. 221–22; Heinrich Heppe, *Reformed Dogmatics: Set Out and Illustrated from the Sources* (London: George Allen & Unwin, 1950), 222.

anthropology on exegesis and argues that Scripture *distinguishes* between a human's body and soul, which he bases on a number of Old Testament texts (Gen. 6:17; Exod. 4:19; Num. 23:10; Judg. 16:30; Ps. 69:2; Job 7:7). In each of these texts Heidegger points to the distinction between body and spirit.[113] Notably, each of these texts in the Septuagint employs the terms *pneuma* or *psychē*, which translate the Hebrew terms *ruah* and *nephesh* respectively. Heidegger correlates these texts with passages from the New Testament, such as Matthew 10:28, "Do not fear those who kill the body but cannot kill the soul. Rather fear him who can destroy both soul and body in hell."[114] Heidegger notes the distinction between body and soul and, like Aquinas before him, says that opinions characterizing the body as merely an instrument of the soul are "absurd."[115]

Heidegger's conclusions clearly do not fit Dooyeweerd's so-called body-soul dualism. Moreover, Heidegger anticipates more recent studies leading to the same result: humans consist of two distinguishable elements, body and soul.[116] In this respect, G. C. Berkouwer (1903–96) offers an important observation regarding the body-soul distinction in light of Dooyeweerd's claims:

> It is important to make the simple observation that duality and dualism are not at all identical, and that a reference to a dual moment in cosmic reality does not necessarily imply a dualism. Trichotomy and dichotomy have this in common, that neither is to be rejected merely because it distinguishes several aspects in man—any more than we can say that the many "spheres" of the Calvinist philosopher Dooyeweerd a priori imply a splitting of man into various parts. A certain duality can be spoken of, for example, in the creation of man and woman, without this implying that God's intention was an opposition, a dualism, between the two (cf. Gen. 2:18). Duality within created reality does not exclude harmony and unity, but is exactly oriented towards it. Duality between man and fellow man, man and the world, becomes a dualism only when there is a polar tension, an inner separation, which destroys the unity between the terms.[117]

The body-soul distinction is not a dualism. Similarly, to distinguish between the secular and the sacred is not dualistic but rather recognizes that God rules over both yet in different ways. In classic Lutheran theology, for example, Martin

113. Heidegger, *Corpus Theologiae Christianae*, 6.92, p. 222.
114. Heidegger, *Corpus Theologiae Christianae*, 6.92, p. 222.
115. Heidegger, *Corpus Theologiae Christianae*, 6.92, pp. 222–23.
116. Cooper, *Body, Soul*, 45, 52–72, 110–78; Hans Walter Wolff, *Anthropology of the Old Testament* (Philadelphia: Fortress, 2012).
117. Berkouwer, *Man*, 211–12; cf. similar comments by A. A. Hoekema, *Created in God's Image* (Grand Rapids: Eerdmans, 1986), 217–18.

Luther characterizes the two kingdoms (sacred and secular) as the kingdoms of the right and left hands. But whose hands, precisely, are in view? God's hands are in view.[118] God sovereignly reigns over both realms but in different ways. Theologians distinguish God's reign through the magistrate from Christ's mediatorial reign in the church.[119] To label anything that has two elements as dualistic may be convenient for one's argument, but in Dooyeweerd's case it seldom has any basis in fact. Dooyeweerd fails to recognize the difference between true separations and distinctions.

Harnack's Hellenization Thesis Redivivus?

Dooyeweerd constantly bangs a drum for purifying philosophy and theology of apostate ground motives, but his attitudes toward Greek philosophy are strangely similar to those of Adolf von Harnack. Both Dooyeweerd and Harnack opposed Old Testament patterns to Greco-Roman philosophical claims,[120] believing that theology had been corrupted by the synthesis of Greek philosophy and biblical truth. Dooyeweerd echoes Harnack's hellenization thesis when he reproves Van Til for being rationalistic because Van Til drew doctrinal propositions from Scripture. Harnack believed that when Christians employed Greek philosophical categories in the defense of the faith, they unwittingly infected the Christian faith with the dogma virus. "Dogma," according to Harnack, "in its conception and development is a work of the Greek spirit on the soil of the Gospel."[121]

Greek philosophy turned the dynamic Christian faith into a series of propositions to which people had to assent. Harnack writes:

> That which Protestants and Catholics call dogmas, are not only ecclesiastical doctrines, but they are also . . . theses expressed in abstract terms, forming together a unity, and fixing the contents of the Christian religion as a knowledge of God, of the world, and of the sacred history under the aspect of a proof of the truth. . . . The only difference is that revelation is here put as authority in the

118. E.g., Martin Luther, *Selected Psalms*, in *Luther's Works*, vol. 12 (St. Louis: Concordia, 1955), 103–4; Luther, *Sermon on the Mount*, in *Luther's Works*, vol. 21 (St. Louis: Concordia, 1956), 211.

119. Cf., e.g., the WCF, which states that *God* is the supreme King of all the world and has ordained civil magistrates to be under him (23.1), whereas the visible church is the kingdom of the Lord Jesus Christ (25.1).

120. Robert Sweetman, "Neo-Calvinism, Antiquity and the Lamentations of Reformational Philosophy: A General Overview," in *In the Phrygian Mode: Neo-Calvinism, Antiquity and the Lamentations of Reformed Philosophy*, ed. Robert Sweetman (Lanham, MD: University Press of America, 2007), 6–10.

121. Adolf von Harnack, *History of Dogma*, 7 vols. (Boston: Little, Brown, 1898–1907), 1:17.

place of human knowledge, although the later philosophic schools appealed to revelation also. The theoretical as well as the practical doctrines which embraced the peculiar conception of the world and the ethics of the school, together with their rationale, were described in these schools as dogmas.[122]

Harnack foreshadows Dooyeweerd's critique against Protestant scholasticism and its failure to purge the Greek philosophical ground motives. And like Dooyeweerd, Harnack also believed that glimmers of light broke through the dense Hellenistic fog hanging low over the church: "The Gospel since the Reformation, in spite of retrograde movements which have not been wanting, is working itself out of the forms which it was once compelled to assume, and a true comprehension of its history will also contribute to hasten this process."[123] In other words, just as Dooyeweerd believed that Calvin broke the grip of the apostate ground motives, so too Harnack believed "the Reformation opened the way for a critical treatment of the history of dogma."[124] Harnack wanted to purge the Hellenistic elements from the church and recover the pure form of the gospel, one unadulterated by dogma. One can substitute Dooyeweerd's term *scholasticism* everywhere Harnack uses the word *dogma*, and the sets of arguments and claims are remarkably similar.

In fact, Harnack believed that the leaven of dogma lay in the apostle Paul's Letters.[125] To a certain extent, J. Gresham Machen (1881–1937) believed Harnack was correct, though to a very different end. Machen held that the history of doctrine was, in many ways, the history and development of Paulinism.[126] In other words, contrary to Dooyeweerd's claims, doctrine rests in exegesis, and this was one of the hallmarks of Reformed scholasticism: rigorous exegesis in the service of theological formulation.[127] Like Dooyeweerd, one of Harnack's concerns was the influx of Greek dualistic thought into Christianity. As Greek philosophy infected the church, faith was subordinated to Greek knowledge, and with this Greek knowledge came docetism and asceticism.[128] Greek philosophy brought three factors with it: "The speculative philosophical, the cultish-mystical, and the dualistic-ascetic." These developments anticipated Neoplatonism and Catholicism. Under the influence of Greek philosophy,

122. Harnack, *History of Dogma*, 1:15.
123. Harnack, *History of Dogma*, 1:21.
124. Harnack, *History of Dogma*, 1:25.
125. Harnack, *History of Dogma*, 1:136.
126. J. Gresham Machen, *The Origin of Paul's Religion* (1925; repr., Eugene, OR: Wipf & Stock, 2002), 7.
127. See, e.g., Muller, *Post-Reformation Reformed Dogmatics*, 2:442–519.
128. Adolf von Harnack, *Outlines of the History of Dogma* (London: Hodder & Stoughton, 1893), 66.

Christians sought "the freeing of the spiritual elements from their union with matter, or the separation of the good from the sensuous world through the Christ-Spirit."[129]

Harnack's hellenization thesis has been subjected to significant criticism.[130] James Barr (1924–2006), for example, diagnosed and addressed the underlying exegetical problems with claims like those of Harnack and Dooyeweerd.[131] Even in Dooyeweerd's day, Herman Bavinck (1854–1921) noted the interplay between Christian theologians and Greek philosophy, but Bavinck points out that theologians were philosophically eclectic and never embraced a single system, whether that of Plato or Aristotle. Instead, most took a critical stance toward philosophy and employed it as a handmaiden: "Just as Hagar was the servant of Sarah, as the treasures of Egypt were employed by the Israelites for the adornment of the tabernacle, as the wise men from the East placed their gifts at the feet of the child in Bethlehem, so, in the opinion of the church fathers, philosophy was the servant of theology."[132] Despite the significant evidence that disproves the hellenization thesis, Dooyeweerd and Harnack were happy to promote their hellenophobia but were blind to their own philosophical Germanophilia with their use of Kantian categories.[133]

Related to his hellenophobia is the question regarding Dooyeweerd's historical-methodological assumptions. Some have suggested that his ground-motives thesis reflects a Hegelian approach to history, as Dooyeweerd sets up dialectical oppositions between form and matter and nature and grace.[134] Can nearly two thousand years of history be summed up by one philosophical observation? Does the so-called nature-grace dualism truly explain medieval, Reformation, and post-Reformation theology? Does the so-called nature-grace dualism explain why medieval theologians supposedly bifurcated life into sacred and secular realms? If one reads neo-Calvinist writers, this is

129. Harnack, *Outlines*, 63.
130. See literature cited in Paul L. Gavrilyuk, *The Suffering of the Impassible God: The Dialectics of Patristic Thought* (Oxford: Oxford University Press, 2004), 4n13; also see William V. Rowe, "Adolf von Harnack and the Concept of Hellenization," in *Hellenization Revisited: Shaping a Christian Response within the Greco-Roman World*, ed. Wendy E. Helleman (Lanham, MD: University Press of America, 1994), 69–98.
131. James Barr, *The Semantics of Biblical Language* (Oxford: Oxford University Press, 1961).
132. Bavinck, *Reformed Dogmatics*, 1:608.
133. For Harnack's Kantian commitments, see Russell Manning, *Theology at the End of Culture: Paul Tillich's Theology of Culture and Art* (Leuven: Peeters, 2005), 34–38; Gary Dorrien, *Kantian Reason and Hegelian Spirit: The Idealistic Logic of Modern Theology* (Chichester, UK: John Wiley & Sons, 2012), 315–77, esp. 321–37.
134. William Rowe, "Vollenhoven's and Dooyeweerd's Appropriation of Greek Philosophy," in *In the Phrygian Mode: Neo-Calvinism, Antiquity and the Lamentations of Reformed Philosophy*, ed. Robert Sweetman (Lanham, MD: University Press of America, 2007), 223.

precisely what they propose. Yet they appear not to deal with two important matters.

First, do such statements accord with the facts of history? Under the medieval church, many who held to the supposed nature-grace dualism believed that the church, under the pope's rule, was ultimately sovereign over all.[135] All of life was unified under the church. Neo-Calvinists also make a faulty assumption when they interpret Plato himself. They would have us believe that a body-soul dualism leads to quietism and a dualism between the sacred and secular realms. Plato most definitely held to a body-soul dualism, but he did not believe in any type of quietism. In his famous *Republic*, he taught that philosopher-kings were ideally suited to govern because they would do so in the pursuit of justice (*dikaiosynē*). According to Plato, a true understanding of forms would enable the citizens of the ideal city to dwell in peace and harmony.[136] Whoever wanted to escape the prison of the body had to live ethically. This would surely not result in disengagement from political life. The best-informed citizens would employ the body-soul dualism for significant cultural engagement, at least according to Plato's theories. An example of Platonic civic-mindedness appears in Cicero's (106–43 BC) account of a dream of Scipio Africanus (236–183 BC):

> You must not depart from human life until you receive the command from him who has given you that soul; otherwise you will be judged to have deserted the earthly post assigned to you by God. Instead, Scipio, be like your grandfather here, and me, your father. Respect justice and do your duty. That is important in the case of parents and relatives, and paramount in the case of one's country. That is the way of life which leads to heaven and to the company, here, of those who have already completed their lives.[137]

Cicero, who admired Plato, did not believe in quietism as a consequence of his commitment to a body-soul dualism. Such observations go unnoticed by Dooyeweerd and other neo-Calvinists because their analysis has become detached from the historical facts.

Second, Dooyeweerd and other neo-Calvinists have not examined their own presuppositions regarding historical methodology. They ultimately employ a central dogma to explain highly complex historical events. In other words, they look for a silver-bullet explanation, one theory that accounts for everything,

---

135. VanDrunen, *Natural Law and the Two Kingdoms*, 32–36.

136. Plato, *The Republic*, trans. Allan Bloom (New York: Basic Books, 1991), 7, pp. 193–221.

137. Cicero, *Republic*, in *The Republic and The Laws*, trans. Niall Rudd (Oxford: Oxford University Press, 2008), 6.15–16, pp. 88–89.

and then explain history in terms of this thesis. Such a methodology is common among nineteenth-century historians such as Harnack but falls short of offering accurate historical analysis.

Conclusion

The so-called dualism claims of some neo-Calvinist theologians fail due to several factors: an idiosyncratic definition of what constitutes a dualism, historical-theological errors and a failure to engage or even cite primary sources, and a commitment to Kantian-influenced theological and historical methods. In spite of these significant shortcomings, the claims against so-called dualisms continue unabated. Whoever tries to raise classic Reformed categories such as natural law or common notions is shouted down as being infected by the nature-grace dualism.

In an overheated letter to the editor of *New Horizons*, the journal of the Orthodox Presbyterian Church, one writer commented:

> Instead of Van Til's militantly antithetical stance against Roman Catholic thought, as well as his consistent starting point of the self-attesting Christ of Scripture applied to all areas of life, we find a compromising position that gives way to a nature-grace dualism that Van Til opposed. In fact, Horton's agenda concerning two kingdoms, natural law, and common grace, which definitely undergirds his article, has more affinity to Aquinas's nature-grace scheme than to Van Til's organic understanding of natural and special revelation being applied to the civil realm.[138]

This one quotation illustrates how widespread is the misunderstanding reflected in the dualism thesis, because it appears in a denominational magazine intended for the person in the pew. The magazine's audience is not academic professionals. Yet this one statement touches on most of the points mentioned in this chapter: dualism, nature-grace, Aquinas, and a methodology defined by a central dogma, starting with the self-attesting Christ of Scripture applied to all areas of life. Ironically, this letter was titled "Militant Reformed Orthodoxy," but the author inveighs against the very categories employed by Reformed Orthodox theologians of the sixteenth and seventeenth centuries, such as natural law. The present climate has become one of outright hostility to classic Reformed theology, but this hostility rests on shaky foundations.

138. William Dennison, "Letter to the Editor: Militant Reformed Orthodoxy," *New Horizons*, January 2012, 20–21.

This chapter has taken at least one small step toward discrediting some neo-Calvinist claims about so-called dualisms. Any who want to claim that classic Reformed theology employs dualisms may do so, but they should ensure that their claims are accurate and supported by primary sources. Acknowledging the confessional and biblical position that humans consist of a body and soul, that such categories as natural and supernatural revelation are valid, and that there are sacred and secular realms need not introduce any noxious dualisms to the theological or apologetic project. Rather, God is the source and author of humans, body and soul, and of all law, naturally and supernaturally revealed, and God is sovereign over both the sacred and the secular. Only by recognizing these distinctions can we properly understand our relationship to God and the broader world. With this understanding, we can then engage unbelievers in the task of apologetics. Such distinctions do not bifurcate or divide our existence but merely help us to see how God operates in these distinct areas of life.

8

THE BOOK OF NATURE
AND APOLOGETICS

For understanding is the reward of faith. Therefore do not seek to understand in order to believe, but believe that you may understand; since, "except you believe, you shall not understand."

Augustine of Hippo

Although the proofs may be insufficient to move someone to believe in the truth of Christianity, on the other hand belief in that truth would certainly have no right to exist if this revelation could be proved to be unhistorical. For faith is not only trust, it is also knowledge and assent and cannot live by cunningly devised fables.

Herman Bavinck

We have pulled the book of nature from the shelf, dusted it off, perused its pages, and examined the historic Reformed understanding of the use of common notions and the broader created order. How does one, therefore, employ the book of nature in the defense of the faith? In what follows, I present a basic sketch of how the books of nature and Scripture can work in concert in apologetics. This is neither a comprehensive presentation of apologetics nor a programmatic proposal. Rather, I merely seek to demonstrate how Christians can stand on the authority of Scripture to press the claims of Christianity while at the same time using and appealing to the book of nature.

This chapter first addresses starting points, the necessary commitments for a biblical apologetic methodology. I explain the nature of epistemology (how we know) within the framework of classic covenant theology: the covenants of redemption, works, and grace. In this section I demonstrate two goals of a covenant epistemology, namely, love and eschatology. Epistemology is ultimately about loving God and submitting to his authority, not simply the acquisition of knowledge. In the language of biblical and older dogmatic categories, epistemology is about wisdom.[1] Epistemology is also eschatological: it is linear and has a *telos*, a goal that transforms the knower. I also address the nature of epistemology in the prefall and postfall contexts. How does epistemology function in a postfall world? What are the noetic effects of sin on the mind of fallen humanity?

Second, I address the goals of apologetics. If fallen humanity cannot be saved through natural knowledge, then what role do intellectual arguments play in one's apologetic system?

Third, I expound the various points of contact that believers and unbelievers share. To acknowledge points of contact does not mean that the Christian surrenders to the dictates of fallen human autonomy. Instead, the believer appeals to God's books of nature and Scripture in the defense of the gospel. Yet in the appeal to natural revelation, it is crucial to recognize how epistemology functions in a postfall world. Who is the source of all knowledge? Can fallen humanity have true knowledge? Fundamental to a proper estimation of epistemology in a postfall world is recognizing the redemptive-historical distinctions (not separations) between Christ as *Logos* and as Mediator. This third section then explores the implications for apologetics of epistemology in a postfall world. With a proper understanding of the roles of faith and reason, Christians can and should appeal to the book of nature in defending Christianity.

Fourth, I explain the importance and necessity of employing evidence in the defense of Christianity.

Fifth and last, I discuss the importance of humility in defending Christianity. As I have demonstrated in earlier chapters, some within the Reformed community in the twentieth century have made unfortunate claims about comprehensive views of life and the world. It is one thing to claim that Scripture helps us understand the telos of the creation, but regeneration does not make

1. Ellen T. Charry, *By the Renewing of Your Minds: The Pastoral Function of Christian Doctrine* (Oxford: Oxford University Press, 1997).

us smarter. Scripture, correlatively, does not give us information about all of life. Instead, Christians should be humble in their defense of Christianity. Just because we present true claims about God, the creation, the fall, and redemption does not mean we have an exhaustive knowledge of the world.

Starting Points

In setting forth the basic points of an apologetic methodology, we must come to grips with certain givens. In line with the historic catholic tradition, we do not approach the subject from the vantage point of reason seeking faith but rather faith seeking understanding. In the words of Augustine (354–430): "For understanding is the reward of faith. Therefore do not seek to understand in order to believe, but believe that you may understand; since, 'except you believe, you shall not understand.'"[2] Augustine recognized that faith is a God-given gift, and hence one cannot use reason to acquire the gift. But once we receive the gift, we must employ reason to its fullest. "Faith brought them into the presence of the word of God," writes Augustine, "but this faith which has sprouted needs to be watered, nourished, strengthened."[3] Augustine counsels against blind acceptance whereby one surrenders one's intellect to specious claims, all in the name of faith. Rather, Augustine recognizes that trusting authority lies at the root of all epistemology. This is not something that is unique to Christianity but occurs in many areas of life. When children become cognizant of their parents, they accept by faith that their parents are who they claim to be. Only later do they explore their parents' claims and obtain a greater understanding of what they first accepted by faith.[4] Faith is the internal cognitive foundation (*principium internum cognoscendi*) of revelation and all theology.[5]

Covenantal Context

The dynamic between epistemology and authority appears in the covenant theology of the Bible. God created Adam and Eve within the context of a covenant, a mutual agreement with promises, stipulations, and conditions—what

---

2. Augustine, *Homilies on the Gospel of John* 29.6 (NPNF[1] 7:184, altered spelling).

3. Augustine, "Sermon 43," in *Sermons: (20–50) on the Old Testament*, ed. John E. Rotelle, Works of Saint Augustine, series III (Brooklyn: New City, 1991), 2:242.

4. Augustine, *The Advantage of Believing* 10.26, in *On Christian Belief*, ed. Boniface Ramsey, Works of Saint Augustine, series I (Hyde Park, NY: New City, 2005), 8:138.

5. Herman Bavinck, *Reformed Dogmatics*, ed. John Bolt, trans. John Vriend, 4 vols. (Grand Rapids: Baker Academic, 2003–8), 1:565.

Reformed theologians have called the covenant of works (WCF 7.2).[6] God issued the command not to eat from the tree of the knowledge of good and evil: "And the LORD God commanded the man, saying, 'You may freely eat of every tree of the garden, but of the tree of the knowledge of good and evil you shall not eat, for in the day that you eat of it you shall surely die'" (Gen. 2:16–17; cf. Exod. 3:14). God, the covenant Lord, commanded his covenant servant, Adam, not to eat of the tree of knowledge. Would Adam trust God's authority and acquire knowledge in accordance with God's instruction, or would he seek this knowledge on his own terms? Before we proceed to discuss the implications of God's command and the relationship between epistemology and authority, we should mention several concomitants.

God created humanity within a covenantal context, which means that covenant characterizes created reality, humanity's ontology, and epistemology. We can begin with created reality, the cosmos, simply because the Scriptures indicate that God first created the cosmos and then filled it with creatures. God created humans on the sixth day (Gen. 1:26–31) and then placed them in the garden-temple (Gen. 2). This world exists regardless of whether people accept its existence. Moreover, contrary to the claims of dualists, such as gnostics, the material world is good, in fact "very good" (Gen. 1:31). But this created cosmos is not merely a physical stage upon which humanity stands. The cosmos is ultimately a macrocosmic temple for the Triune God.[7] The earthly temple was adorned with symbolic imagery such as the cherubim, the ark, the temple accoutrements, and images of trees, all of which revealed information about God's being, character, and relationship both to the creation and to humanity.

As the earthly temple reveals God, so does the macrocosmic temple of creation. The psalmist famously writes:

> The heavens declare the glory of God,
>   and the sky above proclaims his handiwork.
> Day to day pours out speech,
>   and night to night reveals knowledge.
> There is no speech, nor are there words,
>   whose voice is not heard.
> Their voice goes out through all the earth,
>   and their words to the end of the world. (Ps. 19:1–4a)

6. Unless otherwise noted, all quoted confessions come from Jaroslav Pelikan and Valerie Hotchkiss, eds., *Creeds and Confessions of Faith in the Christian Tradition*, vol. 2 (New Haven: Yale University Press, 2003).

7. G. K. Beale, *The Temple and the Church's Mission* (Downers Grove, IL: InterVarsity, 2004), 32–38; Beale, "Eden, the Temple, and the Church's Mission in the New Creation," *Journal of the Evangelical Theological Society* 48 (2005): 5–31.

The cosmos therefore reveals the existence and character of the covenant Lord. The very rhythms of the creation reflect God's covenantal activity within the prefall and postfall cosmos, whether in God's covenants with the day and the night, or his covenant to preserve the postdiluvian world (Gen. 9:8–10; Jer. 33:20).

Created reality does not end with the cosmos but finds its zenith in the creation of humanity, the creature who alone bears the image of the Triune God (Gen. 1:27; 1 Cor. 11:7; 2 Cor. 4:4; Col. 1:15). If the creation is a macrocosmic temple for the Triune God, then humanity is a microcosmic temple.[8] Just as the macrocosmic temple reveals God's existence, character, and power, the microcosmic anthropic temple bears similar characteristics. John Calvin (1509–64) praises the philosophers, such as Aristotle (384–322 BC), who "not improperly called man a *microcosm* (*miniature world*), as being a rare specimen of divine power, wisdom, and goodness, and containing within himself wonders sufficient to occupy our minds, if we are willing so to employ them."[9] God created humanity in his image, which, among other things, means that God wrote his law on their hearts (Rom. 2:14–15).[10] Yet once again, God's law is not abstract but has a context, namely, the covenantal context where Adam and Eve received the command not to eat from the tree of knowledge as well as the command to be fruitful, fill the earth, and subdue it (Gen. 1:28; 2:16–17).

The Goals of a Covenant Epistemology

At this point in preredemptive history, God's natural revelation (the knowledge revealed in the broader creation and written on the human heart) and special revelation (the command not to eat from the tree of knowledge and to fill the earth and subdue it) had a twofold telos. First, God's revelation was the covenantal context in which God placed Adam to submit to his authority by obeying God's natural and supernatural revelation. In this manner, Adam and Eve would have come to greater knowledge: this was the place for the exercise of God's covenantal epistemology. Crucial to this epistemology, however, is the covenantal relationship between God and the first humans. Their knowledge was not a bald submission to authority but was supposed to be the opportunity for them to demonstrate covenantal

8. Bavinck, *Reformed Dogmatics*, 2:562.

9. John Calvin, *Institutes of the Christian Religion*, trans. Henry Beveridge (Grand Rapids: Eerdmans, 1957), 1.5.3; see Aristotle, *Physics*, in *The Basic Works of Aristotle*, ed. R. McKeon (New York: Random House, 1941), 2, p. 359.

10. David VanDrunen, *Divine Covenants and Moral Order: A Biblical Theology of Natural Law* (Grand Rapids: Eerdmans, 2014), 209–62.

fidelity, namely, love. To love means to give oneself entirely to another (cf. John 15:13).

In a number of places, the Scriptures present a nexus between epistemology, revelation, law, and love. Many are familiar with the statements at the beginning of Psalm 19 about general revelation, but the psalmist moves from reflecting on the knowledge of God revealed in the creation to the knowledge revealed in the law:

> The law of the LORD is perfect,
>   reviving the soul;
> the testimony of the LORD is sure,
>   making wise the simple;
> the precepts of the LORD are right,
>   rejoicing the heart;
> the commandment of the LORD is pure,
>   enlightening the eyes. (Ps. 19:7–8)

The two halves of the psalm, the first praising the knowledge of God manifest in the creation and the second celebrating the knowledge of God in the law, echo Genesis 1–3 and in particular evoke the tree of knowledge.[11] The psalmist uses the very same language to characterize the law that Genesis employs to describe the tree of knowledge. The psalmist states that the law enlightens the eyes and makes one wise (Ps. 19:7–8), and the woman saw that the tree was "a delight to the eyes" and "desired to make one wise" (Gen. 3:6). In similar fashion, the first half of the psalm evokes the creation (Gen. 1), and the second half recalls humanity's creation and interaction with the tree (Gen. 2–3).[12] Both creation and law point back to the Creator.

But the law is not merely legal legislation, rules by which one must live, the cold and lifeless judicial bar before which humanity must appear. Rather, the covenant charter of the Old Testament, Deuteronomy, links law, love, sonship, and covenant. God reveals his law within his covenant and expects his covenant subjects to obey that law, yet such obedience is ultimately a manifestation of love.[13] When asked what the most important commandment is, Jesus responds by quoting Deuteronomy 6:5, "You shall love the LORD your God

---

11. D. J. A. Clines, "The Tree of Knowledge and the Law of Yahweh (Psalm XIX)," *Vetus Testamentum* 24 (1974): 8–14.

12. Peter C. Craigie, *Psalms 1–50*, WBC (Nashville: Nelson, 1983), 182.

13. Sherri Brown, *Gift upon Gift: Covenant through Word in the Gospel of John* (Eugene, OR: Pickwick, 2010), 38, 57; Rekha M. Chennattu, *Johannine Discipleship as a Covenant Relationship* (Peabody, MA: Hendrickson, 2006), 65; Jason S. DeRouchie, *A Call to Covenant Love: Text, Grammar, and Literary Structure in Deuteronomy 5–11* (Piscataway, NJ: Gorgias, 2014), 237–50.

with all your heart and with all your soul and with all your might" (see Matt. 22:37; Mark 12:30; Luke 10:27). Here Christ explains that love involves giving one's entire being to service, submission, and dedication to God by carrying out his will.[14] Israel, God's covenanted child (Exod. 4:22), was supposed to study God's law, gain knowledge by it, obey it, and in this way demonstrate love for God the Father.

The prophet Hosea wraps together all of these ideas (covenant, knowledge, obedience, and love) in his indictment against Israel:

> Hear the word of the LORD, O children of Israel,
>   for the LORD has a controversy [ryb] with the inhabitants
>   of the land.
> There is no truth ['emet] or steadfast love [hesed],
>   and no knowledge [da'at] of God in the land;
> there is swearing, lying, murder, stealing, and committing adultery.
> . . . .
> My people are destroyed for lack of knowledge;
>   because you have rejected knowledge,
>   I reject you from being a priest to me.
> And since you have forgotten the law of your God,
>   I also will forget your children. (Hosea 4:1–2a, 6, ESV altered)

The prophet brings his covenant lawsuit (ryb) because there is no truth ('emet) or covenant love (hesed). Israel lacks knowledge (da'at) and hence, like Adam, will be rejected: "Like Adam they transgressed the covenant" (Hosea 6:7). Hosea repeats the very terminology of the Decalogue in his indictment of Israel's treachery. To forget God's covenant law is tantamount to rejecting his covenant knowledge. In Hosea's prophecy, forgetting is the opposite of knowing and typically means disobeying. Knowledge, consequently, requires a constant awareness of and obedience to the requirements of God's covenant, and it must be a relationship characterized by love.[15]

Epistemology, therefore, is not only about the acquisition of knowledge but has love as one of its goals. Love and epistemology are not separate but are distinctly united.[16] In other words, the covenant defines the relationship between God and humanity: God creates humanity in love and gives humans the cosmos as a gift, and they in turn love their covenant Lord in submitting

14. J. A. Thompson, *Deuteronomy*, TOTC (Downers Grove, IL: InterVarsity, 1974), 122.
15. Douglas Stuart, *Hosea–Jonah*, WBC (Waco: Word, 1987), 72–78.
16. Jean-Luc Marion, *The Erotic Phenomenon* (Chicago: University of Chicago Press, 2008), 2, 13, 20, 28, 46, 70–71, 221–22; Esther Lightcap Meek, *Loving to Know: Covenant Epistemology* (Eugene, OR: Cascade Books, 2011), 395–424.

to his authority.[17] Epistemology is ultimately about submission to and trust in authority, and in this case, it means submission to the revealed will of the covenant Lord in order to know and love him.[18] Epistemology is about the call and response, the dialogue, engagement, and transformation of two people, an interplay poetically captured in the Wisdom literature. Song of Songs captures the dialogue between husband and wife, two lovers interacting through speech. Unlike a monologue, the lovers in Song of Songs influence and change one another through their mutual communication.[19]

In Song of Songs 4:12–14, the husband describes his bride as a garden of spices; she hears his words and invites him in: "Let my beloved come to his garden, and eat its choicest fruits" (Song 4:16). The husband hears her call and accepts the invitation: "I came to my garden, my sister, my bride, I gathered my myrrh with my spice, I ate my honeycomb with my honey, I drank my wine with my milk" (Song 5:1). This interactive and transformative dialogue characterizes the entire book.[20] Michael Fox describes the nature of this dialogue: "The communication of these lovers is more than transmission of thoughts. It is *communion*, intimate and reciprocal influence through language. The words of each lover penetrate the other's thought and speech. Love in Canticles is thus the interanimation of two souls."[21] Similarly, marriage is a microcosm of Christ's relationship to his bride, the church (Eph. 5:22–33). Epistemology, therefore, is not only about the acquisition of raw data but is ultimately about a covenantal communion with the living God and submitting to his transformative word.

The second telos of revelation, and hence epistemology, is eschatology. We must recognize that eschatology precedes soteriology. In other words, eschatology existed prior to the need for soteriology.[22] God revealed his will to Adam and Eve with the intent of setting the goal of indefectible eschatological life before them. If they had passed their probation and successfully completed the command to be fruitful, fill all the earth, and subdue it apart from eating from the tree of knowledge, they would have ushered in the age to come, the eschatological outpouring of the Spirit. As Paul writes: "But it is not the spiritual that is first but the natural, and then the spiritual" (1 Cor.

17. Jean-Luc Marion, *Being Given: Toward a Phenomenology of Givenness* (Redwood City, CA: Stanford University Press, 2002), 5, 72–73.

18. See Jeffrey Mallinson, *Faith, Reason, and Revelation in Theodore Beza (1519–1605)* (Oxford: Oxford University Press, 2003).

19. Michael V. Fox, *The Song of Songs and the Ancient Egyptian Love Songs* (Madison: University of Wisconsin Press, 1985), 315.

20. Fox, *Song of Songs*, 317–18.

21. Fox, *Song of Songs*, 322.

22. Geerhardus Vos, *The Pauline Eschatology* (Phillipsburg, NJ: P&R, 1979), 60–61.

15:46). Adam and Eve and their descendants would have filled the earth with image-bearers and claimed the entire earth for their covenant Lord, thereby completing the purpose of all things natural and ushering in the age of the Spirit. Paul does not pit the natural against the spiritual, and he does not posit a flesh-spirit antithesis in which the material is inferior to the spiritual. Paul's point is primarily redemptive historical and secondarily ontological. In other words, the natural probationary period is first, which upon successful completion by humans ushers in the spiritual. Paul's contrast, therefore, is epochal, not a gnostic body-soul dualism.

With Adam and Eve's successful probation, they would have entered an indefectible glorified state in which they would have been further enrobed in the glory of God and reflected the divine image with greater clarity and fullness. This means that epistemology is not only about the acquisition of data but also about a fundamental transformation.[23] Epistemology, or the submission to authority, leads to greater conformity to the image of the covenant Lord. Apart from a telos, epistemology is ultimately self-referential. Divorced from its covenantal context, epistemology serves the abstract and endlessly cyclical quest for knowledge instead of serving its linear, eschatological, and transformative purpose, a process that leads to greater conformity to the divine image. Adam bore the natural image of God and was to seek the indefectible eschatological image. He was to accomplish this transformation through an epistemic pursuit of wisdom in submission to God's authority, not in rebellion against it.

Postfall Epistemology

Epistemology and authority, therefore, go hand in hand, but the foregoing exposition treats epistemology in a prefall context. How does epistemology function in a postfall world? In the initial covenant between God and the first humans, sin was absent, but in a postfall world, humanity's rejection of God's authority has led to a disruption in this covenantal relationship. Fallen humans do not submit to God's authority, do not love God, and love only themselves (Rom. 1:18–25). They dwell in epistemic, moral, and covenantal exile from God. In contrast to the sage, fools say in their hearts, "There is no God" (Ps. 14:1). Humanity's epistemology has also been separated from its transformative and eschatological goals, evident in the splintered opinions scattered throughout the history of philosophy. But this does not mean that we are without hope. One "like a son of man," one like Adam, has come and

23. Meek, *Loving to Know*, 131–44.

submitted to God's authority: he has loved his Father, submitted to his will, even unto death, and thus passed the probation and rightly merited eschatological life for himself and for those whom he represents.[24] The last Adam, Jesus, is the incarnation of true human epistemology in action as he employs it to its divinely ordained covenantal purposes and ends. Christ's obedience and rightly aimed epistemology were ordained in the pretemporal covenant of redemption, the intratrinitarian covenant in which the Father appointed the Son as covenant surety to perform the work of redemption.[25]

Through his successful probation as the last Adam, Jesus has inaugurated the age to come, the eschaton. The initial covenantal relationship between Adam and God, though broken due to Adam's sin, was still functional and operative for the last Adam. Epistemology did not change, general revelation did not change, and God's supernaturally revealed commands to Adam did not change. Rather, God sent one who would faithfully fulfill the commands. The problem for the rest of humanity, however, is that the effects of original sin hamper fallen humanity's existence, including all their faculties. This means that the noetic effects of sin shackle fallen humanity's epistemological abilities. How, then, does the fallen human's ability to know function in a postfall world, in a covenantally exilic state?

Given the absence of sin in a prefall world, humanity's existence was unified, but in a postfall world, all of humanity exists in one of two states, as either a covenant breaker or a covenant keeper.[26] Only the covenant fidelity of the last Adam can redeem fallen human beings from the devastating effects of sin. Only the regenerative work of the Holy Spirit restores proper epistemological function to fallen sinners; Christ through the Spirit restores the God-human relationship by fulfilling the covenant broken by Adam and Eve (1 Cor. 2:6–16). In Christ, the Spirit restores human ability so that we may submit to the authority of divine revelation (2 Cor. 3:14). The last Adam covenantally, ontologically, and epistemologically restores the shattered divine-human relationship. Christ fulfills the broken covenant, repairs and regenerates fallen human nature, restores one's ability to submit to the authority of divine revelation, and resumes his divine dwelling among humanity through the indwelling presence of the Holy Spirit. In other words, the Triune God takes up residence within redeemed sinners by means of mystical union with them.

24. Cf. Gen. 1:28; Ps. 8; Dan. 7:1–28; Matt. 24:30; 26:64; Mark 13:26; 14:62; Luke 21:27; Rev. 14:14. J. V. Fesko, *Last Things First: Unlocking Genesis with the Christ of Eschatology* (Fearn, UK: Mentor, 2007), 145–82.

25. For a more detailed explanation of the covenant of redemption, see J. V. Fesko, *The Trinity and the Covenant of Redemption* (Fearn, UK: Mentor, 2016).

26. Cornelius Van Til, *Christian Apologetics* (Phillipsburg, NJ: P&R, 1976), 26–27.

But what about fallen humanity, those who have a broken covenantal relationship, refuse to submit to divine revelation, and dwell in exile from the Triune God? How do redeemed covenant keepers interact, live, and communicate with covenant breakers? This is where we must delineate the rest of the points in the sketch for how the book of nature functions for the defense of the faith: the goals of apologetics, points of contact with unbelievers, evidence used in the apologetic process, and the humility that must mark Christians as they engage in apologetics with unbelievers.

Goals of Apologetics

We must recognize the specific aims and goals of apologetics, since this is vital in setting the boundaries for the book of nature within apologetics. Over against biblical rationalists such as Jean-Alphonse Turretin (1671–1737), who argued that natural revelation gives access to the knowledge of God that is equal to Scripture, we should recognize that natural revelation has a limited function in a postfall world.[27] Given the absence of the noetic effects of sin in a prefall world, natural and special revelation worked in tandem apart from a need for the Holy Spirit's regenerative work. In short, reason functioned perfectly, which means that natural and special revelation were equally accessible. In a postfall world, natural revelation still carries the same information about God's existence, being, and character so that fallen humanity can accurately perceive and interpret this information. But in their fallen condition, sinful people do not submit to it and instead "by their unrighteousness suppress the truth" (Rom. 1:18; see also 1:19–32). Humanity's will and intellect are corrupt; hence humans are unable to submit to divine revelation and are unable to love.[28] The problem lies not with natural revelation but with fallen humanity's inability to use it properly. This means that no amount of rational argumentation, evidence, or cajoling will persuade sinful covenant breakers to turn to God in repentance. Only a sovereign work of the Holy Spirit can remove the detrimental noetic effects of sin and enable fallen people to love God and submit to his authoritative word in Scripture. Apologetics, narrowly construed as a rational defense of Christianity, does not convert fallen sinners.

27. Jean-Alphonse Turretin, *Dissertations on Natural Theology* (Belfast: James Magee, 1777), 1–28; see also Martin I. Klauber, *Between Reformed Scholasticism and Pan-Protestantism: Jean-Alphonse Turretin and Enlightened Orthodoxy at the Academy of Geneva* (Selinsgrove, PA: Susquehanna University Press, 1996), 62–103.

28. This doctrine has been classically defended by Martin Luther, *Bondage of the Will*, in *Luther's Works*, vol. 33 (Minneapolis: Fortress, 1972).

So then, what role is left for apologetics and the book of nature? In line with Thomas Aquinas (1225–74) and Calvin after him, I argue that apologetics has a threefold purpose: (1) to refute intellectual objections to the Christian faith, (2) to clarify our understanding of the truth, and (3) to encourage and edify believers in their faith.[29] To this we can add the opinion of French Reformed theologian Philippe du Plessis-Mornay (1549–1623), who believed that apologetics was necessary to refute unbelievers of all sorts, even heretics within the church.[30] Unbelievers employ intellectual arguments against Christianity, arguments that Christians can and should refute. To say, for example, that Jesus is a mythological figure runs counter to the historical evidence. Christians can present the historical evidence to prove Jesus Christ's existence. Unbelievers claim that the Christian faith is filled with contradictions and errors. How can Christians worship the God of the Old Testament and at the same time worship Jesus Christ as God? Does this not violate the cardinal principle of Old Testament monotheism? Do not Christians worship three gods, Father, Son, and Holy Spirit, in contradiction to the Old Testament's injunction against polytheism? Christians can present biblical arguments to clarify the scriptural truth-claims in the face of such objections. Concomitant with refuting intellectual objections and clarifying the truth is edifying the faith of believers. As believers reflect on, study, and defend the faith, they can by God's grace strengthen their own resolve and convictions. But as believers submit to the revealed knowledge of God, the covenant Lord transforms them and further conforms and prepares them for life in the consummated eschaton.

Apologetics, therefore, is important and necessary. Sometimes the church has employed apologetics to clear intellectual obstacles for the purpose of evangelism, but at other times the church has presented apologetic arguments to stave off persecution. The early church, for example, suffered persecution under various Roman emperors, from Trajan (53–117, emperor 98–117) to Commodus (161–92, emperor 180–92), where the legal basis for this persecution was not evident. Christian apologists appealed to the emperors and magistrates, some of whom were willing to listen to reasoned arguments, to establish civil tolerance for Christianity.[31] Apologetics, therefore, serves other important functions beyond the task of evangelism.

29. Thomas Aquinas, *Summa Theologica*, 5 vols. (repr., Allen, TX: Christian Classics, 1948), Ia q. 1 art. 8; Calvin, *Institutes*, 1.8.8.

30. Philippe du Plessis-Mornay, *A Work concerning the Trueness of Christian Religion* (London: George Potter, 1604), "Epistle Dedicatorie."

31. Avery Cardinal Dulles, *A History of Apologetics* (1971; repr., San Francisco: Ignatius Press, 1999), 28.

Points of Contact

Since believers live among and interact with unbelievers, the question naturally arises, "Given the fall, do believers have a point of contact with unbelievers?" In the previous chapters, we have explored the various means by which believers can and do communicate with unbelievers in the apologetic process. Since God has created all people in the image of God, they all have his law written on their hearts. Even fallen humans still possesses the knowledge of God; if all knowledge of God were destroyed, humanity would cease to exist because there would be nothing left of God's image. All human beings possess God-given common notions. Yes, the noetic effects of sin twist humanity's faculties so that they refuse to submit to the authority of divine revelation, but this does not mean that believers and unbelievers are epistemologically severed from one another. Sin has damaged human nature and its faculties, but it has not completely obliterated the image of God. Moreover, the Triune God still reigns as the Lord and sovereign over all creation and all humanity. Humanity's collective violation of the covenant of works does not somehow nullify God's rule over creation.

We can agree with Abraham Kuyper's (1837–1920) famous statement about Christ's sovereignty over the creation: "There is not a square inch in the whole domain of our human existence over which Christ, who is Sovereign over all, does not cry, Mine!"[32] But the key question is this: In what way is Christ sovereign over creation? Does he rule over the covenant breaker and the covenant keeper in the same way? The short answer is no. Christ does not rule over believers and unbelievers in the same way, yet he rules over both in such a way as to preserve his sovereignty, enable communication between the two groups, and propel the redemptive-historical shift between this present age and the age to come. In other terms, we must distinguish between the Son's protological rule over the creation and his eschatological reign as Mediator over the church. We must distinguish between the natural and the spiritual. We must account, therefore, for the epochal shifts between preredemptive history, inaugurated eschatology, and consummated eschatology.

Epistemology in Redemptive History

Historically, Reformed theologians have accounted for these epochal shifts through two sets of terminological distinctions (not separations): (1) the distinction between the *principia* (foundations) for general knowledge and for

---

32. Abraham Kuyper, "Sphere Sovereignty," in *Abraham Kuyper: A Centennial Reader*, ed. James D. Bratt (Grand Rapids: Eerdmans, 1998), 488.

saving knowledge, and (2) the distinction between the Son's lordship in terms of his ontological procession and his mediatorial mission. The Triune God is the *principium essendi* (the essential foundation or principle of being) of all that exists, whether in the material or immaterial creation. Hence, if everything owes its existence to God, then correlatively, God must provide the *principium cognoscendi* (foundation of knowing, or cognitive foundation) for all knowledge.[33] The only reason we know anything is because God has chosen to reveal it; he reveals an ectype (*theologia ectypa*), which is an analogical counterpart to his own archetypal knowledge (*theologica archetypa*).[34] The ectypal copy is suited for finite creatures. God's revelation is the *principium cognoscendi externum* (external cognitive foundation), which we find either in nature or Scripture. In a postfall context, a Spirit-wrought faith is the *principium cognoscendi internum* (internal cognitive foundation).[35] For nontheological knowledge—meaning the natural knowledge of God—general revelation is the external cognitive foundation, and reason is the internal cognitive foundation, but just because we shift from supernatural to natural knowledge does not mean that God has been sidelined.

Christ as Creator and Redeemer

At this point we must distinguish (not separate) between the Son's ontological procession and his mediatorial mission, or his identity as *Logos* and

33. Bavinck, *Reformed Dogmatics*, 1:212; Richard A. Muller, *Dictionary of Latin and Greek Theological Terms: Drawn Principally from Protestant Scholastic Theology*, 2nd ed. (Grand Rapids: Baker Academic, 2017), s.v. *principia theologiae* (288–89); Louis Berkhof, *Introduction to Systematic Theology* (1932; repr., Grand Rapids: Eerdmans, 1996), 95–97.

34. Bavinck, *Reformed Dogmatics*, 1:213; Thomas Aquinas, *Summa Theologica*, 5 vols. (repr., Allen, TX: Christian Classics, 1948), Ia q. 1 art. 1; Francis Junius, *A Treatise on True Theology*, trans. David C. Noe (Grand Rapids: Reformation Heritage Books, 2014), theses 7–10, pp. 107–20; Franciscus Gomarus, *Disputationes Theologicae*, in *Opera Theologica Omnia*, vol. 2 (Amsterdam: J. Janssonius, 1644), pars tertia, 1:7, p. 1; Gisbert Voetius, *De Theologia*, in *Diatribe de Theologia, Philologia, Historia, & Philosophia* (Utrecht: Simon de Vries, 1668), 1.12–15, pp. 13–15; Bernardinus De Moor, *Continuous Commentary on Johannes Marckius' Didactico-Elenctic Compendium of Christian Theology*, trans. Steven Dilday, vol. 1 (Culpeper, VA: L&G Reformation Translation Center, 2014), §11, pp. 109–15; Francis Turretin, *Institutes of Elenctic Theology*, ed. James T. Dennison Jr., trans. George Musgrave Giger, 3 vols. (Phillipsburg, NJ: P&R, 1992–97), 1.2.6. These are the sources that Bavinck cites in the Dutch edition of his *Reformed Dogmatics*, sources not mentioned in the English translation; see David S. Sytsma, "Herman Bavinck's Thomistic Epistemology: The Argument and Sources of His *Principia* of Science," in *Five Studies in the Thought of Herman Bavinck: A Creator of Modern Dutch Theology*, ed. John Bolt (Lewiston, NY: Edwin Mellen, 2012), 17–18n49; Herman Bavinck, *Gereformeerde Dogmatiek* (Kampen: J. H. Bos, 1895), 1:145. For other sources cited, see Bavinck's *Gereformeerde Dogmatiek*, 1:145.

35. Bavinck, *Reformed Dogmatics*, 1:213; cf. Sytsma, "Bavinck's Thomistic Epistemology," 17n49.

his role as *Christos*. The Triune God created the heavens and earth through the *Logos*. John writes in his gospel, "All things were made through him [the *Logos*], and without him was not any thing made that was made" (John 1:3). Moreover, the *Logos* is the "true light, which gives light to everyone" (1:9). This means that by virtue of humanity's creation in the image of God and through natural revelation, human beings have the ability to know God and the world around them.[36] Amandus Polanus (1561–1610) explains the significance of this point: "The author of *right reason in the human mind*, is that eternal Logos, that is, the Son of God, as John the Evangelist testifies, 'This eternal Word was that true Light which illumines every man who comes into this world.' For by these words *he necessarily reveals the Son as the Giver of human reason and wisdom*."[37]

In a fallen world, humans still use reason, albeit corrupted by sin, to access and interpret the world around them. Corrupted by sin, people are unable and unwilling to submit to the authority of general revelation. Instead, they use and twist it to their own ends. Because of the noetic effects of sin, humanity's divinely given, naturally acquired, but sin-infected knowledge is inadequate for salvation.[38] But this does not mean, contrary to the claims of Van Til, that testimony of the Holy Spirit is therefore necessary even for general human knowledge. Van Til writes:

> Theologically expressed, we say that the validity of human knowledge in general rests upon *testimonium Spiritus Sancti*. In addition to this, Christian theism maintains that since sin has come into the world, no subject of knowledge can really come into contact with any object of knowledge, in the sense of interpreting it properly, unless the Scripture give the required light and unless the regeneration of the Spirit give a new power of sight.[39]

Scott Oliphint, a disciple of Van Til, says that Scripture is "the ground and foundation for our epistemology."[40] However, to say that fallen sinners require

---

36. Bavinck, *Reformed Dogmatics*, 1:233.

37. Amandus Polanus, *Syntagma Theologiae Christianae* (Hanovia: apud Claudium Marnium, 1610), 5.32, col. 3003, quoted in Sytsma, "Bavinck's Thomistic Epistemology," 44–45n141; see also Richard A. Muller, *Post-Reformation Reformed Dogmatics*, 4 vols. (Grand Rapids: Baker Academic, 2003), 3:397–402; Jean-Luc Marion, *The Visible and the Revealed* (New York: Fordham University Press, 2008), 151–52.

38. Junius, *On True Theology*, theses 18–19, pp. 154–57; Turretin, *Institutes*, 1.4.1–23.

39. Cornelius Van Til, *A Survey of Christian Epistemology*, In Defense of Biblical Christianity 2 (Phillipsburg, NJ: P&R, 1969), 184; cf. Sytsma, "Bavinck's Thomistic Epistemology," 18.

40. K. Scott Oliphint, "Bavinck's Realism, the Logos Principle, and *Sola Scriptura*," *Westminster Theological Journal* 72 (2010): 390.

the testimony of the Holy Spirit to understand anything and that Scripture is the ground of our epistemology represents a departure from both the catholic and Reformed traditions.[41] It also inadvertently scuttles what the Westminster divines called the "common operations of the Spirit" (WCF 10.4). In other words, there are common and special operations of the Spirit, but if general knowledge requires the regeneration of the Spirit, then what exactly are the common operations of the Spirit?

Such claims fit an Enlightenment worldview-driven epistemology, a system that begins with a central dogma from which one deduces an entire system of thought, but these claims run counter to Scripture. They collapse creation and the eschaton, or Christ's identity as *Logos* and his role as Mediator.[42] According to this view, the fall is so devastating that the Holy Spirit through Scripture must explain every fact. However, the Scriptures paint a different picture, as we saw in Paul's encounters with the Gentiles at Lystra and at Athens (Acts 14:8–18; 17:22–31). Paul appealed to nature, providence, and even pagan poets.[43] On two separate occasions, when the apostle Paul was about to be wrongly punished, he did not appeal to Scripture or the testimony of the Holy Spirit but instead to natural law and the principles of justice. Paul reminded his persecutors of his Roman citizenship and that it was unlawful to lash citizens of Rome (Acts 16:37–38; 22:25–29).

We must, of course, always uphold Scripture's teaching that natural persons do not accept the things of the Spirit of God because spiritual things are folly to them. The natural person (*psychikos*) does not understand them because they are spiritually discerned. "The spiritual person [*pneumatikos*]," Paul writes, "judges all things" (1 Cor. 2:15). Only those who have the "mind of Christ" can accept and receive supernatural revelation (2:16). One of the Westminster divines, Thomas Goodwin (1600–1680), explains Paul's point:

> For what is the Reason why a Natural man cannot know them? Because, saith he, they are spiritually discerned. (He speaks just like our Schoolmen, for we use to express in a way of distinction, in a Spiritual manner, that is, spiritually.) The meaning is, To see it in its own Spiritual nature, abstracted from all considerations besides, so he cannot see it; that is the meaning of this, "He cannot discern it spiritually." If he would know it aright, he must know it as it is in itself, now so he hath not a principle suited and fitted to this object as it is

41. Sytsma, "Bavinck's Thomistic Epistemology," 43.
42. Sytsma, "Bavinck's Thomistic Epistemology," 18.
43. Bruce A. Demarest, *General Revelation: Historical Views and Contemporary Issues* (Grand Rapids: Zondervan, 1982), 153.

Spiritual in itself; he may know it otherwise in other considerations, but take it as it is Spiritual and he cannot know it.[44]

Goodwin explains that Paul employs something akin to a scholastic distinction when he delineates between natural and supernatural knowledge. Only through regeneration does a person embrace and receive supernatural knowledge.[45] Or in the words of John Owen (1616–83), Paul demonstrates that the natural man cannot receive "the principal mysteries of the gospel."[46]

But this blindness should never sideline the use of the book of nature in the process of defending the gospel. As Bavinck explains, "Although the proofs may be insufficient to move someone to believe in the truth of Christianity, on the other hand belief in that truth would certainly have no right to exist if this revelation could be proved to be unhistorical. For faith is not only trust, it is also knowledge and assent and cannot live by cunningly devised fables."[47] Proofs, evidence, and the book of nature do not convert unbelievers, but they are an integral part of God's revelation and thus necessary, important, and useful. Again, Bavinck captures the necessity of both books, nature and Scripture: "Revelation in nature and revelation in Scripture form, in alliance with each other, an harmonious unity which satisfies the requirements of the intellect and the needs of the heart alike."[48]

44. Thomas Goodwin, *An Exposition of the First and Second Chapters of Ephesians*, in *The Works of Thomas Goodwin*, vol. 2, ed. Thankfull Owen and James Barron (London: [Thomas Goodwin, Jr.], 1681), serm. 25, p. 323.

45. General epistemology is not in view but rather the ability to accept *spiritual things*, or the gospel, *pace* Richard B. Gaffin Jr., "Some Epistemological Reflections on 1 Cor 2:6–16," *Westminster Theological Journal* 57 (1995): 103–24, esp. 116–22. The following is a cross-section of early modern Reformed theologians who offer this type of explanation of the text: William Perkins, *Golden Chaine*, in *The Works of That Famous and Worthy Minister of Christ, in the Universitie of Cambridge, Mr. William Perkins* (Cambridge: John Legatt, 1616), 20–21; John Downame, *The Christian Warfare against the Devill, World and Flesh Wherein Is Described Their Nature, the Maner of Their Fight and Meanes to Obtaine Victorye* (London: William Stansby, 1634), 167; John Davenant, *An Exposition of the Epistle of St. Paul to the Colossians* (1627; London: Hamilton, Adams, 1831), 304, 392, 452; William Twisse, *The Doctrine of the Synod of Dort and Arles Reduced to Practise* (Amsterdam: Successors to G. Thorp, 1631), 23, 101, 126; James Ussher, *A Body of Divinity* (London: Jonathan Robinson, 1702), 46, 126, 517; John Owen, *Of Communion with God* (London: William Marshall, 1700), 159; Owen, *Pneumatologia, Or a Discourse concerning the Holy Spirit* (London: Nathaniel Ponder, 1674), 217–27; Theodore Haak, *The Dutch Annotations upon the Whole Bible* (London: Henry Hills, 1657), comm. 1 Cor. 2:15; *Annotations upon All the Books of the Old and New Testament* (London: Evan Tyler, 1657), comm. 1 Cor. 2:15.

46. Owen, *Pneumatologia*, 222.

47. Herman Bavinck, *The Certainty of Faith*, trans. Harry der Nederlanden (St. Catharines, ON: Paideia, 1980), 59.

48. Herman Bavinck, *The Philosophy of Revelation* (repr., Grand Rapids: Baker, 1979), 310.

In spite of the noetic effects of sin, human faculties still function sufficiently well for a number of purposes. The Canons of Dordt (1618–19), for example, state the following regarding postfall human abilities:

> There is, to be sure, a certain light of nature remaining in man after the fall, by virtue of which he retains some notions about God, natural things, and the difference between what is moral and immoral, and demonstrates a certain eagerness for virtue and for good outward behavior. But this light of nature is far from enabling man to come to a saving knowledge of God and conversion to him—so far, in fact, that man does not use it rightly even in matters of nature and society. Instead, in various ways he completely distorts this light, whatever its precise character, and suppresses it in unrighteousness. In doing so he renders himself without excuse before God.[49]

Similar statements appear in the Westminster Standards (1647). The Standards speak of the light of nature, which governs and orders society and human actions, as the means by which unbelievers can morally frame their lives, set standards of ethical propriety, and "[show] that there is a God, who hath lordship and sovereignty over all, is good, and doth good unto all, and is therefore to be feared, loved, praised, called upon, trusted in, and served, with all the heart, and with all the soul, and with all the might."[50] The overall intent of these points is to show that human nature is fallen but not obliterated. As such, believers and unbelievers can dwell together, communicate, and comprehend one another's claims.

We must remember that fallen humanity dwells in covenantal exile from the Creator, but this does not mean that everything they do is wrong and that they have no accurate knowledge of the natural world. Although I wholeheartedly support Christian education, I disagree with Van Til's sweeping verdict: "Christian education is not even a fraction of one percent like public education."[51] He argues that because of their different presuppositions, God versus autonomous reason, "no teaching is possible except in Christian schools."[52] Yet the Bible paints a very different portrait of life in covenantal exile.

Genesis 4 presents the covenantally exilic line of Cain in somewhat dispassionate terms. There is certainly an underlying negative assessment that marks Cain's line. For example, Lamech wrongly takes two wives and

49. Canons of Dort, III/IV art. 4.
50. WCF 1.6; 10.4; 20.4; 21.1.
51. Cornelius Van Til, *Essays on Christian Education* (Phillipsburg, NJ: P&R, 1971), 189.
52. Van Til, *Christian Education*, 203.

perverts God's natural law (Gen. 4:19, 23–24). But conversely, the narrative also states that Cain built a city, Jabal was the father of nomadic herdsmen, Jubal was the father of musicians, and Tubal-Cain invented "instruments of bronze and iron" (Gen. 4:17, 20, 22). Calvin explains, "The sons of Cain, though deprived of the Spirit of regeneration, were yet endued with gifts of no despicable kind." Indeed, Calvin believed that Moses wrote of these things to show that the family of Cain "was not so accursed by the Lord but that he would still scatter some excellent gifts among his posterity." Calvin taught that the harp and similar musical instruments had been created for our pleasure rather than for our necessity. Nevertheless, he did not believe that music was therefore altogether superfluous, nor did he think it should be condemned. Rather, Calvin believed that pleasure as a self-referential end, pleasure for the sake of pleasure, should be condemned. But pleasure is appropriate when combined with the fear of God and with the common benefit of society in view.[53]

Through the spectacles of Scripture, Christians can appreciate the liberal arts and sciences, even if generated by unbelievers. The believer can appreciate the beauty and order of music. Calvin writes, "The use of God's gifts is not wrongly directed when it is referred to that end to which the Author himself created and destined them for us, since he created them for our good, not for our ruin."[54] The knowledge of covenantally exiled humanity, therefore, is not totally devoid of truth. Rather, it fails on two counts: it is self-referentially motivated and teleologically misdirected. In other words, rather than use God's good gifts to glorify God, unbelievers direct these things to their own selfish pleasure. Rather than using these gifts for their God-intended goal, unbelievers fail to exalt the Triune Lord. Christians employ the same knowledge motivated ideally by a love for God and directed toward the teleological goal of glorifying God, whereas the non-Christian is motivated by self-love and self-glorification. But just because such knowledge and action are improperly motivated and misdirected does not mean they are completely false. Exilic humanity can and will misuse God-given knowledge and will reach erroneous conclusions: Lamech's self-serving abuse of justice amply proves this point. But Cain, Jubal, Jabal, and Tubal-Cain also show that covenantal exile does not obliterate the natural knowledge of God. Fallen sinners do not cease to bear the image of God.

53. John Calvin, *Commentary on Genesis*, in *Calvin's Commentaries*, 22 vols. (repr., Grand Rapids: Baker, 1991), comm. Gen 4.20–21, 1:218; see also Paul Helm, *John Calvin's Ideas* (Oxford: Oxford University Press, 2004), 386–87.
54. Calvin, *Institutes*, 3.10.2.

Implications for Apologetics

Apologetically, this means that believers can present the gospel in conjunction with rational arguments and evidence and know that unbelievers can intellectually receive and comprehend the message. From the foundation of the authority of Scripture, believers can and should use the book of nature: we can appeal to common notions, the created order, and historical evidence. But as the Canons of Dordt indicate, although unbelievers can intellectually comprehend arguments and claims regarding Christianity, this does not mean that they will accept and trust in those arguments. Nevertheless, if the message were utterly incomprehensible apart from the testimony of the Holy Spirit, then it would be unjust for God to hold unbelievers accountable for rejecting the message. How can God hold one accountable for a message never received? True, God holds all humanity accountable for the sin of Adam by means of imputed guilt, but imputed guilt is not the sole basis for fallen humanity's condemnation. Reformed theologians have historically distinguished between original and actual sins. God holds fallen humanity accountable for both; condemnation rests upon both.

The traditional Reformed distinctions within the doctrine of faith account for the relationship between faith and reason and how unbelievers can intellectually understand the basic claims of Christianity: *notitia* (the facts), *assensus* (comprehension of the facts), and *fiducia* (trust).[55] Herman Witsius (1636–1708), for example, explains:

> But reason, although depraved, yet reason still remains; that is the faculty whereby man knoweth and judgeth, insomuch that man can know and judge of nothing whatever except by his reason, as the first principle and cause of knowledge and judgment; therefore if Divine things, if the mysteries of religion be known, it can be no other way than by reason. Faith itself, considered as knowledge [*cognitio*] and assent [*assensus*], is an operation of reason, or understanding; and this is so clear that he who doubts of it ought not to be considered as a rational being.[56]

The unbeliever has access to the facts, since they are part of God's natural revelation; they are universally available to all. Witsius appeals to *koinas ennoias*

---

55. Turretin, *Institutes*, 15.8.1–20; Bavinck, *Reformed Dogmatics*, 4:113; Muller, *Dictionary*, s.v. *notitia* (235), *assensus* (42–43), *fiducia* (123).

56. Herman Witsius, *An Essay on the Use and Abuse of Reason in Matters of Religion* (Norwich: Crouse, Stevenson & Matchett, 1795), §10, p. 10; Witsius, "Exercitatio XVII: De Usu et Abusu Rationis circa Mysteria Fidei," in *Miscellaneorum Sacrorum: Tomus Alter* (Herbornae: Johannis Nicolai Andreae, 1712), 588.

(common notions), or "the dictates of common sense."[57] The unbeliever also receives the facts of supernatural revelation (Scripture) when believers press scriptural claims in the presentation and defense of the gospel. Unbelievers can also have a certain degree of comprehension of the facts. They understand, for example, that Christians present Christ as the only way of salvation. But apart from the sovereign work of regeneration by the Spirit, the unbeliever will never trust in the message and will ultimately reject the presented arguments and evidence that corroborate the Christian's gospel defense. In Pauline terms, in unrighteousness they will suppress in unrighteousness the truth that they have comprehended (Rom. 1:18).

One of the missing categories in contemporary apologetics discussions is *axiology* (rightly valuing something), a common category in classic Reformed Orthodoxy. Under Van Til's influence, some of his disciples have confused epistemology with axiology, or how we know with the evaluation of that knowledge. William Dennison, for example, writes, "[The unbeliever] will say that the bass weighs three pounds or that $2 + 2 = 4$ (which is metaphysically correct), but he will not describe or explain the truthfulness (epistemological) of the bass or the mathematical proposition in the context of a Christian theistic universe (concrete understanding)."[58] Problems arise with this statement on two fronts: (1) Dennison fails to acknowledge that weighing a bass and adding $2 + 2$ have metaphysical *and* epistemological dimensions; (2) he conflates epistemology with axiology. As Francis Turretin (1623–87) explains: "There is a difference between the 'truth of propositions' and the 'truth of conclusions.'"[59] Fallen human beings can rightly know that $2 + 2 = 4$ or accurately weigh a fish; their ability to know has not been so damaged by the fall that they fail accurately to use reason. But the axiological evaluation of the fish and the simple math equation are a different matter; only the believer will rightly evaluate the ultimate significance of the existence of one of God's creatures and the truth of a mathematical formulation. As with the use of common notions, Reformed theologians distinguished between knowledge and judgment, or principles and conclusions.[60] Even in a fallen world, believers and unbelievers share a common epistemology due to their creation in the image of God. Recall, however, Calvin's distinction between two types of knowledge, the earthly and the heavenly. Just because unbelievers are blind

57. Witsius, *Use and Abuse of Reason*, §11, p. 11.
58. William D. Dennison, "Van Til and Common Grace," *Mid-America Journal of Theology* 9, no. 2 (1993): 238.
59. Turretin, *Institutes of Elenctic Theology*, 1.8.11.
60. E.g., Francis Junius, *The Mosaic Polity*, ed. Andrew M. McGinnis, trans. Todd M. Rester (Grand Rapids: CLP Academic, 2015), thesis 4, p. 46.

as moles regarding the things of heaven does not mean they are equally blind regarding the things of earth.[61]

Evidence

This means that believers and unbelievers share multiple points of contact by which the believer can convey and defend the gospel message. The believer has been regenerated by the Holy Spirit and through the corrective lenses of Scripture rightly sees and ultimately comprehends the revelatory telos of the book of nature. Scripture does not make believers smarter, but the Holy Spirit does enable them to trust in its message and hence embrace Christ and understand the eschatological telos of the creation. From this scriptural foundation Christians can and should appeal to evidence to corroborate the Christian message. We can appeal to the world, such as in Aquinas's teleological argument for the existence of God, and explain that the Creator designed and created the world for a distinct purpose.[62] Or we can and should appeal to historical evidence, for example, to corroborate scriptural claims regarding the resurrection of Christ.[63] We can and should appeal to the natural world around us to demonstrate to the unbeliever that Christ's gospel is about this very real world that God has created. Believers, like the apostle Paul, can appeal to pagan authorities insofar as they rightly understand the world around us. To appeal to these things, whether natural revelation, natural law, common notions, or the light of nature, is not in any way a capitulation to a so-called autonomous neutral zone; to appeal to these things is to appeal to *God's* revelation. In defense of the faith, Christians have two books in their apologetic arsenal, the book of nature and the book of Scripture.

We must and should incorporate the use of evidence in our apologetic methodology for several reasons. First, we can do so because such appeals are ultimately to God's revelation. Second, we can and should appeal to our sensory experience, but such experience must never be divorced from God's authoritative interpretation of those experiences. We can know the world through the senses because God has created us with the capacity to do so, but only the sovereign work of the Spirit can enable us to turn our gathered knowledge into wisdom so that we may love God. And third, against the

---

61. Calvin, *Institutes*, 2.2.18.

62. For more recent versions of the classic arguments, see, e.g., Neil A. Manson, *God and Design: The Teleological Argument and Modern Science* (New York: Routledge, 2003).

63. See, e.g., Gary R. Habermas and Michael R. Licona, *The Case for the Resurrection of Jesus* (Grand Rapids: Kregel, 2004).

claims of idealism, human beings do not impress their understanding upon the world. The world objectively exists, whether human beings rightly or wrongly perceive it; the world is God's natural revelation. Human beings can, to a certain degree, rightly understand the world around them in matters concerning general knowledge,[64] but ideally, general knowledge should work in tandem with supernatural revelation to lead people to submit to God's authority and love him. Submission to God's authority can happen only through the regenerative work of the Spirit, but God has objectively revealed himself in the creation, which is no human projection, as idealist philosophers would have us believe. Thus the Belgic Confession (1561) states concerning the means by which we know God: "First, by the creation, preservation, and government of the universe, since that universe is before our eyes like a beautiful book in which all creatures, great and small, are as letters to make us ponder the invisible things of God: his eternal power and his divinity, as the apostle Paul says in Romans 1:20."[65]

Humility

In the church's efforts to defend the faith, Christians must always take a humble stance toward the world. Like the sons of Zebedee, whom Jesus nicknamed "the Sons of Thunder," we can be all too eager to call down fire on unbelievers (Mark 3:17; Luke 9:54). Add in the misguided claim that the Bible provides a comprehensive view of life and the world that encompasses all knowledge, and this can easily turn into Christian imperialism. Christians today often speak less about saving the lost than about conquering the world. Especially in the secularized West, the problem with such rhetoric is that it does not align with the more modest claims of the Bible. The church is a pilgrim people: this world is not our home. Abraham, Isaac, and Jacob were princes among the people of God and were heirs of the covenant promises, yet they dwelled in tents. As the book of Hebrews tells us, "By faith [Abraham] went to live in the land of promise, as in a foreign land, living in tents with Isaac and Jacob, heirs with him of the same promise. For he was looking forward to the city that has foundations, whose designer and builder is God" (Heb. 11:9–10).

---

64. Generally, e.g., see John Wild, *Introduction to Realistic Philosophy* (New York: Harper & Brothers, 1948), 6; Thomas Reid, *An Inquiry into the Human Mind, on the Principles of Common Sense* (Edinburgh: Anderson & MacDowell, & James Robertson, 1818), 123, 310–11, 318, 351, 353–54, 394; Ben F. Meyer, *Critical Realism and the New Testament* (Eugene, OR: Pickwick, 1989), ix–56.

65. Belgic Confession, art. II, in Pelikan and Hotchkiss, *Creeds*, 2:407.

Correlatively, too many contemporary Reformed Christians have unwittingly imbibed Enlightenment ideas, such as the concept of a central dogma,
a principle from which one constructs an entire system of thought, the Archimedean fulcrum from which one moves the world, the *pou stō*. As noted in
earlier chapters, Kuyper, Dooyeweerd, Van Til, and others have taken the idea
of the central dogma and infused it with Christian content: the sovereignty
of God, creation-fall-redemption, the self-attesting Christ of Scripture, or
Scripture. They then claim that from this one starting point Christians can
develop a comprehensive view of life and the world. Such thought patterns
align well with the notion of a central dogma but fall significantly short when
we hold the claims up to the scrutiny of Scripture, especially what we find in
the Wisdom literature.

The Scriptures undoubtedly present truth-claims that intersect with a host
of general-knowledge claims. The Bible is not a science textbook, but it does
teach that God immediately created Adam. Some scientists are entertaining
the idea that the universe did not begin with the big bang but has always existed, that the universe is in some sense eternal.[66] The Bible, however, claims
that God created the universe out of nothing (Heb. 11:3). So the Bible does
provide Christians with important facts about the world, but as important as
these facts are, the Bible does not provide comprehensive knowledge.

For example, one of the chief themes in Ecclesiastes is epistemology. What
can we know, and how do we know it?[67] The Preacher writes: "I applied my
heart to seek and to search out by wisdom all that is done under heaven"
(Eccles. 1:13). Experience, then, is a source of knowledge for the Preacher. He
sought out pleasure but concluded that it "was vanity" (2:1). Sensory experience, therefore, is a path to insight and understanding.[68] The Preacher is no
idealist, but neither is he a raw empiricist. He draws numerous conclusions
about his investigations, such as the importance of wisdom: "For the protection
of wisdom is like the protection of money, and the advantage of knowledge
is that wisdom preserves the life of him who has it" (Eccles. 7:12).[69] But these
conclusions come nowhere close to anything resembling the contemporary
claims regarding a comprehensive view of life and the world. At the end of his
investigation, the Preacher rests in wisdom, the fear of the Lord, and God's
revealed will: "Fear God and keep his commandments, for this is the whole

66. Stephen Hawking, *A Brief History of Time: The Updated and Expanded Anniversary
Edition* (1988; New York: Bantam, 1996), 119–46.
67. Michael V. Fox, *A Time to Tear Down and a Time to Build Up: A Rereading of Ecclesiastes* (Grand Rapids: Eerdmans, 1999), 71–72.
68. Fox, *Ecclesiastes*, 77.
69. Fox, *Ecclesiastes*, 86.

duty of man" (12:13). The Preacher's point is that in spite of many unanswered questions, we must submit to God's authoritative revelation. If epistemology is all about submission to and trust in authority—the creature submitting to the covenant Lord's authoritative revelation—then the last thing this submission should do is foster pride, arrogance, or triumphalism in our hearts.[70]

Too often, Christians thunder about transforming and conquering the world, but such rhetoric is far from Christ's conduct. Rather than seeking to conquer the world, Christians in defending the gospel must be willing to roll up our sleeves, drop to our knees, and wash the feet of unbelievers. Even Christ washed the feet of Judas, one who would eventually betray him. To claim, as Van Til does, that no true learning occurs outside of Christian education, casts an unintended but nevertheless real shadow of contempt on God's natural gifts, which he has abundantly given to the world, even to the apostate line of Cain. Christians have much to learn from the unbelieving world about many things: science, mathematics, engineering, literature, art, music, and even ethics. Acknowledging that Christians have something to learn from unbelievers does not require that we embrace *in toto* what unbelievers claim. Rather, to learn from the unbelieving world ultimately means to submit to God's natural revelation in the world and the general wisdom he has so liberally bestowed on his good but nevertheless fallen creation. We dig amid the muddy soil of this sin-marred world in search of pearls and gems of God's wisdom. We must always interrogate and compare any claim against the canon of Scripture to determine whether truth-claims are accurate. In our use of the book of nature, we must never set aside the book of Scripture. Scripture must always regulate our understanding of the book of nature, lest we abandon the truth and imbibe the world's erroneous and sinful interpretations of the book of nature. But we must not forget that all truth is God's truth, regardless of its human point of origin.

The apostle Peter captures the humble posture in his oft-quoted statement about always being ready to defend the faith: "But in your hearts honor Christ the Lord as holy, always being prepared to make a defense to anyone who asks you for a reason for the hope that is in you; yet do it with gentleness and respect" (1 Pet. 3:15). Calvin explains this verse in the following manner:

> It should be noted that Peter is not commanding us to be prepared to solve any question about any matter that may be raised, for it is not the duty of everyone to speak on every subject. It is the general doctrine that is meant, which applies to the ignorant and the simple. Peter has in view simply that Christians should

70. Stephen T. Pardue, *The Mind of Christ: Humility and the Intellect in Early Christian Theology* (London: Bloomsbury T&T Clark, 2013), 157–82.

make it plain to unbelievers that they truly worship God, and have a holy and true religion.[71]

Calvin's explanation does not fit the comprehensive life-view and worldview claims of neo-Calvinist theologians but instead argues that Peter has much more modest and humble goals in mind.

Making claims about a comprehensive view of life and the world sets unnecessarily high expectations regarding the Christian's truth-claims. If our so-called biblical claims about science, art, mathematics, engineering, brain surgery, or the like are proved false, then we have unwittingly given the unbeliever an extra intellectual obstacle and another reason for rejecting the gospel. If, on the other hand, Christians refuse to attach the adjective *biblical* to anything except what the Scriptures truly address, then they are less likely to set themselves up unnecessarily for failure. To claim, for example, that the earth is the center of the universe, as the church historically argued, needlessly pitted the book of Scripture against the book of nature. Christians, consequently, must be very circumspect when they apply the adjective *biblical* to natural knowledge.

It is true that those who hold the truth in unrighteousness resist the very source of the order, pattern, purpose, freedom, and beauty in nature. They ineluctably presuppose the theism that they willfully distort and resist. Nevertheless, nowhere in the New Testament do we find language touting the superiority of Christian knowledge, claiming that Christians understand math or science better than unbelievers. Instead, we encounter the humility and love of Christ for sinners, the same characteristics that should mark the church. Hence, Peter counsels Christians to adopt a humble posture in the face of persecution as they testify and give a defense for the hope that is in us. We do not conquer through cultural domination and making claims about the world's ignorance. Rather, if love is one of the goals of epistemology, and epistemology is ultimately the submission to God's authoritative revelation, then we are not cultural conquerors but beggars showing other beggars where they can find a meal. We conquer the world by laying down our lives in testimony for and defense of the gospel, not in making claims of cultural conquest or epistemological superiority. As a pride of ferocious lambs, Christians testify to and defend the truth of the gospel with the books of nature and Scripture always in hand.

71. John Calvin, *Hebrews and 1 and 2 Peter*, Calvin's New Testament Commentaries, ed. T. F. Torrance and David F. Torrance (1960; repr., Grand Rapids: Eerdmans, 1996), comm. 1 Pet. 3:15, p. 289.

Conclusion

Christians need not shun the book of nature. We can rejoice because Christ looks out on the creation and all truth and rightfully claims "Mine!" Every square inch belongs to Christ, and therefore every square inch belongs to Christians. But just because it all belongs to Christ does not mean that Christians are somehow automatically intellectually or culturally superior to their unbelieving counterparts. Christians know the right motivational foundation and teleological goal of all knowledge, though they frequently forget them, and never succeed this side of glory in living in full conformity to them. Nevertheless, with this proper understanding of epistemology, we can fruitfully interact with unbelievers, because we share the image of God. We can defend the gospel, knowing that apologetics can clear away intellectual obstacles to the gospel, clarify our own understanding of the truth, protect the church from false teaching, and encourage our own hearts as we further immerse ourselves in the truth.

BIBLIOGRAPHY

Adams, Jay E. *Competent to Counsel: Introduction to Nouthetic Counseling*. Grand Rapids: Zondervan, 1986.

Adams, Marilyn McCord. "Praying the Proslogion: Anselm's Theological Method." In *The Rationality of Belief and the Plurality of Faith*, edited by Thomas D. Senor, 13–39. Ithaca, NY: Cornell University Press, 1995.

Alighieri, Dante. *The Divine Comedy: Inferno, Purgatorio, Paradiso*. Translated by Allen Mandelbaum. 1980. Reprint, New York: Knopf, 1995.

Allen, Diogenes, and Eric O. Springsted. *Philosophy for Understanding Theology*. 2nd ed. Louisville: Westminster John Knox, 2007.

Allen, R. Michael. *Doing Reformed Theology*. London: T&T Clark, 2010.

Allison, Henry E. *Kant's Transcendental Idealism: An Interpretation and Defense*. New Haven: Yale University Press, 2004.

Althusius, Johannes. *Dicaeologicae Libri Tres*. 2nd ed. Frankfurt: Corvinus, 1649.

———. *On Law and Power*. Translated by Jeffrey J. Veenstra. Grand Rapids: Christian's Library, 2013.

Annotations upon All the Books of the Old and New Testament. 3rd ed. London: Evan Tyler, 1657.

Anselm. *Anselm of Canterbury: The Major Works*. Edited by Brian Davies and G. R. Evans. Oxford: Oxford University Press, 1998.

Aquinas, Thomas. *See* Thomas Aquinas.

Aristotle. *De Anima*. Translated by R. D. Hicks. Cambridge: Cambridge University Press, 1907.

———. *The Basic Works of Aristotle*. Translated by Richard McKeon. New York: Random House, 1941.

Armstrong, Brian. *Calvinism and the Amyraut Heresy: Protestant Scholasticism in Seventeenth-Century France*. 1969. Reprint, Eugene, OR: Wipf & Stock, 2004.

Arrowsmith, John. *Armilla Catechetica: A Chain of Principles*. Cambridge: John Field, 1659.

Aubert, Annette G. *The German Roots of Nineteenth-Century American Theology*. Oxford: Oxford University Press, 2013.

Augustine, bishop of Hippo. *Confessions*. Translated by Henry Chadwick. Oxford: Oxford University Press, 1991.

———. *Homilies on the Gospel of John*. In *A Select Library of Nicene and Post-Nicene Fathers of the Christian Church*, 1st series, edited by Philip Schaff, 7:1–452. 14 vols. New York: Christian Literature, 1886–89. Reprint, Grand Rapids: Eerdmans, 1994.

———. *On Christian Belief*. Edited by Boniface Ramsey. Works of St. Augustine I/8. Hyde Park, NY: New City Press, 2005.

———. *Sermons on the Old Testament.* Edited by John E. Torelle. Works of St. Augustine III/2. Brooklyn, NY: New City, 1991.

———. *Tractates on the Gospel of John, 28–54.* Fathers of the Church 88. Washington, DC: Catholic University of America Press, 1993.

Backus, Irena. "Calvin's Concept of Natural and Roman Law." *Calvin Theological Journal* 38 (2003): 7–26.

Baglow, Christopher. "Sacred Scripture and Sacred Doctrine in Saint Thomas Aquinas." In *Aquinas on Doctrine: A Critical Introduction*, edited by Thomas Weinandy, Daniel Keating, John Yocum, 1–24. London: T&T Clark, 2004.

Bahnsen, Greg L. "The Impropriety Evidentially Arguing for the Resurrection." *Synapse* 2 (1972). http://www.cmfnow.com/articles/PA003.htm.

———. *Presuppositional Apologetics: Stated and Defended.* Edited by J. McDurmon. Nacogdoches, TX: Covenant Media, 2008.

———. "Socrates or Christ: The Reformation of Christian Apologetics." In *Foundations of Christian Scholarship: Essays in the Van Til Perspective*, edited by Gary North, 191–239. Vallecito, CA: Ross House Books, 1976.

———. *Theonomy in Christian Ethics.* Nacogdoches, TX: Covenant Media, 2002.

———. *Van Til's Apologetic: Readings and Analysis.* Phillipsburg, NJ: P&R, 1998.

Barker, William S., and W. Robert Godfrey, eds. *Theonomy: A Reformed Critique.* Grand Rapids: Zondervan, 1991.

Barr, James. *The Semantics of Biblical Language.* Oxford: Oxford University Press, 1961.

Barrett, C. K. *Acts.* Vol. 2. ICC. Edinburgh: T&T Clark, 1998.

Barron, Robert. *Thomas Aquinas: Spiritual Master.* New York: Crossroad, 1996.

Barth, Karl. *Church Dogmatics.* Edited by G. W. Bromiley and T. F. Torrance. 14 vols. Edinburgh: T&T Clark, 1936–68.

Baur, Michael. "Law and Natural Law." In *The Oxford Handbook of Aquinas.* Edited by Brian Davies and Eleonore Stump, 238–54. Oxford: Oxford University Press, 2012.

Bavinck, Herman. *The Certainty of Faith.* Translated by Harry der Nederlanden. St. Catharines, ON: Paideia, 1980.

———. "Foreword to the First Edition (Volume 1) of the *Gereformeerde Dogmatiek*, Translated by John Bolt." *Calvin Theological Journal* 45 (2010): 9–10.

———. *Gereformeerde Dogmatiek.* Vol. 1. Kampen: J. H. Bos, 1895.

———. *The Philosophy of Revelation.* Reprint, Grand Rapids: Baker, 1979.

———. *Reformed Dogmatics.* Edited by John Bolt. Translated by John Vriend. 4 vols. Grand Rapids: Baker Academic, 2003–8.

Baxter, Richard. *More Reasons for the Christian Religion and No Reason against It.* London: Nevill Simmons, 1672.

———. *The Practical Works of Mr. Richard Baxter.* 4 vols. 1660. London: Thomas Parkhurst, et al., 1707.

Beale, G. K. "Eden, the Temple, and the Church's Mission in the New Creation." *Journal of the Evangelical Theological Society* 48 (2005): 5–31.

———. *The Temple and the Church's Mission.* Downers Grove, IL: InterVarsity, 2004.

Beiser, Frederick C. *After Hegel: German Philosophy 1840–1900.* Princeton, NJ: Princeton University Press, 2014.

Berkhof, Louis. *Introduction to Systematic Theology.* 1932. Reprint, Grand Rapids: Eerdmans, 1996.

———. *Systematic Theology: New Combined Edition.* 1932. Reprint, Grand Rapids: Eerdmans, 1996.

Berkouwer, G. C. *Man: The Image of God.* Grand Rapids: Eerdmans, 1962.

Bierma, Lyle D., et al., eds. *An Introduction to the Heidelberg Catechism: Sources, History, and Theology.* Grand Rapids: Baker Academic, 2005.

Billings, J. Todd. "The Catholic Calvin." *Pro Ecclesia* 20, no. 2 (2011): 120–34.

Blankenhorn, Bernhard. *The Mystery of Union with God: Dionysian Mysticism in Albert the Great and Thomas Aquinas.* Washington, DC: Catholic University of America Press, 2015.

Blanton, Ward, and Hent de Vries, eds. *Paul and the Philosophers.* New York: Fordham University Press, 2013.

The Book of Church Order of the Orthodox Presbyterian Church. Willow Grove, PA: Committee on Christian Education of the Orthodox Presbyterian Church, 2015.

Bos, A. P., and D. F. M. Strauss. "Greek Ontology and Biblical Cosmology: An Unbridgeable Gap." In *In the Phrygian Mode: Neo-Calvinism, Antiquity and the Lamentations of Reformed Philosophy,* ed. Robert Sweetman. Lanham, MD: University Press of America, 2007.

Bradley, F. H. *Appearance and Reality: A Metaphysical Essay.* 6th ed. 1893. Reprint, London: George Allen & Unwin, 1916.

Bratt, James D. *Abraham Kuyper: Modern Calvinist, Christian Democrat.* Grand Rapids: Eerdmans, 2013.

———. "Abraham Kuyper: Puritan, Victorian, Modern." In *Kuyper Reconsidered: Aspects of His Life and Work,* edited by Cornelis van der Kooi and Jan de Bruijn. VU Studies on Protestant History. Amsterdam: VU Uitgeverij, 1999.

Briggs, Charles A. *The Bible, the Church, and the Reason: The Three Great Fountains of Divine Authority.* 2nd ed. New York: Charles Scribner's Sons, 1893.

Brown, Peter. *Augustine of Hippo.* Oakland, CA: University of California Press, 2013.

Brown, Sherri. *Gift upon Gift: Covenant through Word in the Gospel of John.* Eugene, OR: Pickwick, 2010.

Brunner, Emil, and Karl Barth. *Natural Theology: Comprising "Nature and Grace" by Professor Emil Brunner and the Reply "No!" by Dr. Karl Barth.* 1946. Reprint, Eugene, OR: Wipf & Stock, 2002.

Bucanus, Guillaume. *Body of Divinity, or Institutions of Christian Religion.* London: Daniel Pakeman et al., 1659.

———. *Institutiones Theologicae.* Geneva: Jacob Stoer, 1625.

Bucer, Martin. *Metaphrases et Enarrationes in Epist. D. Pauli Apostoli ad Romanos.* Basel: Peter Perna, 1562.

Bultmann, Rudolf. *New Testament and Mythology and Other Basic Writings.* Edited by Schubert M. Ogden. Philadelphia: Fortress, 1989.

Burgess, Anthony. *The Difficulty of and the Encouragements to a Reformation: A Sermon Preached before the Honourable House of Commons at the Publik Fast, Septem. 27, 1643.* London: Thomas Underhill, 1643.

———. *Vindiciae Legis: A Vindication of the Morall Law and the Covenants.* London: Thomans Underhill, 1647.

Burnett, Richard. "Point of Contact." In *The Westminster Handbook to Karl Barth,* edited by Richard E. Burnett, 165–67. Louisville: Westminster John Knox, 2013.

Burnside, Jonathan. *God, Justice, and Society: Aspects of Law and Legality in the Bible.* Oxford: Oxford University Press, 2011.

Buswell, J. Oliver. "The Fountainhead of Presuppositionalism." *The Bible Today* 42, no. 2 (1948): 41–64.

Butler, Joseph. *Analogy of Religion, Natural and Revealed to the Constitution and Course of Nature.* New York: Harper & Brothers, 1860.

Calvin, John. *Acts 14–28.* Calvin's New Testament Commentaries, edited by T. F. Torrance and David F. Torrance. 1966. Reprint, Grand Rapids: Eerdmans, 1995.

———. *Calvin's Commentaries.* 22 vols. Reprint, Grand Rapids: Baker, 1993.

———. *Commentarii Integri in Acta Apostolorum.* Geneva: Nicolas Barbirius & Thomas Courteau, 1564.

———. *Commentary on Genesis.* Reprint, Grand Rapids: Baker, 1991.

———. *Hebrews and 1 & 2 Peter*. Calvin's New Testament Commentaries, edited by T. F. Torrance and David F. Torrance. Grand Rapids: Eerdmans, 1996.

———. *Institutes of the Christian Religion*. Translated by Ford Lewis Battles. Edited by John T. McNeill. Philadelphia: Westminster, 1960.

———. *Institutes of the Christian Religion*. Translated by Henry Beveridge. Grand Rapids: Eerdmans, 1957.

———. *Institutes of the Christian Religion*. Translated by John Allen. Grand Rapids: Eerdmans, 1948.

———. *Romans*. Translated by John Owen. Edinburgh: Calvin Translation Society, 1849.

———. *Romans and Thessalonians*. Calvin's New Testament Commentaries. Edited by T. F. Torrance and David F. Torrance. 1960. Grand Rapids: Eerdmans, 1996.

———. *Sermons on Timothy and Titus*. Translated by Arthur Golding. 1579. Edinburgh: Banner of Truth, 1983.

Casselli, Stephen J. *Divine Rule Maintained: Anthony Burgess, Covenant Theology, and the Place of the Law in Reformed Scholasticism*. Grand Rapids: Reformation Heritage Books, 2016.

Catechism of the Catholic Church. Mahwah, NJ: Paulist Press, 1994.

Charry, Ellen T. *By the Renewing of Your Minds: The Pastoral Function of Christian Doctrine*. Oxford: Oxford University Press, 1997.

Chennattu, Rekha M. *Johannine Discipleship as a Covenant Relationship*. Peabody, MA: Hendrickson, 2006.

Clark, R. Scott. "Calvin on the *Lex Naturalis*." *Stulos Theological Journal* nos. 1–2 (1998): 1–22.

Clark, R. Scott, and Carl R. Trueman, eds. *Protestant Scholasticism: Essays in Reassessment*. Carlisle, UK: Paternoster, 1999.

Cicero, *De Naturam Deorum*. Translated by H. Rackham. Loeb Classical Library.

Cambridge, MA: Harvard University Press, 1972.

———. *De Officiis*. Translated by Walter Miller. Loeb Classical Library. Cambridge, MA: Harvard University Press, 1913.

———. *De Republica, De Legibus*. Translated by Clinton Walker Keyes. Loeb Classical Library. Cambridge, MA: Harvard University Press, 1928.

———. *The Republic and The Laws*. Translated by Niall Rudd. Oxford: Oxford University Press, 2008.

Cleveland, Christopher. *Thomism in John Owen*. Surrey, UK: Ashgate, 2010.

Clines, D. J. A. *Job 1–20*. WBC. Dallas: Word, 1989.

———. "The Tree of Knowledge and the Law of Yahweh (Psalm XIX)." *Vetus Testamentum* 24 (1974): 8–14.

Collett, Don. "Van Til and Transcendental Argument." *Westminster Theological Journal* 65 (2003): 289–306.

Collins, C. John. "Echoes of Aristotle in Romans 2:14–15; or, Maybe Abimelech Was Not So Bad after All." *Journal of Markets and Morality* 13, no. 1 (2010): 123–73.

Cooper, John W. *Body, Soul, and Life Everlasting: Biblical Anthropology and the Monism-Dualism Debate*. Grand Rapids: Eerdmans, 2000.

Cowen, Steven, ed. *Five Views on Apologetics*. Grand Rapids: Zondervan, 2000.

Craigie, Peter C. *Psalms 1–50*. WBC. Nashville: Nelson, 1983.

Daneau, Lambert. *A Fruitfull Commentarie upon the Twelve Small Prophets*. Cambridge: University of Cambridge, 1594.

———. *The Wonderfull Woorkmanship of the World: Wherein Is Conteined an Excellent Discourse of Christian Naturall Philosophie*. London: Andrew Maunsell, 1578.

Davenant, John. *An Exposition of the Epistle of St. Paul to the Colossians*. 1627. London: Hamilton, Adams, 1831.

Davies, Brian. *Thomas Aquinas's "Summa contra Gentiles": A Guide and Commentary*. Oxford: Oxford University Press, 2016.

———. *The Thought of Thomas Aquinas*. Oxford: Clarendon, 1992.

Davis, William C. "Contra Hart: Christian Scholars Should Not Throw in the Towel." *Christian Scholar's Review* 34, no. 2 (2005): 187–200.

De Bruijne, Ad. "'Colony of Heaven': Abraham Kuyper's Ecclesiology in the Twenty-First Century." *Journal of Markets and Morality* 17, no. 2 (2014): 445–90.

Demarest, Bruce A. *General Revelation: Historical Views and Contemporary Issues*. Grand Rapids: Zondervan, 1982.

De Moor, Bernardinus. *Continuous Commentary on Johannes Marckius' Didactico-Elenctic Compendium of Christian Theology*. Translated by Steven Dilday. Vol. 1. Culpeper, VA: L&G Reformation Translation Center, 2014.

Dennison, William D. "Militant Reformed Orthodoxy." *New Horizons* (January 2012): 21–22.

———. "Van Til and Common Grace." *Mid-America Journal of Theology* 9, no. 2 (1993): 225–47.

DeRouchie, Jason S. *A Call to Covenant Love: Text, Grammar, and Literary Structure in Deuteronomy 5–11*. Piscataway, NJ: Gorgias, 2014.

Descartes, René. *Meditations on First Philosophy*. 3rd ed. New York: Hackett, 1993.

———. *The Philosophical Writings of Descartes*. Translated by John Cottingham et al. Cambridge: Cambridge University Press, 1991.

Dewan, Lawrence. "Faith and Reason from St. Thomas Aquinas's Perspective." *Science et Esprit* 58, no. 2 (2006): 113–23.

De Witte, Petrus. *Catechizing upon the Heidelbergh Catechisme*. Amsterdame: Gillis Joosten Saeghman, 1664.

Dilthey, Wilhelm. *Dilthey's Philosophy of Existence: Introduction to Weltanschauungslehre*. Translated and edited by William Kluback and Martin Weinbaugh. New York: Bookman Associates, 1957.

Dodds, Michael J. *Unlocking Divine Actions: Contemporary Science and Thomas Aquinas*. Washington, DC: Catholic University of America Press, 2012.

Donnelly, John Patrick. *Calvinism and Scholasticism in Vermigli's Doctrine of Man and Grace*. Leiden: Brill, 1976.

Dooyeweerd, Herman. "Centrum en Omtrek: De Wijsbegeerte der Wetsidee in een veranderende wereld." *Philosophia Reformata* 72 (2007): 1–20.

———. "Cornelius Van Til and the Transcendental Critique of Theoretical Thought." In *Jerusalem and Athens: Critical Discussions on the Theology and Apologetics of Cornelius Van Til*, ed. E. R. Geehan. [Nutley, NJ]: P&R, 1971.

———. *In the Twilight of Western Thought*. Grand Rapids: Paideia, 2012.

———. "Kuyper's Wetenschapsleer." *Philosophia Reformata* 4 (1939): 193–232.

———. *A New Critique of Theoretical Thought*. Translated by David H. Freeman and H. de Jongste. 4 vols. Phillipsburg, NJ: P&R, 1969.

———. *Reformation and Scholasticism in Philosophy*. Edited by D. F. M. Strauss. Translated by Ray Togtmann. Collected Works, series A, vols. 5/1–3. Grand Rapids: Paideia, 2012.

———. *Transcendental Problems of Philosophic Thought: An Inquiry into the Transcendental Conditions of Philosophy*. Grand Rapids: Eerdmans, 1948.

Dorner, Isaac. *A System of Christian Doctrine*. 4 vols. Edinburgh: T&T Clark, 1888.

Dorrien, Gary. *Kantian Reason and Hegelian Spirit: The Idealistic Logic of Modern Theology*. Chichester, UK: John Wiley & Sons, 2012.

Douma, Douglas J. *The Presbyterian Philosopher: The Authorized Biography of*

Gordon H. Clark. Eugene, OR: Wipf & Stock, 2017.

Downame, John. *The Christian Warfare against the Devill, World and Flesh Wherein Is Describe Their Nature, the Maner of Their Fight and Meanes to Obtain Victory.* London: William Stansby, 1634.

Dulles, Avery Cardinal. *A History of Apologetics.* 1971. Reprint, San Francisco: Ignatius, 1999.

Du Moulin, Pierre. *The Anatomy of Arminianisme.* London: Nathaniel Newbery, 1620.

Du Plessis-Mornay, Philippe. *A Worke concerning the Trunesse of Christian Religion.* Translated by Philip Sidney Knight and Arthur Golding. London: George Potter, 1604.

Emery, Gilles, and Matthew Levering, eds. *Aristotle in Aquinas's Theology.* Oxford: Oxford University Press, 2015.

Esler, Philip F. *The Early Christian World.* 2 vols. New York: Routledge, 2000.

Estella, Diego. *In Sanctum Iesu Chrisi Evangelius Secundum Lucam Doctissima Pariter & Piissima Commentaria.* Verdussen, 1655.

Euclid. *The Thirteen Books of The Elements.* Translated by Thomas L. Heath. 2nd ed. 1956. New York: Dover, 2016.

Evans, C. Stephen. *Faith beyond Reason.* Edinburgh: Edinburgh University Press, 1998.

Fenner, Dudley. *The Sacred Doctrine of Divinitie.* London: Felix Kyngston, 1613.

Feser, Edward. *Scholastic Metaphysics: A Contemporary Introduction.* Piscataway, NJ: Editiones Scholasticae, 2014.

Fesko, J. V. *The Covenant of Redemption: Origins, Development, and Reception.* Göttingen: Vandenhoeck & Ruprecht, 2016.

———. "The Days of Creation and Confession Subscription in the OPC." *Westminster Theological Journal* 63 (2001): 235–49.

———. *Last Things First: Unlocking Genesis with the Christ of Eschatology.* Fearn, UK: Mentor, 2007.

———. *The Theology of the Westminster Standards.* Wheaton: Crossway, 2014.

———. *The Trinity and the Covenant of Redemption.* Fearn, UK: Mentor, 2016.

Fesko, J. V., and Guy Richard. "Natural Theology and the Westminster Confession of Faith." In *The Westminster Confession into the 21st Century*, edited by J. Ligon Duncan, 3:223–66. 3 vols. Fearn, UK: Mentor, 2009.

Feuerbach, Ludwig. *Das Wesen des Christenthums.* Leipzig: Otto Bigand, 1841.

Fisher, Edward. *Marrow of Modern Divinity.* 1645. Reprint, Edinburgh: John Boyd, 1778.

Flavel, John. *The Whole Works of the Reverend Mr. John Flavel in Two Volumes.* London: D. Midwinter et al., 1740.

Fox, Michael V. *The Song of Songs and the Ancient Egyptian Love Songs.* Madison: University of Wisconsin Press, 1985.

———. *A Time to Tear Down and a Time to Build Up: A Rereading of Ecclesiastes.* Grand Rapids: Eerdmans, 1999.

Frame, John. "Cornelius Van Til." In *Handbook of Evangelical Theologians*, edited by Walter Elwell, 156–67. Grand Rapids: Baker, 1993.

———. *Cornelius Van Til: An Analysis of His Thought.* Phillipsburg, NJ: P&R, 2009.

———. "In Defense of Something Close to Biblicism: Reflections on *Sola Scriptura* and History in Theological Method." *Westminster Theological Journal* 59 (1997): 269–91.

———. *John Frame's Selected Shorter Writings.* 2 vols. Phillipsburg, NJ: P&R, 2015.

———. "Reply to Richard Muller and David Wells." *Westminster Theological Journal* 59 (1997): 311–18.

———. "Transcendental Arguments." In *New Dictionary of Christian Apologetics*, edited by Gavin J. McGrath and W. C. Campbell-Jack, 716–17. Downers Grove, IL: InterVarsity, 2006.

Franks, Paul W. *All or Nothing: Systematicity, Transcendental Arguments, and Skepticism in German Idealism.* Cambridge, MA: Harvard University Press, 2005.

Friesen, J. Glenn. *Neo-Calvinism and Christian Theosophy: Franz von Baader, Abraham Kuyper, Herman Dooyeweerd.* Calgary: Aevum Books, 2015.

Gaffin, Richard B., Jr. "Some Epistemological Reflections on 1 Cor 2:6–16." *Westminster Theological Journal* (1995): 103–24.

Geehan, E. R., ed. *Jerusalem and Athens: Critical Discussions on the Theology and Apologetics of Cornelius Van Til.* [Nutley, NJ]: P&R, 1971.

Gerhart, Emmanuel V. *Institutes of Christian Religion.* 2 vols. New York: Armstrong & Son, 1891.

Gerrish, Brian. *Grace and Reason: A Study in the Theology of Luther.* Oxford: Clarendon, 1962.

Gerstner, John H., et al. *The Westminster Confession of Faith: A Guide.* Signal Mountain, TN: Summertown Texts, 1992.

Gillespie, George. *A Dispute against the English-Popish Ceremonies Obtruded upon the Church of Scotland.* Edinburgh, 1660.

Gilson, Etienne. *The Christian Philosophy of St. Thomas Aquinas.* Notre Dame, IN: University of Notre Dame Press, 1956.

Goheen, Michael W. *Living at the Crossroads: An Introduction to Christian Worldview.* Grand Rapids: Baker Academic, 2008.

Gomarus, Franciscus. *Opera Theologica Omnia.* Vol. 2. Pars tertia. Amsterdam: J. Jansonius, 1644.

Goodwin, Thomas. *The Works of Thomas Goodwin.* Edited by Thankfull Owen and James Barron. London: Thomas Goodwin Jr., 1683.

———. *The Works of Thomas Goodwin.* 12 vols. Edinburgh: James Nichol, 1863.

Goudriaan, Aza. "Theology and Philosophy." In *A Companion to Reformed Orthodoxy,* edited by Herman J. Selderhuis. Leiden: Brill, 2013.

Grabill, Stephen J. "Althusius in Context: A Biographical and Historical Introduction." In *On Law and Power,* by Johannes Althusius, trans. Jeffrey J. Veenstra. Grand Rapids: Christian's Library, 2013.

———. *Rediscovering the Natural Law in Reformed Theological Ethics.* Grand Rapids: Eerdmans, 2006.

Grajewski, Maurice. "The Formal Distinction of Duns Scotus and Its Philosophic Applications." *Proceedings of the American Catholic Philosophical Association* 20 (1945): 145–56.

Gravilyuk, Paul. L. *The Suffering of the Impassible God: The Dialectics of Patristic Thought.* Oxford: Oxford University Press, 2004.

Green, Joel B. *Body, Soul, and Human Life: The Nature of Humanity in the Bible.* Grand Rapids: Baker Academic, 2008.

———. "Scripture and the Human Person: Further Reflections." *Science and Christian Belief* 11 (1999): 51–63.

Grislis, Egil. "Calvin's Use of Cicero in the *Institutes* I:1–5: A Case Study in Theological Method." *Archiv für Reformationsgeschichte / Archive for Reformation History* 62, no. 1 (1971): 5–37.

Haak, Theodore. *The Dutch Annotations upon the Whole Bible.* London: Henry Hills, 1657.

Haas, Günther H. "Ethics and Church Discipline." In *The Calvin Handbook,* ed. Herman J. Selderhuis. Grand Rapids: Eerdmans, 2008.

Habermas, Gary R., and Michael R. Licona. *The Case for the Resurrection of Jesus.* Grand Rapids: Kregel, 2004.

Hale, Matthew. *Of the Law of Nature.* Edited by David Sytsma. Grand Rapids: CLP Academic, 2015.

Hankey, W. J. *God in Himself: Aquinas's Doctrine of God as Expounded in the*

"Summa Theologiae." Oxford: Oxford University Press, 1987.

Harnack, Adolf von. *History of Dogma.* 7 vols. Boston: Little, Brown, 1898–1907.

———. *Outlines of the History of Dogma.* London: Hodder & Stoughton, 1893.

Harper, Robert Francis. *The Code of Hammurabi, King of Babylon, about 2250 BC.* Eugene, OR: Wipf & Stock, 2007.

Harris, Murray J. "Resurrection and Immortality: Eight Theses." *Themelios* 1, no. 2 (1976): 50–55.

Hart, D. G. "Christian Scholars, Secular Universities, and the Problem with Antithesis." *Christian Scholar's Review* 30, no. 4 (2001): 382–402.

Hawking, Stephen. *A Brief History of Time: The Updated and Expanded Anniversary Edition.* 1988. New York: Bantam, 1996.

Heidegger, Johannes. *Corpus Theologiae Christianae.* 2 vols. Tiguri: ex Officina Heideggeriana, 1732.

Helm, Paul. "Calvin (and Zwingli) on Divine Providence." *Calvin Theological Journal* 29 (1994): 388–405.

———. *John Calvin's Ideas.* Oxford: Oxford University Press, 2004.

———. "Reprise: Calvin, the Natural Knowledge of God, and Confessionalism." *Helm's Deep: Philosophical Theology* (blog), November 13, 2015. http://paulhelpsdeep.blogspot.com /2015/11/reprise-calvin-natural -knowledge-of-god.html?m=1.

Heppe, Heinrich. *Reformed Dogmatics: Set Out and Illustrated from the Sources.* London: George Allen & Unwin Ltd., 1950.

Heslam, Peter S. *Creating a Christian Worldview: Abraham Kuyper's Lectures on Calvinism.* Grand Rapids: Eerdmans, 1998.

Hodge, A. A. *The Confession of Faith: A Handbook of Christian Doctrine Expounding the Westminster Standards.* Reprint, Edinburgh: Banner of Truth, 1958.

Hodge, Charles. *Romans.* 1835. Reprint, Edinburgh: Banner of Truth, 1989.

Hoekema, A. A. *Created in God's Image.* Grand Rapids: Eerdmans, 1986.

Homer, *Odyssey.* Translated by A. T. Murray. Revised by George E. Dimock. Loeb Classical Library. Cambridge, MA: Harvard University Press, 1919.

Horowitz, Maryanne Cline. "The Stoic Synthesis of the Idea of Natural Law in Man: Four Themes." *Journal of the History of Ideas* 35, no. 1 (1974): 3–16.

Horton, Michael. *Lord and Servant: A Covenant Christology.* Louisville: Westminster John Knox, 2005.

The Humble Advice of the Assembly of Divines, Now by Authority of Parliament Sitting at Westminster. London, 1648.

Hütter, Reinhard. *Dust Bound for Heaven: Explorations in the Theology of Thomas Aquinas.* Grand Rapids: Eerdmans, 2012.

Illyricus, Flacius Matthias. *De Peccati Originalis aut Veteris Adami Appellationibus et Essentia,* in *Scripturae S. sue Sermone Sacrarum Literarum.* [Basel]: Eusebius Episcopius, 1580.

Ingersoll, Julie J. *Building God's Kingdom: Inside the World of Christian Reconstruction.* Oxford: Oxford University Press, 2015.

Isidore. *The Etymologies of Isidore of Seville.* Translated by Stephen A. Barney et al. Cambridge: Cambridge University Press, 2006.

Jersild, Paul. "Natural Theology and the Doctrine of God in Albrecht Ritschl and Karl Barth." *Lutheran Quarterly* 14, no. 3 (1962): 239–57.

Joachim, Harold H. *The Nature of Truth.* Oxford: Clarendon, 1906.

Johnson, Dennis. "Between Two Wor(l)ds: Worldview and Observation in the Use of General Revelation to Interpret Scripture, and Vice Versa." *Journal of the Evangelical Theological Society* 41, no. 1 (1998): 69–84.

Jordan, Mark D. *Rewritten Theology: Aquinas after His Readers.* Oxford: Blackwell, 2006.

Junius, Francis. *The Mosaic Polity.* Translated by Todd M. Rester. Edited by

Andrew M. McGinnis. Grand Rapids: CLP Academic, 2015.

———. *A Treatise on True Theology*. Translated by David C. Noe. Grand Rapids: Reformation Heritage Books, 2014.

Justinian. *Justinian's Institutes*. Translated by Peter Birks and Grand McLeod. London: Duckworth, 1987.

Kant, Immanuel. *Critique of Judgment: Including the First Introduction*. Translated by Werner S. Pluhar. Indianapolis: Hackett, 1987. Original German edition, 1790.

———. *Critique of Pure Reason*. Translated by Paul Guyer and Allen W. Wood. Cambridge: Cambridge University Press, 1998.

Kerr, Fergus. *After Aquinas: Versions of Thomism*. Oxford: Blackwell, 2002.

Kerr, Gaven. *Aquinas's Way to God: The Proof in "De Ente et Essentia."* Oxford: Oxford University Press, 2015.

Kirkham, Richard L. *Theories of Truth: A Critical Introduction*. Cambridge: MIT Press, 1992.

Klauber, Martin I. *Between Reformed Scholasticism and Pan-Protestantism: Jean-Alphonse Turretin (1671–1737) and Enlightened Orthodoxy at the Academy of Geneva*. Selinsgrove, PA: Susquehanna University Press, 1996.

Knudsen, Robert D. "The Transcendental Perspective of Westminster's Apologetic." *Westminster Theological Journal* (1986): 223–39.

Kossel, Clifford G. "Natural Law and Human Law (Ia IIae, qq. 90–97)." In *The Ethics of Aquinas*, edited by Stephen J. Pope, 169–93. Washington, DC: Georgetown University Press, 2002.

Kuyper, Abraham. *A Centennial Reader*. Edited by James D. Bratt. Grand Rapids: Eerdmans, 1998.

———. *Common Grace: God's Gifts for a Fallen World*. 2 vols. Bellingham, WA: Lexham and Acton Institute for the Study of Religion and Liberty, 2016.

———. *Lectures on Calvinism*. Grand Rapids: Eerdmans, 1931. Original Dutch edition, 1898.

Lactantius. *The Divine Institutes: Books I–VII*. Translated by Mary Francis McDonald. Fathers of the Church 49. Washington, DC: Catholic University of America Press, 1964.

Lang, August. "The Reformation and Natural Law." In *Calvin and the Reformation*, translated by J. Gresham Machen, 56–98. New York: Revell, 1927.

La Rocca, Robert. "Cornelius Van Til's Rejection and Appropriation of Thomist Metaphysics." Master's thesis, Westminster Theological Seminary, 2012.

Leclercq, Jean. *The Love of Learning and the Desire for God: A Study of Monastic Culture*. Translated by Catharine Misrahi. New York: Fordham University Press, 1961.

Leibniz, G. W. *Discourse on Metaphysics and Other Essays*. Translated by Daniel Garber and Roger Ariew. Indianapolis: Hackett, 1991.

Leigh, Edward. *A Systeme or Body of Divinity*. London: 1654.

Leinsle, Ulrich G. *Introduction to Scholastic Theology*. Translated by Michael J. Miller. Washington, DC: Catholic University of America Press, 2010.

Leiter, Brian. "The Hermeneutics of Suspicion: Recovering Marx, Nietzsche, and Freud." In *The Future for Philosophy*, edited by Brian Leiter, 74–105. Oxford: Clarendon, 2004.

Leithart, Peter. "Stoic Elements in Calvin's Doctrine of the Christian Life, pt. 1: Original Corruption, Natural Law, and the Order of the Soul." *Westminster Theological Journal* 55 (1993): 31–54.

———. "That Eminent Pagan: Calvin's Use of Cicero in *Institutes* I:1–5." *Westminster Theological Journal* 52, no. 1 (1990): 1–12.

Levering, Matthew. *Proofs of God: Classical Arguments from Tertullian to Barth*. Grand Rapids: Baker Academic, 2016.

Levering, Matthew, ed. *Aristotle in Aquinas's Theology*. Oxford: Oxford University Press, 2015.

Locke, John. *Essays on the Law of Nature.* Edited by W. von Leyden. Oxford: Clarendon, 2002.

Lombard, Peter. *The Sentences.* Translated by Giulio Silano. 4 vols. Toronto: Pontifical Institute of Medieval Studies, 2007–10.

Long, A. A. *Epicetus: A Stoic and Socratic Guide to Life.* Oxford: Clarendon, 2002.

Longenecker, Richard N. *Acts.* EBC. Grand Rapids: Zondervan, 1995.

Luther, Martin. *Bondage of the Will.* Vol. 33 of *Luther's Works,* edited by Jaroslav Pelikan. Minneapolis: Fortress, 1972.

Lyotard, Jean-François. *The Postmodern Condition: A Report on Knowledge.* Manchester: Manchester University Press, 1984.

Maccovius, Johannes. *Scholastic Discourse: Johannes Maccovius (1588–1644) on Theological and Philosophical Distinctions and Rules.* Edited by Willem J. Van Asselt et al. Apeldoorn: Instituut voor Reformatieonderzoek, 2009.

Machen, J. Gresham. *Christianity and Liberalism.* 1923. Reprint, Grand Rapids: Eerdmans, 1999.

———. *The Origin of Paul's Religion.* 1925. Reprint, Eugene, OR: Wipf & Stock, 2002.

Magee, Rosemary M., ed. *Conversations with Flannery O'Connor.* Jackson: University Press of Mississippi, 1987.

Mallinson, Jeffrey. *Faith, Reason, and Revelation in Theodore Beza (1519–1605).* Oxford: Oxford University Press, 2003.

Manning, Russell. *Theology at the End of Culture: Paul Tillich's Theology of Culture and Art.* Leuven: Peeters, 2005.

Manson, Neil A. *God and Design: The Theological Argument and Modern Science.* New York: Routledge, 2003.

Marion, Jean-Luc. *Being Given: Toward a Phenomenology of Givenness.* Redwood City, CA: Stanford University Press, 2002.

———. *The Erotic Phenomenon.* Chicago: University of Chicago Press, 2008.

———. *The Visible and the Revealed.* New York: Fordham University Press, 2008.

Marsden, George M. *The Outrageous Idea of Christian Scholarship.* Oxford: Oxford University Press, 1998.

———. "Reformed and American." In *Reformed Theology in America: A History of Its Modern Development,* ed. David F. Wells. Grand Rapids: Baker, 1997.

Marshall, Bruce D. "Faith and Reason Considered: Aquinas and Luther on Deciding What Is True." *The Thomist* 63, no. 1 (1999): 1–48.

———. *Trinity and Truth.* Cambridge: Cambridge University Press, 2000.

McConnel, Timothy. "The Historical Origins of the Presuppositional Apologetics of Cornelius Van Til." PhD diss., Marquette University, 1999.

———. "The Influence of Idealism on the Apologetics of Cornelius Van Til." *Journal of the Evangelical Theological Society* 48, no. 3 (2005): 557–88.

McDowell, Josh. *Evidence That Demands a Verdict.* 2 vols. San Bernardino, CA: Here's Life, 1986.

McFate, Sean. *The Modern Mercenary: Private Armies and What They Mean for World Order.* Oxford: Oxford University Press, 2014.

McGovern, Arthur F. "John Locke on Knowledge of the Natural Law." Master's thesis, Loyola University, 1958.

McLuhan, Marshall. *Understanding Media: The Extensions of Man.* Edited by Terrence Gordon. 1964. Reprint, Corte Madera, CA: Gingko, 1994.

McVicar, Michael J. *Christian Reconstruction: R. J. Rushdoony and American Religious Conservatism.* Chapel Hill: University of North Carolina Press, 2015.

Meek, Esther Lightcap. *Loving to Know: Covenant Epistemology.* Eugene, OR: Cascade Books, 2011.

Melanchthon, Philip. *The Chief Theological Topics: Loci Praecipui Theologici 1559.* Translated by J. A. O. Preus. 2nd ed. St. Louis: Concordia, 2011.

———. *Commentary on Romans*. Translated by Fred Kramer. St. Louis: Concordia, 1992.

Meyer, Ben F. *Critical Realism and the New Testament*. Eugene, OR: Pickwick, 1989.

Miccoli, Giovanni. "Monks." In *Medieval Callings*, edited by Jacques Le Goff, translated by Lydia G. Cochrane, 370–74. Chicago: University of Chicago Press, 1987.

Middleton, Richard. *A New Heaven and Earth: Reclaiming Biblical Eschatology*. Grand Rapids: Baker Academic, 2014.

Moreland, Anna Bonta. *Known by Nature: Thomas Aquinas on Natural Knowledge of God*. New York: Herder & Herder, 2010.

Moreland, J. P., and William Lane Craig. *Philosophical Foundations for a Christian Worldview*. Downers Grove, IL: IVP Academic, 2003.

Muether, John R. *Cornelius Van Til: Reformed Apologist and Churchman*. Phillipsburg, NJ: P&R, 2008.

Muller, Richard A. *After Calvin: Studies in the Development of a Theological Tradition*. Oxford: Oxford University Press, 2003.

———. *Calvin and the Reformed Tradition: On the Work of Christ and the Order of Salvation*. Grand Rapids: Baker Academic, 2012.

———. *Christ and the Decree: Christology and the Decree in Reformed Theology from Calvin to Perkins*. Grand Rapids: Baker Academic, 2008.

———. *Dictionary of Latin and Greek Theological Terms: Drawn Principally from Protestant Scholastic Theology*. 2nd ed. Grand Rapids: Baker Academic, 2017.

———. "The Dogmatic Function of St. Thomas' 'Proofs': A Protestant Appreciation." *Fides et Historia* 24 (1992): 15–29.

———. "Emmanuel V. Gerhart on the 'Christ Idea' as Fundamental Principle." *Westminster Theological Journal* 48, no. 1 (1986): 97–117.

———. "Henry Boynton Smith: Christocentric Theologian." *Journal of Presbyterian History* 61, no. 4 (1983): 429–44.

———. "Historiography in the Service of Theology and Worship: Toward Dialogue with John Frame." *Westminster Theological Journal* 59 (1997): 301–10.

———. "A Note on 'Christocentrism' and the Imprudent Use of Such Terminology." *Westminster Theological Journal* 68 (2006): 253–60.

———. *Post-Reformation Reformed Dogmatics*. 4 vols. Grand Rapids: Baker Academic, 2003.

———. *Scholasticism and Orthodoxy in the Reformed Tradition: An Attempt at Definition*. Grand Rapids: Calvin Theological Seminary, 1995.

———. *The Unaccommodated Calvin: Studies in the Foundation of a Theological Tradition*. Oxford: Oxford University Press, 2000.

Murphy, Nancey. *Bodies and Souls, or Spirited Bodies?* Cambridge: Cambridge University Press, 2006.

Murphy, Roland E. *The Tree of Life: An Exploration of Biblical Wisdom Literature*. Grand Rapids: Eerdmans, 1990.

Naugle, David K. *Worldview: The History of a Concept*. Grand Rapids: Eerdmans, 2002.

Noe, David Craig. "*Oikeiosis, Ratio*, and *Natura*: The Stoic Challenge to Cicero's Academism in *De Finibus* and *Natura Deorum*." PhD diss., University of Iowa, 2003.

Noll, Mark A. *The Scandal of the Evangelical Mind*. Grand Rapids: Eerdmans, 1994.

Notaro, Thom. *Van Til and the Use of Evidence*. Phillipsburg, NJ: P&R, 1980.

Novak, David. *Natural Law in Judaism*. Cambridge: Cambridge University Press, 1998.

Oberman, Heiko. A. *The Dawn of the Reformation: Essays in Late Medieval and Early Reformation Thought*. Edinburgh: T&T Clark, 1986.

O'Connor, Flannery. *Mystery and Manners: Occasional Prose*. New York: Farrar, Straus, & Giroux, 1970.

O'Donnell, Laurence R., III. "Kees Van Til als Nederlandse-Amerikaanse, Neo-Calvinistisch-Presbyteriaan Apologeticus: An Analysis of Cornelius Van Til's Presupposition of Reformed Dogmatics with Special Reference to Herman Bavinck's *Geerformeerde Dogmatiek*." ThM thesis, Calvin Theological Seminary, 2011.

———. "Neither 'Copernican' nor 'Van Tillian': Re-reading Van Til's *Reformed Apologetics* in Light of Herman Bavinck's *Reformed Dogmatics*." *Bavinck Review* 2 (2011): 71–95.

Ogilvie, Brian W. "Natural History, Ethics, and Physico-Theology." In *Historia: Empiricism and Erudition in Early Modern Europe*, edited by Gianna Potmata and Nancy G. Siraisi, 75–103. Cambridge, MA: MIT Press, 2005.

Oliphint, K. Scott. "Bavinck's Realism, the Logos Principle, and *Sola Scriptura*." *Westminster Theological Journal* 72 (2010): 359–90.

———. "The Consistency of Van Til's Methodology." *Westminster Theological Journal* 52 (1990): 27–39.

———. *Covenantal Apologetics: Principles and Practice in Defense of Our Faith*. Wheaton: Crossway, 2013.

———. "Covenant Model." In *Four Views on Christianity and Philosophy*, edited by Paul M. Gould and Richard Brian Davis. Grand Rapids: Zondervan, 2016.

———. "Prolegomena Principle: Frame and Bavinck." In *Speaking the Truth in Love: The Theology of John Frame*, edited by John J. Hughes, 201–32. Phillipsburg, NJ: P&R, 2009.

———. *Reasons for Faith: Philosophy in the Service of Theology*. Phillipsburg, NJ: P&R, 2006.

Orr, James. *The Christian View of God and the World as Centering in the Incarnation*. Edinburgh: Andrew Elliot, 1907.

Owen, John. *Communion with God*. London: William Marshall, 1700.

———. *Pneumatologia, or a Discourse concerning the Holy Spirit*. London: Nathaniel Ponder, 1674.

Pardue, Stephen T. *The Mind of Christ: Humility and the Intellect in Early Christian Theology*. London: Bloomsbury T&T Clark, 2013.

Pareus, David. *In Divinam ad Romans S. Pauli ap. Epistolam Commentarius*. Frankfort, 1608.

Pelagius. *Pelagius's Commentary on St. Paul's Epistle to the Romans*. Translated by Theodore de Bruyn. Oxford: Clarendon, 1998.

Pelikan, Jaroslav, and Valerie Hotchkiss, eds. *Creeds and Confessions of Faith in the Christian Tradition*. 3 vols. New Haven: Yale University Press, 2003.

Penner, Myron B. "Calvin, Barth, and the Subject of Atonement." In *Calvin, Barth, and Reformed Theology*, edited by Neil B. MacDonald and Carl R. Trueman. Milton Keynes, UK: Paternoster, 2008.

Perkins, William. *A Commentarie or Exposition, upon the First Five Chapters of the Epistle to the Galatians*. Cambridge: John Legat, 1604.

———. *The Works of That Famous and Worthy Minister of Christ, in the University of Cambridge, Mr. William Perkins*. Cambridge: John Legatt, 1616.

Philipp, Wolfgang. "Physicotheology in the Age of Enlightenment: Appearance and History." *Studies on Voltaire and the Eighteenth Century* 57 (1967): 1233–67.

Pictet, Benedict. *Christian Theology*. Translated by Frederick Reyroux. London: L. B. Seeley & Sons, 1834.

Pinnock, Clark. "The Philosophy of Christian Evidences." In *Jerusalem and Athens: Critical Discussions on the Theology and Apologetics of Cornelius Van Til*, ed. E. R. Geehan. [Nutley, NJ]: P&R, 1971.

Placher, William C. *Unapologetic Theology: A Christian Voice in a Pluralistic*

Conversation. Louisville: Westminster John Knox, 1989.

Plantinga, Alvin. "The Reformed Objection to Natural Theology." In *Philosophy of Religion: Selected Readings*, edited by Michael Peterson et al. Oxford: Oxford University Press, 2001.

Plantinga, Cornelius. *Engaging God's World: A Christian Vision of Faith, Learning, and Living*. Grand Rapids: Eerdmans, 2002.

Plato. *Plato: Five Dialogues*. 2nd ed. Indianapolis: Hackett, 2002.

———. *The Republic*. Translated by Allan Bloom. New York: Basic Books, 1991.

Platt, John. *Reformed Thought and Scholasticism: The Arguments for the Existence of God in Dutch Theology, 1575–1650*. Leiden: Brill, 1982.

Polanus, Amandus. *Syntagma Theologiae Christianae*. Hanovia: apud Claudium Marnium, 1610.

Poythress, Vern S. *Redeeming Mathematics: A God-Centered Approach*. Wheaton: Crossway, 2015.

———. *Redeeming Science: A God-Centered Approach*. Wheaton: Crossway, 2006.

Pruss, Alexander R. *The Principle of Sufficient Reason: A Reassessment*. Cambridge: Cambridge University Press, 2006.

Pseudo-Seneca. "The Correspondence of Paul and Seneca." In *The Apocryphal New Testament*, translated by M. R. Jones. Oxford: Clarendon, 1924.

Reeling, Rinse H. *Karl Barth and Post-Reformation Orthodox*. London: Routledge, 2015.

Rehnman, Sebastian. "Alleged Rationalism: Francis Turretin on Reason." *Calvin Theological Journal* 37 (2002): 255–69.

Reichenbach, Bruce. *Is Man the Phoenix? A Study of Immortality*. Grand Rapids: Eerdmans, 1983.

Reid, Thomas. *An Inquiry into the Human Mind, on the Principles of Common Sense*. Edinburgh: Anderson & MacDowell, & James Robertson, 1818.

Ridderbos, Herman. *Paul: An Outline of His Theology*. Grand Rapids: Eerdmans, 1975.

Rist, John M. *Human Value: A Study in Ancient Ethics*. Leiden: Brill, 1997.

Robinson, John. *Essayes, or Observations Divine and Morall: Collected out of Holy Scriptures, Ancient and Modern Writers, Both Divine and Human*. London: I. Bellame, 1638.

Rogers, Eugene F., Jr. "The Narrative of Natural Law in Aquinas's Commentary on Romans 1." *Theological Studies* 59 (1998): 254–76.

Rouwendal, Pieter L. "The Method of the Schools: Medieval Scholasticism." In *Introduction to Reformed Scholasticism*, ed. Willem J. Van Asselt et al., trans. Albert Gootjes. Grand Rapids: Reformation Heritage Books, 2011.

Rowe, William V. "Adolf von Harnack and the Concept of Hellenization." In *Hellenization Revisited: Shaping a Christian Response within the Greco-Roman World*, edited by Wendy E. Helleman, 69–98. Lanham, MD: University Press of America, 1994.

———. "Vollenhoven's and Dooyeweerd's Appropriation of Greek Philosophy." In *In the Phrygian Mode: Neo-Calvinism, Antiquity and the Lamentations of Reformed Philosophy*, ed. Robert Sweetman. Lanham, MD: University Press of America, 2007.

Royce, Josiah. *Lectures on Modern Idealism*. New Haven: Yale University Press, 1919.

Rutherford, Samuel. *The Divine Right of Church-Government and Excommunication*. London: John Field, 1646.

Ryken, Philip Graham. *What Is the Christian Worldview?* Phillipsburg, NJ: P&R, 2006.

Sandlin, P. Andrew. "Gospel or Law, or Gospel and Law." *Reformation and Revival Journal* 11, no. 2 (2012): 124–35.

Schaff, Philip. *Theological Propaedeutic: A General Introduction to the Study of Theology*. New York: Charles Scribner's Sons, 1893.

Schneemelcher, Wilhelm, ed. *New Testament Apocrypha*. 2 vols. Louisville: Westminster John Knox, 1992.

Schreiner, Susan. *Theater of His Glory: Nature and the Natural Order in the Thought of John Calvin*. Grand Rapids: Baker, 1995.

Schultz, Robert C. "Original Sin: Accident or Substance—the Paradoxical Significance of FC I, 53–62 in Historical Context." In *Discord, Dialogue, and Concord: Studies in the Lutheran Reformation's Formula of Concord*, edited by Lewis W. Spitz and Wenzel Lohff, 38–57. Philadelphia: Fortress, 1977.

Selden, John. *De Iure Naturali & Gentium, Iuxta Disciplinam Ebraeorum, Libri Septem*. London: Richard Bishop, 1640.

———. *De Successionibus in Bona Defunti Secundum Leges Ebraerorum*. London: Richard Bishop, 1636.

Selderhuis, Herman, ed. *The Calvin Handbook*. Grand Rapids: Eerdmans, 2008.

Shapiro, Barbara J. *Probability and Certainty in Seventeenth Century England: A Study of the Relationships between Natural Science, Religion, History, Law, and Literature*. Princeton: Princeton University Press, 1985.

Shaw, Robert. *Exposition of the Westminster Confession of Faith*. 1845. Reprint, Fearn, UK: Christian Heritage, 1998.

Sinnema, Donald, and Henk van den Belt. "The *Synopsis Purioris Theologiae* (1625) as a Disputation Cycle." *Church History and Religious Culture* 92, no. 4 (2012): 505–37.

Sire, James W. *Naming the Elephant: Worldview as a Concept*. Downers Grove, IL: IVP Academic, 2015.

Smith, Henry Boyton. *System of Christian Theology*. New York: Armstrong & Son, 1884.

Smith, James K. A. *Desiring the Kingdom: Worship, Worldview, and Culture Formation*. Grand Rapids: Baker Academic, 2009.

———. *Imagining the Kingdom: How Worship Works*. Grand Rapids: Baker Academic, 2013.

———. *Introducing Radical Orthodoxy: Mapping a Post-secular Theology*. Grand Rapids: Baker Academic, 2004.

———. Introduction to *In the Twilight of Western Thought*, by Herman Dooyeweerd. Grand Rapids: Paideia, 2012.

———. *Who's Afraid of Postmodernism? Taking Derrida, Lyotard, and Foucault to Church*. Grand Rapids: Baker Academic, 2006.

———. "Will the Real Plato Please Stand Up? Participation versus Incarnation." In *Radical Orthodoxy and the Reformed Tradition: Creation, Covenant, and Participation*, ed. James K. A. Smith and James H. Olthuis. Grand Rapids: Baker Academic, 2005.

Sommerville, J. P. "Selden, Grotius, and the Seventeenth-Century Intellectual Revolution in Moral and Political Theory." In *Rhetoric and Law in Early Modern Europe*, edited by Victoria Kahn and Lorna Hutson, 318–44. New Haven: Yale University Press, 2001.

Sproul, R. C., John Gerstner, and Arthur W. Lindsley. *Classical Apologetics: A Rational Defense of the Christian Faith and a Critique of Presuppositional Apologetics*. Grand Rapids: Zondervan, 1984.

Steinmetz, David. *Calvin in Context*. 2nd ed. Oxford: Oxford University Press, 2010.

———. "The Scholastic Calvin." In *Protestant Scholasticism: Essays in Reassessment*, ed. R. Scott Clark and Carl R. Trueman. Carlisle, UK: Paternoster, 1999.

Strauss, David Friedrich. *Der alte und der neue Glaube: Ein Bekenntniss*. Bonn: Emil Strauss, 1895.

Stuart, Douglas. *Hosea–Jonah*. WBC. Waco: Word, 1987.

Suarez, Francisco. *Tractatus de Legibus ac Deo Legislatore*. London: J. Dunmore, 1679.

Sudduth, Michael. *The Reformed Objection to Natural Theology*. Burlington, VT: Ashgate, 2009.

Summers, Kirk M. *Morality after Calvin: Theodore Beza's Christian Censor and Reformed Ethics*. Oxford: Oxford University Press, 2017.

Sweetman, Robert, ed. *In the Phrygian Mode: Neo-Calvinism, Antiquity and the Lamentations of Reformed Theology*. Lanham, MD: University Press of America, 2007.

Synopsis Purioris Theologiae / Synopsis of a Purer Theology. Vol. 1. Edited by Dolf te Velde et al. Translated by Riemer A. Faber. Leiden: Brill, 2014.

Sytsma, David S. "'As a Dwarfe Set upon a Gyants Shoulders': John Weems (ca. 1579–1636) on the Place of Philosophy and Scholasticism in Reformed Theology." In *Die Philosophie der Reformierten*, edited by Günter Frank and Herman Selderhuis, 299–321. Melanchthon-Schriften der Stadt Bretten. Stuttgart: Frommann-Holzboog, 2012.

———. "Herman Bavinck's Thomistic Epistemology: The Argument and Sources of His *Principia* of Science." In *Five Studies in the Thought of Herman Bavinck, A Creator of Modern Dutch Theology*, edited by John Bolt, 1–56. Lewiston, NY: Edwin Mellen, 2011.

———. "The Use of Reason in Francis Turretin's Arguments for God's Existence." *Stromata* 47 (2006): 1–27.

Taylor, Charles. *Hegel*. Cambridge: Cambridge University Press, 1975.

Themistius. *Aristotle: On the Soul*. Translated by Robert B. Todd. London: Bloomsbury, 2014.

Thomas Aquinas. *Commentary on Aristotle's "Posterior Analytics."* Translated by Ralph McInerny. Notre Dame, IN: Dumb Ox Books, 2007.

———. *Commentary on the Book of Job*. Translated by Brian Thomas Becket Mullady. Latin/English Edition of the Works of St. Thomas Aquinas. Vol. 32. Lander, WY: Aquinas Institute for the Study of Sacred Doctrine, 2016.

———. *Commentary on the Letter of St. Paul to the Romans*. Latin/English Edition of the Works of St. Thomas Aquinas 37. Lander, WY: Aquinas Institute for the Study of Sacred Doctrine, 2010.

———. *Commentary on the Letters of St. Paul to the Philippians, Colossians, Thessalonians, Timothy, Titus, and Philemon*. Translated by F. R. Larcher. Latin/English Edition of the Works of St. Thomas Aquinas 40. Lander, WY: Aquinas Institute for the Study of Sacred Doctrine, 2012.

———. *Disputed Questions on Truth*. Translated by Robert W. Mulligan. 3 vols. Chicago: Henry Regnery, 1952.

———. *An Exposition of "On the Hebdomads" of Boethius*. Washington, DC: Catholic University of America Press, 2001.

———. *Summa contra Gentiles*. 5 vols. Notre Dame, IN: University of Notre Dame Press, 1975.

———. *Summa Theologica*. Editio alter romana. Rome: Forzani et S., 1894.

———. *Summa Theologica*. Reprint, Allen, TX: Christian Classics, 1948.

Thompson, J. A. *Deuteronomy*. TOTC. Downers Grove, IL: InterVarsity, 1974.

Todd, R. B. "The Stoic Common Notions: A Re-examination and Reinterpretation." *Symbolae Osloenses* 48, no. 1 (1973): 47–75.

Tolstoy, Leo. *What Is Art?* New York: Penguin Books, 1996.

Toomer, G. J. *John Selden: A Life in Scholarship*. 2 vols. Oxford: Oxford University Press, 2009.

Trelcatius, Lucas. *A Brief Institution of the Common Places of Sacred Divinity*. London: Francis Burton, 1610.

Troxel, A. Craig, and Peter Wallace. "Men in Combat over the Civil Law: 'General Equity' in WCF 19.4." *Westminster Theological Journal* 64 (2002): 307–18.

Tuckney, Anthony. *Praelectiones Theologicae*. Amsterdam: Stephen Swart, 1679.

Turner, Denys. *Faith, Reason and the Existence of God*. Cambridge: Cambridge University Press, 2005.

Turretin, Francis. *Institutes of Elenctic Theology*. Edited by James T. Dennison Jr. Translated by George Musgrave Giger. 3 vols. Phillipsburg, NJ: P&R, 1992–97.

———. *Institutio Theologiae Elencticae*. Geneva: Samuel de Tournes, 1688.

Turretin, Jean-Alphonse. *Dissertations on Natural Theology*. Belfast: James Magee, 1777.

Twisse, William. *A Discovery of D. Jackson's Vanity*. Amsterdam, 1631.

———. *The Doctrine of the Synod of Dort and Arles Reduced to Practise*. Amsterdam: Successors to G. Thorp, 1631.

Ursinus, Zacharias. *The Commentary of Dr. Zacharias Ursinus on the Heidelberg Catechism*. Columbus, 1852. Reprint, Grand Rapids: Eerdmans, 1954.

———. *Corpus Doctrinae Orthodoxae*. Heidelberg: Jonah Rodius, 1616.

Ussher, James. *Body of Divinity*. London: Thomas Downes & George Badger, 1645.

Van Asselt, Willem J. "Introduction: What Is Reformed Scholasticism?" In *Introduction to Reformed Scholasticism*, ed. Willem J. Van Asselt et al., trans. Albert Gootjes. Grand Rapids: Reformation Heritage Books, 2011.

Van Asselt, Willem J., and Eef Dekker, eds. *Reformation and Scholasticism: An Ecumenical Enterprise*. Grand Rapids: Baker Academic, 2001.

Van der Walt, B. J. *Heartbeat: Taking the Pulse of Our Theological and Philosophical Heritage*. Potchefstroom: Potchefstroom University, 1978.

Van Dixhoorn, Chad. *Confessing the Faith: A Reader's Guide to the Westminster Confession of Faith*. Edinburgh: Banner of Truth, 2014.

———. *Minutes and Papers of the Westminster Assembly*. 5 vols. Oxford: Oxford University Press, 2012.

VanDrunen, David. *A Biblical Case for Natural Law*. Grand Rapids: Acton Institute, 2012.

———. *Divine Covenants and Moral Order: A Biblical Theology of Natural Law*. Grand Rapids: Eerdmans, 2014.

———. *Living in God's Two Kingdoms: A Biblical Vision for Christianity and Culture*. Wheaton: Crossway, 2010.

———. "Medieval Natural Law and the Reformation: A Comparison of Aquinas and Calvin." *American Catholic Philosophical Quarterly* 80, no. 1 (2006): 77–98.

———. *Natural Law and the Two Kingdoms: A Study in the Development of Reformed Social Thought*. Grand Rapids: Eerdmans, 2010.

Van Til, Cornelius. *Christian Apologetics*. Phillipsburg, NJ: P&R, 1976.

———. *Christianity and Idealism*. Philadelphia: P&R, 1955.

———. *Christianity in Conflict*. 1962. Reprint, Glendside, PA: Westminster Campus Bookstore, 1996.

———. "Christian Philosophy of Life: Address Presented to the Association for the Advancement of Christian Scholarship." March 29, 1968.

———. *Christian Theistic Evidences*. Phillipsburg, NJ: P&R, 1978.

———. *A Christian Theory of Knowledge*. Phillipsburg, NJ: P&R, 1969.

———. *Common Grace and the Gospel*. Phillipsburg, NJ: P&R, 1972.

———. *The Defense of the Faith*. Phillipsburg, NJ: P&R, 1955. 3rd ed., 1967.

———. *Essays on Christian Education*. Phillipsburg, NJ: P&R, 1971.

———. "God and the Absolute." *Evangelical Quarterly* 2, no. 4 (1930): 358–88.

———. "Herman Dooyeweerd (A Personal Tribute)." *Westminster Theological Journal* 39, no. 2 (1977): 319–27.

———. *Herman Dooyeweerd and Reformed Apologetics*. 3 parts. Philadelphia: Westminster Theological Seminary, 1972.

———. *Immanuel Kant and Protestantism.* Philadelphia: Westminster Theological Seminary, 1960s.

———. *Introduction to Systematic Theology.* Phillipsburg, NJ: P&R, 1974.

———. Introduction to *The Inspiration and Authority of the Bible*, by Benjamin B. Warfield. Edited by Samuel G. Craig. Reprint, Phillipsburg, NJ: P&R, 1948.

———. "My Credo." In *Jerusalem and Athens: Critical Discussions on the Theology and Apologetics of Cornelius Van Til*, ed. E. R. Geehan. [Nutley, NJ]: P&R, 1971.

———. *The New Synthesis Theology in the Netherlands.* Phillipsburg, NJ: P&R, 1975.

———. *Paul at Athens.* Phillipsburg, NJ: P&R, n.d.

———. *The Protestant Doctrine of Scripture.* In Defense of Biblical Christianity 1. [Philadelphia]: Den Dulk Christian Foundation, 1967.

———. *The Reformed Pastor and Modern Thought.* Phillipsburg, NJ: P&R, 1980.

———. "Response by C. Van Til to G. R. Lewis." In *Jerusalem and Athens: Critical Discussions on the Theology and Apologetics of Cornelius Van Til*, ed. E. R. Geehan. [Nutley, NJ]: P&R, 1971.

———. "Response of Van Til to Knudsen." In *Jerusalem and Athens: Critical Discussions on the Theology and Apologetics of Cornelius Van Til*, ed. E. R. Geehan. [Nutley, NJ]: P&R, 1971.

———. "Response to Herman Dooyeweerd." In *Jerusalem and Athens: Critical Discussions on the Theology and Apologetics of Cornelius Van Til*, ed. E. R. Geehan. [Nutley, NJ]: P&R, 1971.

———. *A Survey of Christian Epistemology.* In Defense of Biblical Christianity 2. Phillipsburg, NJ: P&R, 1969.

Van Til, Henry. *The Calvinistic Concept of Culture.* 1959. Reprint, Grand Rapids: Baker Academic, 2001.

Velde, Rudi A. te. *Aquinas on God: The "Divine Science" of the "Summa Theologiae."* Surrey: Ashgate, 2006.

Vermigli, Peter Martyr. *Most Learned and Fruitfull Commentaries of D. Peter Martir Vermilius.* London: John Daye, 1568.

———. *Philosophical Works: On the Relation of Philosophy to Theology.* Edited by Joseph C. McLelland. Peter Martyr Library. Vol. 4. Kirksville, MO: Sixteenth Century Essays & Studies, 1996.

Virgil. *Eclogue, Georgics, Aeneid Books 1–6.* Edited by G. P. Goold. Loeb Classical Library. Cambridge, MA: Harvard University Press, 1999.

Voetius, Gisbert. *Diatribe de Theologia, Philologia, Historia, & Philosophia.* Utrecht: Simon de Vries, 1668.

von Harnack, Adolf. *See* Harnack, Adolf von

Vos, Antoine. *The Philosophy of John Duns Scotus.* Edinburgh: Edinburgh University Press, 2006.

Vos, Arvin. *Aquinas, Calvin, and Contemporary Protestant Thought: A Critique of Protestant Views on the Thought of Thomas Aquinas.* Washington, DC: Christian University Press, 1985.

Vos, Geerhardus, "Christian Faith and the Truthfulness of Bible History." *Princeton Theological Review* 4, no. 3 (1906): 289–305.

———. *The Pauline Eschatology.* Phillipsburg, NJ: P&R, 1979.

———. *Reformed Dogmatics.* Edited by Richard B. Gaffin Jr. Bellingham, WA: Lexham, 2012–14.

Wallace, Ronald S. *Calvin's Doctrine of the Christian Life.* Eugene, OR: Wipf & Stock, 1997.

Walsh, Brian, and Richard Middleton. *The Transforming Vision: Shaping a Christian Worldview.* Downers Grove, IL: InterVarsity, 1984.

Ward, Rowland. *The Westminster Confession of Faith: A Study Guide.* Melbourne, Australia: New Melbourne Press, 1992.

Watson, Thomas. *A Body of Practical Divinity.* London: Thomas Parkhurst, 1692.

Webster, John. "The Place of Christology in Systematic Theology." In *The Oxford*

Handbook of Christology, 611–28. Oxford: Oxford University Press, 2015.

Wells, David F. "On Being Framed." *Westminster Theological Journal* 59 (1997): 293–300.

Whitaker, William. *A Disputation on Holy Scripture*. Cambridge: Cambridge University Press, 1849.

White, Thomas Joseph. "How Barth Got Aquinas Wrong: A Reply to Archie J. Spencer on Causality and Christocentrism." *Nova et Vetera* 7, no. 1 (2009): 241–70.

———. *Wisdom in the Face of Modernity: A Study in Thomistic Natural Theology*. 2nd ed. Ave Maria, FL: Sapientia, 2016.

White, William, Jr. *Van Til: Defender of the Faith*. Nashville: Nelson, 1979.

Wild, John. *Introduction to Realistic Philosophy*. New York: Harper & Brothers, 1948.

Willett, Andrew. *A Six-Fold Commentary upon the Most Divine Epistle of the Holy Apostle S. Paul to the Romans*. Cambridge: Leonard Greene, 1630.

Williamson, G. I. *The Westminster Confession of Faith for Study Classes*. Philadelphia: P&R, 1964.

Wippel, John F. "Thomas Aquinas on Philosophy and the Preambles of Faith." In *The Science of Being as Being: Metaphysical Investigations*, edited by Gregory T. Doolan, 196–220. Washington, DC: Catholic University of America Press, 2012.

Witsius, Herman. *An Essay on the Use and Abuse of Reason in Matters of Religion*. Norwich: Crouse, Stevenson, & Matchett, 1795.

———. *Miscellaneorum Sacrorum: Tomus Alter*. Herborn: Johannes Nicolas Andreas, 1712.

Witte, John, Jr. "A Demonstrative Theory of Natural Law: The Original Contribution of Johannes Althusius." In *Public Theology for a Global Society*, edited by Deirdre King Hainsworth and Scott R. Paeth, 21–36. Grand Rapids: Eerdmans, 2001.

Witte, John, Jr. and Harold J. Berman. "The Integrative Jurisprudence of John Selden." In *Great Christian Jurists in English History*, edited by Mark Hill QC and R. H. Helmholz, 139–61. Cambridge: Cambridge University Press, 2017.

Wolff, Christian. *Philosophia Prima, sive Ontologia, Methodo Scientifica Pertractata qua Omnis Cognitionis Humanae Principia Continentur*. 9th ed. Frankfurt: Occicinia Libraria Rengeriana, 1736.

Wolff, Hans Walter. *Anthropology of the Old Testament*. Philadelphia: Fortress, 2012.

Wolters, Albert M. *Creation Regained: Biblical Basics for a Reformational Worldview*. Grand Rapids: Eerdmans, 1985.

Wood, John Halsey, Jr. *Going Dutch in the Modern Age: Abraham Kuyper's Struggle for a Free Church in the Nineteenth-Century Netherlands*. New York: Oxford University Press, 2013.

Wright, David P. *Inventing God's Law: How the Covenant Code of the Bible Used and Revised the Laws of Hammurabi*. Oxford: Oxford University Press, 2009.

Wright, N. T. *The New Testament and the People of God*. Vol. 1 of *Christian Origins and the Question of God*. Minneapolis: Fortress, 1992.

———. *Paul and the Faithfulness of God*. Vol. 4 of *Christian Origins and the Question of God*. Minneapolis: Fortress, 2013.

Zalta, Edward N., ed. *Stanford Encyclopedia of Philosophy*. http://plato.stanford.edu.

Zanchi, Girolamo. *Omnium Operum Theologicorum*. Vol. 4. Geneva: Joannis Tornaeusij, 1649.

———. *On the Law in General*. Translated by Jeffrey J. Veenstra. Grand Rapids: Christian's Library, 2012.

AUTHOR INDEX

239

SUBJECT INDEX

Adam, prefall nature of, 36–37, 38
Adam and Eve, 197–201
aevum, 168–69
antithesis, 98, 99, 106, 107, 109, 112, 120, 128, 130
apologetics
  evidence in, 7, 95, 140, 150, 157, 212, 214–15
  goals of, 203–4
  humility in, 215–18
Aquinas. *See* Thomas Aquinas
Aquinas-Butler method, 85
archetypal knowledge, 206
Archimedean principle, 182
argument from design
  Calvin on, 62
  Thomas on, 79
argument from motion, 79
Aristotelian philosophy, 72, 111, 138, 143, 148–49, 153–54, 157, 162, 172, 175–76, 179

Barth, Karl
  on Calvin, 51–52
  Christocentrism of, 52–53
Belgic Confession, 1–2, 68, 129, 215
body-soul anthropology, 168, 175, 176, 178, 179–80, 185–86, 190
book of nature, xiii, 1–4, 7–9, 11, 23, 96, 118, 120, 135, 157–58, 193, 209, 214, 217–19
book of Scripture, 1–3, 8–9, 11, 23, 157–58, 214, 217, 218
Burgess, Anthony
  on common notions, 28–31
  on natural law, 5, 13–26

Calvin, John
  on common notions, 34–35, 57–60, 68–69
  continuity with Thomas Aquinas, 50, 64–65, 68
  difference from Thomas Aquinas, 67–68
  on learning from non-Christians, 132–33
  on natural knowledge of God, 4, 5, 48, 60–61
  on natural law, 50–53, 57–58, 68–69
  on scholasticism, 53–56, 68
Calvin College, 150
Calvinism as worldview, 127–28
Calvin of myth and history, 6, 67
Calvin versus the Calvinists, 49–50, 177–78
Canons of Dordt, 14–15, 27, 38–39, 40, 46, 210, 212
central dogma, 3, 104, 182–83
Christian counseling movement, 113
Christian education, 210, 217
Christian liberty, 17
Christocentrism, 52–53
  principial, 104–5, 108n67
  soteriological, 104–5
Christology as central dogma, 104
coherence theory of truth, 8, 137, 138, 149–54, 157
Commodus, 204
common grace, 8, 66, 97, 100, 106, 109–11, 120, 130, 131, 179, 181
common ground, 73, 99, 111
common notions, xii, 4–5, 9, 14–15, 24–25, 31–48, 61, 96, 99–100, 109–11, 114, 135, 213
  before and after the fall, 15
  Burgess on, 28–31

245